RENASCENT RATIONALISM

by

Helier J. Robinson

Professor Emeritus, Department of Philosophy,
University of Guelph, Guelph, Ontario, Canada.

Fifth edition, revised.

Sharebooks Publishing, Fergus, Ontario, Canada
www.sharebooks.ca

The first edition of this book was published with the help of a grant from the Humanities Research Council of Canada, using funds provided by the Canada Council.

Library and Archives Canada Cataloguing in Publication

Robinson, Helier J., 1928-
    Renascent rationalism / by Helier J. Robinson. -- 5th ed., rev.

Also published in electronic format.
Includes index.
ISBN 978-0-9783635-9-9

    1. Rationalism. I. Title.

B833.R63 2007   149'.7
C2007-905626-1

CONTENTS

Be not afraid to multiply entities up to necessity.

Introduction.

The history of western philosophy can be characterised as a history of a quarrel: the quarrel between the two schools of philosophy called, broadly, empiricism and rationalism. Empiricism makes perception the main, sometimes only, source of knowledge and rationalism makes reason the main source. Rationalism was represented in the past by such figures as Plato, Descartes, Spinoza and Leibniz. For the past three centuries, however, rationalism has been out of fashion, for a very simple reason. This period has seen the rise of modern science, which is so powerful a cure for ignorance that any philosophic system that cannot accommodate it is doomed. It was, and is, widely believed that science is exclusively empirical and hence it is believed that the only philosophical approach that can accommodate science is empiricism. I contend that this is an error. Some of science — empirical science — is empirical and well accommodated by empiricism; but, also, some of science — theoretical science — is non-empirical and, in fact, accommodated only by rationalism. The reason for this is that empiricism allows only perceptible entities, hence those things which cannot be perceived either do not exist or else are "radically unknowable." Rationalism, on the other hand, allows such entities, on the grounds that we can have speculative knowledge of them. The key point here is that the entities of theoretical science are non-empirical, imperceptible. Their effects may be empirical, of course, and these effects provide the basis for rational speculation concerning them. In particular, some of their effects are empirical measurements. It is widely believed that if something can be measured then that thing is empirical, which is quite false. Something is empirical only if it is known through the senses, and theoretical entities are never so known; indeed, that is why they are called theoretical. For example, mass is a theoretical entity which cannot be perceived. If it could be perceived then Newton would never have supposed it to be material, as opposed to the energetic mass of Einstein. We can of course perceive some of the effects of mass, and also measure them: that is, forces, such as weights, and inertial forces. But we cannot perceive mass itself so our knowledge of it must be theoretical, speculative.

This one fact alone demands a renaissance of rationalism.

There is one major difficulty in doing this. It arises from the fact that common sense, which is sacrosanct to almost everybody, contains errors. Hume and Kant both perpetuated these errors, while Spinoza and Leibniz denied them — which partly explains both why Hume and Kant prevailed among men of common sense, and why they are wrong. These errors are unimportant in daily life — common sense could not have survived if they were not — but in philosophy they are comparable to those former errors of common sense at which we now smile: a flat earth, geocentricism, celestial spheres, and the immutability of species. These errors can be discovered through a rigorous treatment of the philosophic problems of perception. This was first done by Leibniz (so far as we know) but his discovery remained unnoticed until Bertrand Russell rediscovered it, and recognised Leibniz' priority. Russell in his turn has been almost completely ignored.

The Leibniz-Russell solution, although logically simple and elegant, is psychologically difficult because of the adjustments to common sense that it requires. Part One of this book is devoted to an exposition of it.

A major consequence of the Leibniz-Russell solution is the possible synthesis of theoretical science and metaphysics, in a new departure in philosophy of science. This means that we no longer have to strain our credulity with the doctrine that theoretical science is really empirical, or else fictitious. Nor do we have to worry about the empiricists' problem of induction. And other problems currently ignored by philosophers, such as how it is possible for theoretical science to predict empirical novelty, frequently and successfully, are easily solved. Such things are dealt with in Part Two.

A particular result of all this is a liberation from the behaviourist proscription against theoretical psychology. Part Three deals with the nature of mind, ego, consciousness, internal conflict, feeling, thought and many other features of mind which could have been explained long ago had it not been for the taboo against speculation.

Finally, in Part Four the concepts used in earlier parts of the book are used to make sense, it is hoped, of the mystical goal of the major rationalists. Pythagoras, Parmenides, Plato, Plotinus, Spinoza, Leibniz, Hegel and others all maintained, in their various ways, that the limits of rationality can be both reached and passed, with the result of suprarationality: the most valuable of all possible achievements for a human being.

Typographic notes.

Square brackets represent cross-references, the numbers within them being page numbers. Forward cross-references should be ignored on a first reading.

When a word is first defined or introduced, it is presented in **boldface**.

Sections within chapters are marked by triple asterisks, and subsections of these by single asterisks.

Part One. Perception.

1. On Indubitabilities.

Philosophy should begin with indubitabilities, things which cannot be doubted, of which there are four kinds:

    1. Consciousness,
    2. Existence within consciousness,
    3. Necessary truths within consciousness, and
    4. Necessary falsities within consciousness.

Merely to state these is to reveal the need to philosophise, since philosophy develops from necessary falsities within consciousness, and from the desire to correct them, by means of necessary truths about what exists within consciousness. Consequently I will first amplify and clarify the statements of the four classes of indubitabilities, and then introduce the kind of philosophy that arises from them.

✷

1. First, the consciousness whose existence is indubitable is, of course, one's own. No one in fact usually doubts that other people are conscious, but one *can* doubt it; which is to say that other people's consciousness is dubitable. But one's own consciousness is indubitable because doubting it at all is impossible unless one is conscious. The traditional way of making this point is Descartes' *cogito ergo sum* — "I think therefore I am." In the present context this might be better phrased as "I am conscious therefore I exist." The use of the concept 'I' excludes other people's consciousness from the statement; but whatever 'I' refers to — soul, self, ego, or subject — the indubitability of its existence may be questioned, so that the concept is better left out. So I can say "Consciousness exists indubitably" and implicit within this is a limitation: the indubitability covers only a certain range of consciousness — a range that I characterise by "Mine, now." If anyone else is also considering this matter then they have a similar indubitability. We may also note that this indubitability precedes and includes the other three.

✷

2. The second indubitability, existence within consciousness, is, for me, the existence of all that I am conscious of, now. For example, if I see a woman then it is indubitable that she exists. What *kind* of existence she has may, of course, be dubitable. She may be a genuine woman, a corpse, a store window dummy, a robot, an illusion, a hallucination, a fantasy, or a dream. Whichever she is, it is indubitable that, as such, she exists. It is a curious fact that to date all existence is either indubitable in this way, or else unproved; this is a matter that will be examined in detail later (Chapter 4). This kind of indubitability will be called **existential indubitability**.

✳

3. The third indubitability, necessary truth, consists of the truths of logic and mathematics. They take the form of intuitions that are indubitable. No one who has such intuitions can seriously consider a contradiction to be true, for example, or doubt that $2+2=2\times2$ or that $3+4=7$ or that $\sqrt{2}+\sqrt{8}=\sqrt{18}$. This kind of indubitability will be called **logical indubitability**.

It is the preference for one of these two latter kinds of indubitability over the other that divides philosophers into, broadly speaking, empiricists and rationalists. There is a widespread belief that the historical rationalists — Descartes, Spinoza, and Leibniz — tried to deduce the truth about the world by relying entirely on logic and mathematics. This is as foolish as supposing that empiricists rely entirely on fact and have no use for logic or mathematics. The distinction between rationalists and empiricists appears when there is a clash between logical and existential indubitability. In such a case the rationalists prefer the logical indubitability and the empiricists the existential. Such a clash occurs when two seeming facts contradict each other, as in illusion. On the question of illusion (which will be discussed in greater detail shortly) empiricists prefer to ignore a contradiction in favour of existential indubitability; this takes the form of asserting the reality of that object having the illusory qualities. Rationalists, on the other hand, question this reality because of the contradiction.

✳

4. Finally, necessary falsities occur either in the world that each of us perceives around himself or herself, or else in the conscious mind. The former are illusions, the latter false memories, false expectations, false beliefs, and false statements. That illusions are falsities we know because

they are discovered through contradictions within sense perception. A **contradiction** is anything that is at once true and false. Thus I am now holding a pen and looking at it with my eyes crossed. My fingers inform me that there is one pen, my eyes that there are two. Either my tactile perception or my visual perception must be false, or else there are in fact three pens — two visual and one tactile — and my combined perception, which assures me that there is only one pen, is false. The indubitability of part of this perception being illusory — false — arises when I consider the nature of contradiction, since I have an indubitable logical intuition that a contradiction cannot be true.

The indubitability of false belief exists because I now believe that at least one of my beliefs is false. This present belief is either true, in which case at least one of my beliefs is false; or else it is false, in which case at least one of my beliefs — that is, this belief itself — is false. It is consequently indubitable that at least one of my beliefs is false.

Similarly, I can remember an occasion on which I discovered one of my memories to be false, hence it is indubitable that some memories are false. The fact of false memory is less significant, philosophically, than the facts of false perception and false belief, except in one respect. It is false memory that acquaints us with the nature of falsity. A memory is false when it does not resemble its original. Non-resemblance, or dissimilarity, is the key feature of each of false memory, false perception and false belief. Conversely, of course, a memory is true when it resembles its original; such truth by resemblance or similarity is called **similarity truth**. So falsity by non-resemblance may be called **dissimilarity falsity**, to distinguish it from other kinds of falsity. False expectations differ from false memories only in their temporal direction and greater frequency. Their indubitability is established similarly: I now expect some of my expectations to be false.

A self-contradictory statement is indubitably false for the same reason as the other falsities — a contradiction is indubitably false — but in this case the falsity is not dissimilarity falsity but what might be called nominal falsity — which will be discussed in Chapters 14 and 15.

✶

In short, I cannot doubt that I am conscious of existents, that I have logical intuitions, and that I perceive, believe, expect and remember, and know statements; and that these logical intuitions are true, and that some of these perceptions, beliefs, expectations, memories and statements are false.

It should be noted that although perception, memory, expectation and belief are sometimes indubitably false, they are never indubitably true. The indubitable is that which *cannot* be doubted, not that which is never *in fact* doubted[1]. Only intuitions of logical necessity, and statements of these, are indubitably true.

Of course, most of what I am conscious of — externally and internally, materially and mentally — is dubitable. It is neither necessarily true nor necessarily false. Still, *some* of it is necessarily true, and *some* of it is necessarily false. It is because of necessary falsity that anyone ever begins to philosophise. For to ask the nature of this falsity, and how much of the dubitable is false, and how it may be corrected and what the resulting truth is, is to begin philosophy. There are, quite possibly, people who do not ask such questions, being unaware of logical intuitions, oblivious of illusions and convinced that all their own beliefs are true; but such are not rational people, and so disqualified for, as well as unmotivated to, philosophy.

So this philosophy proceeds with an inquiry into false perception and false belief, and the inquiry is possible at all because we can trust our logical intuitions.

For the present, in undertaking such an inquiry, we will confine ourselves to perception, leaving the question of belief until later.

✶ ✶ ✶

Before ending this chapter, it will be convenient to give the definitions of some basic terms. They are all simple enough, but inconveniently long to define as they arise. They need not be mastered, or even memorised, on a first reading: a first familiarisation is all that is needed. The concepts to be defined are *appearance* and *reality*; *mental* and *material*; the *empirical* and the *theoretical*, including *empirical* and *theoretical perception*; two interpretations of theoretical perception, called the *realistic* and the *metarealistic* interpretations; two kinds each of *publicity* and *privacy*; and *representation* or *image*.

---

[1] This is an example of the distinction between necessity and universality, which is discussed later [244].

✱

1. The **apparent**, or **appearance**, is anything that is within someone's consciousness. It may be either material or mental.

✱

2. The word **real** has at least five distinct meanings. There is first the major meaning, which is the meaning intended throughout this book unless otherwise stated: something is real if it exists independently of being perceived: that is, it exists regardless of whether it is perceived or not. This definition, if required, can be enlarged to existence independently of consciousness, if perception is so defined as to include introspection. This meaning of *real*, if it has to be distinguished from the others, will be called **theoretical reality**.

The second meaning is called **empirical reality**: anything we perceive around us that is both public and non-illusory is empirically real. We know that those contents of consciousness that are private, such as dreams and hallucinations, are unreal simply by the fact of being private; and illusions are necessarily unreal. In fact, although some illusions are fairly public, such as the railway lines meeting in the distance for a group of people standing together, or the Sun and the Moon appearing to be the same size during a total eclipse, they are not universally public; and, furthermore, this publicity need not be actual: if something is potentially public, like the tree that falls in the forest and is heard by only one person, then it is empirically real. So we may define the empirically real as all that we perceive around us that is potentially, universally, public.

The third meaning is *real* in the sense of *true*: we speak of a portrait being a real likeness, for example, meaning that it is true to its original.

The remaining two meanings of *real* are mentioned here only to dismiss them. One of them is *genuine*: we speak of real leather, real flowers and real flavours as opposed to simulated leather, plastic flowers and artificial flavours. The other is the legal meaning of immovable property, such as land or a house; it occurs most often these days in the phrase *real estate*.

Given this clarification we can define the **real world** as everything that exists independently of being perceived.

✱

3. The **mental** and the **material** [159] are concepts used in classifying the contents of consciousness, which is why they are mentioned here. But they are not ultimately useful because their demarcation is unclear. It is difficult, perhaps impossible, to decide whether, for example, physical pains or perceived relations are mental or material. Indeed, there are no generally agreed definitions of *mental* and *material*. It was long supposed that the material is anything having mass, but this does not work. Another definition is that the material resists one's will — it disallows levitating in spite of willing it — while the mental does not — one can daydream to one's heart's content about levitating. Perhaps the best definition is that the material obeys the laws of empirical science while the mental does not. We will be using these terms for a while for their convenience, but will later abandon them.

✴

4. The **empirical** is anything known through the senses. The **theoretical** is non-empirical. These two terms belong, of course, to science.

The *empirical* is almost synonymous with our other, philosophical, term, the *apparent*: the difference is that the apparent includes introspection while the empirical, as usually understood, does not. However it is going to be so useful to us to have them synonymous that we will so use them: we will allow that introspective data is empirical. It is going to be equally useful to make the *theoretical* and the *real* synonymous, even though that may seem very implausible at present. The utility in having these synonyms is that we will later need to make such frequent use of the concepts for technical distinctions that the synonyms will relieve monotony.

✴

5. **Empirical perception** is perception as each of us knows it from experience. Each of us only knows his or her own empirical perception, of course, but our experience of it is generally confirmed by reports from other people, so that there is a consensus on the nature of empirical perception. This consensus is that each of us is *directly conscious*, of *objects*, and of *qualities*, and also of *relationships* between these; all of which includes, of course, *indubitable existence* and *illusions*; and also the consensus includes the facts that all of these are *external* to the body of the

perceiver and are usually *reperceptible*, in that when we return our perception to them they reappear; short-lived things, such as a flash of lightning, are not reperceptible, but these are exceptions that prove the rule. It is also universally characteristic of empirical perception that we each of us perceive from our own *viewpoint*; the location of this viewpoint is our own empirical body, a location that we describe as "I, here, now" and which is the origin of a subjective co-ordinate system whose axes are *in front of me, behind me, my left, my right, above me, below me, my past* and *my future*. What we perceive around us is always bounded by *horizons of the moment*, beyond which we cannot see: the farthest of these is the blue sky on a sunny day or the black sky with stars on a clear night. We do not perceive, but have good grounds for believing, that what is empirically perceived is *material*, as opposed to mental; and *public* — perceptible by others — as opposed to the mental content of consciousness, which is *private* to each of us. Finally, subsequent to empirical perception is memory: when remembering empirically perceived things we are conscious of mental, and hence private, *representations* or *images* of them.

The two most important features of empirical perception are that most of what we perceive is *external* and *public*. But not everything we perceive is external and public, since physical pleasures and pains are internal, to one's own body, and private; so, while not excluding these from empirical perception, we will for a while ignore them. This is in order to simplify our argument, without in any way invalidating it.

These fourteen concepts are the significant features of empirical perception, so far as philosophy is concerned: *direct consciousness, objects, qualities, relations, indubitable existence, illusions, externality, publicity, reperceptibility, viewpoint, horizons, materiality,* and *memory*. Note that with all of them we have left the realm of indubitability. Some are indubitable in so far as our own experience is concerned, but not other people's — which is to say that they depend upon word of mouth, which is dubitable. The rest of them involve belief, memory or word of mouth and so are dubitable. However, although empirical perception is dubitable in these ways, we hardly ever do in fact doubt the truth of any of these fourteen points.

✳

6. **Theoretical perception** is a belief, invented originally in order to explain one particular feature of empirical perception. This feature is illusion. Originally theoretical perception was only the bare bones of a theory, called the **representational theory of perception**. This said merely that illusions are *misrepresentations* of reality. As such, they are mere appearances. The modern version of theoretical perception is the bare-boned representational theory filled out with the flesh of scientific detail. As such it is often known as the **causal theory of perception**. The detail includes the physics of light and sound — frequency, rectilinear propagation, velocity, reflection, refraction, etc. — the chemistry of olfactory vapours, the physiology of afferent nerves and the brain, and so on. The basic features of theoretical perception are that a real object causes, by a process of information transfer, a representation or image of itself to appear in the brain of the perceiver, where, by a process that will be explained in Part 3, this perceiver becomes directly conscious of it. I deliberately say *it* ambiguously here because there are two quite different ways of interpreting theoretical perception. They differ in what this *it*, the object of immediate consciousness, is: the real object, or the image of it.

✳

7. One of these interpretations, which I will call the **realistic interpretation** of theoretical perception, incorporates empirical perception such that the *it* of which the perceiver is directly conscious is *the real object*; and this object is external, material, and public. The representation may also come into consciousness — either at once, in the case of illusions, or later in the form of memory. The realistic interpretation is also sometimes known as **common sense realism**, or, unkindly, as **naive realism**, or as **realism** for short. The most succinct statement of it is: *the empirically real is theoretically real*. In other words, all that we perceive which is external and potentially, universally, public continues to exist when unperceived.

✳

8. The other way of understanding theoretical perception may be called the **metarealistic interpretation**. This is that the *it* of immediate consciousness is *the representation of the real object*. Consequently the object of consciousness is *internal*, *mental*, and *private* and, since it exists only as a result of being perceived, *unreal*, or merely apparent. It is a

feature of the metarealistic interpretation that it requires that *everything* perceived is a representation, received via the afferent nerves — not merely illusions and memories, as in the realistic interpretation. In this interpretation real objects are always beyond any possibility of immediate consciousness, always beyond the horizons of the moment; because of this they are sometimes said to be **radically unknowable** according to this theory. I will use the term **strict imperceptible** for this: that is, a strict imperceptible is anything which is not empirically perceived by anyone, ever.

There are two more differences between empirical perception and theoretical perception: one is that empirical perception is an *act*, while theoretical perception is a *causal process*. The other is that empirical vision, introspectively, is as if we see through holes in the head: we do not see our eyes by looking through them; but theoretical vision is through eyes consisting of lens, vitreous humour, retina, and optic nerve — and these together are not holes.

★

9. There are two kinds of publicity (that is, two ways in which things may be public to many observers), and it is an important feature of realism that it particularly adopts one of them. One is **publicity by identity**; if many observers are all directly conscious of *one* and the same object, then that object is public by identity. The Moon is a good common sense example: we all perceive one and the same Moon. Although the word *identity* is often used ambiguously, its technical meaning, which is the one used here, is not: it means *oneness*: if A and B are identical then they are one and the same. The ambiguous meaning, avoided here, is similarity: "A and B are identical" meaning they are similar, as in the phrase *identical twins*. A and B may be similar but not identical because they are two, hence not one.

The other kind of publicity is **publicity by similarity**: many observers may be directly conscious each of their own private object, yet all are public by virtue of similarity. Newspapers, radio, and television, are examples. Each reader of a particular edition of a newspaper may have his or her own private copy, yet what he or she reads is public because the content of all the private copies is similar.

Realism has it that the publicity which renders apparent objects empirically real is publicity by identity. And of course this may be potential publicity rather than actual.

It follows from the fact of two kinds of publicity that there are two kinds of privacy: **privacy by plurality** and **privacy by dissimilarity**. For example, if all the bedrooms in a hotel are exactly alike, they are clearly public by similarity; yet the occupant of each none the less has his or her own private room. This is privacy by plurality. In the same way, when all the readers of a particular edition of a newspaper have their own private copy, this is privacy by plurality — even though all the copies are fully public by similarity. Dreams, on the other hand, besides being private by plurality, among different sleepers, are also private by dissimilarity. No two dreamers dream the same dream. It is because of this that newspaper readers, television watchers, and the like may know the content of other people's papers and television programs, but not know, unless told, the content of their dreams.

Equivocation occurs here in common sense. Ordinary language does not usually distinguish between the two kinds of publicity and of privacy: similarity and identity are both referred to by the word *same*, and dissimilarity and plurality are both referred to by the word *different*. Thus we say "Jack's pen is the same as Jill's" because they each own similar pens, and "Jack's house is the same as Jill's" because they live together in the one house. In the first statement *same* means similarity and in the second it means identity. And we may also say "Jack's memories are different from Jill's" because they are dissimilar, and "Jack's concept of the number three is different from Jill's" because, although the two concepts are not dissimilar they are still two — that is, plural. Many uses of *same* and *different* are quite ambiguous because of this lack of distinction. "Jack and Jill are reading the same newspaper" is unclear as to whether they are sharing one copy, and "Jack and Jill own different cars" is unclear as to whether or not these cars are of similar make, model or colour. This ambiguity allows the equivocation that many more or less similar things are one: a move from publicity by similarity to publicity by identity which is quite invalid. Musicians talk, for example, about *the* Messiah — even though Handel wrote many versions and each version has been both printed and played many times; various nearly-similar things are collapsed into one, *the* Messiah — quite illogically. It is, I believe, a very strong desire for simplicity, which here overwhelms reason and makes this error very widespread. We will have many examples of this error in what follows — enough that the error needs to be named: it will be called **the identity error**. The correction of this error is by the principle that qualitative difference entails quantitative difference [25]: that is, that any dissimilarity requires plurality.

We should note at this point that similarity is a matter of degree, while identity is not. Whatever the names A and B may refer to, either they refer to one and the same, identical, thing, or they do not; there is no third possibility. But if A and B are similar or dissimilar, there is a whole range of possibilities, from exact, or perfect, similarity through degrees of diminishing similarity and increasing dissimilarity to exact, or perfect, dissimilarity. In terms of this, we may define **perfect publicity** as that of exact similarity, **perfect privacy** as that of exact dissimilarity, and **imperfect publicity** (or, equally, **imperfect privacy**) as that of any intermediate degree of similarity. That is to say, the imperfectly public has some publicity by similarity and some privacy by dissimilarity.

Because our two kinds of publicity and privacy are consequences of identity, plurality, similarity, or dissimilarity, it follows that various relationships among these four hold between the two kinds. For example, everything is exactly similar to itself at any one time, which is to say that identity entails exact self-similarity. But not *vice versa*: exact similarity allows identity but does not entail it. So publicity by identity entails perfect publicity, but not vice versa: even if two things are perfectly public, they are not necessarily one thereby. And dissimilarity entails plurality (no one thing can be dissimilar to what it is) but not *vice versa* — a plurality of things are not thereby dissimilar to each other — so privacy by dissimilarity entails privacy by plurality but not *vice versa*.

This all becomes more comprehensible if summarised as in Table 1.1. The table is read by considering a column first, choosing a line and then discovering from the intersection of these two whether the column heading makes the kind of publicity or privacy of that line necessary or impossible.

	Perfect publicity (exact similarity)		Plurality	
	Identity	Plurality	Imperfect publicity	Perfect privacy
Publicity by identity	Necessary	Impossible	Impossible	Impossible
Publicity by similarity	Necessary	Necessary	Necessary	Impossible
Privacy by plurality	Impossible	Necessary	Necessary	Necessary
Privacy by dissimilarity	Impossible	Impossible	Necessary	Necessary

Table 1.1

It is important to satisfy oneself that this table is correct, because its two main features are, first, that there are only two ways in which things may be at once both public and private: either they must be plural and exactly similar, or else they must be partly similar and partly dissimilar. In either case they must be plural. That is, imperfect publicity entails plurality. Second, whatever is public by identity cannot be private at all — either by plurality or by dissimilarity.

✸

10. Finally, we may speak variously of a *representation, image, copy, replica, facsimile, map, model, duplicate,* or *reproduction* of some original. All of these terms will be used synonymously, but **representation** and **image** will generally be preferred. As already explained, if a representation such as a memory is similar to its original it is called similarity true and if it is dissimilar it is called dissimilarity false. Since similarity and dissimilarity are a matter of degree, as opposed to a two-valued either-or, so are this kind of truth and falsity.

2. False Perception.

There are many philosophical problems with perception. We begin by looking at eighteen of them, and at seven failed attempts to solve them, and then show that they are all special cases of one general problem of perception. We will then look at this general problem of perception in detail and, in the next chapter, look at the logical solution of it. We do all this because the logical solution is sufficiently difficult, psychologically, that such preparation is helpful.

First, we look at the eighteen examples of problems with perception.

✳

1. If you are looking at this book and you cross your eyes, or press on one eyeball, so that you have double vision, then you see two books. Which is the real book: the book on the left or the book on the right? If each is an image rather than the real book, then as they coalesce when you uncross your eyes, do you now see two coincident images, or do you see the real book?

✳

2. If you watch a car drive down a straight road, it seems to get smaller as it gets farther away. You can hold up your thumb, in the manner of a landscape painter, and the size of the car, relative to your thumb, diminishes. We know that the car does not really get smaller, so we distinguish between the real size of the car, which is constant, and the apparent size, which diminishes. At what distance does the apparent size equal the real size? Or, how far away must an object be for you to see its real size?

✳

3. Real size does not vary with distance and measured size does not vary with distance, so are real size and measured size one and the same? Not necessarily, since to argue so would be to commit **the fallacy of undistributed middle**[2]. And how far from your eyes do a yardstick or a metre rule have to be in order for you to see a real yard or a real metre?

✳

---

[2] Compare "All real sizes are constant with distance, all measured sizes are constant with distance, therefore all measured sizes are real sizes" with "All rats are mammals, all humans are mammals, therefore all humans are rats."

4. There are real things which cannot be perceived, but which can be described, such as atoms. So if colours are real, why cannot they be described to a blind man?

✳

5. We believe things to be real by the fact of their being in public space, which is external to each of us — as opposed to internal sensations, which are private. The space around us is public to everyone, and things in it are public by virtue of being in it. Mountains, trees, and clouds are all in public space, hence public, hence real. But the fuzziness of things seen with unfocussed eyes, or the redness of things seen through red glass, or after-images, are all in public space but unreal. We say that they are unreal, and hence illusions, because they are private. How can private illusions be in public space and remain private? If their externality is itself illusory, how can we know that the externality of the mountains, trees, and clouds is not illusory?

✳

6. A normal swimming pool is cool to an overheated diver, and warm to a cold diver. So is the pool really cool, or warm?

✳

7. When you see a rainbow, the concentric circles, of which the rainbow is a portion, have their centre on a straight line between the Sun, which is behind you, and your eyes: this line, extended forwards, goes to the centre of the arcs of the rainbow. So as you move around, the rainbow moves with you, because your eyes are moving relative to the landscape. Consequently many people looking at a public rainbow each see their own rainbow, in a different place, and do not see the rainbows of the other people. Yet all these people agree that they all see the rainbow, that the rainbow is public. So is there one public rainbow, or are there many private ones?

✳

8. If two people are looking at a house, one from the southwest and one from the southeast, then the first sees the front and west side of the house, and the second sees the front and east side. We say that each sees a different aspect of the house, and that every viewpoint yields a different aspect. So if every observer of the house only sees one aspect of it, at any one time, how can anyone ever perceive the house itself? Alternatively, if

the house is the totality of its aspects, how can anyone ever perceive the house itself?

✻

9. If, by some strange mutation, you were born always to see green as other people see red, and red as they see green, then as you learnt to talk you would have called your red *green* and your green *red*. Could you ever know that your colour perception was different from other people's?

✻

10. If you were asked to point to something that you perceive which is entirely free of illusion, could you do so?

✻

11. And if you could point to something that is wholly free of illusion, how would you know it to be so?

✻

12. When you see the Moon, which is about 250,000 miles away, does your consciousness extend out of your head, for a distance of 250,000 miles, to the Moon, or do you see an image of the Moon, brought to you by reflected sunlight? If you see an image of it then you do not see the real Moon, while if you see the real Moon then your consciousness somehow has to get out of your head to that distance. So do you see the real Moon, or not? The real Moon and the image cannot be one and the same, because the Moon is made of rock, and the image is not made of rock.

✻

13. If you do not see the real Moon, then is anything that you see real?

✻

14. As Bishop Berkeley asked, if a tree falls in the forest and there is no one around to hear it, does it make a sound? The same problem in the realm of sight is: does colour exist in the dark?

✻

15. When you talk on the telephone with a friend, do you talk with your friend, or with a reproduction of your friend's voice?

✻

16. There is a child's riddle: how do you catch an elephant with a telescope, a pair of tweezers, and a matchbox? The answer is that you look at the elephant through the wrong end of the telescope and this makes it

small enough to pick up with the tweezers and put in the matchbox. Children find this funny because they know that the telescope does not really make the elephant smaller. We know that lenses appear to enlarge or to diminish things, and we also know that they do not enlarge or diminish the things themselves, but only images of the things. Photographs are images of things, and a photographic enlarger enlarges these images by means of lenses. Lenses change the sizes of images of things, not the sizes of things themselves. So everything seen through a lens must be an image, not the thing itself. A bacterium seen though a microscope, or a moon of Jupiter seen through a telescope, is only an image of the bacterium or the moon, not the reality. But our eyes have lenses, so everything we see must be an image, not reality. Can this be true?

*

17. What is the difference between hearing the siren of an ambulance, and hearing the sound of the siren? They cannot be one and the same because if you hear a recording of a siren then you hear the sound of the siren but not the siren itself. But in that case do you ever hear a siren?

*

18. If the Sun were to explode we could not know of it until eight minutes later, because that is how long it takes for light to travel from the Sun to Earth. So for eight minutes we would see an unexploded Sun, while the real sun would be exploded. It follows that we do not see the real Sun. But everything we see must be later than reality, because of the time it takes light to travel from reality to our eyes, so nothing we see is real. Can this be true?

* * *

We next look at seven past attempts at solving these problems, and at why they fail.

*

1. Some of these problems are commonly dealt with by supposing that we *project* internal things out into the world. We project secondary qualities such as colours onto external objects, for example, and as a result perceive the colours to be on the surfaces of the objects, even though we know that the colours are really in our brains. Thus, we project the secondary quality of redness out onto the surface of the real tomato. The difficulty with this is: how do we project? We do not project as movies and

slides are projected onto a screen, we do not project mechanically, as stones are projected from a slingshot and bullets from a gun, and we do not project geometrically, as the shapes of our shadows are projected onto walls and the ground. But these are the only mechanisms of projection that there are. Unless an appropriate mechanism can be described, this solution is no better than saying that we can stop the tide by means of the will.

A second difficulty with projection is Problem 5: how can we project private things into public space and have them remain private?

A third difficulty is that some illusions cannot possibly be projected onto real things: how could smallness be projected onto a distant real object and make it small?

✳

2. It is sometimes said that we perceive real objects *by means of* images of them: the images are brought into our brains by the sense organs and the efferent nervous system, and by means of these images we perceive their originals, the real objects. This can only work as a solution if the *means* can be explained. It is true to say that we can calculate quickly by means of computers, or boil water by means of electricity, or fly by means of airplanes; but it is false to say that we can levitate by means of will power, or speak with the dead by means of the Ouija board, or, as above, stop the tide by means of the will. This is because the first three *means* are genuine and the last three *means* are fictitious. So unless the means by which we perceive reality *via* images can be shown to be genuine, by being spelled out in detail, it is fictitious by default, in which case this explanation does not work.

✳

3. It is also sometimes said that we perceive reality *through* images, and so perceive both, as if the images were like a dirty window so that in looking through the window we see the scene outside as well as the dirt on the window. This does not work because the analogy fails. Images are not like windows; nor are the retinas of our eyes like windows. The only window-like features in vision are the lenses and vitreous humour of our eyes, and we do not see through these, we only see the images that they deliver to the retinas.

✳

4. Psychologists sometimes say that we unconsciously *organise* sense data in our brains, into two kinds: external data and internal data. Because of this organisation some of what we perceive is external and some internal: material and mental, as we usually call it. This obscures the fact that such organisation cannot put material data outside the perceiver's head if there is no doorway for it to go through. If you were in a prison cell with no egress, you could shuffle a deck of cards as much as you liked, but could not thereby organise any of the cards outside the prison: if you could so organise the cards, you could organise yourself outside as well.

✶

5. The doctrine of *indirect perception* is the doctrine that to perceive something directly is to perceive its cause indirectly. To perceive something directly is to be immediately conscious of it in perception, while to perceive its cause is to be mediately conscious of this cause. So if we perceive the image of a real object, this real object is the cause of the image and so we perceive the real object indirectly, in which case we perceive the real object. This doctrine is seen to fail as soon as it is pointed out that *indirect perception* is a misleading way of talking about belief. Beliefs, like memories, are perception substitutes: when our perception fails us we substitute a belief. We cannot perceive anything beyond the horizon of the moment, but we believe that the world beyond it exists; and we cannot normally perceive the far side of opaque objects, but believe such objects to have far sides. So if we perceive images of real objects rather than the real objects themselves, then our perception fails us with the real objects: so we can only believe in the real objects, not perceive them. For example, lightning and thunder are caused, we believe, by atmospheric electric discharges; we cannot perceive these discharges, we can only perceive their effects, lightning and thunder. However, can we be certain that they are caused by atmospheric electric discharges? The ancients believed that they were caused by angry gods throwing thunderbolts. If the ancients could be wrong, so could we. Beliefs may be false, but perception of reality, direct or indirect, cannot be false — since reality is the standard of truth. Thus the mere possibility of being wrong proves that indirect perception is belief or memory, not perception, since perception of reality, if it occurred, could not be false. Furthermore, we can ask how far indirect perception might extend: if you read a newspaper, do you indirectly perceive the printing

press, the editor, the journalist, the dramatic events that led to the story, the causes of these events, and so on? Or do you just believe in these things? If we could perceive indirectly to ultimate causes then we could know, rather than believe, whether or not there is a God.

✳

6. It has been suggested that we can perceive *through* causal chains, somewhat as we can perceive through a telescope. Thus, transitively through a neural image, a retinal image, electromagnetic radiation, and molecular excitation, we see a real object. But why the real object? Why not the rods and cones on our retinas, or the electromagnetic radiation, or the Sun that illuminates the real object? Quite apart from this, the analogy is patently wrong: there is as much resemblance between a causal chain and a telescope as there is between a logical argument and a hearing aid. In each case the first consists of necessary connections and the second of amplification of images.

✳

7. Austin's famous distinction between *seeing as* and *it looks to me*, which led to the infamous controversy as to whether illusions are adverbial or adjectival, is misleading. If I see a half-immersed stick and say "What I see is a straight stick but I see it as bent" or "What I see is a straight stick but it looks bent to me" then these statements do suggest that illusions are linguistic. Yet in fact both statements are false. The true statement is: "What I see is a bent stick but I *believe* that it is really straight." The illusion comes before its correction; the illusion is a matter of fact and the correction of it is a matter of belief and language.

✳ ✳ ✳

There is a solution to all of these problems which, although it is logically very simple, is psychologically very difficult. This is the metarealistic interpretation of theoretical perception. If everything we perceive is images of reality, rather than reality itself, all these problems are solved.

So all of these problems boil down to **the general problem of perception**, which is: *do we perceive reality around us, or only images of reality?* To make this as clear as possible we will consider four arguments for the case that we perceive reality around us, and four more for the case that we perceive images of reality; and then, in the next chapter, we will resolve this contradiction by means of the Leibniz-Russell theory of perception. But first we must say something more about the realistic interpretation of theoretical perception.

✳

The realistic interpretation [10] seems, at first, to reconcile empirical and theoretical perception, into one consistent whole. However, it does not do so: all the problems of perception arise because of inconsistencies within the realistic interpretation, and these problems remain insoluble for as long as this realism is presupposed. In other words, the general problem of perception arises because the realistic interpretation cannot possibly be true; and if common sense realism is false then empirical perception and the metarealistic interpretation of theoretical perception seem to be incompatible, even though we can deny neither. Empirical perception gives us real objects, outside our heads, material and public; and theoretical perception gives us images of real objects, inside our heads, mental and private.

The realistic interpretation is part of common sense — so basic a part, in fact, that very few philosophers in the history of philosophy have been able to bring themselves to deny it, in spite of the many contradictions within it. And if philosophers have trouble denying it, it is hardly surprising that the laity do not know that the problem exists.

Before going any further, I hasten to say that common sense is the accumulated practical experience of thousands of generations of people, and quite indispensable in everyday activities. Anyone lacking common sense is unlikely to survive for long, and those who have it in full measure are usually successful and happy. Consequently to deny a basic part of common sense, as I am doing here, is to invite ridicule. But sometimes common sense is in fact wrong.

The situation with realism is comparable to the former common sense beliefs in geocentricism and special creation. In Copernicus' day very few people knew that there was any problem with the Ptolemaic theory of our planetary system; and so basic was the belief that the Earth was flat, immobile, and fixed at the centre of the Universe, that the common sense of the day found it ludicrous to suppose that anything as large as the Earth was spherical, flying very fast through space around the Sun, and rotating as it went. These days we most of us like to think that if we had lived then, we would have preferred reason to prejudice, and sided with Copernicus and Galileo — as did Descartes, Kepler, Newton, and a few others — rather than the cardinals and Pope who favoured common sense. Similarly, we like to believe that we would have sided with Darwin, in his day, in his explanation of our descent from apes, rather than with the then common sense belief that we were specially created. Well, a comparable situation is here. You have an opportunity to discover how rational and open minded you really are.

So the general problem of perception may be stated as: if the realistic interpretation of theoretical perception cannot be true, how can empirical perception be reconciled with the metarealistic interpretation? Do we perceive reality or images of reality?

✶ ✶ ✶

Let us next consider the arguments for each side, starting with those for reality.

✶

1. According to theoretical perception — the causal theory of perception — real objects outside my head cause images inside my head. Since, ignoring introspection, all that I empirically perceive is outside my head, it must all consist of real objects, not images of real objects.

✶

2. Unless everyone is an extraordinarily consistent liar, what I empirically perceive is mostly public, while images inside my head are private. So all that I perceive which is public must be real, not images.

✶

3. Most of what I empirically perceive is reperceptible. When I leave home in the morning I cease to perceive my house, but when I return in the evening I perceive it again, which is what is meant by saying that it is reperceptible. The simplest explanation of reperceptibility is that things are reperceptible because they continue to exist between the times that they are perceived; this means that they exist while unperceived, and so are real, by definition. Also, someone else may perceive my house while I am away, which proves that it exists independently of my perception, and so is real. Particularly convincing cases of reperceptibility are processes, such as a cake baking in the oven, logs burning in the fireplace, a second hand rotating around the dial of a clock, or the aging face of a friend. All of

these can, and usually do, continue while unperceived, so that we perceive results rather than processes — which means that the processes are real, since they exist unperceived.

✷

4. Images in our heads are mental but what we empirically perceive is material, in that it resists our wills while following scientific laws. If you step off a roof while willing yourself to levitate, Newton's laws will prevail over your will, thereby showing your body to be material and real, not mental and an image of reality. Another way of putting this is to say that the material behaves in a causally coherent manner, while the mental — dreams, for example, or political or religious belief systems — is often incoherent. Causal coherence in general means that material objects conform to scientific laws. So what we perceive is real because coherent, unlike less coherent mental images of reality.

Thus we may argue that what we empirically perceive is real because it is external, public, reperceptible, and material. Against this are four arguments that what we empirically perceive is all mental images in our heads.

✷

1. There is the fact that every thing that we perceive is to some degree illusory, and illusions are necessarily unreal. Both these points need expanding.

Among illusions are **secondary qualities**, which are qualities manufactured by the sense organs: colours manufactured by the eyes, sounds manufactured by the ears, tastes, smells, sensations of hard and soft, hot and cold, rough and smooth — all of these are secondary qualities and by that fact illusory. But can you point to any empirical thing that does not have any such qualities? Also, much of what we perceive is distorted during the process of perception: light is reflected and refracted, giving us mirror images, mirages, and the illusions of the half-immersed stick being bent and of objects becoming smaller with distance; sound is reflected, giving us echoes, and it is distorted if its source is moving, as in the Doppler effect; sensed temperatures are distorted by the temperature of the skin, so that a hot hand finds cool the water that a cold hand finds warm; and tastes and smells vary between health and illness.

That illusions are unreal follows from the fact that they are empirical contradictions [271n], and reality cannot contain contradictions. To suppose that reality can contain contradictions is to suppose that contradictions can be true, since reality is the basis of truth, and to suppose that contradictions can be true is to abandon reason. The fact that illusions are empirical contradictions is shown by the half-immersed stick, which is bent to the sight and not bent to the touch; or by Aristotle's illusion, in which a marble or ball-bearing is held between crossed fingers and is two to the touch while it is only one to the sight. Other illusions are contradictions between what is perceived and well-established belief, as in the diminution of size with distance.

The only possible explanation of illusions is that they are misrepresentations of reality, in which case they are representations — false representations, as opposed to true representations; such falsity and truth are dissimilarity falsity and similarity truth [5]. But although empirical things cannot be a mixture of reality and representation, any more than a man can be a mixture of himself and a photograph of himself, they can be a mixture of true and false representations. And since every empirical thing is partly illusory, every empirical thing must be partly a false representation and partly a true representation, in which case it is wholly a representation, or image.

✱

2. The second argument that what we empirically perceive is images arises from the principle that qualitative difference entails quantitative difference. This principle is so often abused, in the form of the identity error [13], that it is worth taking a moment to prove it. Suppose that we have two names or descriptions, A and B, and we want to know if they refer to one and the same thing or not. If we know that there is a qualitative difference between what they refer to, then we know that there is some quality, Q, say, such that A is Q and B is not-Q. If A and B are one, then one thing is at once Q and not-Q, which is impossible. So A and B must be two. So qualitative difference entails quantitative difference. Putting this another way, qualitative difference precludes identity. For example, if the highest mountain in Africa has ice on top and Mount Kenya does not have ice on top then it is impossible for Mount Kenya to be the highest mountain in Africa; Mount Kenya and the highest mountain in Africa cannot be one,

cannot be identical, they must be two. And if the President is clean shaven and Jack Robinson has a beard, then it is impossible for Jack Robinson to be the President; they cannot be one, they must be two.

With this in mind, we may define the **empirical world** of any one person, at any one time, as all that they empirically perceive at that time. Because of viewpoint and perceptual idiosyncrasies, each person's empirical world differs qualitatively from everyone else's; and because of illusion, each person's empirical world differs qualitatively from reality. Since qualitative difference entails quantitative difference, it follows that there must be as many empirical worlds as there are perceivers, and that none of these empirical worlds are the real world. So at best each person's empirical world must be their own private representation of reality, in which case all that we empirically perceive is images: wholly private by plurality and public, to some extent, by similarity.

✶

3. Next, part of the process of perception is a largely unconscious **interpretation** of what we perceive. This includes an automatic *correction* of illusions, such as correction of visible size for distance and of the bending of the half-immersed stick; *compounding* of data from different senses into single objects, such as a bonfire seen, a bonfire heard, a bonfire felt, and a bonfire smelled: four distinct bonfires that are unconsciously compounded into one empirical bonfire (they are four because qualitative difference entails quantitative difference); and *addition of beliefs*, such as the beliefs that perceived opaque objects have far sides and continue to exist between occasions of being perceived. The purpose of interpretation, and its evolutionary survival value, is to make our perceptions more true. The problem is: what is it that we interpret, reality or images of reality? If we interpret reality then we make reality more true, which does not make sense, since reality is our standard of truth. But if we interpret images then we never perceive reality, only images of reality.

✶

4. Last, all that we perceive must be images because there is no intrinsic difference between illusions and non-illusions, and since illusions must be representations, so must be non-illusions. There are intrinsic differences between, say, a woman and a photograph of her, or between an actor and a television picture of him. For a start, they are made of different

stuffs: woman and man are made of flesh and bone, while a photograph is made of dyes on paper and a television picture is made of coloured pixels. There are plenty of other intrinsic differences as well, so that we can easily distinguish the original and its representation. But between illusions and non-illusions there are no such intrinsic differences: if there were we could tell non-illusions from illusions with ease, in which case empirical science would be superfluous. It follows that illusions and non-illusions must all be made of the same stuff: mental images. The difference between them is that illusions are false representations and non-illusions are true representations; but since we cannot perceive such falsity and truth we cannot know non-illusions as such, although we can know illusions by their contradictoriness.

3. The Leibniz-Russell Theory.

The Leibniz-Russell solution to the general problem of perception is bizarre. It is so bizarre that no one would ever seriously consider it, were it not for the fact that it solves all the philosophic problems of perception. Note that the bizarre is not necessarily absurd. The bizarre is anything contrary to established belief, while the absurd, technically, is anything that is self-contradictory and therefore impossible. The Leibniz-Russell solution is not absurd, but it will strain the common sense of the reader considerably. As a result the temptation to reject it out of hand, on the ground of absurdity, will be very strong. The only way to counteract such prejudicial temptation is with reason. And reason may be helped in this undertaking by the adoption of a willing suspension of disbelief — at least until the demonstration of the power of the Leibniz-Russell theory to solve philosophical problems is complete.

Because the Leibniz-Russell solution clashes with common sense, it is worth repeating two things. Common sense, which can be defined as majority belief, is based on the cumulative practical experience of millennia of human living; as such, it is not to be discarded lightly. On the other hand, the history of ideas is a history of corrections to common sense — and we have no grounds for supposing that this history is complete. So it is quite possible that what Leibniz and Russell propose is another such correction. However, their correction will probably be more painful to the uninitiated then were those of Copernicus and Darwin.

I will present the Leibniz-Russell theory here in four ways: (i) by stating the key point of the theory, from which everything else follows; (ii) by explaining the theory with figures; (iii) by analysing the language of perception; and (iv) by sketching the logic of the theory in seven steps.

✶ ✶ ✶

1. The key point in Leibniz-Russell is that if everything you perceive is an image of reality then your own empirical head is an image of your real, theoretical, head: you have two heads. Your entire empirical world, including your own empirical head, is inside your real, or theoretical, head. This means that if you go outside on a sunny day then beyond the blue sky is the inside surface of your real skull.

✶ ✶ ✶

2. The best method for understanding the Leibniz-Russell theory is undoubtedly pictorial, so we next approach it with diagrams. In each of the

following figures the subject of perception is shown as an ego, which is drawn as a force field. The reasons for this will be given in Part Three.

Fig. 3.1 illustrates empirical perception and realism combined. Jack and Jill are empirically seeing a real tree, which means that each is directly conscious, visually, of this tree and of each other. These are external and

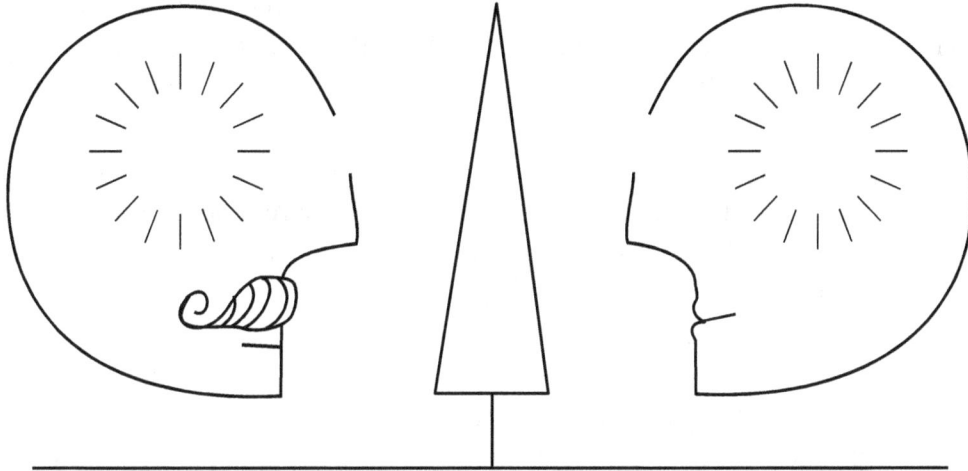

Fig. 3.1.

public by identity [11], and, introspectively, Jack and Jill each see them through holes in their heads.

Fig. 3.2 illustrates theoretical perception. Jack and Jill are theoretically seeing a real tree and the real other, which means that each is directly conscious of representations of this tree and of the other. The representations are internal to each of them, partially public to both (by

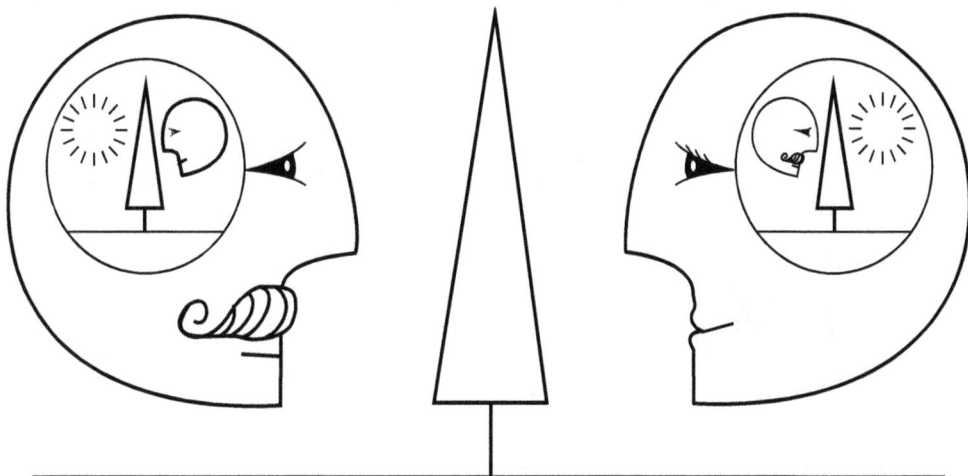

Fig. 3.2.

29

similarity), partially private to each (by dissimilarity, because of viewpoint) and private by plurality [12-14].

The problem is to make Figs. 3.1 and 3.2 both true at once. This is the general problem of perception. It is soluble only if the realism of Fig. 3.1 is omitted, as shown in Fig. 3.3. Here, discussing only the perception of the tree to begin with, Jack and Jill each have two bodies: a real body (with real afferent nerves by means of which they theoretically perceive) and an apparent body (which is a representation of their real body and is composed of empirical sensations). Inside the real body — inside the real brain, that is — is the representation of the real tree; this representation, or apparent tree, is outside the apparent body. The apparent head contains the ego which is directly conscious (through eyes that, visually, are holes) of this apparent tree. That is, the ego empirically perceives this apparent tree.

Thus the tree of which each is directly conscious is both internal and external, because each has two bodies: the tree is internal to the real body and external to the apparent body — the apparent body also being internal to the real body. Each is also conscious of a tree that is partly public by similarity, partly private by dissimilarity, and wholly private by plurality. The tree also is material because, as a representation of a real tree which obeys scientific laws, it copies this behaviour and also obeys scientific laws; and at the same time it is mental because it is a product of a real brain. However, these apparent trees are not real, because their existence depends upon the real tree being theoretically perceived. This does not mean that they are not reperceptible, because if either Jack or Jill returns their theoretical perception to the real tree the representation of it will be

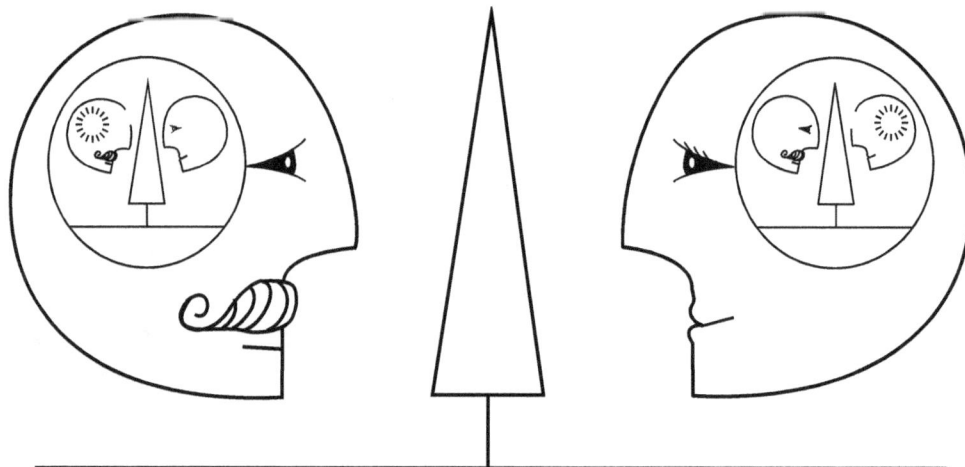

Fig. 3.3.

recreated in their brain — which means that the apparent tree is reperceptible. It is reperceptible even though unreal, because its cause — the real tree — is real; that is, the real tree continues to exist when theoretically unperceived, but the apparent tree does not.

Furthermore, Jack's apparent world, besides containing his own apparent body and an apparent tree, contains an apparent Jill; and, similarly, Jill's apparent world contains an apparent Jack. Some idea of how bizarre this theory is comes from realising that the apparent Jill in Jack's world is composed only of Jack's sensations, such as colours, and nothing else. His apparent Jill has no ego, no reality, and none of the consciousness that Jack attributes to Jill. A close analogy here is a television picture of a real person; the picture, as opposed to the real person, is composed only of colours, is mindless and exists only while the real person is being televised and the receiving set is switched on at that channel. Clearly, there is no problem here for the intellect. But for the emotions it is quite a different story. One has only to look at anyone else, but preferably someone loved, and reflect that they are merely sensations, unconscious and unreal, to realise that the Leibniz-Russell solution is indeed contrary to habitual belief.

So far as everyday practical affairs are concerned, such conclusions should give no one any pause. We are all pre-Copernicans to some extent: we speak of sunrise and sunset, meaning that we regard the sun as coming up over the horizon, travelling across the sky and then sinking below the horizon again — as if the Earth were fixed and the sun travelled around it. So, for common sense daily activities, we may regard apparent external objects as if they were real, and apparent other people as if they were conscious beings. The error in doing this is error of oversimplification. In the same way one can converse by television-telephone and treat the correlated picture of a person and reproduced voice as if it were a genuine person rather than a reproduction of one. Apparent worlds can be treated as if they were real simply because they are fairly good copies of the real world; and apparent people can be treated as if they were conscious beings simply because they are fairly good copies of real, conscious beings. In other words, realism is harmless in day-to-day living, and has the advantage of great simplicity. But so far as philosophy is concerned, realism has long been a poison to sound reasoning. Its oversimplicity has trapped philosophers in narrow, confined systems of thought that were thereby full of problems without solutions. Leibniz and Russell have liberated philosophy as Copernicus liberated astronomy.

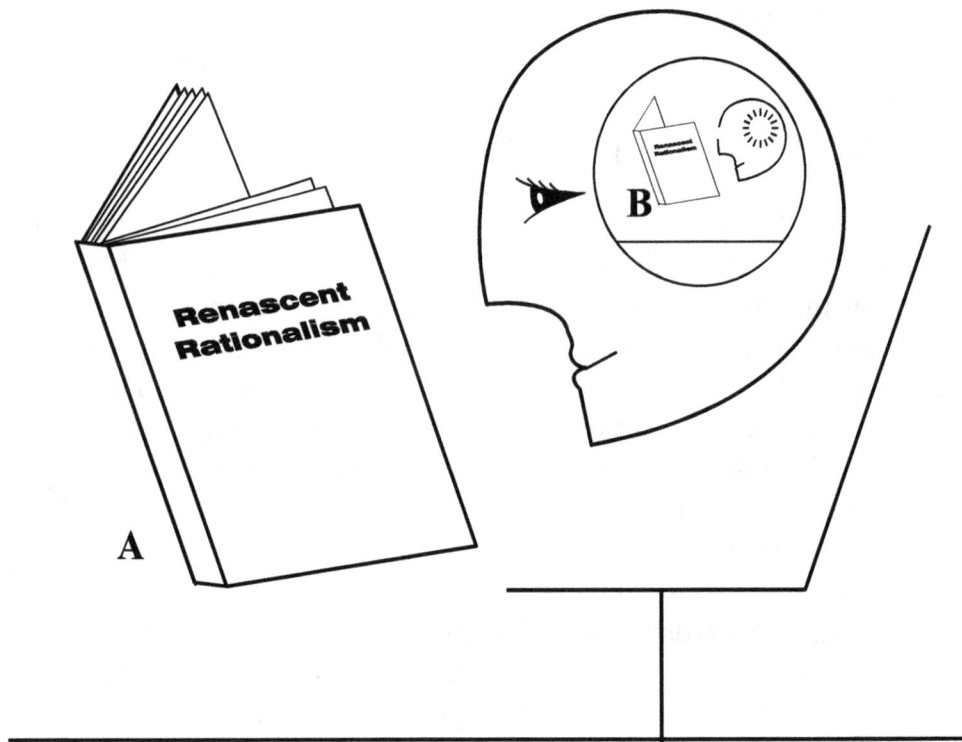

Fig. 3.4.

Fig. 3.4 is given to avoid a misinterpretation that I have occasionally found students to make when they first encounter this theory. Fig. 3.4 may be supposed to represent you, the present reader, reading this book. In terms of empirical perception, you are directly conscious of this book. In terms of Fig. 3.4, is this book, of which you are immediately conscious, book A? Or is it book B? It is, of course, book B — a representation of book A; because book A is a strict imperceptible. It is quite surprising however, how many people answer this question with book A — because their realism still prevails over their intellect.

In Figs. 3.3 and 3.4 each real person perceives by having a little person inside their head, who perceives representations. This suggests an old philosophic problem arising out of this approach to perception. If each little person perceives in the same way as the real person, then they each have a little person in their head, each of whom has a little person in their head, *ad infinitum*. If the Leibniz-Russell solution did indeed require an infinite regress of this kind, it would be fatally flawed. However, it does not. Inside the first little person's head is an ego, which is immediately conscious of representations; a possible explanation of this is given in Part Three. Putting it another way: if the apparent person, inside the real person, theoretically perceived representations then there would have to be another apparent person inside the head of the first. But the apparent person does

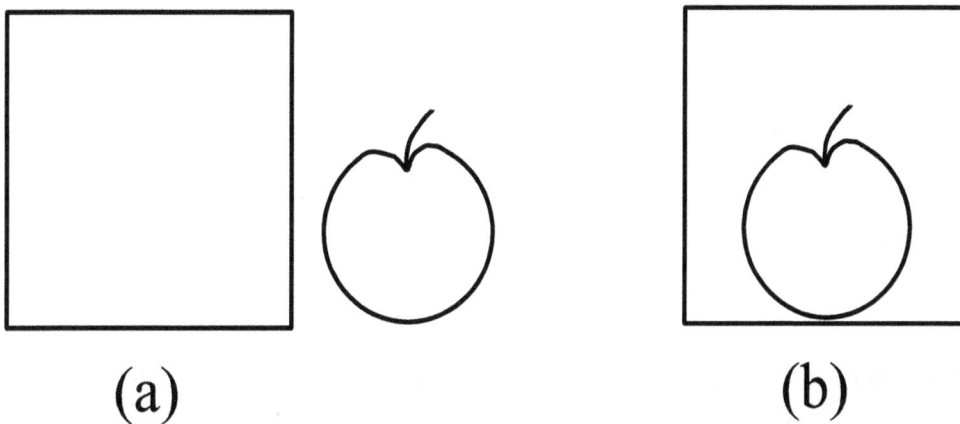

(a)   (b)

Fig. 3.5.

not theoretically perceive representations — it empirically perceives them.
✸✸✸

The logic of the Leibniz-Russell theory, as given in these figures, may be illustrated clearly by an analogy. Suppose that you are told that the apple is outside the box, and also that the apple is inside the box, as in Fig. 3.5, (a) and (b). How can these both be true?

There are three possibilities, shown in Fig. 3.6, (a), (b), and (c). One way, (a), is to deny the first definite article and say that there are two apples, one inside the box and one outside; another way, (b), is to deny the second definite article and say that there are two boxes, one inside the

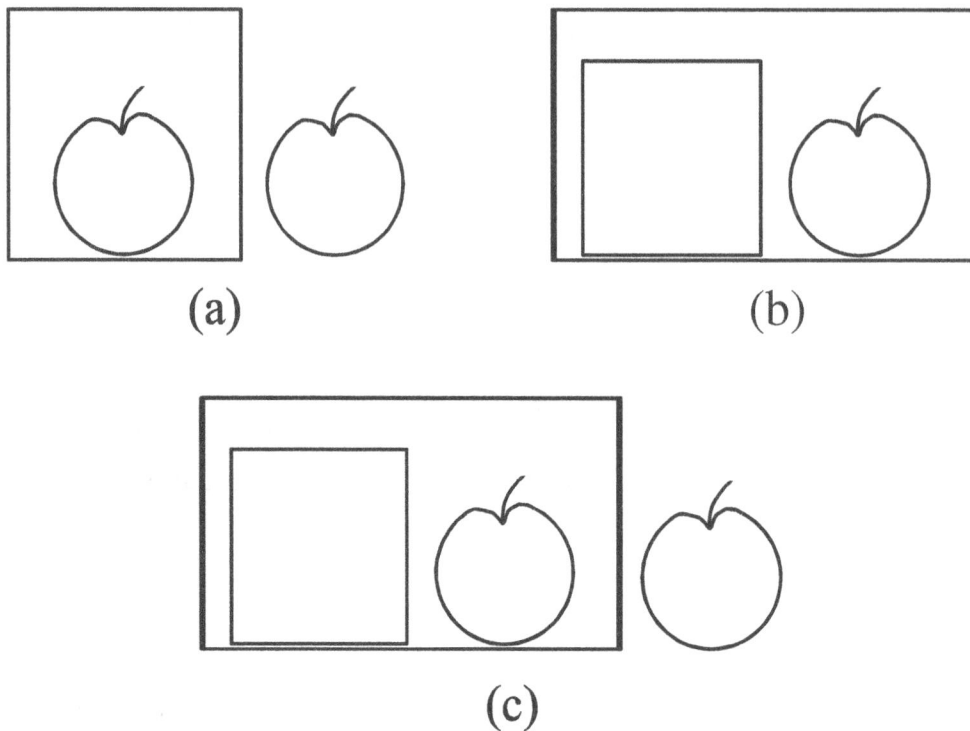

(a)

(b)

(c)

Fig. 3.6

other, with the apple between them; and the third way, (c), is to combine the first two ways. This third way, (c), is the solution used in the Leibniz-Russell theory, because the nature of theoretical perception requires it. So, for *apple* read *object*, and for *box* read *head*: empirical perception requires the object to be outside the perceiver's head, and theoretical perception requires the object to be inside the head, hence there are two objects and two heads, so that the empirical object is inside the theoretical head and outside the empirical head, the theoretical object is outside the theoretical head, and the empirical head is inside the theoretical head.

✱

We may now explain why the words *real* and *theoretical* are used as synonyms [8], in opposition to the words *apparent* and *empirical*. The real, it will be recalled, is all that exists independently of perception, so that the real world is everything real; but according to the Leibniz-Russell theory, the real world is strictly imperceptible, radically unknowable, in the sense of never being given in empirical perception. The theoretical was defined as the non-empirical, which is to say that it is never known through the senses. So the real and the theoretical are one and the same, just as the apparent and the empirical are one and the same.

However, realism, the deeply rooted belief of a common sense to which we are all dearly attached, must be false. This is not such a drastic requirement as it first seems. Realism is a belief, which we hold in order to explain the externality, publicity, reperceptibility, and materiality of things that we empirically perceive — that is, we suppose that empirical things are public by identity, and they are external, material, and reperceptible because they are real. The Leibniz-Russell solution denies this, on the grounds of logical impossibility (given the facts of illusion, viewpoint, imperfect publicity, etc.) and offers an alternative explanation: apparent objects are public by similarity, they are external to the apparent head rather than the real head, and they are material and reperceptible because their causes are real. This alternative explanation I will call **metarealism** because it includes the metarealistic interpretation [10].

∗ ∗ ∗

We turn now to a linguistic approach to the Leibniz-Russell theory. This depends upon the fact that empirical perception and theoretical perception have one common vocabulary. Each uses the same words, but with different meanings. This equivocation turns out to be an extraordinarily effective mask for the contradictions that realism produces. It allows people who have a professional stake in clear objective thinking — scientists and philosophers dealing with perception — to remain muddled and subjective, in order to maintain their belief in realism. (The words *same* and *different*, with their equivocal meanings, also help in this, as we have seen [12].)

I will begin with four key words from this one vocabulary of perception: *object*, *medium*, *representation*, and *subject*. When these are used for theoretical perception I will qualify them with the word *real*, and when they are used for empirical perception I will qualify them with the word *apparent*. Thus in theoretical perception a real object (which I will symbolise as r-O) causes, via a real medium (r-M) a real representation (r-R) of itself to appear in the immediate consciousness of a real subject (r-S). The real medium is electromagnetic radiation in real space, real eyes, real afferent nerves, etc. The real subject is the ego of Part 3. This perception is represented symbolically in Fig. 3.7.

$$\text{r-O} \longrightarrow \text{r-M} \longrightarrow \text{r-R} \longrightarrow \text{r-S}$$

Fig. 3.7.

In empirical perception, on the other hand, an apparent object (a-O) is directly perceived, through an apparent medium (a-M), by an apparent subject (a-S); and an apparent representation (a-R) of it may be remembered later by this apparent subject. The apparent medium is empirical space. The apparent subject, I will assume for the time being, is also the ego of Part 3. (It is in fact an oversimplification to identify r-S and a-S. But the errors that result are not important for the present; they will be corrected in Chapter 11.) This perception is represented in Fig. 3.8.

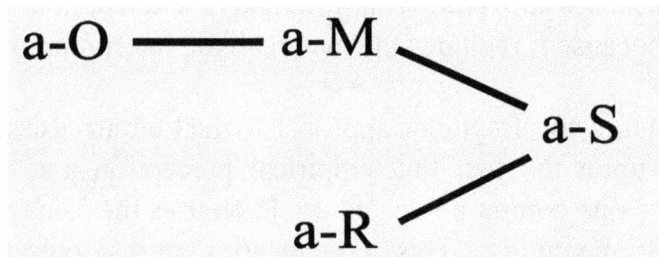

Fig. 3.8.

Realism, in failing to distinguish the two vocabularies, identifies real objects with apparent objects, real representations with apparent representations, and so on. But the relationships shown in Figs. 3.7 and 3.8 cannot be identified in this way. Perceiving and remembering are two different acts, succeeding each other in time; and Fig. 3.7 represents a causal process, while Fig. 3.8 represents two kinds of direct consciousness — of objects and of memories.

Metarealism, on the other hand, according to the Leibniz-Russell solution, identifies the real representation with the apparent object. This can be argued on the grounds that there is only one subject per person because the real subject and the apparent subject are one; hence what is given directly to the consciousness of this one subject (now symbolised as

S) must be identical in both languages. This given (G) is the real representation in the one language and the apparent object in the other. Hence r-R and a-O are one: namely, G. So the relationships of Fig. 3.7 and 3.8 combine into that of Fig.3.9. The identification of the apparent object

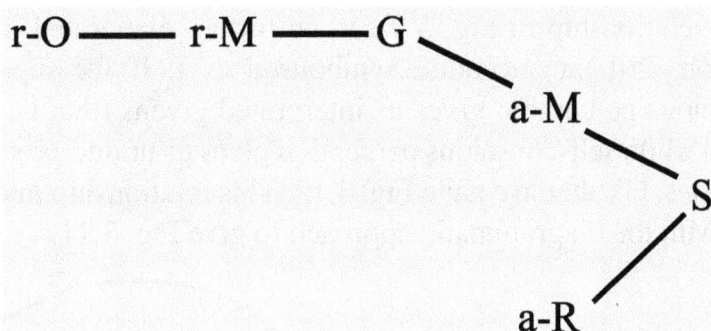

r-O —— r-M —— G
                 a-M
                     S
             a-R

Fig. 3.9.

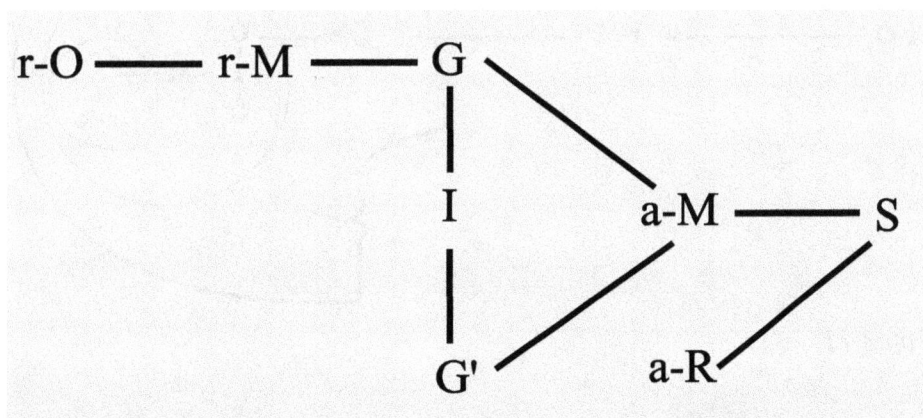

r-O —— r-M —— G
                 a-M —— S
I
             a-R
G'

Fig. 3.10.

with the real representation (metarealism) rather than with the real object (realism) is perhaps the crux of the Leibniz-Russell solution. So it is worth arguing the point once again. We need only consider any illusion. The illusory quality, whatever it might be, is empirically perceived as "out there" — external to the perceiver, and usually public. So the illusory quality belongs to the apparent object. But in theoretical perception the illusory quality always belongs to the real representation; if it were in the real object it would not be illusory. And if it were anywhere else but in the representation the whole theory of perception would be pointless, since the representation is postulated for no other reason than to explain illusion. So the illusory qualities are not in the real object, as realism requires, but are in both the apparent object and the real representation. So these latter are one and the same, identical, as metarealism requires.

✶

The relationship in Fig. 3.9 can be further elaborated if we take interpretation [26] into account, symbolised as I. If we suppose that unselfconscious perception gives us interpreted givens (that is, apparent objects, G′) while self-conscious perception gives us uninterpreted givens (i.e. sensations, G), then we have Fig. 3.10. This relationship may then be combined with the diagrammatic approach to give Fig. 3.11.

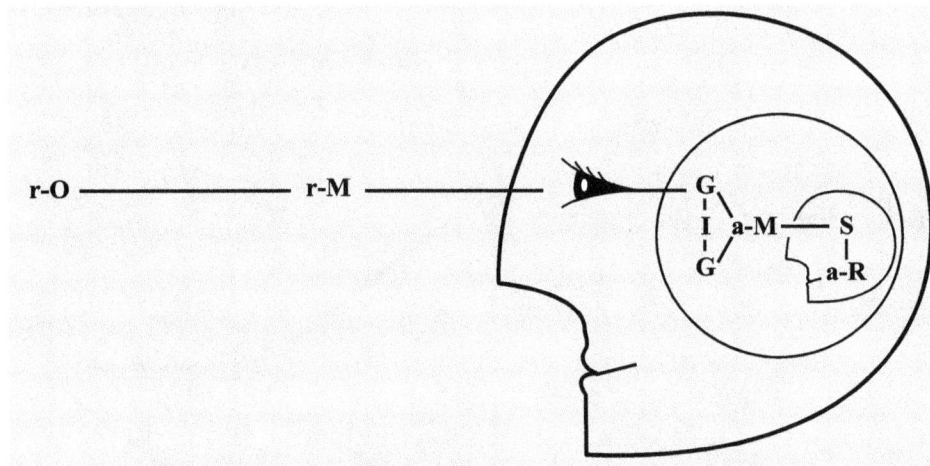

Fig. 3.11.

✶

The distinction between the two vocabularies of perception may be further extended. Thus we have already defined real world and apparent world. We may do the same with mind. An **apparent mind** is all the content of someone's consciousness which would normally be classified as mental: all that which is not subject to the laws of empirical science. A **real mind** (Fig. 3.12) consists of a conscious subject, or ego; all that this ego is conscious of, which is apparent world and apparent mind; and an unconscious mind, repository of memories, etc. Apparent mind is thus empirical — i.e. it is known directly, by introspection; and real mind is theoretical, a product of theoretical neural switchings. The distinction

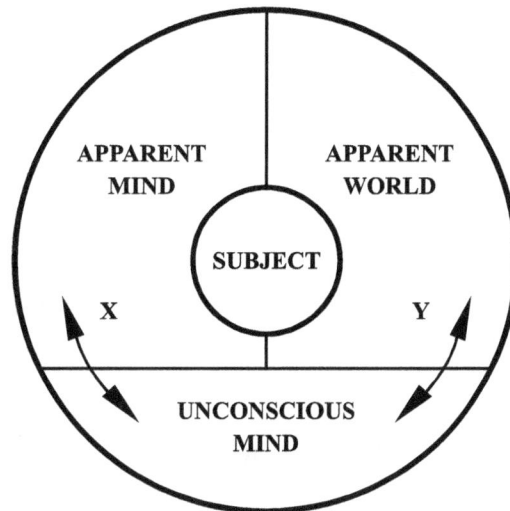

Fig. 3.12.

between real mind and apparent mind resolves the sometimes nagging paradox that if mind is defined in terms of consciousness then the concept of unconscious mind is self-contradictory. Only apparent mind is defined exclusively in terms of consciousness, and the concept of unconscious mind belongs to real mind.

In these terms a possible explanation of what is called projection [196] is movement from one part of the real mind to another: specifically, from the unconscious mind to the apparent world. This, in principle, is no more difficult to explain than remembering, which requires movement from the unconscious mind to the apparent mind. These are shown schematically in Fig. 3.12, which is a schematic representation of the real mind, and in which the arrow X represents remembering and the arrow Y represents projection.

We have also distinguished the apparent body and the real body of the perceiver. If we suppose, crudely but conveniently, that the boundary between the material and the mental is the skin of the person concerned, then we may distinguish real skin and apparent skin. Clearly, the real world contains skins, which contain minds. If we represent such containment by the symbol >, then we have the two relationships of Fig. 3.13.

Realism identifies the corresponding terms of these relationships, equivocally: the real world is the apparent world, the real skin is the

Real world > real skin > real mind

Apparent world > apparent skin > apparent mind

Fig. 3.13.

apparent skin, and the apparent mind is the real mind. However, metarealism does not make this identification; instead it requires that the real mind contains the apparent world, as in Fig. 3.14.

Real world > real skin > real mind > apparent world > apparent skin >

apparent mind

Fig. 3.14.

✳

In Figs. 3.11 and 3.14 the apparent mind is located inside the apparent head. Although this is incorrect, we can allow it for now, for simplicity. Our common sense, or realistic, identification of the corresponding terms of the two relationships in Fig.3.13. make us believe it. The fact that one's apparent memories are external shows that one's apparent mind is outside one's own apparent head, not inside. All that we discover inside our own apparent heads is headaches. In a similar vein, introspectively, the apparent heart is the location of the emotion of love but not the location of the real heart, the blood pump.

✳

A further refinement in the distinction of the two vocabularies of perception is to take into account the person for whom the real exists independently of being perceived, and the person to whom the apparent is given in consciousness. Thus Jack's apparent world is apparent-to-Jack, since Jack is immediately conscious of it. But it is real-for-Jill, since it exists independently of Jill's perception. Similarly, Jill's apparent world is real-for-Jack and apparent-to-Jill. In the same way we can say that the real-world-for-Jack includes all consciousnesses other than his own. The **strictly real world** could then be defined as the world that is real-for-everyone — it is the totality of things that exist independently of anyone's perception. Which is to say, it is the totality of existents that are strictly imperceptible — unlike Jack's apparent world, which is strictly imperceptible to Jill, but not to Jack.

✹ ✹ ✹

4. The fourth approach to the Leibniz-Russell theory is the seven logical steps that lead to it; they are:

1. The facts of perception — illusions, viewpoint, external privacies, etc. — require that we never empirically perceive real objects, we only perceive images, or representations, of them. The real object in theoretical perception, and most of the information transfer that is the causal process of theoretical perception, cannot be empirically perceived; they are strict imperceptibles. Consequently the *representation* within theoretical perception must be the *object* in empirical perception; so *empirical perception is the last stage of theoretical perception.*

2. Theoretical perception requires a duality of cause and effect; or, equally, of object and representation; or, equally, of real object and apparent object. Each perceiver, in empirically perceiving, may be directly conscious of his own body as an apparent object. Consequently *each perceiver must possess two bodies, one real and one apparent*. His or her real body is then the cause of the apparent body, which is a representation of the real body. It is the apparent body that is empirically perceived; the real body is a strict imperceptible.

3. If someone theoretically perceives a real object, which is external to their real body, then three representations will be caused to appear within their consciousness. These three representations are of the real object, of their own real body, and of the relationship of externality between these. And these three representations will appear as an apparent object apparently external to their apparent body. These three appearances (i) will be in their real brain and (ii) they will empirically perceive them — they will be directly conscious of them. Thus *what is empirically perceived is internal to the real head and external to the apparent head.*

4. For any one perceiver the totality of apparent objects — all that they empirically perceive — is their apparent world. As a representation of the real world, this is entirely inside their real head. Consequently, since each person's real head is wholly separate, spatially, from everyone else's,

there is one numerically distinct and spatially distinct apparent world for each perceiver.

5. Every member of a group of real people in one vicinity in the real world will possess representations of this vicinity in their real heads. These representations will be their individual apparent worlds. As representations of the real, they will have some similarity to the real (that is, similarity truth), and therefore some similarity to each other. They will also have some dissimilarity to each other because of viewpoint and perceptual idiosyncrasies. In so far as these apparent worlds are similar, they are public by similarity; insofar as they are dissimilar, they are private by dissimilarity; and they are, of course, private by plurality. Thus *the publicity of apparent worlds is not due to identity, but to similarity.* This error of realism is an instance of the identity error [13].

6. In so far as real objects conform to scientific law, and in so far as apparent objects are true representations of real objects, so will these apparent objects conform to scientific law. It is largely because of this conformity to scientific law that we call apparent objects *material.* Also, in so far as apparent objects are within the consciousness that is a product of a real brain, they are *mental.* Thus *apparent objects are both (apparently) material and (really) mental.*

7. In so far as a representation of a real object exists in a real brain only while the real object causally sustains it there — that is, only while the real object is being theoretically perceived — so is the existence of the apparent object dependent upon perception. In Berkeley's phrase, *esse est percipi* is true of all apparent things: that is, to be is to be perceived so far as apparent worlds are concerned. So apparent objects are unreal, although their causes — real objects — are real. Thus *the reperceptibility of things empirically perceived is not due their being real, but to their causes being real.*

✱

To summarise these points: empirical perception is the last stage of theoretical perception; each perceiver must possess two bodies, one real and one apparent; what is empirically perceived is internal to the real head and external to the apparent head; there is one numerically distinct and spatially distinct apparent world per perceiver; the publicity of apparent worlds is not due to identity, but to similarity; apparent objects are both (apparently) material and (really) mental; and the reperceptibility of things empirically perceived is not due their being real, but to their causes being real.

In short, the Leibniz-Russell theory allows both empirical perception to be true and theoretical perception to be true. Objects of which we are immediately conscious are public (by similarity to other people's), external (to the apparent head), and material (because they obey scientific laws) — as empirical perception requires. At the same time they are representations that are private (by plurality, as well as by some dissimilarity), internal (to the real head) and mental (because a product of the real brain) — as theoretical perception requires. Furthermore, since empirical perception is the last stage of theoretical perception, empirical perception is immediate awareness of an apparent object (that is, of a representation) rather than the causal process that produces that apparent object.

✱ ✱ ✱

We next look at the eighteen problems of perception of Chapter Two, to see how the Leibniz-Russell theory solves them all.

✱

1. The double vision problem [15] is the problem that we explain the experience of seeing double objects when the eyes are crossed by saying that we see two images, one per retina. How, then, do we see a real object rather than two coincident images when the eyes are not crossed? The answer is that we never see a real object, we always see images of real objects.

✱

2. Because the apparent size of visible objects diminishes with distance and their real size does not, we had the problem of how far away an object has to be for its apparent size to equal its real size [15]. The plain answer is that since we never see real size, we can never know. However, visible size can be correlated with tactile size. If you hold a tennis ball in one hand and bring it closer to your eyes, then both the visible ball and the visible hand get larger as they get closer, but the tactile ball stays a constant size. At the shortest distance you have maximum visible size, and this may be compared with your tactile size. So if you clutch your head with both hands — something that the Leibniz-Russell theory is likely to make you

do anyway — then you have a tactile size of your own empirical head, and a correlated maximum visible size. Since this empirical size is an image *inside* your real head, it must be smaller than your real head, in which case visible size is never as large as real size. Some possible exceptions to this are those things seen through a microscope: if you see a bacterium through a microscope, what you see is an image of the bacterium, enlarged by the lenses of the microscope; and it is possible that the enlarged image is the same size as the real bacterium. But since we cannot measure the real size of visual images in brains, we cannot know their relative sizes. (More fully, there is a real optical image, produced by a real microscope, and an apparent optical image, which is a representation of, and smaller than, the real optical image.) In short, we cannot see real size.

✶

3. Connected with this problem was the question of whether real size and measured size are identical [15]. Since we can see measured size but cannot see real size, they cannot be identical. The significance of measured size is that it is public — potentially, universally, public — because it does not vary with distance. Measured size is like tactile size in this respect, and it is noteworthy that in the early days of civilisation the units of measure of length were tactile: they were body parts, such as the foot.

✶

4. The problem of describing colour to a blind man [16] was that if colours are real, as realism requires, then they should be describable in the same way that atoms are describable — but they clearly are not. The reason is that all sensations are absolutely private. This is privacy by plurality, in the same way that dreams and thoughts are private. We can describe dreams and thoughts to anyone who speaks our language because our language is originally learnt ostensively — by pointing to public things and naming them. This is publicity by similarity, in the same way that many copies of the same newspaper, or many television pictures, on different sets, of the same program, are public. Colours are not public to a blind man, so colour-words cannot be ostensively defined for him, so they cannot be meaningful to him.

✶

5. The next problem [16] was that of how private things can be in public space and remain private: the fuzziness of things seen with unfocussed eyes, after-images, hallucinations, and the like. This is a problem for realism because it requires that things are public by virtue of being in *one* public space. This is publicity by identity. We have seen [14] that publicity by identity has to be totally public: it cannot be partially public and partially private. So, since all that we empirically perceive is a mixture of both, the publicity of empirical worlds must be publicity by similarity, it cannot be publicity by identity — as metarealism, or the Leibniz-Russell theory, require.

✶

6. The swimming pool problem [16] was that of how one swimming pool can be at once warm to a cold swimmer and cool to a hot swimmer. The answer is that it cannot: one thing cannot be both warm and not warm at once. So there must be two empirical swimming pools, one warm and one cold, which is what the Leibniz-Russell theory requires. The real pool has one theoretical temperature, which is the average kinetic energy of its molecules, and this is sensed by real swimmers, relative to the theoretical temperatures of their theoretical skins, and experienced by them as their individual empirical temperatures. These empirical temperatures are the temperature, for each of them, of their own empirical swimming pool.

✶

7. The rainbow problem [16] was that of whether many people see one rainbow, as realism requires, or many rainbows, as theory requires. All the people can quickly discover that their empirical rainbows are public, and the problem is that of deciding whether this is publicity by identity, as realism requires, or publicity by plurality, as metarealism requires. This is decided by the fact that some of the rainbows may be partially private — since some of the people may be colour-blind to some degree — and publicity by identity cannot be partially private. And, of course, the Leibniz-Russell theory requires that there be as many rainbows as there are theoretical perceivers, since there are as many empirical worlds as there are perceivers.

✶

8. The aspect problem [16] is that of how we ever perceive a solid object, such as a house, if we only ever perceive aspects of it. This is only

a problem for realism, which wants to identify an aspect of an object with the (qualitatively different) object itself. As we have seen, qualitative difference entails quantitative difference, so that the aspect and the object must be two. This is no problem for the Leibniz-Russell theory, since the object is theoretical and the aspect is empirical.

∗

9. If you were so constituted as to see green when everyone else saw red, and *vice versa*, could you ever know this [17]? The answer, of course, is no, since colours are private by plurality. This is closely related to the problem of describing colour to a blind man: we *assume* that our colour sensations are public, and so define words for them ostensively, but we cannot *know* that they are public; this assumed publicity is publicity by similarity. Realism assumes it to be publicity by identity — but if it were so then your seeing green when others saw red would be impossible.

∗

10, 11. The next two problems [17] are: can you point to something that is entirely free of illusion; and if you can, how would you know it to be so? The simple answer to this is no: we can be certain of illusion, but not of non-illusion, or perceptual similarity truth. What we empirically perceive *could* all be hallucination, or a dream — not images of reality at all; and then none of it would be free of illusion. A more sophisticated answer is that some objects of science might be illusion free; but our knowledge of this would only be probable knowledge, not certain knowledge. This will be discussed further in Part Two.

∗

12. The Moon problem [17] is the problem of consciousness at a distance: if you empirically perceive the real Moon, which is 250,000 miles away, how does your consciousness extend out of your head for that distance? If, on the other hand, you see an image of the Moon, brought to you by reflected sunlight, and this image is in your head, then there is no problem. Obviously the problem exists for realism but not for metarealism. This problem is discussed in more detail later [153].

∗

13. The problem following on this [17] was: if you do not see the real Moon then is anything you see real? The answer, according to Leibniz-

Russell, is no: everything you see is images of reality, not reality itself. The problem exists only for realism.

✶

14. As Bishop Berkeley asked, if a tree falls in the forest and there is no one around to hear it, does it make a noise [17]? The answer is yes and no. According to the causal theory of perception, which is incorporated into the Leibniz-Russell theory, the word *noise* has two meanings: real noise and apparent noise, or theoretical noise and empirical noise. Real noise is acoustical waves in the air, and empirical noise is sensation of sound produced in the ears when real noise vibrates the eardrums. When the tree falls it produces theoretical noise, but if there is no one around to hear it, there is no apparent noise. In the same vein, colour exists in the dark if by *colour* you mean a molecular structure that radiates electromagnetic waves in the so-called visible spectrum, but does not exist if you mean either this radiation or the sensations of colour produced by it.

✶

15. When you talk with a friend on the telephone, do you talk with your friend, or with a reproduction of you friend's voice [17]? According to realism, you talk with your friend, and according to the causal theory of perception, you talk with a reproduction. So also does your friend talk with a reproduction: a reproduction of your voice. There are two distinct conversations, one at each end of the telephone line. Communication between you is possible because the two conversations are public by similarity. They are not public by identity, as realism supposes. The significance of this is that if you talk with your friend in person, the same situation holds: you talk with a representation of your friend, in your empirical world, and your friend talks with a representation of you, in her empirical world. In everyday living the common sense simplification of these, into direct conversations, is harmless and convenient; but in philosophy it leads to problems that cannot be solved within realism.

✶

16. The child's riddle [17] about catching an elephant by making it small, by looking at it through the wrong end of a telescope, requires that everything seen through a lens is an image; and since our eyes have lenses, everything we see must be an image. Clearly, this is a problem for realism but not for metarealism.

＊

17. The difference between hearing the sound of a siren and hearing the siren [18] is the difference between hearing an image and hearing reality. According to the Leibniz-Russell theory we only ever hear images, we never hear reality, so there is no problem; the problem exists only for realism. When we say that we hear a siren, what we should say, if we want to be philosophically correct, is that we hear the sound of a siren and believe that it is caused by a siren.

＊

18. The same answer applies to the exploding Sun [18]: if it exploded, we would continue to see it for eight minutes, even though it no longer existed, because that is how long it takes light to travel from there to here. Realism has it that we empirically perceive the real Sun, and thereby has a problem with this; the Leibniz-Russell theory has it that we only ever see images of the Sun, and thereby has no problem: the real Sun no longer exists, but the image of it continues to exist, for eight minutes.

＊

In short, all these problems arise from the need to say that we empirically perceive reality itself, not images of reality; and they are problems only for as long as one tries to reconcile this with realism. Within metarealism there are no such problems.

＊ ＊ ＊

We end this chapter with a remark on empirical and theoretical reality. These were defined as: theoretical reality is all that exists independently of being perceived and empirical reality is all that is empirically perceived which is potentially, universally, public. In terms of the Leibniz-Russell solution, empirical reality is *truth* of perception. That is, it is the truth of apparent worlds. This truth is truth by resemblance to theoretical reality — the truth that is the similarity between apparent world and real world. That this is so is obvious once it is understood that empirical reality is all of apparent worlds except the illusory and the private — and these latter are empirical perceptions that are resemblance false.

Part Two. The Real World.

4. False Belief.

Having inquired into false perception we now turn to false belief. We begin with belief itself, then consider it as false, and then consider the possibilities of correcting it.

In the first place, we will take for granted that beliefs occur in real minds [38], that they are composed of apparent images, or of concepts, etc. This type of analysis of belief belongs to theory of mind and must wait until we get to Part 3 [160]. For the present we are not concerned with what beliefs *are*, but with what they are *about*. This will mean, as it turns out, that our major concern in Part 2 is with the real world: all that exists independently of being perceived [7]. We are also for the present only concerned with rational beliefs. Irrational beliefs, believed because of wish-fulfilment, prejudice, vanity, superstition, or stereotyping, also will be dealt with in Part 3.

The transition from the concept of perception to the concept of belief comes about most easily with a truism: perception is of perceptibles. This is worth saying because it immediately reveals the basic feature of belief: **belief** is of imperceptibles, belief is a perception substitute.

In other words, when perception fails we substitute a belief. That which we did not perceive, because of the failure of our perception, but which we none the less believe in, is an imperceptible. Perception may fail through false perception, as we have already considered; or through interruption, as with sleep, fog, high walls, horizons, etc.; or through inadequacy of sense organs, as in our failure to see ultra-violet and infra-red, or hear ultrasonic vibrations. In all these cases, if we are conscious of the failure, we substitute a belief.

Memory and expectation are also perception substitutes, of a temporal kind; but here we are mainly going to consider beliefs.

✳

An imperceptible may be defined, initially, as any thing, quality, relation, event, process, or whatever that either is not, or else cannot be, given in consciousness. Imperceptibles are thus empirical imperceptibles, but not necessarily theoretical imperceptibles. For example, a real chair is

Strict perceptibles, (for me, now)	Given to me, now	} Perceptibles
Imperceptibles {	Reportables, not given to me, now, but given to someone, sometime.	
	Given to no one, ever	Strict imperceptibles

Table 4.1.

an imperceptible; it is empirically imperceptible, even though it is theoretically perceptible: it cannot be given in consciousness, but it can be represented in consciousness, as an image, an empirical chair.

The concept of imperceptible, like the concept of real [40], can be confusing because a full definition must specify the subject of the perception. If we do this, it turns out that the definitions most suitable for our purposes involve three classes[3].

Any one person can define a **strict perceptible** as: anything apparent to me, now. In other words, the totality of strict perceptibles for me, now, is my apparent world and my apparent mind, now — thc totality of indubitable existents, the total content of my present consciousness.

There is secondly the class: anything not apparent to me now, but which is apparent to someone, sometime; this will be called the class of **reportables**.

And thirdly, we may define a **strict imperceptible** as: anything apparent to no one, ever.

---

[3] The modern term for *class* is *set*. The two words may be regarded as synonymous, but I usually use *class* because of its derivative concept *classification*, which we will later find to be an irrational thought process.

50

Strict perceptibles are known by being given, now; reportables are known inductively, as will be explained shortly; and strict imperceptibles are known speculatively.

We next define a **perceptible** as anything that is not a strict imperceptible, and an **imperceptible** as anything that is not a strict perceptible. This is perhaps confusing, because the classes of perceptibles and imperceptibles intersect — they have the subclass of reportables in common. However, Table 4.1 clarifies this.

Thus imperceptibles are either strict imperceptibles or else reportables, and perceptibles are either strict perceptibles or reportables.

For example, as I write, my computer is a strict perceptible for me but it is only a perceptible for you, the reader, as are all past and future apparent events. Since I am writing this in Canada, the Houses of Parliament in London are only perceptibles for me, although they are, I believe, strict perceptibles for some of the people now in London. Secondly some things never have yet been perceived by anyone, but they will be — some ocean beds for example; these are perceptibles. Third, among strict imperceptibles are real objects in theoretical perception, and everything that is theoretically imperceptible, such as the interior of the sun. Other things are strictly imperceptible in the trivial sense that they do not exist: perpetual motion machines, mermaids, the philosopher's stone, square circles, and the like.

The importance of the concept of imperceptible is recognised immediately it is understood how much dispute is about imperceptibles — about which do or do not exist, or did or will exist, and what their nature is, was, or will be: God, for example, or the total mass of the Universe.

Three of the concepts in the above classification are also of particular importance: strict perceptibles are everything whose existence is indubitable: that is, every strict perceptible for you, now, exists indubitably for you, now. Also, of the least dubitable existents other than these, empirical science [67] is concerned with perceptibles and theoretical science [67] with strict imperceptibles. These points will be discussed later.

✶ ✶ ✶

There are two kinds of rational belief: empirical beliefs and explanatory beliefs. **Empirical beliefs** are beliefs about the existence of reportables, while all beliefs about strict imperceptibles are explanatory beliefs. Thus if I believe in the existence of something not actually perceived by me, now, but perceived by someone, sometime, then that belief is an empirical belief. For example, I believe that some apparent worlds other than mine contain scenes called by various London names; that some future apparent worlds will contain novel sea beds; and that once my own apparent world contained events of my boyhood. Belief in the truth of memories and expectations, of predictions, of hearsay, and of historical events is based on empirical belief, since the truth of all of these depends on the existence of a reportable.

✳

Along with empirical beliefs should be mentioned the supposed belief in the non-existence of an imperceptible, which seems to be a belief but in fact is not so. It is a denial of a belief, a denial of the belief that this imperceptible exists — and so is a **disbelief**. This point will be significant in the discussion of solipsism below [56].

✳

Explanatory beliefs, besides presupposing the existence of imperceptibles, explain something by means of them. Suppose, for example, that I have a glass on my table and that it suddenly shatters. I can explain this perceptible event by saying that it was a punishment by God for the fact that the glass contained demon rum. Or that "They" are persecuting me by means of invisible rays. Or that a rifle bullet just happened to pass that way. Or that the glass contained uranium salts to give it a yellow-green colour, and a small nuclear explosion occurred. Or that my audio system emitted an ultrasonic note that broke the glass through resonance. Or that the glass was internally stressed when manufactured and finally gave way. All of these possible explanations of the shattering of the glass invoke imperceptibles: God, "They", invisible rays, a travelling rifle bullet, a small nuclear chain reaction, an ultrasonic note, internal stresses. To accept any one of these explanations is to believe in the existence of the imperceptible that it invokes.

An empirical belief may be part of an explanatory belief in that we believe that other people are conscious — in order to explain why they behave as they do — yet the content of their consciousness is the content of my empirical beliefs. This shows that although all beliefs about strict imperceptibles are explanatory beliefs, the converse does not hold: some explanatory beliefs are about reportables.

✳

It is not enough however simply to say that explanatory beliefs explain. We need to know how they explain. The answer to this is that explanatory beliefs explain by the assumption that the imperceptibles to which they refer are causes. The imperceptible is the cause and that which is explained is the effect. Thus the shattering of the glass was an effect, and the various possible explanations of it give various possible imperceptible causes of it.

The difficulty with this answer is that philosophers do not agree on the nature of causation. One reason for this is that, as with perception, there are two kinds of causation that are generally treated as one. We can call them, quite appropriately, **real causation** and **apparent causation**, or, equivalently, **theoretical causation** and **empirical causation**. Broadly speaking, real or theoretical causation occurs in the real world and includes the relation of necessity — that is, the real cause necessitates the real effect — while apparent or empirical causation occurs in apparent worlds and does not include necessity. These definitions are incomplete, in that they leave unclear whether any part of real causation is ever perceptible or not. This will be returned to later [86, 255]. Apparent causation is perceptible. It is Humean, or common sense, causation: a temporal correlation of perceptible events. For example, it is often supposed that lightning causes thunder. Lightning and thunder are both perceptibles, and the occurrence of the earlier, the cause, is always followed by the occurrence of the later, the effect. In theoretical terms, however, lightning does not cause thunder. Instead a strictly imperceptible atmospheric electric discharge in the real world causally necessitates, among other things, perceptible flashes of light and perceptible rumbles of sound in the apparent worlds of real people nearby. Empirical lightning and empirical thunder are thus both effects of the theoretical atmospheric electric discharge — and are thereby correlated.

✳

We have in consequence two kinds of explanation. We may define explanation as: an **explanation** is a description of a cause, such that what it explains are the effects of this cause. Or, more briefly: to describe causes is to explain their effects. Furthermore, the effect can be *deduced* from the cause — or, more precisely, a description of the effect can be deduced from the explanation. This is sometimes stated in the form that an explanation yields its *explicandum* logically. Obviously, **empirical explanation** is a matter of description of apparent causes, and **theoretical explanation** of real causes. Apparent explanation is sometimes known as **covering law type explanation**.

When I use the terms *cause, effect, causation,* and *explanation* subsequently, they will, unless otherwise qualified, always refer to the real, not the apparent, concepts.

✱ ✱ ✱

We now turn to the question of false belief. As we saw in Part 1, rational people cannot doubt that they have at least one false belief. We also discovered two cases of dissimilarity falsity [5] in Part 1: an apparent object is false in so far as it does not resemble its original, the real object; and an apparent representation, or memory, is false in so far as it does not resemble its original, the apparent object. Consequently a belief similarly is false in so far as the images or concepts that constitute it do not resemble the imperceptibles that they represent. There is a variety of ways in which this can happen. Just as an hallucination is false because its real object is non-existent, so is a belief false if an imperceptible to which it refers is non-existent. Or, if a belief attempts to explain a perceptible by means of the wrong imperceptible, then it is false. Or a belief might refer to the right imperceptible, but resemble it incorrectly — for example, by attributing the wrong structure to it — or else relate it incorrectly to other imperceptibles.

Conversely, of course, perception, memory and belief are true when the apparent object, the apparent representation, or the concept, do resemble their originals. This kind of truth (as opposed to logical truth and speaking the truth) is similarity truth [5]. There is no more problem about understanding the nature of similarity truth than there is in understanding the falsity of non-resemblance, or dissimilarity falsity. We are sure of dissimilarity falsity when the perception, memory, or belief contains a contradiction. Unlike dissimilarity falsity, however, we can never be sure that we have similarity truth in perception, memory, or belief. The truth of theoretical perception lies in the resemblance of apparent objects to real objects, and these latter are imperceptible. The truth of memory lies in the resemblance of apparent representations to former apparent objects, and these latter are also imperceptible. The truth of belief lies in the resemblance of apparent representations or concepts to imperceptibles. In each case the similarity truth can be known only by comparing the copy with its imperceptible original; and this requires that we empirically perceive an imperceptible, which is impossible. Secondly, since similarity truth in each case involves an imperceptible, whenever we consider the truth of perception, of memory, or of belief, we are in the realm of belief. We can know perception to be false, but we cannot know it to be true, we can only believe it to be true; we can know memory to be false, but only believe it to be true; and we can know belief to be false, but only believe it to be true. There are no similarity truths among the indubitabilities [3]; all such truth, including the truth of belief itself, are a matter of belief.

In short, although it is indubitable that some beliefs are false, off hand we do not know which, if any, of the remainder are true and which are false — since none of them are indubitably true. We therefore have the problem of how to discover which beliefs are true and which false.

✶

A beginning of an answer to this problem is to consider the extreme possibility that no beliefs are true, that no imperceptibles whatever exist. This is the same as supposing that only strict perceptibles exist — that is, only that of which I am conscious now, exists. This is to suppose that all beliefs are false, including my belief that other people have beliefs, so mine are the totality of beliefs and all beliefs whatever are false. This is the position of extreme doubt. I cannot doubt that of which I am now conscious, because of its existential indubitability; but I can doubt everything else. We need to consider extreme doubt at this point if only to discover whether it is acceptable; that is, if extreme doubt leads to a contradiction then it must be false, in which case some imperceptibles must exist.

If I am an extreme sceptic in this way, and I wish to be consistent, I have to find a meaning for the words *I* and *my* — otherwise I cannot meaningfully claim that only what is given in consciousness to *me* exists. Since only strict perceptibles exist, *I* can only be defined in terms of some or all of them. A little consideration shows that the most satisfactory definition is to say that I am the totality of strict perceptibles, which is to say that I am the totality of the contents of my consciousness. That is, I am defining myself as a conscious subject, not myself as an empirical body: my empirical body is only one among my strict perceptibles. It immediately follows from this definition that I alone exist, since we have supposed that no imperceptibles exist, hence only strict perceptibles exist. This doctrine that I alone exist is known as **solipsism**. Solipsism is a very peculiar doctrine, and is of considerable philosophic interest. We will first look at its peculiarities, and then see why it is none the less interesting.

✳

If solipsism is true then:

    1. *Time* does not exist. I cannot perceive the future, so it is an imperceptible and so does not exist. I cannot perceive the past, so it equally does not exist. So time does not exist.

    2. The *passage of time* of which I am conscious must be an illusion: I am conscious of passage of time, but there cannot be passage of time if there is no time.

    3. All the *memories* that I am now remembering — there are no others — are false. I can remember the past, but to remember it is not to perceive it. Since that which makes a memory true is a past event and none such exist, all memories must be false.

    4. Equally, all *expectations* of the future — all those of which I am now conscious — are false.

    5. Furthermore, the truth of perception as we have understood it so far is similarity truth — similarity to the real; since all the real is imperceptible, none of it exists, so all of the one and only *apparent world* is resemblance false — it is all illusion.

    6. All the *explanations* of which I am now conscious, which are all that exist, are also false, since all explanations explain by means of imperceptible, hence non-existent, causes.

    7. All *beliefs* are also false, since what would make them true is imperceptible and does not exist.

    8. And all *reports* of which I am now conscious are equally false.

✳

This peculiar doctrine is important to philosophy for a number of reasons. In the first place, it results from extreme doubt. Since what is dubitable is all imperceptibles, all that remains after such doubt is all strict perceptibles. Which is to say, all strict perceptibles "for me, now," where "me" refers to whomever might be considering this matter and "now" to the time of this consideration. As we saw in Chapter 1, these are the totality of indubitabilities. Thus solipsism allows the totality of indubitabilities and nothing else. It is the opposite of Leibniz's position: Leibniz said that this is the best of all possible worlds [104], while solipsism requires that this is the worst of all possible worlds.

Within modern times three philosophers have come close to solipsism. Descartes, seeking indubitabilities, invented the method of extreme doubting, which he called hyperbolical doubt, in order to discover what remained at the end. He avoided solipsism by means of arguments, not widely accepted, that God exists (which *ipso facto* denies solipsism, since God is an imperceptible) and, furthermore, that, God not being a deceiver, imperceptible real objects exist in order to make perceptions true. Bishop Berkeley also came close to solipsism with his definition of existence: *esse est percipi*, or to be is to be perceived [42]. Strictly applied, this must mean "perceived by me, now" since to argue that minds other than mine, now, exist because they perceive themselves is to beg the question — they perceive themselves because they exist and they exist because they perceive themselves. But if only what *I* perceive now exists then solipsism is true. Berkeley avoided solipsism by asserting that imperceptibles exist because they are perceived by God — an inconsistent position, since God, being imperceptible, does not exist. Although Hume never asserted the doctrine of *esse est percipi* he wrote in the spirit of it. His position was also one of extreme doubt, but his was sceptical doubt rather than hyperbolical. His position denied the legitimacy of all speculation — "'Tis vain to speculate" was his favourite phrase — yet he evaded solipsism by using a speculative argument to prove that other minds exist.

That Descartes, Berkeley and Hume all escaped from solipsism by invalid means highlights an extraordinary fact: no one has ever proved solipsism to be false. Our inability to escape from solipsism is sometimes called the **solipsistic predicament**. If solipsism is to be shown to be false, and hence at least one belief shown to be true, then we must use either of two criteria of falsification [77]: we must show solipsism to be inconsistent, or else prove that at least one imperceptible exists. Before examining the difficulty of these, however, we will briefly look at a variant of solipsism.

✷

This variant of solipsism arises if we consider the consequence of supposing that no *strict* imperceptibles exist, rather than no imperceptibles whatever. This means that all perceptibles exist, rather than only all strict perceptibles — that is, everything actually perceived by someone, sometime, as well as everything perceived by me, now. This is the basic assumption of empiricism. Historically, empiricism has been muddled because, besides this assumption, it included realism. If realism is excluded, then the resulting **rigorous empiricism** allows the existence of more than one consciousness, and requires that everything that does exist (or did, or will exist) does so within one of these consciousnesses — that is, within an apparent world or an apparent mind. To put it another way, the strictly real world [40] does not exist. This position is nearly as peculiar as solipsism. Although it allows some memories, expectations, and beliefs to be true, it does not allow any perceptions to be true — everything perceived is illusion — nor are any theoretical explanations true. And it does not allow any causal connections between consciousnesses, so that there is no possibility or communication between them. (There is pseudo-communication, of course, as in solipsism: between the whole consciousness and certain mindless parts of it called apparent people.) Thus all true beliefs that I have about imperceptibles that exist now are beliefs about other minds; these imperceptibles serve to explain why apparent people in my apparent world behave as they do. But such explanation is false (the other consciousnesses do not *cause* this behaviour), so there is no good reason for me to believe that other consciousnesses exist. One is almost as well off being a solipsist. Oddly enough, this rigorous empiricism bears a striking resemblance to Leibniz's doctrine of monads [102, 105ff.].

✷

We can next consider an ingenious argument that tries to show that solipsism is inconsistent. In discovering why it fails, we will learn the difficulty of escaping the solipsistic predicament by trying to show solipsism to be self-contradictory. The argument is that if one accepts the doctrine of solipsism then one *believes* it; but, since according to solipsism all beliefs are false, it then follows that solipsism is self-refuting — if it is true then it must be false, in which case it cannot be true.

This is a lovely kind of trick of which philosophers are fond: take the basic principle of a philosophical position that you dislike, and use that principle to refute that position. For example, relativism is the position that all truth is relative to the person who believes it: if you believe it then it is "true for you." This means that there is no absolute truth. But if we ask whether relativism is itself absolutely true or not, then if it is then there is absolute truth — namely, relativism itself — in which case relativism is false; and if it is not absolutely true then not all truth is relative so there must be some absolute truth — in which case relativism is false. Thus relativism is self-contradictory. Another example was logical positivism, which, in its effort to sanctify science, claimed that a statement is meaningful only if it can be verified, either empirically or logically. But this definition of meaningfulness is a statement that cannot be verified and therefore refutes itself.

However, accepting the doctrine of solipsism is not a matter of belief, but a matter of disbelief [52]. Solipsism is extreme disbelief, and so is not self refuting.

✶

There are other arguments against solipsism that are merely plausible: they do not show solipsism to be inconsistent, but plead other grounds for rejecting it. They take the form that it is not possible to accept solipsism because it is not possible to think of any reason why such a peculiar, not to say ridiculous, doctrine should be true. But it is irrelevant whether any such reason can be thought of, since to provide one is to *explain* why solipsism is true, and if solipsism is true then all explanations are false and so irrelevant. Thus one might ask why God would create a world consisting only of illusion and falsity or meaninglessness; but if solipsism is true then God, as an imperceptible, does not exist. Equally, to suppose that all this illusion, falsity, and meaninglessness must be produced by me, since I alone exist, and hence is a product of my unconscious imagination, is to rely on an imperceptible, my unconscious imagination, which does not exist. Solipsism, in short, is consistent; we cannot prove the existence of any imperceptibles by showing that solipsism is self-contradictory.

✸

To escape the solipsistic predicament by showing solipsism to be contrary to fact requires that we prove that an imperceptible exists. The existence of something can be proved easily by the simple device of perceiving it. If I perceive a table then I *know* that this table exists; it may be an illusion or a hallucination, but even then, as an illusion or hallucination, it exists. It exists *indubitably*, as we saw in Chapter 1. But to prove existence in this way is to prove the existence of a strict perceptible, never of an imperceptible. The second, and only other, possibility of genuinely proving the existence of an imperceptible is by logic, either from the fact that one or more particular strict perceptibles exist or else by logic alone. We will consider first the possibility of proof from strict perceptibles — what Hume called "proving one matter of fact from another." For this we must examine some simple logic, the logic of evidence. We will consider first the possibility of proving the existence of a strict imperceptible, and then the possibility of proving the existence of a reportable.

✸ ✸ ✸

There is an important kind of compound statement in logic, which is called a **conditional**. It uses the words *if... then...* to combine two statements into one. For example, "If you close your eyes then your visible apparent world will vanish." The first component statement, immediately following the *if*, is called the **antecedent**, and the second, following the *then*, is called the **consequent**. There are three important ways in which a conditional can be used logically; two of these are valid deductions, and the third is not. We will assume the above example to be true and use it to illustrate these uses; but we will abridge it for convenience to "If eyes closed then world vanished." *Eyes closed* is then the antecedent, and *world vanished* is the consequent. We then can have:

1. Affirmation of the Antecedent. Assume that *eyes closed* is true. Then *world vanished* necessarily is true also. If a conditional and its antecedent are both true, then its consequent is necessarily true.

2. Denial of the Consequent. Assume that *world vanished* is false. Then *eyes closed* necessarily is false also. If the world has not vanished, then the eyes must still be open. If a conditional is true and its consequent is false, then its antecedent is necessarily false.

Note that each of these necessities is an instance of logical indubitability [4].

3. Affirmation of the Consequent. Assume that *world vanished* is true. Then *eyes closed* is neither necessarily true nor necessarily false. The world *might* have vanished because the eyes are closed; but it also might have vanished for the person concerned because of being struck blind by an avenging angel, or by switching off the light. So if a conditional and its consequent are both true, the antecedent is neither necessarily true nor necessarily false.

It is the necessity in affirmation of the antecedent and in denial of the consequent — our first two cases — that makes them valid forms of argument. (We go into this in greater detail in Chapters 14 and 15.) It is the absence of necessity in affirmation of the consequent that makes it an invalid form of argument, a fallacy, known as the **fallacy of affirmation of the consequent**.

A useful alternative way of describing a true conditional is in terms of necessary and sufficient conditions. The truth of the antecedent is a sufficient condition for the truth of the consequent, but the truth of the consequent is only a necessary condition for the truth of the antecedent. Thus for the world to vanish it is sufficient that the eyes are closed. But for the eyes to be closed, although it is necessary that the world vanish, it is not sufficient — because the vanishing of the world may be due to darkness. A clear example of necessary and sufficient conditions is: being female is a necessary condition, but not a sufficient condition, for being pregnant, while being pregnant is a sufficient condition, but not a necessary condition, for being female.

The significance of this is that a real cause is a sufficient condition for the effect, but the effect is only a necessary condition for the cause. If a cause occurs then the effect necessarily follows, but not *vice versa*: if an effect occurs, one of several possible causes will have occurred, but not necessarily any specific one of them. Since all explanation is causal, it follows that all explanations take a conditional form, with the explanation as antecedent and that explained as consequent. Thus: "If this explanation is true then what it explains is true." This amounts to: "If the cause occurred then this effect occurred." Very often in English the consequent is stated first and antecedent second, with *if... then...* replaced by

...because... For example: "The world vanished because my eyes closed", or "Pat is female because Pat is pregnant." *Because* may be thought of as meaning *by cause of*, or *by reason of*. However such a conditional is stated, the consequent of the explanation is true: that which we are trying to explain, "this effect", is an empirical fact. But to try to establish the truth of the antecedent — the causal explanation — on the grounds of this empirical fact is to commit the fallacy of affirmation of the consequent.

Equally, therefore, since belief in any strict imperceptible is for the sake of explanation, to assert the existence of any strict imperceptible because what it explains is a fact, is to commit the fallacy of affirmation of the consequent. I might say, for example, that if a rifle bullet [52] hits my glass then the glass will shatter — which is true; and that my glass has shattered, which is also true; but I cannot assert from the truth of these that it is true that the glass was hit by a rifle bullet — it may have been, and equally it may not have been. Thus to try to prove the existence of an imperceptible cause by asserting the existence of an effect is to commit the fallacy of affirmation of the consequent. The one exception to this rule is when the cause is the *only possible* cause of the effect, in which case the argument from effect to cause is valid. But such necessary causes are rare; one can test any explanation for uniqueness of cause by invoking Descartes' malevolent demon: if the effect could conceivably have been caused by a malevolent demon, trying to deceive you, then there is an alternative possible cause: very implausible, no doubt, but definitely possible.

✶ ✶ ✶

We next consider the possibility of proving the existence of a reportable. For this we need what is called induction. This is a logical move from what is called an I-proposition to an A-proposition. An **I-proposition** is of the form "Some S are P" and an **A-proposition** is of the form "All S are P," where S and P are concepts denoting classes; S stands for subject and P for predicate. For example, "Some beliefs are explanatory" is an I-proposition and "All beliefs are about imperceptibles" is an A-proposition. Suppose now that some man frequently checked his memories and found them accurate; he could rightly claim that some of his memories — all those that he had checked — were true. "Some of my memories are true," he could say, with an I-proposition. If he next generalises from this and supposes *all* his memories to be true, he would state this conclusion with an A-proposition: "All my memories are true." **Induction** is such generalisation: it goes from an I-proposition to an A-proposition that has the same subject and predicate. It is logically invalid — it is fallacious reasoning. Because if some of my memories are true, although it is possible that all are true it is also possible that some are false. The truth of the I-proposition does not necessitate the truth of the A-proposition, and such necessity is required for validity.

(Logicians usually suppose that this fallacy is the same as that of affirmation of the consequent, so that affirmation of the consequent is sometimes called induction. I wish to deny this equivalence, on the grounds that induction belongs to extensional logic and the affirmation of the consequent with which we are concerned belongs to intensional logic. This distinction will be discussed in Chapters 14 and 15.)

It does not take long to discover that the grounds for believing in any reportable are inductive. Consider the different kinds of reportables. There are first of all one's own, known about by means of *memories* and *expectations*; then there are those of one's contemporaries, known about by *word of mouth*; and those for which we have *evidence*, of which *legal* (including *circumstantial*), *historical* and *scientific* evidence are the most important kinds. In all these cases belief is based on previous experience of relative reliability. If I know Jack to have been truthful in the past I am unlikely to disbelieve him now when he tells of a fish he caught — even though what he says is mere talk for me. But in believing that talk to be true I am making an inductive step. Consequently I cannot prove my belief to be true, so I cannot prove the existence of the reportable concerned, the fish. Even if I went home with Jack and saw a fish in his kitchen, I could not prove, beyond any doubt, that this fish was one and the same as the fish of his story. I would *believe* it to be, because I trust Jack not to lie; but my trust is inductively based.

Philosophers of science are particularly concerned about induction because all scientific laws are arrived at inductively. Since superstitions and stereotypes are equally arrived at inductively, it becomes a problem to justify the use of induction in the one case while condemning it in the others. We will discuss this problem of induction later [70].

✶ ✶ ✶

We have arrived at the point that seemingly the truth of no explanatory or empirical belief, and the existence of no imperceptible, can be proved logically from perceived facts. Or, in other words, no combination of logical thought and strict perceptibles can establish the existence of an imperceptible. If true, this does not mean that no imperceptibles exist, so that all statements about them are false; such could be the case, and would be so if solipsism were true. Instead it means that the imperceptibles might or might not exist, so that the statements about them might or might not be true.

In fact, there is an old argument, called the ontological argument, for the existence of imperceptibles which is probably sound; it uses the concept of "necessary existence" — a combination of logical necessity and empirical existence. It is discussed further in Chapter 17.

Meanwhile, we will consider the scientific means of escape from the solipsistic predicament. It does not provide a philosophic proof, but the next best thing: a highly probable argument. We can ask: if we cannot disprove solipsism, why then do we not believe it? Or, more generally, why do we believe that some beliefs are true, that some imperceptibles exist? So far as rational beliefs are concerned, the answers are simple. Rational belief in reportables is based on *objectivity*, and certain other related features of empirical science; which is to say that we believe rationally in existential beliefs in so far as we are objective about the evidence for them. And rational belief in explanation is simply a matter of *quality* of explanation: the more powerful an explanation, the stronger our rational belief in its truth, and in the existence of the imperceptibles that it invokes. In other words, I am claiming that it is a psychological fact that strength of rational belief in reportables is proportional to objectivity, and also that strength of rational belief in strict imperceptibles is proportional to their explanatory power; these psychological facts are not certain, they are merely probable.

This in turn brings us to science, because science lays particular stress on objectivity and produces more powerful explanations than any other discipline. But before considering science, we should note that solipsism's power of explanation is nil — it can explain nothing whatever, since it requires all explanations to be false. So the strength of our belief in solipsism is also nil. Equally so with rigorous empiricism.

Another way of putting this is to say that if we cannot *prove* that an imperceptible exists then the next best thing is to *believe* it. Thus the escape from the solipsistic predicament is by an act of faith. This act of faith may take any of three forms: common sense belief, religious belief, or scientific belief. The common sense belief is realism, which we have found to be necessarily false. The religious belief is belief in a pre-eminent imperceptible, called God; we will not consider this until Part 4. And the scientific belief is belief in the imperceptible entities of science — which is the route we are about to take.

5. Physics.

We have seen that there are two kinds of proof: empirical and logical. I can *prove* empirically that Jack is taller than Jill by requesting them to stand back to back and saying "See for yourself"; the existence of Jack, of Jill, and of the relationship *taller than* all exist indubitably by virtue of being perceived. And I can *prove* logically that 51 is not a prime number by showing that it is divisible by 17. In the strict sense of *proof*, there is no third kind. This is because there are only two kinds of positive indubitability, existential and logical, as we saw in Chapter 1. However there is another meaning of *proof*, which, although it is not strict proof, is one on which we place great reliance: scientific proof. As was pointed out in Chapter 1, most of the content of consciousness is neither indubitably true nor indubitably false — it is merely dubitable. But within the dubitable, that which, rationally, is least dubitable is that which is scientifically proved.

The reason we consider science rather than anything else at this point is that science is successful — spectacularly successful. One form of success in science is in generalisation. We all make generalisations, and most of the time they are quite unreliable guides for further behaviour; for example, about other people (all Scotsmen wear kilts, all women are dominated by their emotions, all men are naturally aggressive, etc.) or about fortune (black cats are lucky, breaking a mirror is unlucky). We have even constructed entire disciplines of generalisations, such as magic, astrology, and alchemy. But one such discipline works, and is a reliable guide to future behaviour: empirical science, generalisations out of which are so good that they are called **laws**.

A second form of success in science is successful explanation. Specifically, explanation of scientific laws, by means of **theories**. One mark of this success is that theoretical scientists can predict novelty, accurately and often. Any generalisation can predict simply, because generalisation is the inductive move from "All known instances of X are Y" to "All X are Y" — and this includes generalisation into the future, which is prediction. It is the kind of prediction that promises more of the same — such as the prediction that the sun will rise tomorrow. This is **prediction of repetition**. But **prediction of novelty** is not prediction of repetition, by definition; it is prediction that something, never before observed, will happen. Although predictions of novelty are frequently made (the end of the world will come on Wednesday next week at 4:00 p.m.; or, when they are discovered, the elixir of youth will cure age and the philosopher's stone will convert base metals into gold) they are usually characterised by non-fulfilment — except in science, where they succeed daily. Sometimes in science they are of very great social significance as well — as with Maxwell's equations, which led Hertz to discover radio waves, and Einstein's $e=mc^2$, which predicted nuclear energy. Anti-particles, lasers, holograms, and black holes were other theoretically predicted empirical novelties.

Science can succeed in this manner for only one credible reason: it is true, or largely so. There are other possible explanations of its success, such as the successes being an extraordinary series of coincidences, or a series of miracles sent by God to test our faith, or sent by Satan to deceive us; but when we have examined the criteria for good explanation, these alternative explanations will be found to be unacceptable.

✱ ✱ ✱

So we now examine the basic features of science. There are six steps in scientific investigation, of which three constitute empirical science and the other three theoretical science. They are:

✱

1. **Observation and measurement**. Sometimes called **data collection**, this is concerned with discovering and describing public features of apparent worlds. It is stringent insistence on publicity that makes this undertaking scientific — as opposed to other investigations such as alchemy and astrology. Publicity is important in two ways. All experiments in empirical science must be repeatable (which is to say that they must be public) and all work must be objective [69]. All observations and measurements are of perceptibles. Recall that empirical reality was defined as all that is potentially, universally, *public*.

✱

2. **Formulation**. This is the process of condensing a mass of data into a succinct formula: a correlation, a classification, or a numerical

formula. For example, if two kinds of event, A and B are observed to be correlated, the earlier may be said to apparently cause the later — as lightning is said to cause thunder. Or if the data are of measurements of two correlated properties, they may be plotted as a graph and then described by means of the equation for that graph. Kepler's work provides another example: he described a vast amount of detailed measurements of the positions of the planets at various times by means of the formula that the planets travel in elliptical orbits, with the sun at one focus, and that they sweep out equal areas in equal times. Linnaeus provided formulation of a different kind by means of a structure of classes in which all living things could be classified: kingdom, phylum, class, order, family, genus, species.

✶

3. **Generalisation**. The formula is generalised. Instead of being true only for the cases actually observed or measured, it is said to be true for all similar cases. Thus it will be said that lightning *always* causes thunder. Or if the graph represents the pressure and volume of a gas at constant temperature, and the formula is that they are inversely proportional, this is generalised to be true of *all* gases at constant temperature. Kepler's formula concerning elliptical orbits is generalised to include *all* future measurements of positions of the planets, and also other orbiting celestial bodies, such as the satellites of the planets. When a formula is generalised it becomes a **scientific** or **empirical law**. Logically, the generalisation takes the form of induction, of going from "*Some* X are Y" to "*All* X are Y" [63]. For example, from "Some men (that is, all those so far observed to die) are mortal" to "All men are mortal." More generally, this form of reasoning goes from "The formula is true in *some* cases" (that is, those so far perceived) to "The formula is true in *all* cases". When we consider *all* cases, we find that (i) we are still dealing with perceptibles, since every one of these cases will be observed by someone, sometime (because each case occurs in an apparent world); and (ii) we are dealing with imperceptibles since it is not possible for all the cases to be strict perceptibles for any one person. The technical way of putting this is to say that all the instances of a scientific law are individually perceptible but collectively strictly imperceptible. It is because they are all perceptible that the law is called empirical; and it is

because most are imperceptible to any one person that the truth of the generalisation cannot be known and so is a matter of belief. It is because of this dubitability of the conclusion that the reasoning from *some* to *all* is deductively invalid, and so is called induction.

It should be observed that the belief which is an empirical generalisation is an empirical belief. It is a belief in the existence of reportables — of what is perceived by someone, sometime. It is not meaningful to speak of instances of an empirical law perceived by no one; being empirical means occurring in somebody's apparent world, and in apparent worlds to be is to be perceived [42]. As empirical beliefs, empirical laws have no explanatory power. We believe in them, in the first instance, because we believe in superstitions and other generalisations: we have an inherited learning process by which we expect observed patterns to repeat. This is sometimes called **association of ideas**, sometimes **conditioning**. Because of it, when we see lightning we expect thunder and when we click a wall switch we expect the light to come on. This conditioning contributes in an important way to interpretation, in that it adds anticipations of changes to the apparent world, such that the subject can act accordingly, to his or her advantage. As we saw [26], interpretation has survival value because it increases the truth of the given. It does this by making the given more public. The success of empirical science is a refinement of this. Empirical science succeeds because of **objectivity**, which is best defined as **attention to the public**. The correctness of this definition is most obvious when considering its opposite: subjectivity is attention to the private. If the results of an empirical investigation are determined or affected by private elements in the scientist concerned — prejudice, wish-fulfilment, malice, etc. — then the results are subjective. If all such private elements (including perceptual privacies such as viewpoint or colour-blindness) are eliminated then the scientist is attending only to the public. The scientific emphasis on publicity is quite general. For example, Einstein developed his theories of relativity because of recognising that the velocity of light must be the same for all observers, despite their relative motion — which is to say that it must be a public velocity. And he enunciated one of the most fundamental principles of all science: his Principle of Relativity, which requires all the basic laws of science to be true for all observers, despite their relative motion. This principle says, in effect, that these laws must be public: potentially, universally, public. Again, what is sometimes called verification of empirical laws is the process of an increasing number of repetitions of the observations, measurements or experiments that are instances of the law. It is frequently supposed that verification occurs because this increases the number of the "some," and so brings it closer to the "all"; as, for example, in going from "Some crows are black" (that is, all those observed) to "All crows are black," the greater the proportion of the total are included in those observed, the more probable the truth of the generalisation. But this is incorrect: instead, verification establishes publicity; it is this publicity that makes repeatability of experiments important in empirical science. On the matter of publicity, we may also note: (i) that the most potentially universally public features of apparent worlds are the quantitative ones, which is why quantitative data are so much more important than qualitative data in empirical science; (ii) that consensus among scientists is publicity of belief; and (iii) that reason is the most potentially universally public feature of minds. Thus we have a solution to the problem of induction. Induction, unlike superstitious or stereotypical generalisations, works because of objectivity, or attention to the public; and the potentially universally public is most likely to be true. Indeed, we have more than this solution; we have a justification of all the criteria of empirical science. These are usually listed as: science must be objective, experiments must be repeatable, and quantitative data are preferable to qualitative data; and all of these are justified by saying that they work towards the potentially, universally, public — empirical reality — which is most likely to be true by resemblance to theoretical reality. This last point is dealt with later [221].

Strictly speaking, the term *empirical law* is a misnomer. The empirical is what is observed or perceived, and a law is imperceptible, as we have seen. Knowledge of imperceptibles is theoretical knowledge, so that properly speaking the stage of science called generalisation is theoretical, not empirical. The misnomer dates from the days when theoretical science was not recognised as being distinct from empirical science: scientists believed that all of science was empirical, so that laws were also. Hereinafter the term *scientific law* will be used in preference to *empirical law*.

∗

4. **Explanation**. This consists of what are called variously theories and hypotheses[4]. They consist initially of undefined, or primitive, concepts of strict imperceptibles, and unproved propositions about these concepts, called **axioms** in mathematics, or **principles** in science. From these two starting points further concepts of strict imperceptibles may be defined, and further propositions may be deduced as theorems. Some of these theorems will have the same form as scientific laws. The whole conceptual system — primitive and defined concepts, axioms and theorems — is a theory. It explains all the scientific laws for which it contains analogical theorems. When a theory is properly organised in terms of an explicit and ordered statement of primitive terms, axioms, defined terms, and deductions leading to theorems, it is called an axiomatic system. For example, Newton assumed four strict imperceptibles: mass, absolute space, absolute time, and action at a distance; and three axioms — his famous miscalled "Laws of Motion." The resulting theory not only contained theorems corresponding to Kepler's laws, but could explain all other then known mechanical phenomena, such as the paths of projectiles and the tides.

Darwin, to take another example, explained the multitude of species described by Linnaeus, to which Darwin himself added considerably. He did this with three principles — chance variations, natural selection, and survival of the fittest — and a host of imperceptibles, namely, all the ancestors of all living things.

To take a third example, one scientific law is the famous ideal gas law: $PV=aRT$. In this, P is the pressure of the gas, usually defined as that quantity measured by a manometer: a glass U-tube, containing water or mercury; V is the volume of the gas, measured usually in a graduated cylinder; T is the temperature of the gas, defined as that quantity measured by a thermometer; and a and R are constants that depend upon

---

[4] The term *hypothesis* is widely used equally for a theory and for a generalisation which is not yet verified. For this reason it can be misleading, and will not usually be used here.

the chemical composition and mass of the gas. A theory that used to be called the kinetic theory of matter, and is now called statistical mechanics, due originally to Boltzmann in Austria, Maxwell in Britain, and Gibbs in the USA, explains this law, among many others, by assuming that a gas consists of a statistically significant number of tiny, perfectly elastic, particles called molecules, and that they all have an equal mass; and that these obey Newton's laws of mechanics. The temperature, T, of a gas is then defined as the average kinetic energy of the molecules, and the pressure, P, as the average force of reaction of the molecules bouncing off their container and off each other. It can then be deduced that $PV=aRT$. This is a theorem, within the axiomatic system, which is analogous to the scientific law. The scientific law says, very economically and much more precisely than in ordinary language, that if you heat a gas, its pressure increases; if you expand it, it cools; if you compress it, it gets hot; and so on. The theory explains all this by saying that if you heat a gas you add kinetic energy to its molecules, so its temperature rises; that if you expand it, molecular kinetic energy is used up in the expansion and so its temperature falls; *vice versa* if you compress it; and so on.

✳

5. **Prediction of Novelty**. As we saw [66], there are two kinds of prediction in science. Empirical prediction is generalisation into the future; it is the "more of the same" kind of prediction, prediction of repetition. Theoretical prediction goes further than this because theories can predict empirical novelty. We will later see that the correct description of the origin of such novelties is that they **emerge** within the theory. Prediction of empirical novelty occurs when a theorem is deduced within a theory and there is no known law that corresponds to it, or even no known perceptibles that correspond to the defined terms in the theorem. If the law — and the new perceptibles, if any — are then empirically sought and discovered, then the theory has successfully predicted empirical novelty.

✳

6. Such seeking of theoretically predicted empirical novelties requires **design of experiments**, which is the last stage of science. Two of the greatest designers of experiments were Faraday and Rutherford.

Their designs were so simple and elegant that in retrospect they seem obvious and easy, so that anyone might have designed them. However, the easy solution to a difficult puzzle is obvious once you know it, but while still unknown it is exceedingly difficult. So the design of good experiments is often underrated.

Experiments designed to test theories produce results which constitute data collection, so that at this point the scientist returns to the first type of scientific investigation. In healthy sciences such as physics and chemistry there is repeated progress through the six stages in this way — a cyclic process of a type called **successive approximations to the truth**, since each time round the laws and theories are more probable. It is possible, of course, that the predicted novelty does not appear; if neither the deduction nor the experiment was defective, this means that the theory is false in some respect; correction of the falsity is established when a modified theory produces predictions of novelty that are successful.

✳

So **empirical science** consists of the stages of data collection, formulation, and design of experiments, and **theoretical science** consists of generalisation, explanation, and prediction of novelty.

It should be emphasised that the power to predict novelty successfully is not merely a socially valuable feature of theoretical science, as Maxwell's equations led to radio, and Einstein's to nuclear energy; this power is an essential step in the process of successive approximations to the truth. By far the most common form of novelty that is predicted by theorists is novel experimental results.

✳ ✳ ✳

The strength of our belief in a law or theory is usually called the **probability** of that theory. Before discussing how the probability of a theory increases with its power to explain, something must be said about the word *probability*, which has three distinct meanings.

✳

1. One kind of probability is statistical; it is usually called **relative frequency**. This is the type that is found in actuarial tables and opinion polls. The proportions of something are found in a sample, and then generalised. This kind of probability is sometimes called **empirical**

probability. It is widely used in the inexact sciences — economics, sociology, behavioural psychology, etc. — in which correlations are sought between perceptibles, such that future occasions of one of these perceptibles will each have an empirical probability, equal to the appropriate correlation, of being accompanied by the other. For example, if a psychologist discovers that 80 per cent of his rats take ten minutes or more to run a maze, then the empirical probability of new, untested rats requiring at least ten minutes is 4/5.

✳

2. The second kind of probability is called *a priori*, or **mathematical probability**. This is the kind that is the probability of compound events, calculated in terms of the supposedly "equiprobable" elementary events that constitute them. It is used in calculating the probability of different hands of cards, the chances of drawing so many white balls from a jar that holds known quantities of black and white, etc. If the number of possible elementary events is p, then the probability of any one of them is $1/p$. Compound events are various combinations of elementary events; and given the probabilities of the latter, the former can be calculated. For example, the probability of drawing any one particular card from a well shuffled deck of 52 cards is 1/52; or, since there are four aces in a deck, the probability of drawing one ace is 4/52, or 1/13. Having drawn one ace the probability of drawing another is then 3/51, since there are 3 aces and 51 cards left in the deck. Consequently the probability of the compound event of successively drawing two aces is the product of these: $(1/13) \times (3/51)$ or 1/221. This type of probability is called *a priori* because it is calculated prior to the event in question; as opposed to empirical probability, which is sometimes known as *a posteriori* probability because it is only known after the event, when it has been measured. Mathematical probability is used in theoretical science. For example, in statistical mechanics it is assumed, as an axiom, that every microstate, or arrangement of molecules, is equiprobable. A macrostate, which is the empirical state of the system, may be constituted by any one of a variety of microstates, and some macrostates are based on a larger variety than others. It then follows that the macrostate which results from the largest number of microstates is the most probable. Such

a macrostate is called the one of maximum **entropy** — a matter to be discussed later [127].

✳

3. The third kind of probability is strength of belief — usually called **subjective probability**. Originally this was expectation. A man might be asked if he expected rain and reply that rain was highly probable — meaning that he very much expected it. Expectation is based on learned association, and animals exhibit it as much as humans. For example, if you pick up a dog's leash, the dog will expect to go for a walk, through association. Such association is the basis of Humean, or empirical, causation and hence of empirical generalisation. A strong expectation is, of course, a strong belief, and the concept of probability can be extended from expectations (beliefs in future perceptibles, which are present imperceptibles) to all beliefs. For example, "I think the existence of God is very improbable" or "God's existence is highly probable" both express strength of explanatory belief; and "Einstein's mechanics are more probable than Newton's" expresses a stronger belief in Einstein's explanation of physical movement than in Newton's.

✳

The use of the word *probable* for qualifying laws and theories arose because, as we have seen, we can never know when they are true. So scientists, wanting not to be dogmatic, spoke of them as probable. A great effort has been made by philosophers of science to show that the probabilities of laws and theories are either empirical or mathematical probabilities. One reason for this is a tradition in modern philosophy called positivism, which regards empirical facts and mathematical truths as the only meaningful knowledge. If this is so, the probabilities of laws and theories are meaningless if they are not either measured or calculated. But even without the over-stringent positivist criterion of meaning, there is a general reluctance to allow subjective probabilities into science. To say that the probability of laws and of theories is the strength of belief of scientists in these laws and theories seems to introduce the kind of subjectivity into science that scientists have always avoided so carefully. Strength of belief seems not to be public, in the way that public features of apparent worlds and mathematical truths are public. Each scientist has his or her own beliefs, and can neither measure nor compute their strengths, so cannot directly compare them for strength with other people's beliefs. Another way of putting this is that empirical probabilities are *measured*, mathematical probabilities are *calculated* but subjective probabilities are only *evaluated*; since laws and theories are scientific, their probabilities ought to be measured or calculated, ought not to be merely evaluated: measurement and calculation are objective, evaluation is subjective.

A second reason for widespread contemporary denial that the probability of a theory is strength of belief in it, is that if this is so then in principle the theory is either true or false. In positivist philosophy, and for most empiricists, strict imperceptibles do not exist, so they are all regarded as fictions. But in such a case speaking of a theory being true is meaningless, so belief in its truth is necessarily false. In the present context, of course, this is no problem: true theories are true by resemblance to the theoretical world.

It is not difficult to eliminate both empirical and mathematical probability as interpretations of the probability of laws and of theories. But first, a distinction is necessary. The probability *of* a law must not be confused with a probability *stated by* a law. For example, it is a trivial law that the probability of any one particular person being killed by a meteorite is exceedingly small. This law is highly probable — that is, almost certainly true — but the probability that it states is very low. Since they have different values, they have to be two different probabilities.

Clearly, the probabilities *stated* by scientific laws are relative frequencies, and the probabilities *stated* by theories are calculated probabilities. However, the probabilities *possessed* by laws and theories cannot be relative frequencies, because laws and theories are not individuals having relative frequencies in populations. Nor can laws and theories possess *a priori* probabilities, because they are not compound events composed of equiprobable elementary events.

Consequently, unless there should be a previously unsuspected fourth meaning for the word probability, the probability of laws and theories is our strength of belief in them. There is, furthermore, a good measure of objectivity in strength of scientific beliefs — a good measure of public content, that is — simply because of consensus among scientists. There is consensus among scientists because they avoid as far as possible being influenced by private (that is, subjective, irrational) feelings in forming their beliefs, leaving public evidence to be the determining factor for scientific laws, and certain other criteria for theories. So we next turn to these other criteria.

* * *

We have already examined the criteria for good empirical science — objectivity, repeatability of experiments, and the preference for quantitative data — so we now consider those of theoretical science.

Scientists rely on at least nine criteria for or against the truth of a theory. The first two listed here, when applicable, falsify a theory; the others are evidence for its truth. Just why they are evidence for its truth will be explained in Chapter 14; for the present, with some of them at least (that is, 3, 4, and 9) it should be obvious that the more applicable the criterion the better the explanation — and so the greater its probability. The criteria are:

*

1. The theory must be logically consistent. If it contains contradictions, it is necessarily false.

*

2. The theory must not be contrary to empirical fact. That is, its theorems must not contradict empirical formulae or empirical fact. If they do, the theory is false — by denial of the consequent, as we have seen [60]. These two criteria each overrule all the other criteria; this is because they falsify a theory, whereas the others verify it — and such falsities may be indubitable but such verifications not so.

*

3. The larger the scope of explanation of a theory, the more strongly we believe in it. That is, the larger the range of scientific laws that a theory explains, the more probable the theory. For example, the principle of conservation of energy originally applied only in mechanics, to kinetic energy and potential energy. The principle said that kinetic energy and potential energy could be converted one into the other, and no energy was ever created or destroyed in the process. Later internal energy (popularly, heat) was included in the principle; and then electric and magnetic energy, followed by mass. With each addition of another type

of energy, the scope of explanation of the principle increased, and with each increase of scope, the principle became more probable.

✳

4. The greater the density of detail in a theory, within a given scope, the more strongly we believe in it. For example, Newton's mechanics explains all mechanical phenomena but for two exceptions: those in which two systems have a very high relative velocity, and those systems in which the masses are very small. Einstein's special theory of relativity explains everything that Newton's theory does, plus these high velocity phenomena. The special theory of relativity thus has a greater density of detail, within the scope called dynamics, than the Newtonian theory and so is more probable. Similarly, Newton's theory does not explain the mechanics of the very small, while quantum mechanics does; so within this realm, quantum mechanics is the more probable of the two.

The difference between scope and density of detail is most easily understood by an analogy with photographs. The larger the view contained in a photograph (that is, the wider the angle of the lens used on the camera) the greater is its scope. While the more minute the detail is within the photograph, the greater the density of detail. Thus, in a photograph of a forest the scope increases with the number of square miles of forest shown, while the density of detail increases with the number of individual trees, or even leaves, that can be distinguished.

✳

5. If two theories are otherwise equal — that is, they are not falsified and they have identical scope and density of detail — then the simpler is more probable. This is sometimes called the principle of parsimony of hypothesis. A medieval maxim known as Occam's Razor is an instance of it; originally it read: "Do not multiply entities beyond necessity." In the present context this could be rephrased as "Do not include more imperceptibles in the theory than are necessary to explain the perceptible facts." The converse of this, though rarely stated, is also true: "Do not reduce entities beyond necessity — do not have fewer imperceptibles than will explain the facts[5]." However, simplicity through

---

[5] When I was a graduate student I was presumptuous enough to call this principle *Robinson's Restorative*. I would not so call it now, although some other

a minimum of imperceptibles is not the only kind. Logical or mathematical simplicity is also relevant; and what are called **stationary principles** are a form of simplicity — the path of least resistance, the principle of least action, the path of least time, etc. An example of application of the criterion of simplicity is realism. One reason that this belief has persisted for so long, within common sense and most philosophic systems, is its beautiful simplicity, which provides a strong ground for believing it; but the reason we have to reject it is the falsification criterion of inconsistency, which applies here and overrules the criterion of simplicity. That is, the contradictions arising out of the belief that the real world and all apparent worlds are one — i.e., theoretically real objects are given in perception — show that the assumption is inconsistent and so false, despite its simplicity.

✶

6. The harmony of a theory with other theories is a quite important criterion, although it is perhaps not a criterion in its own right, since harmony between two theories leads to their integration into one theory with the scope of each combined — so that harmony of theories could be considered to be simply enlargement of scope. However, it may be used negatively, and then this argument does not apply. An example of this negative use is its application to parapsychology [140] — telepathy, clairvoyance, psychokinesis, etc.; the meagre theory of this subject does not harmonise with other theoretical science, which is a large reason so many scientists are sceptical about the entire field. (Other reasons, of course, are that so much of the evidence for it is private, not public; and that its proponents seem to have a very strong desire to believe in it — which is subjective.) A positive instance of the criterion of harmony is quantum mechanics and theoretical chemistry, each of which is much more probable because of its harmony with the other.

✶

7. Elegance of a theory is another criterion that sometimes plays a strong part in determining a scientist's belief in it. On the whole scientists seem reluctant to make much of this criterion — possibly because it seems subjective, like the enjoyment of art, and so a sin

---

people do, but I have used it as the motto of this book.

against objectivity. However, surprisingly enough, the common factor of all these criteria of good explanation is not objectivity at all, but something else — as we will see in Chapter 14. Objectivity is most important in empirical science, but it only appears indirectly in the criteria for theoretical science, in the sense that logical necessity is in principle the most public feature of apparent minds.

✱

8. Symmetry is another criterion that scientists value considerably. Principles of conservation — of energy or momentum, for example, involve symmetry over time: they require the given quantity to be the same before and after a given event. The second law of thermodynamics, on the other hand, is not symmetrical with time: it requires entropy to increase generally. No one would suggest that the law is false because of this asymmetry, but none the less it leaves some people unhappy. Other, more abstract, symmetries are also important in physics because, through Noethe's theorem, they explain principles of conservation.

✱

9. Finally, successful theoretical prediction of empirical novelty is a most convincing ground for believing an explanation. If a theory predicts novelty successfully then either it is true to a considerable extent or else the prediction succeeded by chance. Again, absence of the conditions of this criterion does not falsify, but presence greatly strengthens.

✱ ✱ ✱

We may consider three non-scientific explanations in terms of these criteria, by way of illustration.

✱

1. One is solipsism, given that this philosophic position can be considered an explanation at all. We may note first that solipsism is neither contrary to fact nor inconsistent, as far as anyone has proved so far, so we cannot know it to be false. It has the great merit of extreme simplicity, which is probably the only reason anyone might be tempted to believe it. Its scope is very small: no more than that which exists indubitably, for me, now. And the density of detail explained within this scope is zero — which means that its power of explanation is zero so its probability — our rational strength of belief in it — is zero.

∗

2. We next consider rigorous empiricism [58]. It will be recalled that ordinary empiricism, although attractive because of its simplicity, fails because it is inconsistent — it includes realism. Once this is corrected, within empiricism, rigorous empiricism results. In this doctrine no strict imperceptibles exist, although other imperceptibles — reportables — do exist. This explanation has the same scope as solipsism, all strict perceptibles for me now, and the same density of detail, nil, but it is not nearly so simple. This is because it multiplies entities beyond necessity: it posits the existence of more imperceptibles than are needed to explain the facts that it does explain. Namely, it posits the content of all other consciousnesses but mine, now. So if we had to choose exclusively between rigorous empiricism and solipsism, then solipsism would be preferable.

∗

3. Last, we may examine the theory that the world exists, and everything happens as it does, because of the will of God. The scope of this theory is the maximum — the theory explains everything. This is the only reason, other than irrational grounds, why anyone can find any probability in the theory — since the density of detail that it provides also is zero. Every possible detail within this scope is explained the same way, as resulting from the unknowable will of God, and so there is no way of distinguishing one detail from another within the explanation, so there is no detail.

∗ ∗ ∗

Our next two tasks are to explain how explanations explain, and how theoretical science successfully predicts empirical novelty. We have already considered the first briefly, in saying that explanations are causal explanations; and we distinguished between real causation and apparent, or Humean, causation. We are now able to relate these to the fundamental difference between empirical science and theoretical science.

This difference is that empirical science describes true features — potentially, universally, public features — of apparent worlds, while theoretical science describes, or tries to describe, the real world. In other words, empirical science describes empirical reality and theoretical science describes theoretical reality [7].

We defined explanation earlier [53, 71] by saying that an explanation of an effect is a description of its real cause. Since theoretical perception is a process of real causation, in which apparent objects are really caused by real objects, it follows that what scientific laws describe is caused by what theories describe. Consequently theoretical science explains empirical science.

This may be summarised as follows. We have four elements:

(a) empirical, or apparent, reality, symbolised by A;
(b) empirical science, symbolised by E;
(c) theoretical science, symbolised by T;
(d) the real world, symbolised by R.

Between these elements are four relationships:

1. A is described by E;
2. R is described by T;
3. R causes A;
4. therefore T explains E.

This is only the bare bones of the matter, of course. The process in all its detail is complex, but it is well worth understanding because of its explanatory power. Some of this detail is given schematically in Fig. 5.1. This begins with a real cause, A_1, and its real effects, L_1 and T_1. We may suppose, for clarity, that A_1 is a real atmospheric electric discharge, L_1 is a real flash of lightning, and T_1 is a real clap of thunder. That is, L_1 is a burst of electromagnetic radiation in the visible[6] spectrum and T_1 is a burst of acoustical vibration, both of these radiating outwards in all directions as waves. Each of them really causes, through the process of theoretical perception, a real image of itself in an apparent world; these — L_2 and T_2 — are phenomena, or givens, for the subject of that

---

[6] It is theoretically visible, but not empirically visible; the rest of the electromagnetic spectrum is not visible in either way.

apparent world: apparent lightning and apparent thunder. Each phenomenon really causes an apparent representation — a memory — of itself in that subject's apparent mind. Each such apparent image — remembered lightning and remembered thunder, L_3 and T_3 — then really causes the formation of concepts — L_4 and T_4 — by a process that we will not much worry about until we discuss the real mind in Part 3. For the present we can simply assume that a concept is a combination of a word or symbol and the abstract idea that is its meaning, taking *abstract idea* on faith for the present. So L_4 and T_4 are concepts of lightning and thunder. The heavy arrows in Fig. 5.1 represent the relation of necessity. Thus A_1 causally necessitates L_1 and T_1; L_1 causally necessitates L_2, which necessitates L_3 which necessitates L_4; and T_1 similarly causally necessitates T_2, T_3, and T_4 successively. (It is of course assumed that all other necessary conditions are present; for example, L_1 would not necessitate L_2 if there was no person present to theoretically perceive, and L_3 would not necessitate L_4 if the person concerned did not think about what he or she empirically perceived.) The broken arrows represent correlation — which is apparent, or Humean, causation. In an apparent world this is simply constant conjunction of contiguous and successive events. In an apparent mind it is association of ideas. Thus the correlation between L_2 and T_2 is an instance of the scientific law that lightning empirically causes thunder; and a remembering or thought of lightning, L_3 or L_4, is followed by a remembering or thought of thunder, T_3 or T_4.

If the person in whose mind all this is occurring has some basic physics, he or she will have a concept, A_4, of an atmospheric electric discharge, and of how this causes thunder and lightning. The heavy arrow between A_4 and L_4 represents the relation of necessity within the theory that contains A_4 and L_4, such that within this theory A_4 necessitates L_4 mathematically. In other words, the arrows from A_4 represent logical necessity, as opposed to the causal necessity of all the other heavy arrows lower in the diagram. Similarly A_4 logically necessitates T_4. Thus L_4 and T_4 can be deduced from A_4, and so can their correlation; so the law is explained in the sense of being deducible from the theory.

If the theory in the apparent mind of Fig. 5.1 is true, it is because it accurately copies a state of affairs in the real world: A_4 accurately copies A_1, L_4 accurately copies L_1, T_4 accurately copies T_1, and the

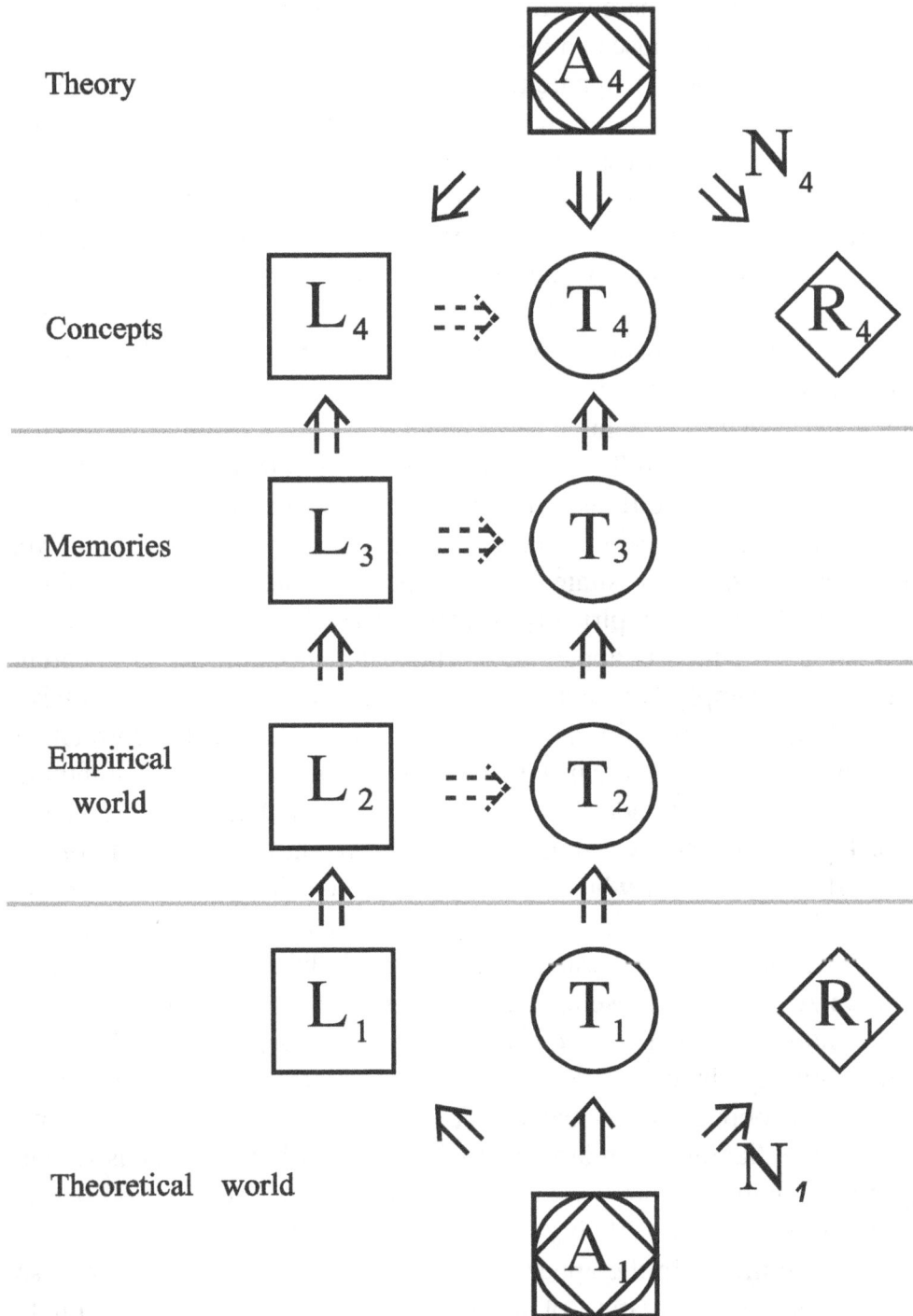

Theory

Concepts

Memories

Empirical
world

Theoretical   world

Fig. 5.1

logical necessities between A_4 and L_4 and between A_4 and T_4, accurately copy the causal necessities between A_1 and L_1 and between A_1 and T_1.

It is such *logical necessities* that enable theoretical predictions of empirical novelty to be made, and such *causal necessities* that make them come true. Suppose that A_1 regularly causes R_1, as shown by the arrow N_1, but that R_1 is not perceived as R_2 because R_1 is outside the range of human perception, so is theoretically imperceptible. In the present example, R_1 is electromagnetic radiation outside the visible spectrum. If the theory in which A_4 necessitates L_4 and T_4 is true, then A_4 will logically (mathematically) necessitate R_4, as shown by the arrow N_4. When the scientist deduces R_4 from the theory, he is predicting novelty. In this particular case he would be predicting radio noise. An experimentalist should then be able to figure out what is needed — some experimental apparatus — to make R_1 theoretically perceptible. When she has built this apparatus, a radio receiver, and set it up during an electric storm — a situation such that her apparent world will contain L_2 and T_2 — then, provided the radio works, she will hear radio noise, R_2, correlated with every flash of lightning, L_2, by means of it. The prediction of novelty will then have come true. It comes true because of the causal necessity, N_1. I do not know whether any scientist ever made this particular prediction of novelty or not, but it could easily have been made and it serves well as an illustration even if it should be historically inaccurate.

Thus the possibility of prediction of novel empirical facts by theoretical deductions is explained. Minimum conditions for this are a three-way resemblance between (i) the structure of the real world (ii) the structure, jointly, of the public features of apparent worlds and scientific laws, and (iii) a theory that is both a construct out of (ii) and a reconstruct of (i). Without the real world, theoretical prediction of empirical novelty is inexplicable, because there are no necessary connections in apparent causation to correspond to the logical necessity in the theory. In other words, if prediction of novelty is to be explained then believing in the existence of a world described by theoretical science is necessary; and, in particular, a world containing causal necessities described by the mathematical necessities in theoretical science. Without the mathematical necessities, such as N_4, the prediction of novelty would be mere guesswork, and without the causal necessities, such as N_1, the success of the prediction would be pure chance.

It is worth reiterating at this point that four pairs of L and T are necessary because of the facts of perception. L_2 and T_2 are bad copies of L_1 and T_1 — just as correlation is a bad copy of necessity — and L_3 and T_3 are bad copies of L_2 and T_2. We require this because of the facts of illusion and of defective memories, and we know of these because of contradictions within our experience. L_4 and T_4, on the other hand, are better copies of L_1 and T_1 because they are reconstructions, out of the data that are L_2 and T_2, and other apparent representations, so as to exclude contradictions.

There is some possibility of confusion with Fig. 5.1, concerning what of all these processes are perceptible. Of necessity — the heavy arrows — only logical necessity is ever a perceptible. Of real effects, all those of Fig.5.1 that are in the real mind are perceptibles: apparent objects, apparent representations, and concepts. Of real causes, although an apparent object is the real cause of an apparent representation, or memory, and this in turn of a concept, they are not empirically perceived as such because the necessities are empirically imperceptible; and all real objects, as real causes, are strict imperceptibles. So with the provision that some contents of real minds are real causes but not perceived as such, we can say that all real causes are imperceptibles [51].

★ ★ ★

Finally, concerning science, we need to examine further the relations between the theoretical world, empirical reality, empirical science, and theoretical science. For this we need, as a preliminary, to discuss the concept of homomorphism. If two structures X and Y are similar in all but one respect, namely that X has a lesser density of detail than Y, then X is a homomorph of, and homomorphic to, Y. A road map is an excellent example of this. The roads in the map are similar to the roads in the terrain that the map represents, but only in their gross detail. Their relative directions, lengths and intersections are similar, but much detail is lacking; the map does not show ditches, traffic lights, trees, etc. So the map has a much lower density of detail than the terrain, although the detail that it does have is true, hence the map is homomorphic to the terrain.

The concept of homomorphism is important because it is a special case of similarity truth [5]. We would not normally label a road map false for omitting ditches, for example, although it is clear that there is a sense in which it is false for this reason. In other words, if a structure is a perfect homomorph of another, the first is perfectly true as far as it goes, but it is not a complete truth because it does not go far enough — it lacks fine detail.

This can be applied to our four elements [82]: the true features of apparent worlds, or empirical reality, A; empirical science, E; theoretical science, T; and the real world, R. Each of these is a structure — either a set of relationships (empirical reality and the real world) or a mathematical structure (empirical science and theoretical science).

There are clearly homomorphic relationships between these four

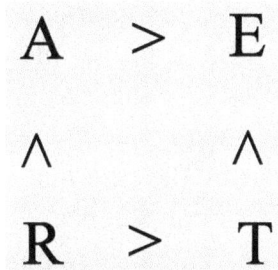

$$
\begin{array}{ccc}
A & > & E \\
\wedge & & \wedge \\
R & > & T
\end{array}
$$

Fig. 5.2

structures (ignoring, for simplicity, that there may be falsities in empirical science or theoretical science). These are:

1. Empirical reality is a homomorph of the real world.
2. Empirical science is a homomorph of empirical reality.
3. Empirical science is a homomorph of theoretical science.
4. Theoretical science is a homomorph of the real world.

These can all be represented graphically if we represent the homomorphic relation by '>', where the symbol points from large density of detail to small, as in Fig. 5.2.

Each of these may be explained quite simply. Empirical reality, A, is a homomorph of the real world because there is much loss of detail in the process of theoretical perception — we do not perceive atoms and molecules, for instance. Empirical science, E, is a homomorph of empirical reality partly because empirical science is incomplete — it has not yet described all possible public features of apparent worlds — and partly because it leaves out most of the concrete detail of empirical worlds: secondary qualities such as colours, smells, and tastes. Note, however, that there is one respect in which the converse holds: empirical reality is homomorphic to empirical science in that empirical reality lacks the mathematical necessity within empirical science. Empirical science is also a homomorph of theoretical science, T, because a good theory, although it has analogues of all the laws of that portion of empirical science that it explains, also has much that empirical science lacks — such as axioms, or scientific principles, primitive terms, and novelties. And theoretical science is a homomorph of the real world, R, partly because, again, it is incomplete — there is presumably much in the real world not yet thought of by any theorist; and also because theoretical science *cannot* have the detail of the real world — the human brain cannot handle it: think only of the fact that every one of the countless molecules in a gas has a specific velocity, while the corresponding theory deals only with an average velocity.

Of these four homomorphs the one that is important for our present purposes is that between empirical science and theoretical science. The structure of empirical science, E, is a homomorph of the structure of theoretical science, T, because the theoretical scientist has added to empirical science to create theoretical science. This is why, to digress briefly, although there are methodological rules for some of empirical science, there are none for theoretical science: making a theory is a creative act, for which, for a major theory, just as for a major work of art or for design of a major new scientific experiment, genius is required. There is no scientific method because there is no method for genius.

Note that all of this is an explanation both of how theoretical science successfully predicts empirical novelty and how theoretical science explains empirical science. As such, it requires that if prediction of novelty is to succeed, and the other criteria of theoretical explanation are to be met, then the theory, and the scientific laws out of which it grew, must be similarity true or nearly so. Thus the successful prediction of empirical novelty by a theory, and the fulfilling of the other criteria of good explanation, are good grounds for believing in the truth of the theory.

★ ★ ★

Embedded in this philosophy of science is an instance of a very common principle of rationalist philosophy. Once it is realised that, because of the solipsistic predicament [57], all our knowledge of the real world is a matter of belief, rather than of perception, then the question arises as to what the basic nature of the real world is. The answer, for a rationalist, is that the real world is rational. That is, it not only does not contain logical impossibilities — contradictions — but it also does contain logical necessities. These necessities are causal necessities.

With this principle we have ceased to be in the realm of theoretical science and entered that of metaphysics. **Metaphysics** is the philosophical investigation of the real world. This definition is incomplete because theoretical science, as we have just seen, is also the investigation of the real world. So we need next to distinguish between the two disciplines.

In terms of two of our positive criteria for the explanatory power of a theory — scope and density of detail — obviously no human mind could possibly contain an explanation for everything, in full minute detail. So whoever seeks explanations must, to some extent, sacrifice either scope for the sake of detail, or else detail for the sake of scope. Those who sacrifice scope for detail are specialists. Their knowledge can become increasingly detailed in proportion as the field in which they specialise becomes smaller. According to an old joke, the specialist knows more and more about less and less until he knows everything about nothing. On the other hand, those who sacrifice detail for the sake of scope are anti-specialists, generalists, metaphysicians, seeking synoptic knowledge, and they may be said to know less and less about more and more until, like Socrates, they know nothing about everything. Scientists are specialists and metaphysicians are anti-specialists.

A second difference between theoretical science and metaphysics is that theoretical science must correspond directly with empirical fact. Metaphysics must also correspond with fact, but because metaphysics is synoptic rather than minutely detailed, the facts that it must correspond with are the accepted theories and laws of science, rather than particular observations. Metaphysics thus has a second order resemblance to empirical facts, while science has a first order resemblance. Metaphysics and theoretical science are obviously very closely related, and indeed very interdependent. But since the time of Hume and Kant they have been divorced, in spite of their compatibility. It is high time that they were remarried. Nevertheless, before we arrange a wedding we must look at metaphysics in greater detail.

6. Metaphysics.

If we are reconstructing the real world conceptually, it is not enough to apply the rationalist principle that the real world is rational, because this only establishes relations between whatever the real world is composed of. Deciding what is the "stuff" of the real world poses a problem that has always divided philosophers. Given our criteria of probability of theories, there are only two plausible answers to this problem; that is, of all possible answers, only two are of maximum simplicity. This is because in conceptually reconstructing the real world we have no choice but to use categories with which we are familiar. There are three such categories, and any one person's apparent world can be fully described in terms of these three categories alone. They are the categories of *thing*, *quality* and *relation*.

Thus I may describe what I see in my apparent world as "A yellow book on a wooden table." This description invokes *things* (book, table), *qualities* (yellow, wooden), and a *relation* (on). Although it might seem at first that there are perceptibles that are not describable in terms of these three categories, this is not in fact so. For example, in describing the place and date of a certain event it would seem that each of the place, date, and event are not thing, or quality, or relation. As it turns out, however, all three reduce to relation. An event is located in space and time by means of its spatial and temporal relations to things or to other events — for example, *later* than W but *earlier* than X, four miles *to the NNE* of Y, and five feet *above* Z. And an event itself is a change (of either quality or relation) and a change is a combination of a temporal relation and a dissimilarity — both of which are relations. Thus to say that something changed at four o'clock is to say that *before* four o'clock it was *dissimilar* to what it was *after* four o'clock, and this change was an event.

Each of these three concepts — thing, quality, and relation — has a history of associated philosophical problems. I will briefly examine each concept and then some of their associated problems, as a preliminary to looking at the above mentioned two simplest answers to the problem of what is the stuff of reality.

The category of thing has always seemed to be the most basic of the three because it appears to be existentially prior to qualities — that is, qualities are dependent upon things for their existence: if there are no things then it seems that there cannot be any qualities. And the category of relation has seemed least basic because relations cannot exist without their terms, and these terms must, in the first instance, be either things or qualities; so that relations are dependent upon both things and qualities for their existence. I will consequently use this hierarchical order in my exposition even though, as we will see, it is false.

✷ ✷ ✷

1. A **thing** is what, in describing empirical perception earlier, was called an apparent object. Strictly speaking, we do not empirically perceive things, we only believe we do. That is, thinghood is a belief that we add to the content of empirical perception by means of interpretation [26]. This is because thinghood, traditionally, is something that is reperceptible. Reperceptibility, as we saw, is empirically perceived (in conjunction with memory) and is normally explained realistically: that is, things are reperceptible in empirical perception because they are real, they continue to exist when unperceived. This is false, as we now know; we have substituted metarealism [35] for realism, so that apparent things are reperceptible because their causes are real — that is, their causes are real objects, which continue to exist between occasions of being theoretically perceived. However, the traditional problem of thinghood applies as much to the real objects of metarealism as it does to the supposedly real objects of realism. This is the problem of what it is that is thinghood. What makes a thing a thing? We return to this problem on page 95.

✷

2. In ordinary use the word *quality* has a wide meaning. We may say, for example, that the number of teeth that a man has is a quality of that man, or that he has the quality of having many friends. But here I will use the word quite narrowly, such that these two examples will not be qualities but intrinsic and extrinsic relations respectively, as they will be explained shortly [100]. The reason for this is that the totality of the content of empirical perception, before anything is added by interpretation, is sensations and relations. Sensations are the basis of the category of quality, and I propose to confine qualities to them in all that follows: sensations, and nothing but sensations, are **qualities**. Thus to experience particular sensations of colour, warmth, texture, taste, smell, sound, or sensual pleasure or pain, is to empirically perceive qualities. Sensations, and hence qualities, are basic; they may be defined ostensively, by pointing, but cannot be described — they are definitionally primitive.

✳

3. When it comes to **relations** there is a great deal to be said, which cannot be said all in a rush. Consequently what follows here should be regarded as a preliminary only. A preliminary, moreover, which will be much more comprehensible once the remainder of Part 2 has been read. Empirically perceived relations are, in the first instance, relations between qualities. This red is *darker* than that, for example, but the *same shape* as that blue, which is located *between* the yellow and the orange; the orange is *bigger* than the yellow but is a *similar shade*. *Warmer than, sweeter than, louder than, rougher than* are others — the possible list is long. In the second place, relations may have other relations as their terms, as in: these two reds are similar, and so are these two yellows, but the similarity between the reds is *greater than* that between the yellows. Certain sets of relations are what will later be explained to be structures: all the relations within an apparent object are its total structure [100], and various subsets, of similar relations, are parts of its structure — such as shape, uniformity of colour, rate of change of some quality, etc. Structure consists only of relations — not of the qualities which are their terms. It is what Aristotle called form. Various parts of the structure of a thing, or the qualities that are their terms, or both, are **properties** of that thing. Some properties may be the terms of relations in a larger structure. For example, the shape of an object, the number of blue spots on it and the shape of the blue spotted area, are all properties. Thus qualities are properties but not all properties are qualities, since some properties may be relations or properties of relations.

So quality and relation are basic categories, while property is not a basic category, since it is one or the other or both of the first two. That quality and relation are basic categories is shown by the fact that one cannot be described, empirically, wholly in terms of the other. This can be demonstrated by observing that qualities are concrete and relations are abstract, as is shown by a simple test. The concrete can be imagined in isolation, while the abstract cannot. Thus one can fill the visual field of one's imagination with a single colour, which shows colour to be concrete. But one cannot imagine shape visually without imagining at least two colours as well — so shape is abstract. I will later [116] contend that the converse of the above relationship holds: everything **concrete** is a quality, or a property that includes qualities, and everything **abstract** is a relation or a property of a relation. This will only make good sense, however, once the problem of universals has been discussed, in Chapter 14.

We can now see that the traditional hierarchy of existential dependence of thing, quality, and relation is false. Apparent thinghood is added, by interpretation [26], to apparent worlds and so is consequent to, rather than prior to, qualities and relations. And these latter are existentially dependent upon theoretical perception, not on each other. In fact, arguing priority here is pointless because qualities are representations of relations. That is, they are representations of real micro-structures whose detail is theoretically imperceptible. Sensations of colour, for example, may be representations of molecular structures which reflect or transmit different frequencies of electromagnetic radiation. In other words, qualities are homomorphs of structures in the real world [158]. Apparent relations also are representations of real relations, so the seemingly fundamental difference between qualities and apparent relations is not very important.

One further general point needs to be made about relations. This is the possibility of **emergence**. If two relations are created, a third may emerge as well — as we saw above in the case of the two relations of *similarity* of colour: one was *greater than* the other, and this *greater than* is a relation between the two, and emergent from them. Philosophers have in the past talked of emergent *qualities* (for example, Samuel Alexander and Lloyd Morgan), on the basis that a sufficient increase of quantity, beyond a so-called threshold value, leads to a new quality emerging. However it is my contention that the emergence of qualities is either inexplicable, or else explicable only in terms of emergent relations — such that the concept of emergent quality is a secondary one at best.

We will have many examples of emergent relations in later pages. For the present, the following possible emergent relations, although complex and imprecise, will illustrate the concept of emergence. If the number of people in a room is increased from one to two, the possibilities of a love affair and a quarrel emerge. With a third person, the possibilities of an eternal triangle and a casting vote emerge, and with a fourth person, a bridge game. And so on up. Three other examples of emergent relations are a *melody*, the *working order* of a machine, and *knots*. A melody is a temporal relation between notes; working order is a relation between the parts of a machine; and knots are relations between loops and crossings in pieces of string. Still other examples of emergence are pattern, order, homogeneity, organisation, and life.

The opposite of emergence is **submergence**: if some terms of a relation are removed, or sometimes simply rearranged, the relation ceases to exist, it submerges. For example, if your feet are *under* the table, and you get up and walk away, the relation of *under* submerges because its terms are rearranged.

★ ★ ★

Two problems arise out of these characterisations of thing, quality, and relation. One is the problem of identity and change, and the other is the problem of the nature of thinghood. The two problems are related.

★

The problem of identity and change is the problem of how one thing can change with time. We all normally believe that things, including ourselves, have identity through time, and also change over time. But it is logically impossible for one thing to change with time: if it changes it must be two, and so loses its identity, or oneness. This extraordinarily anti-common-sensical claim is easily proved, using the principle, proved earlier [25], that qualitative difference entails quantitative difference. Remember that a change is a qualitative difference over time. Now consider supposedly one thing, A, at two different times: call it A_1 at the earlier time and A_2 at the later time. By the principle that qualitative difference entails quantitative difference, if there is any change in A between these two times then A_1 differs qualitatively from A_2 and so A_1 and A_2 are two — they *cannot* be one. Conversely, if A_1 and A_2 are one, then there cannot be any qualitative difference between them and then they *cannot* have changed during this time. In other words, it is logically impossible for one thing to change with time: identity and change are mutually incompatible. The early Greek philosophers understood this well. Heraclitus denied identity: he claimed that "All is change; only the fact of change is permanent" and "You cannot step into the same river twice"; and Parmenides denied change: he claimed that "Only the One is" and "All change is illusion." Plato argued that there are two worlds: the sensible, or empirical, world, in which there is change but no identity; and the other, the world of forms, or real world, beyond heaven, in which there is identity and no change. Later Greeks, and subsequent philosophers, adopted a pseudo-solution to this problem by dividing all things into two parts: stuff (either atoms or substance) and qualities, such that the stuff provided identity and the qualities were what changed. But if a part changes then so does the whole, while if a whole is unchanging then so is every part of it. (See the distinction made later [277] between compositional and distributive properties.) So if a thing is stuff and qualities together then it can have either identity or change but not both.

An important special case of this problem is the problem of personal identity: we are each of us normally quite sure of being one and the same person, changing from day to day. But, logically, this must be an illusion.

✳ ✳ ✳

The problem of thinghood, as we saw, is: what makes a thing a thing? It is related to the problem of identity and change because it is things which have identity or which change. There are three known possible answers to the problem of thinghood, all unsatisfactory to some extent within realism. One is that thinghood is *substance*; another is that it is *totality of qualities*; and the third is that it is *spatio-temporal continuity*. And there is only one satisfactory answer to the problem of identity and change.

✳

1. The concept of substance arises out of Aristotelian logic, as will be explained shortly. One definition of it is that it is that in which qualities inhere. If one thinks analogously of the chips of stone in a mosaic as qualities, then the substance of the mosaic is the mortar in which the chips inhere. In ordinary language substance is the stuff of which an object is made: the substance of bread is flour and water, for example. But this is a debased usage. Philosophically, substance is strictly imperceptible. It is a concept invented to explain, not only reperceptibility of apparent objects, but the reperceptibility of the configuration of their qualities — their *form*. As a concept, substance was particularly useful historically in connection with the problem of personal identity. A human being was supposed to consist of two substances; one material, constituting the body, and one spiritual, constituting the soul. Then no matter how the body changed — growth and cutting of hair, loss of a limb, death, etc. — the soul remained intact and personal identity, to say nothing of immortality, was assured. A major disadvantage with substance as the basis of thinghood is that if the parts of something are successively replaced, the whole must eventually gain an entirely new substance and hence identity. Each part of a car, for example,

could be replaced in turn: a second car would then result because of the new substance of the parts. This leads to further difficulties concerning the identities of the two cars at various stages of the transformation. It would be necessary for one identity to fade away while the other faded into existence, and this is not possible with identity — identity is not a matter of degree.

✳

2. To say that thinghood is totality of qualities provides a simple answer to the problem of thinghood, but no answer to that of identity. I might say that all the qualities of this apple — roundness, redness, sweetness, etc. — constitute its thinghood, but if I want to claim that it is one and the same apple as the one I perceived yesterday I have to suppose that each of these qualities is one and the same as the corresponding one I perceived yesterday. This means that the problem of identity is merely transferred from the thing to its qualities, without being solved. This solution also has a difficulty with the problem of thinghood. If two things — two mass-produced pens, for example — have exactly similar qualities then they must be one thing. This difficulty can only be avoided by an *ad hoc* denial of the possibility of such exact similarity, which is unsatisfactory. (Leibniz had such a principle — the principle of identity of indiscernibles — but not for this reason.) Thirdly, this solution makes it impossible for one thing to change with time. If I paint my table a different colour then one of the table's qualities changes, which means that the table is now a different totality of qualities, so a numerically different table. Every change in quality implies *another* new thing, rather than a change in *one* thing.

✳

3. Spatio-temporal continuity requires that whatever has such continuity (i) exists continuously in space — that is, if it moves from point A to point B then it passes through every intermediate point on some path from A to B; and (ii) it exists continuously in time — if it existed last night and exists this morning then it existed through all intermediate times. We have met this before [23], with the argument for the reality of apparent objects on the grounds of reperceptibility. Reperceptibility is most simply explained by spatio-temporal continuity: spatio-temporal continuity of empirical objects in realism, and spatio-temporal continuity of theoretical objects in metarealism. This approach fits well into modern physics, according to which a real thing is a world tube: a four-dimensional volume, of which the fourth dimension is

temporal. Any temporal slice of a world tube is then a three-dimensional, spatial, volume at that particular time — which is how we normally think of things. Rather than speak of one thing enduring through time, it is better to speak of the world tube. As a whole, its oneness provides identity, while it is composed of many temporal slices — many "things" — which may differ from each other. It is these latter things that change with the time and the former that is one. That is, the momentary things differ from each other, and these temporal differences are changes; and the totality of these things and changes, the world tube, has identity and does not change. In fact, this is the only satisfactory solution to the problem of identity and change.

However, spatio-temporal continuity is a set of relations, and is conceptually incomplete unless the terms of these relations are specified. That is, it is not enough to speak of spatio-temporal continuity alone, we must be prepared to answer the question: spatio-temporal continuity of *what*? The usual answer is: spatio-temporal continuity of qualities. (It may be noted that substance implicitly had spatio-temporal continuity, as well as the ability to cement, as it were, qualities into thinghood.) The major disadvantage of this approach is in the problem of personal identity. The one indispensable quality of this is consciousness — and the continuity of consciousness is frequently interrupted. A dreamless sleep while a passenger on an aircraft, for example interrupts both the spatial and the temporal continuity of one's consciousness. So every time this happened and one recovered consciousness, one would have a new identity, according to this approach.

✳

In a metarealistic context it might seem at first that these two problems, of thinghood and identity, are compounded, in that they apply to both apparent things and real things. But in fact they are resolved. In the first place, we have seen [42] that *esse est percipi* — to be is to be perceived — applies to apparent worlds: in any apparent world, what is unperceived does not exist. Substance is a strict imperceptible, so cannot exist in apparent worlds; hence apparent thinghood and identity are not substantial. And spatio-temporal continuity is also imperceptible. That is, we perceive small segments of it — whenever we are perceiving one apparent thing continuously — but we never perceive it otherwise, and so it does not otherwise exist in apparent worlds. This means that the thinghood of apparent objects is totality of qualities. We can in fact improve on this traditional concept by saying that rather than a mere totality of qualities, apparent thinghood is *structure* of totality of qualities. A structure is a set of relations [100]. And, secondly, there is no such thing as identity of apparent objects between occasions of their being perceived. Many representations of one real object cannot be one; they are inescapably many, as many photographs of one object are many. If Jack sees Jill for 365 mornings in a row, then he empirically perceives 365 numerically distinct apparent Jills. His common sense attributes numerical identity to these, falsely. The falsity is of little practical significance, because the many apparent Jills are representations of temporal parts of a real Jill who does have identity over time: she is a world tube. It is, again, falsity of oversimplification; an instance of the identity error [13], because many qualitatively different things are supposed to be numerically one. Philosophically, on the other hand, the error is intolerable.

Real thinghood cannot be totality of qualities because qualities are illusory, hence unreal: they are sensations, mere secondary qualities manufactured by the sense organs, at the earliest. So real thinghood could be substantial, or it could be spatio-temporal continuity of structure. In either case world lines and world tubes are possible, so that we can speak meaningfully of real identity. We will see, in particular, that personal identity is found in the world tube of a real ego; the nearest one can get to an apparent self is the succession of perceptions of one's own apparent body — and these, as representations of one's real body, do not have identity.

The substantial and structural answers are the two answers, of maximum simplicity, to the problem of what is the stuff of reality, that were mentioned earlier [90]. One of these two plausible answers is that of Pythagoras and Plato: the real world consists only of relations. We will not discuss this answer until we have considered the other: that the real world contains no relations, but consists of substances only. The first of these metaphysical positions I will call the abstract answer and the second I will call the concrete answer. The abstract answer is more important philosophically but the concrete answer is more important historically — which is why we are considering it first.

✳ ✳ ✳

Although Aristotle denied the abstract answer, he allowed what he thought of as the real world to have relations, and so did not fully accept the concrete answer — although he inclined towards it. Nevertheless, Aristotle is very important historically in this context because he laid the logical groundwork for the concrete answer, such that Spinoza and Leibniz were able to complete it. In this answer the real world is composed of metaphysical things, called substances, which have metaphysical properties called attributes; these are theoretically perceived as empirical things and qualities in empirical worlds. The real world of substances and attributes is then rational in that the relations between substances and between attributes are the relations of, and so described by, Aristotelian logic.

Aristotelian logic is now one of many formal logics. A formal logic consists of statements, in words or symbols, and relations of validity between them. In logic one statement validly implies another if and only if the truth of one necessitates the truth of the other, or else the falsity of one necessitates the falsity of the other. The rationalist view is that the statements in a logical calculus are statements of propositions, and that propositions are composed of ideas — usually abstract ideas. This is a matter that will be developed in Part 3. For the present we need only the historical information that for Aristotle — and for all subsequent philosophers until late in the nineteenth century — all propositions in logic were of a kind called categorical propositions. A **categorical proposition** consists of two concepts called the subject, stated first, and the predicate, stated second. For example, in "All men are mortal" the word *men*, and the idea that is its meaning, together are the concept that is the subject; and the concept *mortal* is the predicate. All subjects and predicates generate classes — such as the class of all men and the class of all mortals — and so they are sometimes called class concepts. The distinction between subject and predicate is not necessarily fixed for a given concept; in the propositions "The book is red" and "Red is a colour," the concept *red* is first a predicate, then a subject. Aristotle found that there are four possible kinds of categorical proposition — of which we have met two already in connection with induction [63]. If subject and predicate are represented by S and P then these four are of the form: "All S are P," "No S are P," "Some S are P" and "Some S are not P." A special case of the first kind is a singular proposition, in which the subject class has only one member; for example, "The S is P," or "Socrates is mortal." Logic, as a discipline, then consisted of discovering which categorical propositions can be deduced from which. We need not concern ourselves with these deductions (which may be found in any good elementary logic text); we are concerned only with Aristotle's supposed similarity of structure between this logic and the world. (Aristotle was a realist rather than a metarealist: his metaphysics incorporated the identity error [13].)

Obviously, the basic similarity between this logic and the world is that substances correspond to subjects and attributes correspond to predicates. Since, however, a predicate can have predicates — that is, be a subject — Aristotle defined a substance as that which is always a subject, never a predicate.

When it comes to describing things and their qualities or properties — whether these are real or apparent — categorical propositions are clearly sufficient. But when it comes to describing relations, difficulties arise. To understand this, we must distinguish two kinds of relation.

✶

Intrinsic relations are relations between the parts of one subject. For example, the relation between a man's head and his shoulders is an intrinsic relation; because there is one subject, the man, and two parts of him, such that this one subject has the predicate "head *above* the shoulders." In other words, an intrinsic relation can be stated as part of a predicate, and consequently be treated as a property or an attribute. It is the totality of the intrinsic relations of one thing that is here called its structure, and that Aristotle called its form.

✶

Extrinsic relations, on the other hand, are relations between two or more subjects. For example, "Winnipeg is *west* of Montreal" has two subjects, Winnipeg and Montreal. There is no one definite way of translating this proposition into categorical form — that is, of making it a proposition with just one subject and one predicate. Instead, there are three ways of doing this, and no satisfactory way of choosing between them. We can consider that Winnipeg is the subject, with the predicate *west of Montreal*; or we can treat Montreal as the subject, with the predicate *east of Winnipeg*; or we can introduce another subject, Canada, with the predicate of having a city, Winnipeg, west of a city, Montreal. Each of these translations is unsatisfactory furthermore because each requires a subject to become part of a predicate; it then cannot be a substance, according to Aristotle's definition. In fact, if the third approach is taken seriously then the whole world, or universe, must consist of one substance, and all the relations in it — such as spatial, temporal, and causal relations — must be attributes of this one substance; this is essentially the approach of Spinoza.

∗

Whether a particular relation is intrinsic or extrinsic is generally only a linguistic matter, a matter of how it is described: with its terms as parts of one subject, or with its terms as subjects in their own right. But there are occasions when describing a relation as an intrinsic one is most inconvenient, and it is then that the difficulty with Aristotle's logic arises.

This difficulty turns out to be significant. Among such extrinsic relations are spatial and temporal relations, similarity and difference, and causation. These have all been the centres of some of the more intractable problems in the history of philosophy. What are space and time? "I know what time is," St. Augustine said, "until somebody asks me what it is; and then I find that I do not know what it is." Are space and time finite or infinite; infinitely divisible, or not; or substances, or not? Where is space? The relation of similarity leads us to collect similar things into classes, and name everything in one class with a type of word called a universal. The meanings of universals leads to the problem of universals which is notoriously disputed in philosophy [227]. So is the nature of causation: do causes necessitate their effects, or not [53]? If they do, why cannot we perceive such necessities? If they do not, then we cannot distinguish between causation and correlation, and so have to say that day causes night and night causes day, and that cockcrow causes the dawn.

Consequently the focus of these problems — their common factor of extrinsic relations — is of considerable importance. If the rationality of the real world is to be that of subject-predicate logic, then the problem of extrinsic relations must be solved. Spinoza and Leibniz each solved it by constructing a metaphysical system without relations. Each claimed that all relations are *entia rationes* — things of the mind, fictions.

∗

Spinoza's way of doing this was to say that the entire real world is one substance, and that no more than one substance exists. Consequently there are no extrinsic relations; so everything that we might be tempted to

101

call a relation we would have to call an intrinsic relation — intrinsic to this one substance — and as such it is really a predicate. This one substance Spinoza called God; he claimed that it has an infinity of attributes, of which we can know two: thought and extension — that is, we can be conscious of apparent mind and apparent world, or, more vaguely, mind and matter. However, the importance of Spinoza in the history of philosophy is not this metaphysics, but his claim, like Plato's, that we can get to know this one substance, the real world. This claim is examined in Part 4.

★

Leibniz's solution was to say that the real world consists of an infinity of substances, each with an infinity of attributes, but no relations. Each substance is, he said, *simple* and *windowless*. Which is to say that it has no intrinsic relations — that is, no parts — and so is simple; and has no extrinsic relations, and so is "windowless".

Each substance Leibniz called a monad. His concept of a monad is extraordinarily similar to what in the present work is called a real mind [38]. Consequently it is worth while to examine Leibniz's system in greater detail — in spite of the fact that it seems at first to be bizarre to the point of incredibility.

Leibniz began with the idea of **analyticity**. An analytic proposition — a proposition which is so called analytically true — is one in which the predicate is contained in the subject[7]. That is to say, the idea which is the predicate is a part of the idea which is the subject. (The possibility of this will be explained in Part 3. We are here concerned with what will there be called intensional analyticity, as opposed to extensional analyticity or nominal analyticity.)

The best examples of analyticity — for us, if not for Leibniz — are found in axiomatic systems. We have already encountered these in discussing explanation in science and met specific cases with scientific theories [71]. The oldest and best known axiomatic system is Euclid's geometry — indeed, for Leibniz this was the only known one. Since then, most notably, arithmetic and all other mathematics was axiomatised, with

---

[7] This is called truth because a statement to the effect that the subject has that predicate cannot be false: the subject *must* have that predicate.

primitive terms and axioms from modern logic, by Frege, Peano, Whitehead, and Russell.

An axiomatic system may be thought of as consisting of primitive ideas — each of which is an abstract structure — and primitive propositions, or axioms, which are structures of primitive ideas. These together constitute a further structure that is the axiomatic system. (These structures are not the systems of mathematical symbols by which the axiomatic system is described; they are structures of abstract ideas.) A crude analogy is a complicated structure of scaffolding, in which can be discerned substructures — such as the part standing in the pond, the dome-shaped part, etc. — and these are composed of various designs of basic unit of scaffolding. These latter are like primitive ideas, and the substructures are like axioms. If, now, in the total structure, new substructures are discernible, these can be *defined*. And if new relations between these defined structures can be discovered, these are theorems. For this is what happens when we construct and examine an axiomatic system. Having constructed it — a task usually requiring creativity of genius order — we examine it for novel substructures and relations between these substructures — emergent relations, in other words. These are respectively the meanings of defined terms, and the propositions stated by theorems. They are abstracted from the axiomatic system in the process called deduction.

If we next call the axiomatic system as a whole — the entire structure — a subject, and every defined term and every deduced theorem a predicate, then it is easy to see that all the predicates are contained in — are a part of — the subject; and that in consequence the truth of the theorems, and the validity of their deductive proofs, is all analytic, by the above definition of analyticity.

Leibniz did not think of analytic truth in quite the above way. He thought of the subject simply as an idea, containing sub-ideas or predicates. Consequently all analytic truths could, for Leibniz, be expressed in categorical form; and they were related as categorical propositions are related in logic. Because if a subject S contains P as a predicate then it is true that "All S are P." And Leibniz's system as a whole is an axiomatic system, although not explicitly so in his writings. It begins with just one axiom. The result is the most nearly logically perfect system of metaphysics ever produced.

*

Leibniz's one axiom is: *All truth is analytic.*

From this we can deduce the following.

1. All true propositions have their predicates contained in the subject and so must be categorical propositions.

2. Hence the principle that Leibniz called *The Principle of Sufficient Reason*. Because the existence of a whole is a sufficient condition for the existence of its parts, the existence of a subject is a sufficient condition, or reason, for the existence of each of its predicates. Consequently the Principle means that for every predicate there must be a subject, which is the sufficient reason for that predicate; and to state this sufficient reason is to explain that predicate.

3. All factual truth must be analytic — that is, all statements about what exists must be analytic. So whatever exists must be a substance having attributes, such that an adequate idea of a substance contains as part of itself an adequate idea of each attribute of this substance. These adequate ideas are subject and predicates respectively.

Leibniz gave as an example of this the claim that an adequate idea of Julius Caesar contains the idea of his crossing the Rubicon, so that the historical fact of Caesar's crossing the Rubicon can in principle be *deduced* from the adequate idea of Caesar. Such an adequate idea is of infinite magnitude however (see five below) and hence not possible within human consciousness.

4. The total number of substances that exist in reality is either a minimum or a maximum, or some number in between. Any number in between would be arbitrary — there would be no sufficient reason for it. The minimum number of substances is zero, and it is false that zero substances exist, since I exist — my own existence is indubitable. Consequently a maximum number of substances exist, and this maximum number is infinity.

5. An analogous argument applies to the number of attributes of each substance. This number is neither arbitrary nor zero, hence infinite. It follows that an adequate idea of each substance contains an infinity of predicates.

Another way of putting items 4 and 5 is to say that a world consisting of an infinity of substances, each with an infinity of attributes, is the best of all possible worlds. Best in the sense that any alternative possible world would have to contain fewer attributes. Hence the sufficient reason for this world's existence is that it is the best of all possible worlds. This dictum, which is perhaps the best-known part of Leibniz, should not be confused with Voltaire's misunderstanding of it in *Candide*, where it becomes a superficial justification of *laissez-faire* conservatism. Voltaire was a common sense realist, who did not understand that Leibniz's best of all possibles referred, not to any empirical world, but to the metaphysical, or theoretical, world of metarealism.

Each of the infinity of substances Leibniz called a **monad**.

6. Because all true propositions are categorical and analytic there are no true propositions about relations, which is to say that no relations exist. All relations are *entia rationes*, said Leibniz — things of the mind, hence illusory.

7. Consequently there are no intrinsic relations in a monad: that is, every monad is indivisible — it has no parts, it is a *simple* substance. (An attribute of a substance is not a part of it, for substance-attribute metaphysicians: attributes "inhere" in substances, and inhering is not a relation.)

8. And there are no extrinsic relations between monads — for example, no spatial or temporal relations, no causation and no similarity. Leibniz described this metaphorically by saying that every monad is *windowless*.

9. So the infinity of monads occupies no space at all, and is timeless — that is, eternal.

10. And there is no causation between one monad and another, each is wholly independent of every other.

11. And no two monads are alike, since there is no similarity between any of them. This is Leibniz's famous *Principle of the Identity of Indiscernibles*: no two things differ numerically alone. If they are two, it must be because of a qualitative difference — a difference of predicates. It should be noted here that for Leibniz similarity would be exact similarity; anything else is dissimilarity, and dissimilarity is not a relation, since it is merely the absence of similarity. Consequently every monad has some characteristic, qualitative difference from every other. This characteristic difference Leibniz called its *viewpoint*.

12. If monads were to be ordered according to the closeness of their viewpoints, they would seem to be in a spatio-temporal-causal ordering. This ordering Leibniz called the pre-established harmony.

13. Because both the world and each monad are, as it were, of maximum richness, each monad is in this respect a copy of the world; it *mirrors* the world, as Leibniz said. Consequently among its attributes each monad contains a copy of every other monad plus a copy of the pre-established harmony; yet at the same time each monad differs from every other. So each monad contains a spatio-temporal-causal copy of the real world, which is unique in its viewpoint. Or, to put it another way, the pre-established harmony is a spatio-temporal-causal assemblage of viewpoints, which, when mirrored, is mirrored at and from each of these viewpoints. As such, it is in each mirroring the empirical world given in perception to the monad at that viewpoint.

14. Within each mirroring — each world given in perception to a monad — are *things*. Things are mirrorings of assemblages of monads of closely related viewpoints. Such assemblages Leibniz called compound substances. They are compound as compared with simple substances, or monads.

15. Finally, among monads are human souls. These perceive, each in its own world, its own human body. This body is a mirroring of a compound substance. Each compound substance consists of an infinity of monads, so it follows that each human being has an infinity of souls — a strange doctrine that Leibniz disguised in his published writings by the supposition that one of these monads is dominant over all the others. This dominant monad was then the one soul required by Christian teaching.

✱

It is not difficult to relate this sketch of Leibniz's metaphysics to the theory so far developed in this book.

Thus a real mind, which we defined as a subject plus all of which that subject is conscious — apparent world and apparent mind — plus an unconscious mind, is in Leibnizian terms a monad. A monad is itself a subject of consciousness, conscious of some of its attributes and unconscious of others. Those attributes of which it is conscious are either a mirroring of the real world, and as such constitute the apparent world, or a reflecting on the apparent world and as such constitute the apparent mind. (Leibniz, who was the inventor of the concept of unconscious mind, invented it in order to explain how a monad with an eternal infinity of attributes was not conscious of all of them at once.) A real object is what Leibniz called a compound substance — a collection of monads whose viewpoints are close together. The mirroring of the real object within a monad is an apparent object. But this mirroring is not, of course, for Leibniz a causal process of theoretical perception, but simply an arrangement of attributes within the monad in accordance with the pre-established harmony. One's own apparent body is thus a mirroring of one's own real body, which is a compound substance.

There are, of course, differences in detail between a monad and a real mind. A real mind is neither simple nor windowless; and it contains a subject, rather than is itself a subject. But these, although they need to be pointed out, are not important when it comes to understanding one system in terms of the other.

Historically, the most important feature of Leibniz's philosophy is that, by providing one distinct apparent world per consciousness, each a copy, from its own viewpoint, of the real world, Leibniz resolved all the philosophical problems of perception. Notice that he did so by providing two bodies per consciousness: a compound substance, and a mirroring of this compound substance; that is, a real body and an empirical body. It is indicative of the irrational power of common sense prejudice over men's reason that this achievement of Leibniz was not recognised until the twentieth century, when Bertrand Russell pointed it out; and that on this point Bertrand Russell has been almost totally misunderstood and ignored by professional philosophers. Indeed, Leibniz's system is so impressive that, concerning the wedding mentioned at the end of the last chapter [89], between metaphysics and theoretical science, Leibniz's system at first sight seems to be a perfect mate for theoretical science. In fact, however, his system has certain defects, all analysable into one fundamental flaw.

These defects appear when we ask the sufficient reason for a number of things. For example, what is the sufficient reason for dominant monads to have apparent minds? They mirror the real world, and as such have apparent worlds; but apparent minds are not a mirroring of anything. So either the real world is defective, in not having a universal mind to be mirrored, or else dominant monads are over-endowed. Again, except for the peculiarities of perception arising from viewpoint, Leibniz's system has made illusion and other peculiarities of perception logically *possible*, but not — at least overtly

— *necessary*. Which is to say that there is no recognisable sufficient reason for illusion — including the illusion of relations. The same may be said for dominance of monads. The Principle of Identity of Indiscernibles makes it necessary for a plurality of monads to differ qualitatively, and one way they differ is in their dominance. But they already differ in their viewpoints. Differing viewpoints are a sufficient reason for plurality, and dominance is a sufficient reason for plurality, but plurality does not need two sufficient reasons. Again, given differing dominance, why is the imperfect human monad the highest? It is imperfect because of illusion in its apparent world and error in its apparent mind. Surely, in the best of all possible worlds there should be an infinity of higher degrees of dominance, all the way to perfection? That this is not so, requires a sufficient reason.

The only answer possible for Leibniz is to say that the sufficient reason for all these things is to be found — in principle, if not in fact — in the pre-established harmony. Thus it is incomplete to say of any monad that the sufficient reason for any of its attributes (such as illusion or error) is the monad itself — even though the sufficient reason for any predicate is the subject that contains it. Rather, the nature of each monad is determined by the pre-established harmony; which is to say that the sufficient reason for any monad having just the set of attributes that it does, rather than any other, is the pre-established harmony. The pre-established harmony, in its turn, has the sufficient reason that it is the best of all possible harmonies. Hence for Leibniz the sufficient reason for apparent minds, illusion and error, dominance and its finitude is to be found in the best of all possible pre-established harmonies — the ultimate logical subject.

One objection to this is that to explain everything in terms of the pre-established harmony is no better than to explain everything in terms of the will of God [81]. Each explanation, although of universal scope, is wholly lacking in detail. The same objection applies to Spinoza's one substance. Perhaps this is why old style metaphysics was largely swept aside by science. Another objection to the pre-established harmony being the ultimate sufficient reason is that, according to Leibniz's axiom, the pre-established harmony should be a substance — in which case all the monads are predicates of that one substance and therefore not themselves substances. This would make Leibniz's pre-established harmony indistinguishable from Spinoza's one substance, or God.

Much more interesting than these defects, however, is the actual nature of the pre-established harmony. If we ask what it has to be — substance, attribute, or relation — it is obvious that it is a relation. It is an infinitely complex relation, with an infinity of terms — namely, each of the infinity of attributes of each of the infinity of monads. Leibniz has not excluded relations from his real world, he has only compounded them into one infinite-adic [111] relation. The ultimate metaphysical subject — the sufficient reason for everything else — is not a substance at all, but a relation. To claim that the real world is relational is the second answer, of maximum simplicity, to the question of what is the stuff of reality.

Furthermore, as we will see early in the next chapter, the monads, *qua* substances, are not logically necessary; and their function of mirroring the pre-established harmony is superfluous. Hence we can argue that the real world does not consist of substances and attributes, but of relations.

★

Before developing this theme, two minor points should be made. First, those who are familiar with Hegelian dialectic will notice that we have encountered an elegant exercise in it. For Leibniz's metaphysics has *destroyed* itself, yet *preserved* itself, and *elevated* itself. It has destroyed itself in that, starting with the thesis that the logic of the real world is subject-predicate logic, it has arrived at the antithesis that the logic of the real world is relational; but in the process of arriving at this, the structure of the real world that the thesis required is preserved, in that much of what Leibniz says of the real world is probably true; and it is elevated in that it can now harmonise with empirical and theoretical science — something that no subject-predicate metaphysics can do, since science is relational.

Secondly, to argue that the real world is relational produces as great an outrage to common sense as to argue that there is one separate empirical world per consciousness. This is because all relations are abstract entities. Hence everything concrete in any apparent world — colour, sound, texture, etc. — is illusion. In other words, sensible qualities — sensations — exist in apparent worlds and minds, and nowhere else. Their causes — electromagnetic waves, sound waves, vapours, etc. — exist in the real world, but the concrete qualities themselves do not. This does not mean that the rich glory of apparent worlds — sunsets, autumn colours, gourmet delights, etc. — are lost to a thin, bleak world of abstractions, but the reverse. Apparent worlds, rich as they often seem, are far less rich than the real world.

Compare the richness of a single colour sensation, and that of the molecular structure that gives rises to it. Concreteness [158], in fact, is illusory because it is an oversimplification, a homomorphism, of reality. It is illusory precisely because of loss of richness.

7. Relational Metaphysics.

We said in the last chapter that there are two answers, of maximum simplicity, as to what is the "stuff" of reality. These are (i) that reality is substantial — its rationality is the Aristotelian subject-predicate logic — and (ii) that reality is structural, it consists of relations — its rationality is mathematics. In choosing between these we have to opt for the second, and so side with Pythagoras and Plato, because theoretical science is mathematical. So this chapter is an examination of relational metaphysics.

∗ ∗ ∗

The concept of relation is primitive, so far as the present work is concerned: it can neither be defined nor explained. We can, however, gain some idea of the concept by discussing the characteristics of relations. There are six that will be discussed here. Further details will be found in Chapter 15.

∗

1. First, all relations have two or more terms, or *relata*, which are what it is that the relation relates. The number of terms a relation has is called its **adicity**. For example, dyadic, triadic, tetradic, and polyadic relations are relations with two, three, four, and many terms, respectively. Examples of each of these, in order, are: A is *larger* than B; C is *between* D and E; Jack *gave* Jill a message for John; and all human beings are *descended from* common ancestors. Empirical relations — relations which we perceive in our empirical worlds — usually have as their terms empirical concrete objects or empirical concrete qualities; the exceptions are those empirical relations which have other empirical relations as their terms. Among empirical relations are those in the imagination, known introspectively. But theoretical relations, with a few exceptions, have other theoretical relations as their terms, as will be explained shortly. Note that there are no monadic relations — relations having only one term, such as self-similarity: the least number of terms that a relation may have is two. We may describe or define monadic relations, but they do not exist. This is because monadic relations multiply extravagantly, and so must be denied by Occam's Razor. For example, if everything is self-similar then this relation of self-similarity is self-similar, and this second self-similarity is self-similar, as is this third, and so on to infinity. Some other relations, besides monadic relations, multiply extravagantly in this way: the relation *term of*, between a

relation and each of its terms, for example; such relations, which may be defined verbally but which do not exist, are called **nominal relations**.

✷

2. All relations have properties. For example, some relations are **symmetrical** and some are **asymmetrical**: the relation *equal* is symmetrical because if A is equal to B then B is equal to A, while *greater than* is asymmetrical because if C is greater than D then D is not greater than C. The exceptions, mentioned above, to relations having other relations as their terms are relations which have *properties of* relations, rather than relations themselves, as their terms: two of these are the relations of **similarity** and **dissimilarity**: any matching properties of any two relations are either similar or else dissimilar. Given any two relations, if they have a number, s, of similar properties and a number, d, of dissimilar properties, and one has m more properties than the other, then the **degree of similarity** between them is $s/(s+d+m)$, and the **degree of dissimilarity** between them is $(d+m)/(s+d+m)$. So if we have a degree of similarity k, then $1-k$ is the degree of dissimilarity[8].

For example, suppose that we want to compare triangles and squares in Euclidean geometry. Let us suppose that each of them is a simple, closed, figure: simple in that no sides cross each other, and closed in that each side joins two others; each such figure has an adicity, which is the number of sides that it has; and each has two emergent properties: area, and shape. These can be described by the lengths of some or all of the sides, and the angles between them. So they all have five properties: simple figure, closed figure, adicity, area, and shape. Any two similar triangles (in the geometric

---

[8] The definitions of degree of similarity and degree of dissimilarity may be extended from those of single relations to those of structures by defining corresponding terms of the relations, and the degrees of similarity or dissimilarity of corresponding terms, and of relations between the terms, and repeating this for lower and lower levels, down to prime relations (see below). The degrees of similarity at each level could then be averaged, and the averages for different levels weighted to form an overall average, with the weights decreasing with level. If desired the weights for a given level and lower could be made zero, for convenience. For example, in comparing the degree of similarity between two monozygotic twins, it is hardly necessary to go lower than the level of their genes.

sense of *similar*) have all five properties similar, and hence a degree of similarity of one. Any two congruent triangles of unequal area have four similar properties, and hence a degree of similarity of 4/5. A triangle and a square of equal area differ in their adicity and shape and so have a degree of similarity of 3/5. And a triangle and a square of unequal area differ in their adicity, area, and shape and so have a degree of similarity of 2/5.

There is a problem with relations of similarity and dissimilarity. Although some of them undoubtedly exist, they also multiply extravagantly, since any two relations of similarity are similar, as are any two relations of dissimilarity, and any pair of a similarity and a dissimilarity are dissimilar. We have no rule which specifies those that exist while denying existence to the ones that multiply extravagantly, other than to require that we do not multiply them beyond necessity, while multiplying them up to necessity — the necessity being the necessity of explaining the empirical facts.

✶

3. All relations exist as particular, individual entities. This needs to be stated because the contemporary formal view of a relation is that it is a fiction, a logical construct, defined in terms of class extensions of ordered pairs, ordered triads, etc. In the present context, if we suppose that the real Jack is taller than the real Jill, then each of Jack and Jill is a structure of structures — of cells, molecules, atoms, etc. — and as such each structure level is a single structure, unified into a whole (see the fifth property, below) by a higher level relation. We then can consider three individual relations: *real Jack*, *real Jill*, and *taller than*. Each relation is an entity, a particular existent. It is a peculiarity of such existents that they cannot exist unless their terms exist; and, furthermore, their terms must be appropriately arranged.

✶

4. Relations easily come into, and go out of, existence. This coming into existence of relations is **emergence**, and their going out of existence is **submergence**. Relations emerge when (i) there exists a sufficient number and variety of terms for them, and (ii) these terms are arranged appropriately. For example, the *melody* that is an emergent relation emerges only if the right number and variety of notes exist, and they are suitably arranged; or a machine, such as an old fashioned weight-driven pendulum clock, has the emergent relation of *working order* only if all of its parts exist and they are suitably arranged. In the first example the arrangement is temporal, in the

second it is spatial. With the exceptions of those empirical relations which have concrete qualities as their terms, and a few other relations such as similarity and dissimilarity which have properties as their terms, the terms of relations are always other relations. This means that if enough relations exist at the lowest level, then relations may emerge out of them and be themselves terms of higher level emergent relations, and again, up to higher and higher levels. This is called **cascading emergence**. An example of it is structures in the real world: wave-particles such as neutrons, protons, and electrons; atoms, or chemical elements; molecules, or chemical compounds; living cells; plants and animals; societies and ecosystems; and the biosphere. At each level novel emergents appear: atomic properties, chemical properties, life, photosynthesis and mobility, money, parasitism, etc. Another example of cascading emergence is an axiomatic system [71, 102, 308], in which definitions and theorems cascadingly emerge from the axiom set; this feature is sometimes called **axiom generosity**. It is a fact that at the lowest level of structure at which many kinds of emergent relation appear, those relations have emergent properties not possessed by their terms; this is called the **principle of novel emergence**. For example, *patterns* of grains of silver in a black and white photograph, or of dots of ink in a printed page, or of pixels on a computer screen, possess properties not possessed by grains of silver, dots of ink, or pixels: properties which make us call them patterns generally, and pictures or letters more particularly. There may also be patterns of patterns, such as pages of text or books of pictures, and both these and their terms have pattern properties. In other words, a particular property of a relation may emerge at levels higher than the lowest level at which its relation emerges, but not at lower levels.

That every emergent relation has a lowest level at which it can exist is shown by our earlier examples of emergent relations: a melody, working order, and knots. Working order cannot appear at a level lower than that of an arrangement of machine parts. Consider the mechanical clock, with weights, a pendulum, escapement, gears, dial, and hands: none of these parts has the property of working order because none of them are machines — only the assembled clock can have this working order. Again, the notes that form a melody are not melodious: a single note cannot be melodious. And knots not only possess properties not possessed by loops and crossings, but different knots have different properties, none of them possessed by their terms: for sailors, for example, a reef knot has the property of being easily released and a bowline has the property of not yielding under a load; for knitters, a sock or a sweater is a single knot possessing emergent properties appreciated by their wearers; and for mathematicians knots have many topological properties. None of these emergent properties are possessed by an unlooped piece of string or yarn. Again, life does not emerge below the molecular level, and money does not emerge below the societal level.

✱

5. Most relations unify their terms. There are three kinds of unification: unification of terms into *classes*, into *compound relations*, and into *wholes*. Classes, also called sets, are unified by a kind of relation called a **set relation**, which has only one property: a particular adicity. **Compound relations** are characterised by having a property similar to a property possessed by all of their terms, their terms being called **compoundable relations**. For example, a compound length is a unified set of unit lengths which has a length. (It is all the terms which are compound, properly speaking, not their unifying relation.) Other compound relations are *durations*; *boundaries*, which are compounds of contiguous dissimilarities; *changes* which are compounds of dissimilarities and durations; *processes* which are compounds of causes; *orderings* which are compounds of ratios; and *transitive relations*: a relation R is transitive if, given that aRb and bRc, then aRc. All transitive relations which relate more than two relations are compound relations.

Wholes are unified by relations which have a property not possessed by any of their terms, or any lower level terms: a **novel property**, of which we saw examples in the previous paragraph. As is well known, a whole is greater than the sum of its parts; the excess of the whole over the sum of the parts is the unifying relation, and the sum of the parts are all of its terms.

✱

6. As entities, relations are **abstract**. This is one of the reasons why many people have difficulty with them. For example, the question as to whether relations can be perceived or not frequently causes difficulty when first encountered. One can perceive that the chair is *in front of* the table, say, so it seems that one can perceive the relation *in front of*. But if asked what this relation looks like, one discovers that it does not have any looks or feels whatever, and this leads to the supposition that it is not perceptible, after all.

For how can one perceive something that has no perceptible qualities? However, it is perceptible: one perceives it because it is there, it exists. But it does not have any looks or feels because all of these are qualities, concrete — and relations, being abstract entities, do not have any concrete qualities. Another difficulty arises with imagining relations. One can imagine, as we saw, that Jack is taller than Jill by imagining Jack and Jill side by side. But many relations cannot be imagined. Most mathematical relations cannot: the relation between a number and its logarithm, for example. To imagine the mathematical symbols is no answer, since this is not to imagine what the symbols stand for. Many people identify imagining with thinking, including some philosophers: Berkeley will be an example given when this point is discussed in greater detail [235]. For these people, what is unimaginable is impossible: it cannot, hence does not, exist. Consequently, since, as we saw [92], the abstract is unimaginable in isolation, nothing abstract exists for these people. However, if a distinction is made between thinking and imagining — that is, they are respectively abstract and concrete — then the impossible is that which is unthinkable, rather than unimaginable; which is to say that the impossible is self-contradictory. In other words, although the unthinkable is unimaginable, the unimaginable is not necessarily unthinkable.

On this sixth point, more will be said later. A problem exists now, however, because the ordinary use of *abstract* does not quite coincide with the use here. The difference is in universal words for concrete qualities, which ordinarily are called abstract concepts, but are not so here. Redness, for example, is usually considered an abstract concept, referring to all particular, and concrete, instances of red. I will later contend that although it is a universal, it is not abstract in the sense of it referring to an abstract idea, as most universals do. Consequently, in order to clarify this, a precise definition of **abstract** and **concrete** should be given. This is possible, but not very helpful to the immediate understanding, since it must be in terms of relations and sensations: namely, the characteristic difference between these is that relations are always abstract, and everything abstract is either a relation or a relational property; while sensations, or qualities, are always concrete [158], and everything concrete is a sensation, a structure of sensations (which is a concrete object), or ideas or memories of these.

✱

7. Every emergent relation possesses an absolute value, called its **hekergy**. This is sufficiently important that it merits a chapter of its own: the next chapter, Chapter 8.

✻ ✻ ✻

The distinction between imagining and thinking brings us to our next point. Imagining is easy and thinking is difficult — as will be understood immediately once it is recognised that the best thinking is mathematical.

In other words, the language of relations is mathematics. Arithmetic is concerned with relations between numbers — such as greater and less, equality, and sum and difference — and numbers themselves are relational: they are adicities [285], which are properties of relations. Geometry equally is concerned with relations — spatial relations, such as relative lengths, angles between lines and planes, curvatures, etc. And similarly with the rest of mathematics.

And this brings us to the reason why we have to conclude that the real world consists of relations, rather than substances and attributes. It is because the most probable beliefs we have about the real world are those that constitute the exact theoretical sciences: astronomy, physics, and chemistry. And the exact theoretical sciences are entirely mathematical. They have no use for subject-predicate logic, and no use for the concepts of substance and attribute. In other words, subject-predicate metaphysics fails on one of our criteria of good explanation: it does not harmonise with other acceptable explanations, such as theoretical physics. Also, subject-predicate metaphysics fails to explain the content of empirical science, which, in so far as it is a product of measurement, is also relational — quantitative — rather than substantial and qualitative. Consequently the rationality of metaphysics should not be that of subject-predicate logic, but that of mathematics. This was advocated by Descartes three centuries ago, although his own metaphysics turned out not to be a mathematical one.

So we now turn to the possibility of a relational metaphysics. It should be made quite clear at the beginning, however, that the relational metaphysics offered here is not intended as definitive. It is merely offered as an illustration of how a competent theorist might proceed in this field. Such a theorist would possess, among other qualifications, a broad and deep understanding both of mathematics and of theoretical physics. These are two qualifications that I lack, which is why the following has to be no more than a pale shadow of what is needed.

The easiest approach to relational metaphysics is with the concept of structure. This is easiest because we are going to think of a real object as a structure; and although a structure is a unified set of related relations, it is in the first instance thinkable as a thing, possessing qualities. In other words, we are going to approach the difficult and abstract via the easy and concrete.

A **structure** is a complete set of relations between the parts of a whole. Any object may be thought of as a number of parts related in such a way as to make a whole: one relation unifies all the parts into a whole by having all of the parts as its terms, and this relation, plus all the other relations among all the parts, constitutes the structure. Most obviously, structure consists of spatial relations: this part is *above* that, to the *north* of this, and *between* those, for example. Less obvious is that structure consists of temporal relations as well, since structures exist through time; and some structures are largely temporal, such as the notes of a piece of music, or the words of a speech. There are other kinds of relation besides these, which contribute to structure.

If we think of the parts of a house as a lot of bricks and pieces of wood, metal, glass, etc., then when the house is about to be built, and all the parts are present at the building site, we have the parts but we do not have a house. What is lacking is the structure, the desired relations between the parts.

Also, portions of structure are emergent relations whose properties constitute properties of the structure, describable by means of predicates. For example, the totality of outer spatial relations constitutes *shape*, the average distance between parts gives *density*, high degree of similarity between parts gives *homogeneity* or *purity*, and so on. It will later be argued that all properties of all real objects are either relations or properties of relations.

The parts of a structure — that is, the terms of the various relations that together constitute the structure — are themselves structures, and hence wholes. We could call them **substructures**, such that substructures are sets of relations between sub-substructures, and so on downwards.

We are in fact quite used to thinking of real objects in this way. For example, a real table is a structure of pieces of wood; each piece of wood is a structure of wood fibres; each fibre is a structure of cells; each cell is a structure of organic molecules, such as cellulose; each molecule is a structure of atoms; each atom is a structure of wave-particles — electrons, protons, and neutrons.

This in turn gives rise to the problem of what is at the lowest level of structure. There are five possible answers, and it is not difficult to eliminate four of them.

✷

1. The first possible answer is that there is no lowest structure. Instead there is an infinite regress of smaller and smaller, lower and lower, substructures. Every structure, at every level, has an infinity of substructures. We can reject this as improbable because of the evidence of modern physics. If every structure had an infinity of substructures then at every level an infinite variety of structures would be possible; whereas if the number of substructures was finite then the possible variety would decrease rapidly as the lowest level was approached. And in fact theoretical physics gives us the latter answer. If, for simplicity, we confine ourselves just to living things, and we ignore the unstable systems at each level — those of very short duration — then it is clear that the number of possible kinds of animal and vegetable is incalculably large; the number of possible kinds of cell is so also, although obviously much smaller; the number of kinds of organic molecules utilisable by cells is still smaller, but still incalculable; the number of kinds of atoms in these molecules is less than a hundred; and the number of kinds of wave-particle in these atoms is three.

✷

2. So we will suppose only a finite regress of substructures. That is to say, there is a smallest part to everything. For the present we may call it an X. A structure of X's will then be a level-1 structure, a structure of level-1 structures will be a level-2 structure, and so on. If now we ask what an X is, then obviously, it is not a structure — because a structure must have parts, since its relations must have terms. So it can be one of the known three possible basic categories of apparent worlds: *thing, quality,* or *relation*; or, since we are concerned with the theoretically real world, *substance, attribute,* or *relation*; or alternatively it could be an unknown category — something not any of these three. This is our second possible answer. In this case we could give X a name but it would be otherwise unthinkable. Fortunately we only need resort to this possibility if it turns out to be

impossible for an X to be any of the three categories — and this is not the case.

✳

3. To say that an X is a substance was Aristotle's choice. In speaking of objects Aristotle sometimes analysed them into substances and attributes, and sometimes into structures. The latter he called form. The parts of a form he called matter; either **prime matter**, which we are calling X, or proximate matter, which is all the immediate parts of a structure. Thus the pieces of wood that constitute a table are the proximate matter of the table. However, to postulate a substance for X if it is possible to have a relation instead, is to multiply entities beyond necessity, contrary to Occam's Razor. In the one case the real world would consist of relations and substances, and in the other of relations only. The latter is preferable, and in fact quite possible.

✳

4. To say that X's are attributes would require at least one substance, of which both the X's and the relations between them are attributes. This possibility, which is basically Spinozistic, suffers from the same defect as Aristotle's — it multiplies entities beyond necessity.

✳

5. To say that X's are relations — what might be called **prime relations**, after Aristotle's concept of prime matter — seems at first impossible because relations must have terms, and the terms of relations are at a lower level than the relations themselves. However, the terms of the X's may be other X's, whose terms are other X's, and so on. Such a series can either expand indefinitely, or it can close in upon itself: either way, each X is both relation and term, hence the terms of X's are not at a level lower than their relations. We will first consider how such a series of X's might expand indefinitely, to form space; and then how it might turn in on itself, to form level-1 structures in space.

✳ ✳ ✳

Imagine a straight line composed of discrete, equal segments: such as a series of hyphens produced on one line by a word processor. Each segment may be thought of as a **separator** — a dyadic relation, whose terms are the two other separators adjacent to it, and which is itself one term of each of these two other separators. Such a series of separators which separate separators clearly makes a line which expands indefinitely. A discrete plane

120

may be imagined simply by having every separator one of a pair, such that each one of a pair crosses the other at right angles. A series of plus signs produced on a series of lines by a word processor illustrates this. Each separator in a pair then separates those two adjacent ones at which it points, and is separated by these two from those next beyond. Similarly, a three-dimensional space will consist of triads of mutually perpendicular separators. A plane of these separators is shown in Fig. 7.2.

This kind of separator will be called a **line separator**. We may assume that they are all of equal magnitude, and that this magnitude is an **atomic length**. In order to emphasise its relational nature it will also be called an **atomic spatial relation**. We are using *atomic* in its original Greek sense of indivisible.

In order to imagine the kind of separator that will produce level-1 structures, imagine a square. Each of its sides separates two of its sides, through two right angles. Each side may be thought of as a separator which is a dyadic relation whose terms are two such separators. And four mutually supporting such separators constitute a structure — a square level-1 structure.

This second kind of separator will be called a **plane separator**. We may assume that they always separate through one or two right angles (see below), that they are all of equal magnitude and that this magnitude is two atomic lengths.

Plane separators easily form three dimensional, level-2, structures.

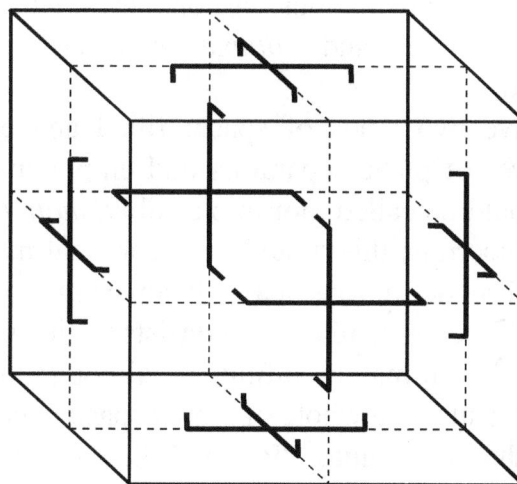

Fig. 7.1.

Imagine a cube, as in Fig. 7.1: it consists of six square sides, each of which may be thought of as a pair of plane separators, at right angles to each other, such that each plane separator separates two similar separators and is itself separated, by these two, from a fourth. Each such group of four is a level-1 structure, and we have three of them together (that is, twelve plane separators) making a level-2 structure. In Fig. 7.1 the thin lines represent the original cube, the heavy lines represent plane separators (with their tails indicating their terms) and the broken lines represent the level-1 structures. The original cube is, of course, merely an aid to the imagination; like the scaffolding used to construct a building, it is disposed of once the building is made. Equally, the broken lines represent nothing real, but serve only to clarify. Only the separators are real.

So far plane separators have been treated as only dyadic — each separates only two separators. But this takes no account of line separators, so that our level-2 structure exists in isolation. To overcome this we must suppose that plane separators can separate through both one and two right angles (in one plane), and that they may sometimes have line separators as their terms. This is illustrated in Fig. 7.2, where a level-2 structure is shown in space. Onl one, partial, plane of space — that is, of line separators — is shown, for clarity; it goes through the centre of the level-2 structure.

The plane separators are now tetradic. Clearly, level-2 structures may be related together in various ways to form level-3 structures. These may then be related to form level-4 structures, and so on up, with cascading emergence [114] of novel relations. Among these emergent relations are *area* in level-1 structures and *volume* in level-2 structures — both compoundable relations.

We now have two kinds of space: filled and empty. Filled space consists of structures of plane separators and empty space consists of line separators. They could be called, not implausibly, *matter* and the *void*, after Leucippus and Democritus; this would be theoretical matter, of course, not empirical matter. The definitions leave it an open question whether this combined space is finite or infinite. If it consists of line separators spreading out in three dimensions, it may be infinite — although the possibility of this will be denied later. But if the whole of empty space is bounded by a shell of level-2 structures then it is finite. "Beyond" the shell would not be empty space — line separators — but non-space, no separators at all. Space could

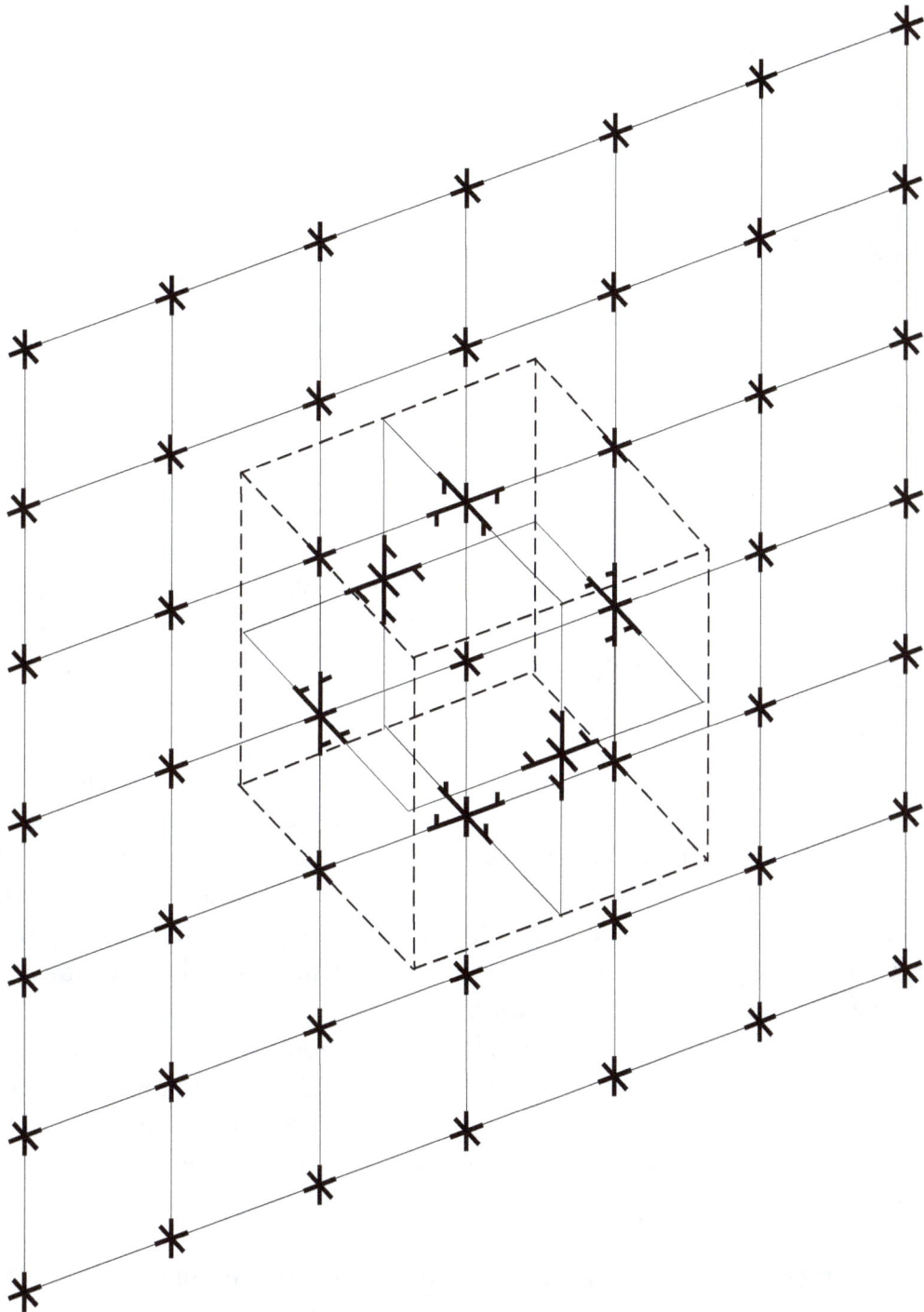

Fig. 7.2.

also be finite but unbounded if it were part of a curved Einsteinian four-dimensional space-time, closed in on itself like the surface of a sphere: this could only happen if plane separators were slightly shorter than two line separators, so that their presence would stretch surrounding line separators according to an inverse-square law.

Given line and plane separators as so far specified, a possible emergent relation results: shape. This happens with level-3 structures, in which a wide variety of shapes is possible. This large variety does not exist with level-2 structures, in which the variety of possible shapes is quite small. This is quite characteristic of emergent relations: as structures get larger, the variety of possibilities increases. An analogy will make this clear. Suppose that a photograph consists of small squares, all equal in size and either black or white. Clearly, the larger the photograph relative to one of these squares, the greater the variety of possible shapes, and of shades of grey, that it will be able to represent.

More generally, we can claim as a metaphysical principle that all properties peculiar to higher level structures are properties of emergent relations. Qualities, as they appear in apparent worlds, are then concrete representations of such properties, as will be explained in Chapter 11 [158].

✶ ✶ ✶

We next consider temporal relations. We may suppose that every spatial separator exists for some small, common duration called an **atomic duration**, or **atomic temporal relation**. All atomic durations may be supposed to be equal. At the end of every atomic duration all spatial separators cease to exist and are replaced with new spatial separators. Some separators are replaced by the other kind (line separator by plane separator or vice versa) and there is then an **atomic change** at that location; others are replaced by the same kind and there is then an **atomic stasis** at that location. That is, an atomic change temporally relates a line separator to a plane separator, and an atomic stasis temporally relates two line separators or else two plane separators. Atomic changes may then be compounded together to produce higher level changes.

✶

Given change, we can now have motion. If we suppose a level-1 structure to disappear, and another just like it to appear immediately afterwards in the next adjacent position, then it is as if one structure had moved from one place to the next. Obviously, a structure of any level can move in this way. And although it can only move in one of three dimensions at each increment of motion, changes of direction at any or all of these increments can add up to motion along any macroscopic path.

If we define this motion as continuous — that is, it is always to an adjacent space, it never jumps intermediate spaces — then clearly there is a maximum velocity of continuous motion: namely, one line separator per atomic duration. And if by *adjacent* we include diagonally adjacent spaces, in the Euclidean sense of diagonal, then there is a maximum velocity in any direction. An interesting sidelight on this is the fact that Max Planck, father of quantum mechanics, proposed a set of units for physical quantities which, unlike the conventional units, are entirely unarbitrary. He did this by taking three fundamental constants in physics, and defining his units by means of them. One was the gravitational constant, G, defined by Newton and first measured by Cavendish; the second was the velocity of light, c, shown by Einstein to be the maximum possible velocity for any causal process; and the third was the constant discovered by Planck himself, and named Planck's constant after him, the quantum of action, symbolised by $\hbar$. In terms of these, Planck defined what is now called the called Planck length as the quantity $(G\hbar/c^3)^{1/2}$, and the Planck time as $(G\hbar/c^5)^{1/2}$. They are small: 1.6×10^{-35} metre and 5.4×10^{-44} second, approximately. But if these are the sizes of the atomic length and the atomic duration, then the maximum continuous velocity is c, the velocity of light, as Einstein's theories require, because a velocity of one Planck length per one Planck time is $(G\hbar/c^3)^{1/2}/(G\hbar/c^5)^{1/2} = c$.

We now have a system of relational metaphysics that in principle allows for an ascending series of levels of structure, from level-1 structures; and of spatial relations within and without these, and temporal relations: a cascading emergence of real structures, in short. We can think of structures of various levels as real objects, and account for their properties in terms of emergent relations within them. These real objects can change their properties and move. All that we still lack in this pale shadow [118] of a theoretical real world is causation; for this we need the concept of that emergent property of every emergent relation called *hekergy*, the subject of the next chapter.

✶

Before ending this chapter we note that separators are not themselves emergent relations. Their existence is instead determined on a top-down basis, as explained in Chapter 17.

8. Hekergy.

The concept of hekergy grew out of the concept of entropy in thermodynamics, and did so because, of all the concepts in science, entropy is the only one that gave promise of providing a scientific, objective, basis of human values: of truth, beauty, and goodness. Speaking very loosely, entropy is a bad thing and its opposite, so-called negative[9] entropy, is a good thing. One can sense this to some extent from the famous Second Law of Thermodynamics, also called the Entropy Law, which says in effect that negative entropy is difficult to acquire but easy to lose. One has only to think by analogy to the things we value, and how they are all hard won but readily lost, to recognize the possibility of their being forms of negative entropy. Wealth is an obvious example, as most people trying to increase their savings in the face of the costs of daily living well know. Good reputation is another example. Purity — particularly chemical purity — is another — as shown by the ease with which lakes, streams, and the atmosphere above cities are polluted. Good health; the beauty of, say, fine porcelain; the weed-free state of a garden; wisdom; a state of cleanliness — of person, clothes, house, etc.; life itself, and civilization, are further examples. All are hard won but easily lost. Forest fires, earthquakes, hurricanes, epidemics, wars, famines, and economic disasters are some of the more spectacular examples of easy loss. This asymmetry of process is, in thermodynamics, called **irreversibility**. Certain processes involve losses of negative entropy, which, being irreplaceable, render the processes irreversible. It is for this reason that perpetual motion machines are impossible: friction makes their motion decrease irreversibly. We are also quite familiar with irreversibility within human values: we cannot restore our youth, awake the dead, or unscramble eggs.

An interpretation of entropy that is a little less vague is that it is a measure of disorder. Negative entropy is in consequence a measure of **order**. The relation of this to value is seen when it is recognized that the difference between diamond and amorphous carbon is one of order; as is the difference between a pile of building materials and a house; between a printed page and

---

[9] Strictly speaking, the term should be *negated entropy*, not *negative entropy*, since a literally negative entropy in physics would require a negative absolute temperature — because entropy is zero at zero degrees Kelvin — and this is impossible. But the usage seems to have become established.

a page spattered with ink; between a regiment and a mob; between music and cacophony; between peace and war; and between healthy growth and cancer. That order is easily lost and hard to gain is shown by how much human activity is spent on restoring order, as in housework, engineering maintenance, and maintenance of health. Order, it may be noted, is a relation.

A more technical kind of negative entropy is a **gradient**. This may be a gravitational gradient, such as a hill down which stones may be rolled; a temperature gradient, without which heat energy is inaccessible; a pressure gradient, as in a meteorological cyclone or anticyclone, a hydroelectric water delivery pipe or compressed air machinery; an electrical gradient, or voltage, without which no current will flow; or an economic gradient. It is because of a dryness gradient that you can dry yourself with a towel; and the absence of such a gradient is why you cannot dry yourself with a wet towel. Without gradients energy is unavailable, so that negative entropy is also a measure of the availability of energy. Gradients may disappear of their own accord, as shown by ice cubes melting in a drink, electric batteries losing their charge during storage, the draining of lakes to the sea, etc.

Possibly it is a symbolic expression of this idea of gradient in ordinary language when values are described in terms of height. We speak of high prices, high finance, higher mathematics, high speeds, high spirits, high numbers, and high standards in general. We raise children, cheer up, catch up, rise above temptation and climb to success. Conversely, we speak of the depth of despair, declining years, down-heartedness, low supply, fallen women, the brink of ruin, falling behind, falling into decay or disuse, and wearing down resistance. We think of heaven as up and hell as down, we name the generative and degenerative seasons Spring and Fall, and, in physics, we speak of high power, high temperature, high voltage, and high frequency.

Again, *work*, and the ability or potential for work, or *power*, are both dependent upon negative entropy, in their technical sense, and, in ordinary language, are expressive of creating or maintaining value, or of the ability to do this. We speak of housework, brain work, manual work, and white collar work, field work, brush work, earth work and, of course, mechanical work. We work for money and make money work for us; and machines and other technical devices are in working order or not. Then there are our uses of *power*: will, purchasing, military, political, spiritual or physical power; power of the spoken word, of the pen, of the sword, of knowledge, of reason and mathematics, or of an ideal. We value such powers, and, like negative entropy, they are generally hard to gain, easy to lose.

Two further general points should be mentioned in connection with entropy. One is a satisfactory definition of life, which, after two and a half millennia of seeking by philosophers, was discovered by a physicist: Erwin Schrödinger, of wave-mechanics fame. He proposed that a living system is one of very high negative entropy, in a state of dynamic equilibrium; and in doing this he began to harmonise physics and biology. Second, Claude Shannon developed a measure of information, and hence a theory of communication, based on entropy.

✳

All this is no more than suggestive. It has been dwelt on at some length because gaining understanding of the concept of hekergy is difficult — although, once understood, it is simple enough. This is largely because the definition of hekergy requires some elementary mathematics. Consequently those readers who feel disinclined to try to gain such understanding on a first reading will have some vague understanding of what is meant by hekergy: it is generalised negative entropy. Such mathematicophobic readers must accept on faith, for now, that hekergy is a property possessed by every emergent relation, that it has a magnitude, and that the greater the magnitude the greater the value of the relation; and then skip the next two paragraphs.

✳

Every emergent relation requires a certain minimum number of terms, of the right kind, in order to emerge. It also requires a suitable arrangement, or structure, of those terms in order to emerge. If the terms are so arranged that the relation emerges, and then rearranged, the relation may submerge, or it may not. The number of arrangements of the terms in which the relation emerges is called the number of equivalent arrangements of the terms of that relation, and this number is represented by e, for *equivalent*. The total number of possible arrangements of those terms is represented by t, for *total*; we assume for now that t is never infinite. The ratio e/t is the *a priori* probability [74] of that relation, and the reciprocal ratio, t/e, its improbability. The **hekergy** of the relation is then the natural logarithm of its improbability, $\ln(t/e)$, while its generalised entropy is the natural logarithm of its probability, $\ln(e/t)$. If the relation is R then its hekergy is symbolised by H_R and its entropy by S_R. So $H_R = \ln(t/e)$ and $S_R = \ln(e/t) = -\ln(t/e) = -H_R$.

The logarithm of the probability is used simply because probabilities combine by multiplication and entropies by simple addition: $\ln(a \times b) = \ln(a) + \ln(b)$. Also, if the entropy of a structure is the logarithm of its probability then the negative entropy is the logarithm of its improbability, since, for any number x, say, $\ln(x) = -\ln(1/x)$, and an improbability is the reciprocal of a probability. Thus a hekergy is a negative entropy, with the proviso that the concept of entropy used here is a generalisation of that used in physics.

✶

Every emergent relation has a hekergy, which may be thought of as its absolute value. The kind of hekergy that it is depends upon the kind of relation that possesses it.

Those familiar with statistical mechanics will recognise that the terms *macrostate* and *microstate* therein are here respectively an emergent relation and an arrangement of its terms. Using our number e, the entropy of a given macrostate is defined in physics as $S = k.\ln(e)$, where k is Boltzmann's constant, which gives the entropy its dimensions of energy per degree of temperature. Physicists do not bother with the term t, since in a closed energy system it is merely an additive constant.

Because hekergies may be defined at any structure level, we must distinguish between summation hekergy and configuration hekergy. At any one level the **summation hekergy** of a structure is the total hekergy of all of its parts, of all the lower level relations, while the **configuration hekergy** is the total hekergies of all the relations emergent at that level. In other words, configuration hekergy is the excess of the value of the whole over the value of the sum of its parts, which latter is summation hekergy.

✶ ✶ ✶

To develop a causal principle with the concept of hekergy we must first distinguish the concepts *local* and *global*. In the first instance anything that can be perceived by one observer is **local** to that observer, or within that observer's locality. This concept may be extended to several observers if they constitute a team — that is, if they are co-operating and communicating about what they perceive; then anything perceived by anyone in the team is local to that team. We may also extend the concept of locality by allowing that measurement is a form of theoretical perception, so that in a sense any measuring instrument, no matter how remote from every team member, whose data are available to the team, is a secondary member of the team.

That which is **global**, on the other hand, applies to the real world as a whole. For example the total quantity of energy in the real world is a global quantity, not locally measurable. An example of a global principle is Clausius' extrapolation of the second law of thermodynamics [127] to a global extent. This item of bad metaphysics required that the total entropy of the universe is steadily increasing, irreversibly; consequently the universe is "unwinding, like a clock" and will end with a "universal heat death."

If the supposition that the real world is finite is correct then the fact that the global is not local is only a matter of practical difficulty, not of principle.

The importance of this distinction between local and global lies in causation. Let us suppose that every real event has a cause, and every real cause necessitates its effects. This is to say that there are no unnecessary, or chance, events: no events that were not necessitated. This is equivalent to Leibniz's principle of sufficient reason [104], since the cause of an event is a sufficient condition for it. We may then distinguish between events that are locally caused, and those that are not. Those that are not locally caused, even in principle, must be globally caused.

Locally caused events include those with which scientists are concerned. A local causal principle, which is usually an axiom in a scientific theory, requires that a series of events — a process — follows a particular pattern — the pattern being a relation emergent out of all of these events. Because a local principle is involved, it is locally verifiable — that is, scientifically verifiable. The principle of conservation of energy is such a local principle; energy is locally conserved and this fact can be locally verified — within the limits of experimental error — that is, evidence for it can be obtained locally. Various stationary, or *extremum*, principles, which are principles of minima or maxima, such as principles of least action, shortest path, least time, and least resistance, are further examples of local principles.

It is a fact that not all events are locally caused. Most scientists regard those that have no local cause as uncaused, and call them chance events.

Philosophically this is unsatisfactory because chance events are inexplicable. As we saw [53], to explain something is to describe its cause or causes; and if chance events are uncaused then we cannot explain them. So we are never able to say why one chance event occurred rather than any of the possible alternatives.

The escape from this predicament is to postulate one or more global causal principles. The one most frequently used in the past was theological: non-locally caused events are caused by the will of God. Most scientists will not accept this because the theology involved contradicts scientific theories, rather than harmonises with them. Even if, as most scientists would concede is possible, the theology contains some truth, there seems to be no way of separating this truth from the dross of myth, superstition, and primitive magic in which it is embedded. However, the concept of hekergy provides an alternative.

The global hekergy principle that I wish to postulate is the principle that the total hekergy of the universe is the maximum possible. This can be stated alternatively as Leibniz did: this is the best of all possible worlds. It is the real world, of course, that we are concerned with here — not anyone's apparent world. A possible proof of the global hekergy principle is given in Chapter 16.

We may suppose because of this a principle of conservation: hekergy is globally conserved. At first sight this latter statement seems to deny the second law of thermodynamics, which denies that entropy is conserved, in that entropy increases; but there is no contradiction, because this non-conservation is local, not global.

We may suppose that within this global conservation some classes of hekergy are locally conserved, and some are not. Those that are locally conserved are such things as energy, linear and angular momentum, mass (in chemical processes) and electric charge. Those that are not locally conserved will be of two kinds: those that decrease locally, and those that increase locally. Those that decrease locally we may suppose to be negative entropies, hekergies. Those that increase locally are those mostly characteristic of animate structures and of some of their products; but they include any increase of hekergy, such as order, gradient, and purity, so that the formation of a galaxy, for example, is a local increase. Global conservation then requires that the global totality of local decreases be equal to the global totality of local increases.

Thus throughout the process of evolution, including the start of life on this planet, every increase of order, of complexity and the like, within vegetable and animal life, as species evolved into higher forms, was an increase of hekergy caused by some equal and opposite decrease of negative entropy. This applies also to artifacts: a coral reef or a computer, a honeycomb or a heat engine, all constitute a hekergy increase in their coming into being. In accordance with Schrödinger's definition of life [129] we may define a living structure to be one of very high hekergy in dynamic equilibrium. The equilibrium is maintained, in the face of hekergy decreases due to the second law of thermodynamics, by replacements through photosynthesis or by feeding on other life. Failure of the equilibrium is death.

One consequence of this approach is to alter one of Darwin's principles of evolution: the principle of chance variations. Or, as it might be stated today, the principle of chance mutations and chance gene combinations. Mutations, to be sure, are supposed to be caused — by cosmic rays or radioactive emissions — but the results are not; favourable or unfavourable, and of what kind, is a matter of chance for biologists. By eliminating this element of chance — in principle, if not in detail — we cure what is perhaps a defect in the theory of evolution. This defect is the fact of some evolutionary advances requiring, not one favourable variation, but many — each of them sufficiently improbable as to make the whole set of them exceedingly unlikely. When this occurs in a way that provides no survival value until the process is complete, one wonders how it could occur so frequently. An example is stereoscopic vision, which requires a series of variations to bring the eyes to the front of the head, so that their fields are co-extensive; and at the same time another series of variations to develop the brain to handle the new kind of data provided and correctly interpret distance from it. Since none of these individual variations has survival value — only the complete series of them does — they are favourable variations only if they occur together as a set, which is highly improbable. This development has occurred in more than one species, as with primates, felines, canines, and owls, and is only one of many such complex ones. To say that such are necessitated by the global hekergy principle, compensating for the second law of thermodynamics, is more satisfactory than to deny the very possibility of explaining them by saying that they are uncaused.

At the same time, the entropy increases of thermodynamics also cease to be a matter of chance, but are explained, in principle if not in detail, by the maximum hekergy of the Universe. In terms of our criteria of good explanation [77] two distinct theories, statistical mechanics and evolution, have been harmonised into one and the asymmetries in each cancel out into a symmetry: decreasing negative entropy and increasing hekergy together constitute a conservation. We may also note that in terms of our rational belief in explanations in proportion to their explanatory power, every explanation that invokes chance thereby decreases its explanatory power and hence its rational credibility.

✱ ✱ ✱

A second, and for us much more important, consequence of the global hekergy principle is that the common factor of every healthy inherited growth and behaviour pattern of every living thing is a need to increase hekergy; or, in the limit, to preserve it; or, if this is not possible, to minimise the loss. This need is, of course, frequently unfulfilled; the second law of thermodynamics applies to animate systems also, with the cumulative result of death. But none the less the need is there, and characterises all healthy growth and behaviour. We might then expect — in minds as high as humans', at least — an ability to assess hekergy magnitudes, directly or indirectly. Such an ability would be *evaluation*, and it would determine values: truth, beauty, and goodness, to name the traditionally honoured ones. In other words, we can say that these values are hekergies, and say why they are desired by all people.

That human values are hekergies can be shown by what we consider perfection to be [216]. A perfect work is one such that, if it is altered in any way, it is diminished and no longer perfect. The value of e for such perfection, in the formula $H = \ln(t/e)$, is thus one — the minimum possible; and so the hekergy of the work is the maximum possible. A similar argument applies to near-perfect works — various paintings, pieces of chamber music, mathematical creations, works in science and philosophy, magnificent moral behaviour, and the like. There are a few possible alterations that would not diminish the whole, and a fewer still that would improve it; so e is very small. But the number of possible ways of ruining the work — of making it mediocre, or even chaotic — is uncountable; t is enormous. So the hekergy of the whole, $\ln(t/e)$, is very large.

This explanation of the basis of human values is a major goal of our excursion into metaphysics. Having it, together with the Leibniz-Russell theory, we are in a position to explain the human real mind in considerable detail. Before we do so, however, I would warn the reader that the metaphysics herein is itself far from having a maximum hekergy. It has many defects, which, although not necessarily irreparable, should be pointed out. This will be the subject matter of the next chapter.

9. Assessment.

As we have seen, a metaphysical system is like a scientific theory in being an explanation. As such, the same criteria of credibility apply: resemblance to empirical fact and logical consistency, scope and density of detail, harmony with other probable theories, simplicity, elegance, symmetry, and prediction of novelty. So let us apply these criteria to our philosophy as so far developed.

✱

As far as *scope* and *density of detail* are concerned, we already saw that to some extent they are mutually exclusive. A theoretical physicist narrows his scope by excluding such things as life phenomena in order to concentrate on the detail within his field. A metaphysician equally is justified in ignoring a great amount of detail in order to be free to concentrate on a synoptic scope. So we need not criticise our relational metaphysics for lack of detail. On the other hand a metaphysical system should not be entirely divorced from detail, as is the explanation of everything in terms of the will of God. Leibniz's explanation is another such: to explain any detail whatever with Leibniz's system requires first an infinite idea, clear and distinct, of the pre-established harmony; and, secondly, an infinite deduction from this, to the detail required. Both of these are humanly impossible, so Leibniz's system in effect has zero density of detail. Spinoza's and Aristotle's metaphysics are other examples.

An example of how the present system lacks detail arises with the global hekergy principle. If there is a life-hekergy decrease somewhere — the fall of a sparrow, perhaps — then the principle requires an equal increase somewhere else — somewhere else, because we are not here dealing with a locally conserved hekergy, so the increase is not local. But the principle in no way specifies where, and of what kind, the resulting increase will be.

✱

Once this need for some detail in metaphysics is recognised, the criterion of harmony with other theories clearly operates in a special way. Any good explanation of the world obviously must be a synthesis between a theoretical science, which provides detail, and a good metaphysics, which provides scope. It is on just this question of synthesis of the present metaphysics with theoretical science that both its strengths and weaknesses lie. Strengths in that this metaphysics holds better promise of synthesis than any previous system, because a subject-predicate metaphysics, if it has any detail, cannot harmonise with a relational physics; and weaknesses because such a synthesis has not been achieved.

In the first place an obvious weakness that must be corrected to obtain a synthesis is the fact that the totality of atomic spatial relations constitutes an absolute Newtonian space, with absolute directions for co-ordinate systems; and the totality of atomic temporal relations constitute an absolute Newtonian time. A synthesis with theoretical physics will require an Einsteinian space-time, in which all co-ordinate systems are relative. This might be achieved by beginning with atomic space-time intervals, rather than with atomic spaces and atomic durations; or by making the space-time of general relativity an emergent out of the quantised absolute space and absolute time of our relational metaphysics. In either case, if the atomic space-time intervals had variable magnitudes, within certain limits, then space-time in the large could have a curvature, and so account for mass in the manner of Einstein's general theory of relativity.

An example of how this metaphysics, if it is a good one, should synthesise with physics lies with level-1 structures. An analysis of all possible kinds of these, or possibly of level-2 or level-3 structures, and all their emergent properties should provide a series of entities corresponding to all known wave-particles, and their properties — mass, charge, spin, etc. More generally, an adequate metaphysics would be an axiomatic system from which all the true theories of science could be deduced, as well as novel true theories not yet constructed. In this sense metaphysics would be the culmination of theoretical science, the ultimate theory. Obviously, the present pale shadow of a system is nowhere near to this.

On the other hand, compared with past subject-predicate systems of metaphysics, the present relational metaphysics has some interesting strengths when it comes to synthesis with physics — above the basic strength of being relational. In the first place, atomicity of relations was assumed originally in order to be able to define hekergy. If space is infinitely divisible then the number of possible alternate structures for any given structure is infinite; hekergy would then depend upon the ratio of two infinities, which is meaningless. But in providing atomicity of relations, space, time, and low level structures are quantised; since, as is well known, the physics of the very small is quantised, this consequence is promising for synthesis. So also is the consequence, within the relational metaphysics, of a maximum velocity, which in a synthesis with physics would obviously be the velocity of light [125].

Another important point that arises concerning this synthesis is field theory. Physicists now talk about gravitational fields, rather than "action at a distance," as they used to, as well as electromagnetic fields and two sub-atomic fields. These are all force fields. Any susceptible thing in a field will be forced to move in the direction of the field at that point, with a force proportional both to the strength of the field and to the magnitude of the susceptible property of the thing: mass in a gravitational field, charge in an electric field, etc. A particularly important feature of field theory is the emergence of waves, of which the best example is electromagnetic radiation — a combination of oscillating, mutually supporting, electric and magnetic fields that travels at the speed of light. So far there is nothing in our relational metaphysics to lead to the notion of fields. However, a possible connection can be found. A field can be thought of, not as an existing set of lines of force, but as a map of the way bodies within it will move. Such movement leads to rearrangement of objects within the field, and by that to a hekergy change. For example, if *like* are attracted to a centre and *unlike* are repelled from it, a chaotic mixture of likes and unlikes will be converted to an ordered state. Positive and negative charges are a possible case: normally they are homogeneously arranged in a macroscopic body — the body is electrically neutral — but in an electric field positive charges are attracted one way and negative charges the other, so that the charges are heterogeneously distributed. Consequently field theory may be a partial answer to the lack of detail, mentioned earlier, in the global hekergy principle — in that fields describe how some hekergy changes will proceed.

✶

The criterion of *symmetry* is well met on at least one point in this metaphysics. The principle of global conservation of hekergy, like all conservation principles, is symmetrical in time. In this respect the metaphysics is preferable to existing theoretical physics, in which the second law of thermodynamics is asymmetrical with time; and to the theory of evolution, in which biological complexity is asymmetrical with time. By unifying these two asymmetries into a symmetry the metaphysics gains probability, becomes more credible.

✶

As for the criteria of *simplicity* and *elegance* there is not a great deal to be said. It is perhaps worth remarking that this relational metaphysics is simpler than any historical metaphysics in that it requires only one of the three categories of thing, quality, and relation to be basic; other historical metaphysical systems required two or three.

✶

Concerning the *prediction of novelty*, not much can be expected from this metaphysics because its density of detail is too low. It is better than a metaphysics which has zero density of detail, but not much better. One detail, however, predicts novelty. Because of time being quantised in this metaphysics there must be — if the metaphysics is true in this respect — a minimum possible period to any oscillation, and hence a maximum possible frequency; consequently the metaphysics predicts a maximum possible frequency, and therefore maximum possible energy for a photon. It also predicts a minimum possible lifetime, and therefore a maximum possible energy for a virtual particle.

✶

So much for the positive criteria. The criteria of *resemblance to empirical fact* and *logical consistency*, as we saw, are negative criteria: if unfulfilled they falsify an explanation, unlike the other criteria that verify it in so far as they are fulfilled. So on these two counts not much can be said at present: there are no obvious contrary to fact or inconsistent features of the metaphysics, although there may quite possibly be hidden ones. In particular it should be mentioned that it has been assumed that a quantised geometry can be created which both is consistent, and approximates to Euclidean geometry as the number of atomic spaces becomes large. This is perhaps the most likely area of danger of inconsistency. I will mention two points in this connection; the first shows how an apparent inconsistency is not really so, and the second shows a lacuna in which inconsistency could lurk. First, if we consider the smallest possible square, having a side whose magnitude is two atomic lengths, then its diagonal is $\sqrt{8}$. It would then follow that the difference in length between diagonal and side of this square is $\sqrt{8}-2$, which is less than an atomic length. So, by *reductio ad absurdum*, an atomic length is not atomic. However, we need only point out that a smallest square does not have a diagonal at all — no separator exists as a diagonal — and the difficulty is resolved. Secondly, there is the question of rotation of macroscopic objects: is it possible with a quantised geometry? I will only raise this point, not explore it.

Turning from physics to psychology, one interesting point may be mentioned. As has already been pointed out, the theory of parapsychology [79] does not harmonise with theoretical physics, which is a major reason for scepticism towards it by physicists. However, if we confine ourselves to the best authenticated cases of telepathy, they all seem to concern death or disaster. A woman will wake in the night crying out that her son is dead, for example, and learn the next day that at that time he was lost overboard from his ship. The death is a hekergy decrease; whereas the knowledge of the death, like all gains in knowledge, is a hekergy increase. It is possible that the one necessitates the other according to the principle of universal conservation of hekergy.

✶

One last point concerning the criteria of good theories is that these criteria are properly described, more generally, as the criteria of good explanation: scientific theories are just one kind of explanation. So these criteria are applicable to all metaphysical systems, as well as to all myths, all theology, and all common sense explanations.

✶ ✶ ✶

I propose to end the present chapter with a partial summary of Parts 1 and 2. This will take the form of listing consequences of one fact: the fact that the explanation of illusion requires a duality. This duality, of reality and appearance, or of the theoretical and the empirical, or of original and mis-representation, entails many other dualities, both epistemological and ontological. The following list of them covers, in outline, what has been discussed so far.

✶

1. There are two *worlds* per perceiver: one real and one apparent.

✶

2. This is possible because each person has two *bodies*: one real and one apparent. Consequently each person has two sets of sense organs: the real are functional and the apparent are not. For example, the real eyes have an optic nerve, a retina, etc. while one's own apparent eyes are, visually, mere holes in the head. Again, real internal organs function, apparent ones, which, strictly speaking, are rarely more than locations within one's own

apparent body, do not. Thus, the real heart pumps real blood, the apparent heart is the location of emotions of love, and of pain in a heart attack.

✶

3. Because there are two worlds, there are two kinds of *science*. Empirical science tries to describe the potentially universally public features of apparent worlds — their similarity-true features — and theoretical science tries to describe the real world.

✶

4. There are also two kinds of *causation*. In apparent, or Humean, causation the cause and effect are both perceptible (apparent, or empirical) and correlated; and there is no relation of necessity between them. In real causation the cause, and the effect as well — unless it is an apparent object or apparent idea — are strict imperceptibles; and there is a relation of necessity between them, which is also a strict imperceptible.

✶

5. So there are two kinds of *explanation*. Apparent, or covering law, explanation, using scientific laws (which are descriptions of apparent causations) to explain instances of them; and real explanation, using theories to explain scientific laws. Both theoretical science and metaphysics are real explanations.

✶

6. There are two kinds of *thinghood*. Apparent things are structures of sensations, or secondary qualities, and real things are spatio-temporal continuities of structure.

✶

7. There are two kinds of *property*. Apparent properties are qualities, sensations, which are reproductions of their originals, which are real properties, which are properties of relations. Apparent properties are concrete and real properties are abstract.

✶

8. There are two kinds of *space*. Apparent space has a fixed origin and coordinate system: I, here, now; my right, my left, etc.; and it is heterogeneous: it diminishes with distance from the origin, such that apparent railway lines meet in the distance and the spacing between their cross-ties gets smaller. Real space is a part of the four-dimensional space-time of the real world and has no fixed co-ordinate systems. It is also

homogeneous, apart from the distortions of gravitation — that is, it is not heterogenous in the manner of apparent spaces.

✶

9. There are two kinds of *time*. Apparent time is either clock time or subjective time. Real time is the fourth dimension of the real world — that is, of four dimensional space-time. Clock time is illusory when it differs from real time, and subjective time is illusory when it differs from accurate clock time.

✶

10. There are two kinds of *perception*. Empirical perception is the last stage of the second kind, which is theoretical perception. The former is a direct or immediate consciousness of appearances and the latter is a causal process in which reproductions of real objects are made to appear to the perceiver.

✶

11. There are, in consequence, two *languages* of perception.

✶

12. There are thus, in perception, two kinds of *representation*. A real representation is an apparent object. An apparent representation is a memory of that apparent object.

✶

13. When these perceptions fail for any reason, they are replaced with two kinds of *belief*. Empirical belief is of reportables, and is arrived at inductively. Explanatory belief is of strict imperceptibles in the real world, and is arrived at speculatively. Empirical science consists of empirical beliefs; and theoretical science and metaphysics consist of explanatory beliefs.

✶

14. Strength of belief is probability, so there are two *bases* of such probability. Potentially universal publicity is the basis of the probability of empirical beliefs, found through objectivity, which is attention to the public content of one's apparent world; and verification of objectivity is public confirmation of one's findings, or consensus among scientists. The various criteria of good explanation are the basis of the probability of explanatory beliefs.

✶

15. There are two kinds of *mind*. Apparent mind is the totality of one's present private content of consciousness; and real mind is the totality of content of one's consciousness, both private and public (that is, apparent mind and apparent world respectively) plus subject and unconscious mind.

✳

16. And there are two kinds of *subject*: the apparent subject is the apparent body and the real subject is the ego, as will be explained in Chapter 11.

✳

17. Last, there are two kinds of *reality*. Theoretical reality is both all that exists independently of being perceived and, in the strictly real world, all strict imperceptibles. Empirical reality is everything in apparent worlds that is potentially, universally, public — that is, it is all similarity-true appearances.

✳

Finally, since many of these dualities demonstrate the incoherence of realism, it follows that ordinary language, in attempting to conform to the realism of common sense, hides many of them by using the same word to refer to each member of a duality, equivocally. Some of these words are *same*, *different*, *real*, *object*, *representation*, *perception*, *cause*, *effect*, and *explanation*.

Part Three.   Real Mind.

10. Basic Concepts.

Theory of mind has until now always been a difficult and largely vacuous subject. But in the present context this is no longer true — simply because the Leibniz-Russell theory, along with relational metaphysics, and the concept of hekergy, provide the necessary foundation.

In Part One the real mind was characterised by four parts: a subject, the two parts of which that subject is conscious — the apparent world and the apparent mind — and an unconscious mind. Here we will begin only with a theoretical mind, containing theoretical ideas, since we cannot have an apparent world or mind until we have a subject to be conscious of them.

We start, then, by postulating what might be called atomic real ideas, which are assumed to be neural switchings in a real brain, and so are of two kinds: an *On* and an *Off*. Because these words are so often used in other contexts, they will be distinguished by always being referred to with capital initial letters: On and Off. I am proposing to ignore almost entirely the physiological basis of mind, if only because a theory of mind is difficult enough by itself, so it is sufficient here to observe that in principle it is quite possible for everything postulated in the present theory to be a feature of, or emergent from, neural switchings in a real brain. Consequently the present theory of mind is in principle an integral part of the metaphysical theory of Part Two.

Between atomic ideas we can have emergent atomic relations, analogous to those of our relational metaphysics, and so obtain structures of atomic ideas. These atomic relations are not, of course, metaphysically atomic; they are only atomic with respect to the real mind. We will begin with four kinds.

★

1. We may suppose that there are atomic spatial relations, analogous with those of line and plane separators in the relational metaphysics, which separate atomic ideas; with these we obtain structures of atomic ideas. We will mostly be concerned with level-3 structures, relative to the level-1 of atomic ideas. Thus various possible level-2 structures will constitute

different kinds of theoretical sensation, and structures of these will be the causes of apparent objects, apparent representations, etc.

Loosely speaking, a neural On may be thought of as a presence, and an Off as an absence. Thus a mental space consisting of atomic spatial relations between Off's is empty, and one consisting of atomic spatial relations between On's is full.

2. Analogously to our relational metaphysics we can expect emergent relations at higher and higher levels, and consequently various magnitudes and kinds of hekergy of real ideas. Among these we will include, for simplicity, atomic likeness relations — similarities and dissimilarities — as emergent relations, as required, since an On is like an On and unlike an Off, and an Off is like an Off and unlike an On.

3. We can also have atomic durations within the real mind — again analogous to those of Part Two. Combining these with atomic unlikes gives us atomic change and atomic stasis and hence of higher level real idea change and stasis: temporal continuity, motion of real ideas within the theoretical mind, internal change, and emergence and submergence. In general, change should be thought of in terms of neural On's in a sea of Off's — that is, in "empty" mental space. An analogy may clarify this. Think of a cinema screen or a computer monitor, consisting of small squares, or pixels, — each too small to be distinguished by the naked eye — such that each is either illuminated, or dark. The total screen then forms a black and white picture, with varying shades of grey, depending upon the density of illuminated squares. The whole picture lasts for a short duration and is then replaced by another, of equal duration; and again and again, indefinitely. Atomic changes between durations add up to large scale changes of the picture as a whole. In particular, if all of the screen is dark except one small portion, which forms a picture of, say, a Pegasus, then the Pegasus may seem to move around the screen, and flap its wings as it goes — all because of an organised series of atomic changes. If this situation is now thought of as a three-dimensional volume, rather than a two-dimensional surface, and the illuminated elements — cubes, now, rather than squares — are neural On's and the dark ones are Off's, then a fair idea of the content of the real mind is obtained. A still better one is obtained if different level-2 structures in this space are thought of as different theoretical sensations — colours, sounds,

etc. — such that level-3 structures may be the causes of everyday objects: coloured, as opposed to black and white, and having other sensible qualities.

4. When it comes to causal relationships within the real mind, and between the real mind and the real world, it will most often be the case in what follows that these are more described, than explained. This will be because either the cause is in the physiological basis of mind — that is, in the real brain — and we are not attempting to go into that; or else the cause is some mechanism that offers no difficulty of explanation in principle, but in detail would further complicate an already complex theory, unnecessarily. In consequence many of the processes to be described in this theory will be based on postulated correlations, rather than derived causations. The critical reader may consider each use of *correlation* in what follows as an inadequacy of the theory; and should satisfy himself or herself that it is only a lacuna in the present work, rather than an unavoidable defect due to a serious deficiency in the theory.

All causation in the real mind will be explained by the overall causal principle derived in Part Two: it is metaphysically necessary that a real mind operates wherever possible in a direction of hekergy increase. This will be called **the mind hekergy principle**. And we will use a special case of this, a specific causal principle of like-attracts-like forces between real ideas in the mind; such forces act to increase the configuration hekergy of otherwise less organised ideas. This principle will be the first subject of the next chapter. Other hekergy increases brought about by this principle will be various correlations, of which the two most important are mappings and bondings.

✶

A **mapping** is a copying, in whole or in part. We are familiar with the concept from Part One, where both a real object is mapped from the real world into the apparent world as an apparent object, and an apparent object is mapped from the apparent world into the real mind as an apparent representation or memory. These mappings are correlations because they are not explained: given the real object, the apparent object comes into existence; and given the apparent object, the apparent representation comes into existence. In each case the former is the cause of the latter, but not the complete cause; a complete description of the cause — and so explanation of the effect — requires a description of the mechanism involved — be it chemical process, neural process, or whatever.

We will also make use of partial mappings, in which only some particular substructure of the original is mapped; this will be the basis of abstraction — to take the most obvious example. Such mappings will be important in the explanation of discrimination [169].

✶

Bonding occurs when two or more real ideas become linked so that they move together. One example is the traditional concept of association: if one memory or concept moves into consciousness and another is bonded to it, the second will follow — a process of one conjuring up another, as with the concepts of lightning and thunder, pen and ink, and strawberries and cream. Such association of ideas is the basis of induction, which, as was explained in Part Two [63], is the basis of all empirical beliefs — that is, beliefs in the existence of reportables [50]. Bonding will be important in analysing universals: in which the real ideas of two words — one written and one spoken — are bonded, together with one or more real ideas which are their meaning; the resulting whole is a **concept**. Bonding will also be necessary in explaining action: the willing, by the subject, of real muscular movement. Emotion will be explained as a bonding of feeling and bodily expression. Another kind of bonding is that behavioural characteristic called imprinting, of which possible examples in human behaviour are the influence of the first sexual arousal on subsequent infatuations [195] and fetishism, in which a particular kind of apparent object is bonded to the sexual appetite. Mapping and bonding are not necessarily the only forms of correlation that we will use. For example, interpretation — consisting of compounding, correcting, and adding, as described in Part One [26] — is a matter of correlations. So is the relationship between the presence of drugs in the real blood-stream and the relief of pain, production of hallucinations, etc. So also are the bodily-mental correlations involved in sleep.

It should be noted that there is no difficulty in principle with the mechanisms of mapping and bonding. We have examples of mappings in the various methods of recording and reproducing sound, in photography and in television. A computer programmed for translating languages is an example of bondings.

✶

So we have a theoretical mind, containing atomic ideas, with various relations between them so as to form structures, structures of structures, and on up, within the mind. These are real ideas, such as theoretical sensations and structures of theoretical sensations, mappings and bondings of these. Out of this we need to get an ego that is conscious and that can act.

11. Some Simple Mental Processes.

Free motion of ideas in the real mind is, I will postulate, on a basis of like attracts like and repels unlike. Working by analogy with the inverse-square law of physics, we can define the force between two theoretical ideas as proportional to:

$$\frac{(L-\frac{1}{2})(H_1 \times H_2)}{d^2}$$

In this formula L is the degree of likeness[10], or degree of similarity [112], or resemblance, between the two real ideas, which has possible values from 0 to 1, inclusively. If L is greater than 1/2 then the force is positive and, by convention, thereby an attraction; while if L is less than 1/2, a negative force, and so repulsion, results. (In electrostatics and in magnetism $(L-\frac{1}{2})$ in effect has only two possible values: -1 and $+1$; and in each of these cases like attracts unlike and repels like; and in gravitation $(L-\frac{1}{2})$ in effect has only one value, $+1$, and like attracts like.) H_1 and H_2 are the total hekergies of each of the two ideas, and d is the distance between them.

There may be a variety of hekergies in the two ideas, at each of their structure levels, so the force between two mid-ideas is usually compound, and may consist of both attractions and repulsions, acting on different substructures of the mid-ideas; and these in turn may lead to torques that bend or twist the mid-ideas.

From now on this principle of motion, like attracts like and repels unlike, will be called L.A.L.R.U., and, even more briefly, L.A.L.

Notice that L.A.L. is a special case of the mind hekergy principle [146], since the ordering of real ideas on a basis of L.A.L., out of less organised input, produces an increase of configuration hekergy.

---

[10] The words *like* and *unlike*, rather than *similar* and *dissimilar*, are used here because of their use in electromagnetism and the analogy of this to the present formula.

We will discover that everything in the real mind that is based on L.A.L. is **irrational**; that is, everything explained by L.A.L. is usually classified as irrational. The **rational**, on the other hand, is any arrangement of theoretical ideas that has maximum configuration hekergy, as will be discussed later. The hekergy of the irrational is less than maximum, but more than that of the input from theoretical perception.

Before we apply the L.A.L. principle to mid-ideas we must first confirm their source. This is a familiar matter. We can think of the real mind as initially empty, like Locke's *tabula rasa*, or blank tablet; which is to say that all atomic ideas in it are Off's. When a real object is theoretically perceived a representation of it is produced in the real mind as a theoretical idea.

✶ ✶ ✶

At this point some new terminology is needed. This representation of a real object is not yet an apparent object, because there is no ego to be conscious of it, but, as we will discover, it will be the cause of the apparent object, once the ego develops. Thus we have a third kind of object, which is the effect of the real object and cause of the apparent object. So we will call it the **mid-object**, since it is causally between the real object and the apparent object. We will refer also to **mid-feelings, mid-meanings,** etc., all of which are midway between reality and consciousness. All of these may be classified together as **mid-ideas**. Mid-ideas are real ideas, never apparent ideas: that is, they are strict imperceptibles.

The mid-object is transient, lasting only for as long as the real object is theoretically perceived, but we may suppose that it may be mapped into a real idea which is permanent. Such a real idea is a **mid-memory** of the mid-object.

A secondary source of mid-ideas is construction, producing constructs. Portions of mid-ideas are mapped, as new mid-ideas, and bonded intimately to others such, to produce novelties. A portion of a mid-memory of a woman and a portion of a mid-memory of a fish produce a mid-idea of a mermaid, for example.

We now can use the principle of L.A.L. to explain the formation of the conscious, active, subject; and also to explain recognition, prejudice, class formation, and other well known features of mind.

✶ ✶ ✶

The formation of the perceiving subject is the most important consequence of L.A.L. This subject will be called the **ego** from now on, rather than subject, because it will be able to act as well as to perceive, and because it will be essentially selfish.

The nearest that one can come to describing oneself, as ego, in terms of introspective data, is to say "I am the totality of my memories and of my beliefs. I am what I am because of what I have experienced and of what I have done. All this is past, but it remains as memories. I am also what I am because of what I believe. The totality of these memories and beliefs is me."

Although at first sight it might seem that this is insufficient for a definition, we will discover that it is in fact an excellent definition. It seems inadequate initially simply because it seems impossible to understand how a bundle of memories and beliefs can be either conscious or capable of acting. But in fact there is no difficulty. This bundle is not a mere totality, a random jumble, but a structure; and as such it possesses emergents, of which consciousness and the power to act are two. All three of these points, structure, consciousness, and action, are explicable by means of L.A.L. Secondly, the memories and beliefs are not those that we are familiar with in consciousness, but theoretical memories and theoretical beliefs — mid-memories and mid-beliefs — which are the causes of conscious memories and beliefs.

✳

In the beginning, before there exists an ego, representations appear in the real mind because they are mapped there; but they are not *apparent* representations, in the sense of Part One, because they are not given to a perceiving subject: there is as yet no subject. But all these representations have a feature in common. They all have an extrinsic relation to a mid-memory of the theoretical body of the individual concerned: **mid-bodies**, we may call these mid-memories. This extrinsic relation is within a fixed subjective co-ordinate system [9]. The mid-body is at the origin, or centre, of that co-ordinate system, which is called *here, now*. The axes of this co-ordinate system are my right, my left, in front of me, behind me, above me, below me, and my past and my future, where this past and future are relative to my now. This *my* refers to the mid-body, but once there is an ego that is conscious of all this, and able to speak, it will always be able to say truly "I am here, now, at the centre of the world that I perceive" since it will be conscious of such a co-ordinate system, with its body at the origin, because the mid-co-ordinate system will be mapped into its consciousness; and this origin is the centre of the apparent world of this ego.

Every mid-memory of the mid-world includes, as a part, such an egocentric co-ordinate system, along with its origin, and a mid-body at that origin. "All my memories include me" a fully developed ego could say. This relation to a mid-body, and one term of this relation, the mid-body itself, constitute a large degree of likeness between mid-memories of the mid-world. As such, these representations are mutually attracted by L.A.L. to form a structure of mid-ideas. The common factor of the mid-ideas within this structure is the mid-body and its co-ordinate system. It is this structure of self-centred representations that is the ego. It is an ego, rather than a mere collection of memories, because it is unified by an emergent relation, which makes it a whole greater than the sum of its parts. This emergent relation is the **essential self**, distinct from all of its terms. Thus the essential you is an emergent relation — which is one reason why it is so difficult to come to terms with self-knowledge.

✷

The **consciousness** of this ego arises from the fact that a mid-object — a structure of mid-sensations — in the vicinity of the ego is either attracted or repelled by L.A.L. These forces must produce a reaction in the ego, and it is this reaction that is consciousness. The mid-object produces a reaction within the ego and this reaction is the empirical object, a structure of empirical sensations, where an empirical sensation is the reaction in the ego to a mid-sensation. The empirical object and the ego's consciousness of it are identical.

Although this may sound far too simple to explain the variety and richness of consciousness, it will be seen not to be so once it is understood that this reaction is not a simple reaction like the flattening of a rubber ball when it bounces, but a highly complex one. This is so first because there are many mid-ideas within the ego, with different hekergies and hekergy magnitudes among themselves, such that different ideas will react with different magnitude, and direction of force as well as kind of force: push, pull, bend, or twist. Secondly, the mid-idea that is the cause of this reaction may be large and complex, with considerable variety of hekergies and hekergy magnitudes, and thereby add further to the complexity of this

152

reaction. For example, different substructures of it are different theoretical sensations, which produce different empirical sensations in the ego. Thirdly, consciousness as so far described is purely passive; once the ego can act, and be conscious of not only the empirical object that triggered the acting but also conscious of the acting and the consequences, in the empirical world, of this acting, plus the inter-relationship of all three, then the quality of this ego's consciousness is in principle close to the richness of that which we know introspectively: apparent consciousness.

This consciousness is entirely within the ego. It consists of reactions, within the ego, to L.A.L. forces between the ego and mid-ideas. The ego is not conscious of the mid-ideas, it is conscious of these reactions to them: consciousness and these reactions are one and the same, identical. Thus, mid-objects are structures of mid-sensations; and empirical, or apparent, objects are structures of empirical, or apparent, sensations. So it follows that all empirical objects — which is to say, the entire empirical world — is within the ego. Not only is the theoretical skull beyond the empirical blue sky, as required by the Leibniz-Russell theory, but so are the outer limits of the ego. This means that there is no consciousness at a distance, although there may seem to be. When looking at the Moon, for example, we seem to be conscious of the Moon, and also conscious of its distance. It is indeed distant from the apparent body, but it is not the apparent body that is the conscious subject: it is the ego, which contains the apparent Moon and the apparent body and their spatial separation within itself. This solves the problem for naive realism of how consciousness can extend out from the head for a quarter of a million miles to apprehend the real Moon.

✱

Among the empirical objects of which the ego is conscious is its own apparent body. It is quite instructive that the words *I* and *me* may refer equally to one's own body, as in "I ache all over," and to one's own ego, as in "I had a dream that I was disembodied." In Part One we located the ego inside the empirical head; this was done for simplicity in understanding the Leibniz-Russell theory, but must now be corrected. Not only is the ego not inside the empirical head, but the empirical head is inside the ego — along with the rest of the empirical world and the subjective, egocentric, co-ordinate system whose origin, the centre of this world, is "I, here, now." Also, mid-objects are composed of mid-sensations, which are structures of

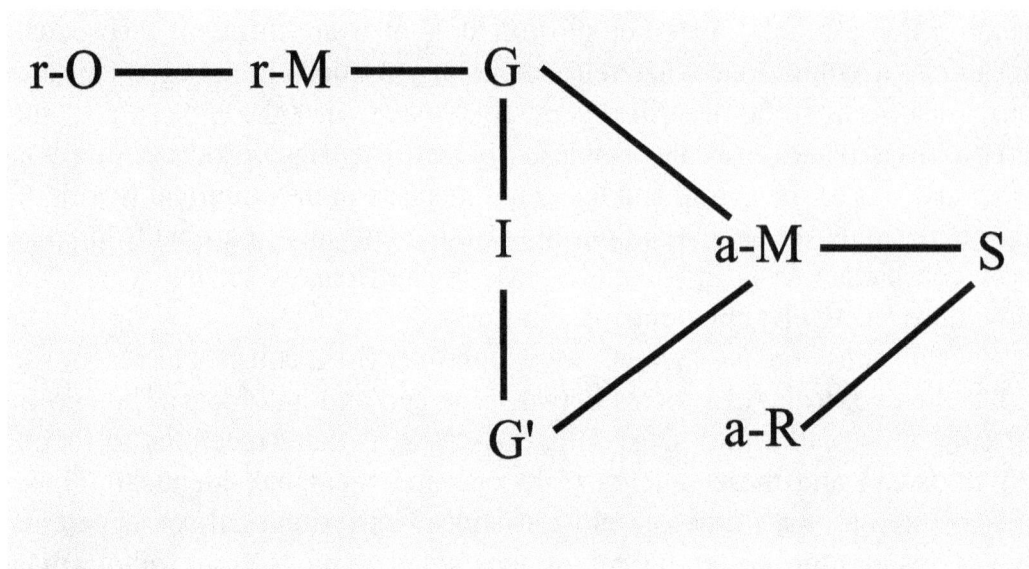

Fig.11.1.

atomic real ideas, On's and Off's, while the empirical objects are composed of empirical sensations, which are concrete. Concrete sensations [158] are the ego's L.A.L. reaction to mid-sensations. So there is a theoretical body, or person — a very complex structure of theoretical cells, a whole unified by the emergent relation called life — and some of this person's vicinity in the theoretical world is mapped, by theoretical perception, into the real mind as a mid-world, which is then mapped into the ego as an empirical world; and the mid-world contains the mid-body of that person, while the empirical world contains his or her empirical body.

In discussing the two languages of perception, those of empirical perception and of theoretical perception, we assumed in Part One that the subject in each was one and the same; and as a result the real image was identified with the apparent object. We know now that these two identifications are not true: the empirical subject is the empirical body and the theoretical subject is the ego, such that the theoretical subject contains the empirical world, which contains the empirical subject, "here, now"; and the real image is the mid-object, which is the cause of the empirical object, not the empirical object itself. This means that the relationship of Fig. 3.10, reproduced here as Fig. 11.1, must be corrected.

In Fig.11.1, G′ is the given, arising by interpretation — correction, compounding, and addition — from G, where G is the real-image-cum-apparent-object, and S is the identified apparent-subject-cum-real-subject.

G and S are now each two, not one. That is, G becomes m-O and a-O, (Fig. 11.2) and S becomes r-S and a-S (Fig 11.3).

In this corrected relationship a new prefix has been introduced: 'm-', standing for 'mid-'. Rather than speak of the given, G, as in Fig. 11.1, we now speak of m-0, the mid-object, midway between the real object, r-0, and the apparent object, a-0 — and the latter is now the given. The m-0 is, of course, what was previously called the real representation; the terminology is introduced so that we can say, for example, *mid-skin* rather than *real representation of real skin*. As in Fig. 11.1, we have both interpreted and uninterpreted m-0's — m-0′ and m-0 — and these produce interpreted and uninterpreted a-0's — a-0′ and a-0; the former is given in unselfconscious perception and the latter in selfconscious perception. The mid-object is a structure of atomic ideas; the apparent object is the reaction, in the ego, to the L.A.L. forces produced by the mid-object. One further new term has been introduced: D, standing for dreams and imagination. We have both m-D (which are real ideas) and a-D (which are the ego's reaction to the former, and hence apparent to the subject). Similarly for memories, m-R and a-R.

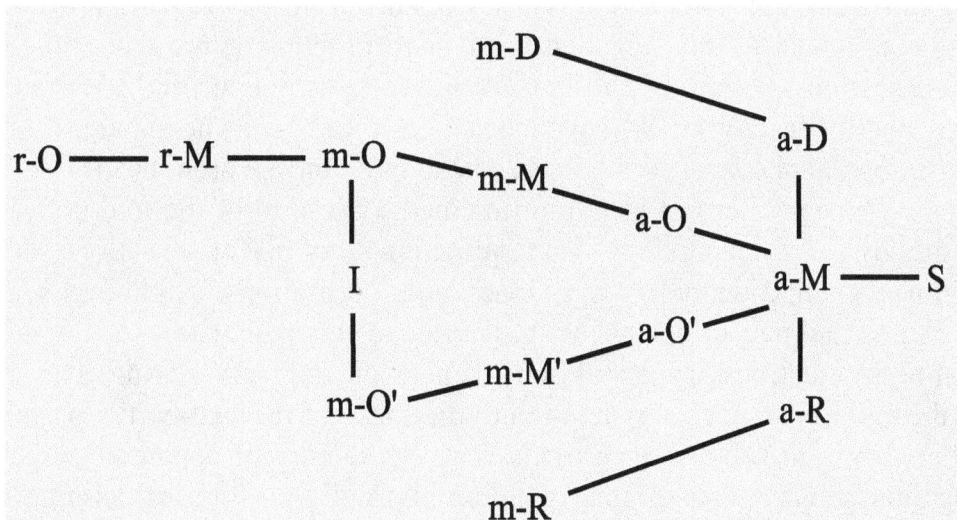

Fig.11.2.

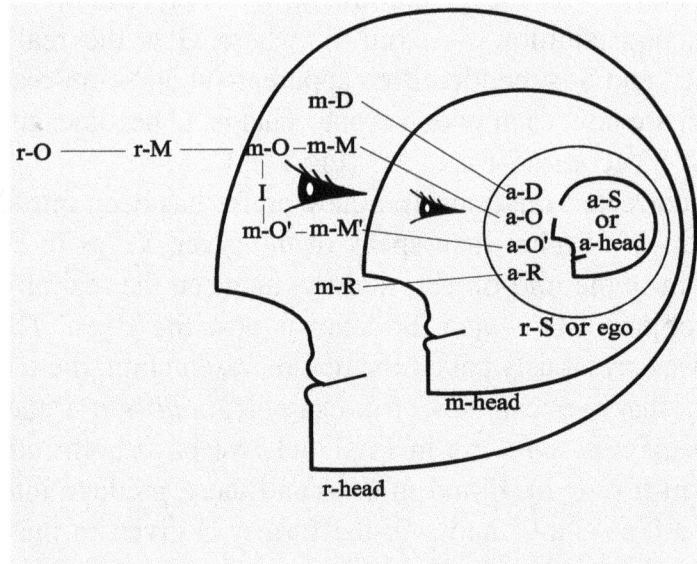

Fig. 11.3.

We can correct the second mis-identification, of real and apparent subjects, by combining the relationship in Fig 11.2 with the kind of schematic bodies used in Part One. The result is Fig. 11.3. Here the outermost body is the real body, containing the real brain and real mind in its head. Within the real mind are real ideas and structures of real ideas, which are mid-ideas and structures of mid-ideas, such as m-O, m-D and m-R. Some of these — beliefs and self-memories — form the structure that is the ego, r-S. Reactions, within this, to mid-ideas and structures of mid-ideas are the contents of consciousness — such as a-O, a-R and a-D. The apparent subject is the apparent body, shown here as a head only: the apparent head.

The ego is drawn as a thin line inside the head of the mid-body. The mid-body is a compounding — interpretation — of bodily sensations such as mid-touch, mid-warmth, mid-kinaesthetic sensations, and mid-sensual pleasures and pains, together with theoretical self-perception such as visual real representations of the real body, self-touch, and self-hearing. The shape of the ego has no necessary relation to the shape of the mid-body; to suppose otherwise is to suppose incorrectly that the identity of apparent body and apparent subject requires that of mid-body and ego. We will assume later [182] that the shape of the ego tends to the spherical; so we may for

156

convenience assume that the ego fits within the mid-head as shown in Fig. 11.3.

The apparent body, or apparent subject, is then the L.A.L. reaction, within the ego, to the mid-body. When the ego refers to its own body it is referring to the apparent body, not the mid-body — because the former is the only one of which it is conscious. So when referring to its own body the ego is referring to a part of itself, rather than to something of which it is a part. Similarly, relations of *mine* are internal to the ego: they are relations between the ego and certain apparent objects, not mid-objects. Indeed, everything whatever of which the ego is conscious is a reaction, within itself, to L.A.L. forces — and so is within the ego.

Within the spaces defined by the three bodies in Fig. 11.3 we may observe first that there is usually nothing at all in the head of the apparent body. This is the location that common sense attributes to mind, but, apart from occasional headaches, introspection shows the head to be empty. So, largely, is the apparent body. Apart from internal sensations and sensual pleasures and pains, and a few emotions such as love in the heart region, fear in the belly, rumblings in the belly, etc., perception reveals nothing in the apparent body. No apparent lungs, apparent heart, apparent liver, apparent stomach, apparent intestines, etc. — none of these are apparent, so they do not exist. They may appear in exceptional circumstances, such as surgery, of course, and then for the duration of that appearance, they exist. *Esse est percipi*, it will be recalled [42], so far as the content of consciousness is concerned. And of course we may perceive evidence of heart, stomach, etc. in the form of pulse, heartburn and the like; but these are evidence of the real organs, not the empirical ones — there are no empirical ones, normally.

Outside the apparent body is the space of consciousness: apparent world, apparent imagining, apparent remembering, apparent dreaming, etc. It is limited by the horizons of the moment, of which the farthest is what the Greeks called heaven; beyond this Plato put the forms (unchanging reality); Aristotle put God, the unmoved mover, of pure form; and fundamental Christians put Heaven, the throne of God, the angelic host, etc. [300]. But beyond heaven are mid-ideas, of which the nearest are those that constitute the mid-head. These are all, of course, inside the real head — that is, in the real brain, which is in the real body, along with the real heart, real lungs, real stomach, etc. Beyond the real body is the rest of the real world.

Actually, theoretical perception is even more complex than this, because it is a process. Light waves reflected off a theoretical object constitute an image of that object, and the image travels through space and onto the theoretical retinas of a perceiver; it is then transduced into a neural image, consisting of On's and Off's, and this image travels down the optic nerve into the brain, where it becomes a real idea; this real idea, a mid-object, then causes a complex reaction in the ego, and this reaction is the empirical object, of which the ego is conscious. So there are a theoretical object and a whole series of images of it, in different media, a process, such that the final image is an empirical object. However, we can confine ourselves to theoretical object, mid-object, and empirical object, for simplicity. Theoretical perception is also a temporal process, in the sense that it produces a series of perceptions, like the series of frames in a movie or television program.

✱

All the real ideas outside the mid-head — mid-objects, etc. — are abstract structures of atomic ideas. All, or most, of the contents of consciousness, outside the apparent head — apparent objects, apparent memories, apparent dreams, etc. — are concrete. Or, more accurately, they are structures of concrete sensations. Since the concreteness is a copy of neither mid-objects nor real objects, it is illusory; and as such it must be explained. This is most easily done in the first place by an analogy. Imagine twelve men pushing a truck. There are twenty-four hands pushing on the truck, and twenty-four feet pushing the ground. The result is that the truck moves. So we have a complex cause — two dozen hands and two dozen feet; and a simple effect, motion of the truck, which shows none of this complexity. In the same way, a mid-sensation is a complex abstract structure and an apparent sensation is a simple concrete structure. In other words the concrete is a representation, of the abstract, which lacks a lot of the detail of the abstract; it is a homomorph [86]. Or, to put it another way, concrete qualities have a much lower density of detail than the abstract structures that cause them. The nature of the concrete is over-simplification, a kind of ignorance. This is at once obvious if we compare the sight of a leaf, say, with what a biochemist and botanist know of leaves. The loss of information that results in concreteness is, fairly obviously, a two-stage one: one loss occurs between real object and mid-object, and another between mid-object and empirical object.

✳

The consciousness of the ego must be focussed; as so far described, it is diffuse. Focussing is a matter of **attention**, which can be explained in terms of **attitude**, and attitude is a matter of ego structure just as the focussing of a lens is due to part of the structure of the lens: its shape. The mid-memories that constitute the ego can be arranged in many equivalent ways without changing the hekergy of the ego, because this hekergy is not a maximum; and, obviously, different ways will give different kinds and degrees of consciousness, of ego reactions to mid-ideas. If we allow that the outer memories the outer structure of the ego can be rearranged, while the inner structure remains more or less constant, then we can distinguish two attitudes. The outer attitude, which is variable, is attention; the inner attitude, which is constant, is egocentric. Both of these attitudes will be determined overall by the mind-hekergy principle: the fundamental need to increase the hekergy of, in this case, the ego. This makes the basic, inner, attitude of the ego the attitude of selfishness: it is attention to the good — the hekergy increase — of the self, of the totality of mid-memories of the mid-body. The outer attitude is one of paying attention to whatever transient empirical object will increase the ego's hekergy; which is to say, the ego attends to that which will give it pleasure, or which will satisfy needs and desires. All these will be explained shortly, as will their opposites, pains, dangers, and aversions.

✳

In principle this explanation of consciousness allows the ego to be conscious of both the apparent world and of apparent ideas, and to distinguish them: it allows the ego to distinguish the **material** from the **mental** [8]. And it also allows the "greater force and vivacity," as Hume put it, or vividness, of the material. The ego can distinguish apparent objects from apparent ideas because in being conscious of apparent objects, their causes, the mid-objects, although subject to L.A.L. forces by the ego, do not as a result move accordingly. (Unless, of course, the ego wills bodily action: advance or retreat. But this is another matter than L.A.L.R.U.) They do not move because their motion is governed, not by L.A.L., but by the motion of the real objects that they copy — that is, in accordance with the laws of physics. This, however, does not prevent forces of reaction in the ego, and hence consciousness of the apparent objects by the ego. Apparent ideas do not have this independent movement that apparent objects have, and this is the basis of distinguishing them: that is, of distinguishing the material from mental. As it is sometimes put: the material resists our will, while the mental does not. Thus our fantasies can run counter to scientific laws but our apparent worlds, when true, cannot.

That apparent representations, or empirical memories, are less vivid than the apparent objects they copy is easily explained, once we have explained remembering. Remembering is not a mapping of empirical object into empirical memory, but a mapping of mid-object into mid-memory. The ego is conscious of an empirical object when a theoretical object is theoretically perceived, and later is conscious of a memory of it when the mid-memory of the mid-object produces an empirical memory. The mapping, from mid-object to a mid-memory of it in the real mind, is a many-one mapping, rather than a one-one mapping. That is, there is only one level-2 structure in the mid-memory for every so many in the mid-object. The mid-memory is a homomorph [86] of the mid-object. This gives the mid-memory a lesser magnitude of hekergy and so the ego undergoes a smaller L.A.L. reaction to it. Which is to say that the ego is less conscious of the memory than of the original: the empirical memory is less vivid than the empirical object.

Concerning the consciousness produced by mid-ideas, we must assume that there is some threshold magnitude of L.A.L. force, below which no consciousness is produced within the ego. That is, below a certain hekergy magnitude of mid-idea, the idea is subliminal. The subliminal is not necessarily the same as the unconscious, since the ego may be unconscious of a supraliminal idea because it is out of range, or masked by other ideas.

✳

The fact that the ego is composed of beliefs as well as memories enables us to explain what believing is. A **belief** [49] is a proposition (see below) or a set of propositions. But not all propositions or sets of propositions are beliefs. We may entertain or consider propositions without believing them. An atheist may consider the proposition that God exists, without believing it; and a theist may think about the proposition that God does not exist, without believing it. The difference between propositions being considered and being believed is that in the first case the ego is simply conscious of them while in the second case the ego incorporates them into itself. To believe a proposition is to make it part of oneself. That is, to believe an apparent proposition is to incorporate its cause, a mid-proposition, into oneself.

✶

We can also explain the distinction, within consciousness, of meaning and feeling. Mid-ideas have both structure and hekergy; the ego's reaction to the structure is its consciousness of **meaning**, and its reaction to the hekergy is its consciousness of **feeling**. The meaning possessed by a structure of mid-ideas — by a **proposition** — is the meaning of both the mid-ideas and the relations between them. Meaning will be mentioned again in this chapter, in connection with language; and will be more fully discussed in Chapters 14 and 15. Feeling, as consciousness of hekergy, is feeling of both the hekergy of empirical objects, ideas, etc., and of hekergy changes to the ego itself. Feeling varies both in kind and in intensity, by virtue of kind and magnitude of hekergy. At present we can only explain very subjective feelings, based on hekergies relative to the ego; but as the ego matures feeling will become more objective; this is shown by the disagreement among immature critics and the agreement among mature ones.

It should also be noted at this point that relations between mid-ideas are themselves mid-ideas. Such relations are emergents and so possess hekergy and are subject to L.A.L. forces, and so may be mapped into the ego's consciousness by L.A.L., along with their terms. So the ego may be conscious of such relations: either empirical relations, in its empirical world, or mental relations, between introspective ideas. Two examples are *similarity* and *dissimilarity*.

✶ ✶ ✶

The possibility of **action** by the ego arises with postulation of **motor-ideas**, which control real muscles, and the bonding of them with mid-ideas. We must first suppose a special part of the theoretical mind, called the **motor-mind**, which contains motor ideas. An understanding of the functioning of motor ideas is most easily gained by means of an analogy with the punched data cards used in the early days of computers. These cards each had a pattern of holes punched in them according to some precise code, such that a pattern of holes was a record of information. This pattern of holes is comparable to a real idea: a pattern of holes is a structure of holes, which is like a structure of On's; and a recording of information is like remembering, as a representation records information in the memory. Secondly, punched cards may be put into a decoding machine that translates the information on them into some other code, on a basis of one-one correspondence. This other code may be data or instructions, expressed in electrical impulses. Data might be alphanumeric strings, or numbers, and instructions might be to print the strings or add the numbers; there is no intrinsic difference between data and instructions, they differ only in their mutual relations, in their positions in a sequence. We may suppose real ideas in the motor mind to be coded structures in this way, such that decoding constitutes the introduction of specific control information into the efferent nervous system, to cause specific muscular movements. Just as a punched card had to be introduced into a decoder in order for its information to produce the desired result, so may we suppose that a motor idea must be taken to its **action point**: some specific location in the real mind so that its specific muscular action may be initiated. It will come to its action point because it is bonded with a mid-idea that is a memory of that specific muscular action. When the ego attracts this mid-idea to its action point in the real mind, the motor idea correlated with it moves to the action point also. Thus, for the ego to act muscularly is for it to attract the idea of this action to an action point. This is an explanation of real willing by the ego — as opposed to apparent willing, which is the ego's consciousness of the effects of real willing in its empirical body. Since the ego will be conscious of the result of the action, there exists a cybernetic loop and feedback can operate; for example, the motion of the hand reaching for food will slow down as the food is approached, and the fingers will close as it is touched.

Needless to say, this explanation of action does not do more than make the ego the first cause in a process. The ego wills real muscles to move, which causes movement of the real body. This movement is theoretically perceived, so that the mid-body moves similarly, and the empirical body does also, in its turn. Thus the ego is conscious of the effect of its willing.

This explanation also does not explain the possibility of choice. This is because our theory of ego is still insufficiently developed. It does not yet have an explanation for discrimination [169], for instance, which is a necessary condition for choice. Choice will also require that the ego, having discriminated among several memories of action, can select one and draw it to the action point; this means that the ego must be able to move ideas regardless of their natural tendencies to move among themselves by L.A.L. However, these deficiencies will be repaired later. For the present it is sufficient that the ego is able in principle to cause muscular action.

★ ★ ★

We next turn to **recognition**. If the ego of Jack is conscious of an apparent object — Jill, say — it is because a representation of Jill appeared in Jack's real mind by theoretical perception. One of two things can now happen. Either by L.A.L. the mid-idea of Jill pulls near to itself a like mid-idea, or it does not. This like mid-idea is a mid-memory of Jill, produced when she was theoretically perceived on an earlier occasion. The current mid-Jill either so pulls if this mid-idea exists, or does not if it does not exist. If the mid-memory exists in the real mind then there will be an emergent hekergy, out of the combination of two like mid-ideas. If the mid-memory does not exist, or if it exists but is inaccessible — that is, if theoretical Jill had never previously been theoretically perceived, or if the mid-memory of her was blocked — then there is no such emergent hekergy. If we call the process that produces this emergent hekergy **theoretical recognition**, then the resulting consciousness of this emergent hekergy will be the feeling of familiarity that is **empirical recognition**. This feeling of familiarity can occur if there was a previous encounter, producing a memory that, on the second occasion, makes possible the feeling; or if the like mid-idea was produced by some other means such as a photograph, a television appearance, or a very good description.

Again, this is only the basic principle of recognition. With nothing else, it would only allow crude recognition; explanation of more refined recognition depends on an explanation of discrimination [169]. Also, recognition is usually followed immediately by identification by name, which cannot be explained until the process of naming [166] has been explained.

★

Prejudice is another mental fact easily explained by L.A.L. We saw that a structure of ideas can be a proposition [161]; and that a proposition or a structure of propositions can be a belief. Such a belief may, by L.A.L., attract like ideas and/or propositions to itself, and repel unlike. Generally these will be, respectively, evidence for, and evidence against, the belief. Consequently when the ego is conscious of this belief, it will be conscious of a great deal of supporting evidence, but not conscious of any contrary evidence, since the supporting evidence is present and the contrary evidence is absent. And if any new counter evidence is presented it will be repelled immediately: it is discounted. So the belief will seem obviously true. We thus explain the major characteristics of prejudice: an automatic, unconscious, selection of evidence; strong conviction, based on favourable evidence; discounting of new unfavourable evidence; and ignorance of the prejudicial nature of this conviction, because of the absence of contrary evidence. As a structure, the prejudice is, of course, a mid-prejudice.

Why some propositions grow into prejudices in this way and others do not depends both on already existing prejudices, and new, day to day, experience just as the new course a river cuts for itself depends both on its existing course, and on fresh possibilities. A particular constellation of prejudices in an ego will thus depend in the first instance on the nature of the first prejudice. That there is a first prejudice should, of course, be obvious: it is the ego itself, as might be expressed by "I am the most important person of all."

*

The final item to be explained by means of L.A.L. in this chapter is the easiest. It is class formation. Mid-ideas form into classes — that is, groups, collections, or sets — simply because like attracts like and so like mid-ideas move toward each other to form a class. Classes are important both because their formation may be an early stage in scientific investigation (classification of data is one kind of formulation, as we saw in Chapter 5 [67]); and because they are very significant in theory of thought, because of their connection with universals — a matter that will be further developed in Chapters 14 and 15. For the present it is sufficient that the possibility of classification is explained.

At this point anticipating a potential confusion is desirable: the seeming lack of key differences between the ego, prejudices, and classes, all of which form by L.A.L. The essential differences here are (i) that the ego is far larger than any ordinary prejudice or class and (ii) that while a class is composed of mid-sensations or mid-objects, a prejudice is composed of propositions. (Readers familiar with the logic of classes, or sets, should understand that the classes here explained are not all of the logically possible classes, but only finite extensions of ideas actually in the real mind: mid-classes, in other words.)

✳ ✳ ✳

We turn next to three more basic features of mind, which are explained other than by L.A.L. These are (i) pleasure and pain, and related features; (ii) language; and (iii) discrimination.

✳

The explanation of sensual pleasure and pain is likely to be confusing if the distinction between apparent body and real body is forgotten. So the reader is here reminded that the apparent body — that which he or she sees in the bath — is not composed of cells, organic molecules, etc. This empirical body — the body given in perception, which is here, now — is composed of empirical sensations: colours, shapes, tactile sensations, etc. It is the real body that is composed of cells, organic molecules, and the like, but this is never given in perception; it is "beyond heaven", beyond the blue sky in the day and the apparent sphere of visible stars at night, beyond all perceptible horizons, beyond the farthest reaches of the ego: a strict imperceptible. And the third body, the mid-body, is composed of mid-sensations, which are also strict imperceptibles.

With this in mind the explanation of pleasure and pain is very simple. **Pleasure** is consciousness of hekergy increase and **pain** is consciousness of hekergy decrease. There are two kinds of each: sensual, or bodily, pleasures and pains, and feelings of pleasure and pain. Feelings of pleasure and pain such as the pleasures of humour or intellectual achievement and the pain of compassion belong entirely to the real mind and are explicable in terms of hekergy changes of mid-ideas there, and consciousness of these changes; we will examine these in Chapter 13. Sensual pleasures or pains originate as hekergy increases or decreases in the real body, and these produce representations in the real mind which cause the ego to be conscious of pleasures or pains in the empirical body.

Naive apprentice philosophers are liable to fall into one of two errors of oversimplification of their consciousness of hekergy: that the good and hence morality is a matter of sensual pleasure (hedonism and utilitarianism) or that the good and hence morality is biological — a matter of survival value. Both of these moral positions are true to a certain point according to the present system because the good is high hekergy, and both survival value and sensual pleasure are a matter of hekergy increase or maintenance; hence their appeal as bases of morality, and the ease of justifying them, to some extent, as such. But the inadequacy of these positions, which will become clear in Chapter 13 and Part 4, lies in the fact that there are other kinds of hekergy increase besides those of survival value and pleasure, so that to reduce the good to one of these latter is to oversimplify.

Related to sensual pleasure and pain are **desire** and **aversion**. These, fairly obviously, are sensations correlative to pleasure and pain, respectively, and are caused by real bodily states correlative to the cause of pleasure and pain; that is, by appetite or need, and by disgust or danger, respectively. A need, clearly, is a need for real bodily hekergy increase, and a danger is a danger of real bodily hekergy decrease.

✶

The principles of **language** to which we turn next, are quite simple in the present context. The starting point is certain mid-ideas that are **mid-words**, spoken or written, which produce empirical words in the consciousness of the ego. The basic principle of language is that words *mean* mid-ideas, or properties thereof, or relations between mid-ideas. *Mean* is used here as a verb: a word *means* a mid-idea in the sense of being bonded to it — in the special sense of correlation described in Chapter 10 [147]. Such a mid-idea, bonded to a mid-word, is a **mid-meaning**. In its simplest form, language requires a triadic bonding: there is (i) the mid-idea that is the mid-meaning of the word, there is (ii) the mid-word bonded to it, and there is (iii) a motor-idea [161] bonded to it as well, which produces the word in, sequentially, the theoretical world, the mid-world, and the empirical world. More fully, we should distinguish between mid-word and the empirical word that it produces in the consciousness of the ego, and also between mid-meaning and the empirical meaning that it produces in the consciousness of the ego. Still more fully, there are two words for the mid-idea, one spoken and one written, hence two mid-words; and also two motor ideas: one to speak the word and one to write it. For each foreign language in which the ego is proficient there will be two more mid-words, written and spoken, of the mid-meaning, and two more motor ideas for producing it; and similarly for each synonym. Thus what we normally think of as one concept is a structure of all of these. There will also be relations between such concepts: logical relations (which are relations between the mid-ideas), and the relations expressed by rules of grammar (which are relations between the words).

This situation is also further complicated when we consider the details of producing a word. Suppose Jack's ego wishes to speak a certain word. The ego acts by bringing the mid-word (which is bonded to a mid-meaning) to the appropriate action point [162] in the mid-mind. This brings the bonded motor idea to the action point in the motor-mind, which causes the real body to speak the word. This produces a complex pattern of acoustical vibrations in the real world that are theoretically perceived by all other real people in that vicinity of the real world. Suppose that there is just one of these, Jill. The mid-word then appears in the mid-worlds of both Jack and Jill. For each, it is immediately mapped into the mid-mind, as a mid-memory. In the case of Jill, another mid-memory, of a similar word, is attracted by L.A.L. — that is, Jill recognises the word; and, because a mid-meaning — similar to the one bonded to the word in Jack's real mind — is bonded to this word in Jill's real mind, Jill has the mid-meaning of the word in her real mind. By L.A.L. Jill's ego then becomes conscious of both the word and its meaning. It is in this way that language communicates. Of course, if Jill's mid-meaning, evoked by Jack's word, is different from Jack's mid-meaning, then each has a different meaning for the same word and communication fails — a very common occurrence when philosophers converse. There is no way that the two meanings can be compared directly, any more than the real world can be known directly; but just as the real world can be known, and investigated, indirectly, so can the mid-ideas in two real minds be compared indirectly. In the first instance, with young children, this is by ostensive definition. Later it is by means of other kinds of definition, and by discussion.

Words, or symbols, need not be correlated with mid-ideas on a one-one basis. A case of one-many occurs when one name may be used for any member of a mid-class of mid-ideas. This will be called a **concrete name**. We could suppose that the concrete name is only bonded to one, representative, member of the class, such that any other member, in order to be referred to, brings this representative one to the action point by L.A.L. Concrete names will be important in that they are one form of universal — a matter that will be further discussed in Chapter 14 [227]. For the present it is sufficient that the ego can say "man," "horse," "dog," etc. without having to learn — that is, bond — the name to each specific individual man, horse, or dog encountered.

It was earlier said [161] that a structure of mid-ideas is a mid-proposition. If the constituent ideas, and the relevant relations between them are named successively then the result is a statement of the proposition. There are four common ways in which mid-ideas are related. One is a direct copy of relations in the apparent world; for example, a series of events or a process in the apparent world is a representation of a series of related mid-ideas; this latter will be mapped and so remembered as a series of corresponding mid-memories and of corresponding relations between them: this produces an **empirical proposition**. A second way in which mid-ideas may be related is by means of logical or mathematical necessity; this produces an **analytic proposition**, which will be explored in Chapters 14 and 15. A third way is in terms of relative kinds of hekergy and their magnitudes; this produces **evaluative propositions** and will be explored in Chapter 13. And a fourth way is the product of L.A.L. ordering, which is an **irrational proposition**. These four kinds of propositions lead to empirical, analytic, evaluative, and irrational statements respectively.

✷ ✷ ✷

Statements, as structures of words, need not be fully determined by their propositions. We can allow certain bondings of motor ideas; some of these, when described, will be rules of grammar; others may be idioms, clichés, etc. Needless to say, in the light of the foregoing, the meaning of a statement should not usually be sought in these bondings, or **language game rules**, as they might be called. In proposing otherwise, Wittgenstein took a trivial feature of language and tried to make it a universal explanation of abstract thought — a defence of nominalism that does not work, although it took a decade or so of work by fashion-conscious philosophers to discover this.

Not all language is propositional, of course. It may be used for such things as commands, appeals, exclamations, and questions. The basis of these other uses will be discussed in the next chapter, which concentrates on interpersonal relationships. Technically, what these kinds of utterances have to communicate is considered not to be propositional because it is neither true nor false — and a proposition is usually defined so as to be necessarily

168

either true or false. So it may be worthwhile at this point to review the various meanings of truth that we have encountered. There is analytic truth, which we discussed in Chapter 6 [102], in connection with Leibniz, and to which we will return in Chapters 14 and 15 [243, 280]; this is the truth of necessity. There is similarity truth [5], which is the degree of likeness, or similarity, between a proposition and that to which it refers. It may refer to one's own apparent world alone, or to many apparent worlds; it is then a so-called synthetic proposition — private, or public, respectively. Or the proposition may refer to the real world, in which case its truth cannot be checked directly; it is thus said to be theoretical, as we saw in Chapter 4. Similarity truth is also the truth of memories, expectations, and beliefs — that is, the degree of similarity between the memory, expectation, or belief, and its reference. Again, similarity truth between apparent and real worlds is empirical reality. Thirdly, there is the truth of correct linguistic usage, which is a matter of having similar linguistic bondings as other people; the absence of such truth — falsity — occurs with verbal mistakes and deceit. Finally, there is a meaning of truth called **coherence truth**. Propositions are said to be coherence true in so far as they are logically consistent among themselves, and the greater the number of propositions in a coherent whole, the greater the coherence truth of the whole; this is a matter of harmony between explanations.

✱

Our next topic is **discrimination**, which arises in the first place because of consciousness of similarity or dissimilarity between real ideas. That is, of likenesses of various degrees among apparent objects, mid-ideas or both; such degrees of similarity and dissimilarity are emergent relations. By itself, recognition of a similarity or likeness may provide a crude form of discrimination, since to be conscious of a relation is to be conscious, to some extent, of its terms. For example, a degree of likeness might exist between two real ideas because of their shape or because of their colour; in the one case the terms of the relation are shapes, in the other colours. But this is not sufficient for fine distinctions and, in particular, it provides no basis for a statement of distinction. The degree of likeness could be named "same" or "different," but naming the entire real ideas between which it exists would not distinguish shape from colour. Separating the shape or colour from the whole idea is necessary. This may be done by a special mapping, and indeed it is special mappings that provide both fine distinctions, and the possibility of stating them. We may suppose then that given a moderately high degree of likeness between two real ideas, this may serve as a signal to start special mappings in order to obtain fine discriminations. Naturally, on the basis of our experience, we have to suppose that both this signal and the special mappings are subliminal — that is, imperceptible, introspectively — which is not implausible, since they are theoretical rather than empirical.

In general, these special mappings operate to reproduce only a portion of the original, according to some principle of selection. They are in consequence processes of abstraction.

We will consider a particular set of possible discriminations, involving size, shape, and colour, based on Fig. 11.4. For these we will need three kinds of abstraction: they are called boundary mapping, scale mapping, and patch mapping.

Boundary mapping consists of a mapping from atomic unlikes only, to On atomic ideas, with the exception that isolated atomic unlikes are not mapped. In other words, the boundaries of a real idea, which are strings of dissimilarities, are mapped as strings of On's; these strings are the same size and shape, very nearly, as the boundaries — which may be either internal or external.

Scale mapping is an otherwise direct mapping except that there is a uniform enlargement or diminution. This occurs by having n atomic spatial relations in the map for every one in the original, where n is a whole number; or one in the map for every n in the original. These two kinds of mapping will be called scale-up and scale-down mappings, respectively. Special cases of each are those in which the scaling occurs in only one dimension, such as a vertical scale-up mapping. A scale-down mapping is, of course, a homomorph [86].

Patch mapping is a direct mapping of some small area of the original — always an area of one size and shape; we may suppose it to be a patch of just sufficient size to make the comparison.   In order to state the discriminations that these abstractings will produce, we have to specify that a likeness, and its approximate degree, is given a concrete name, such as "exactly similar," "nearly similar," "rather different," or "very different." Similarly, the various processes of abstraction constitute relations, between original and map, and may be treated as mid-ideas, hence be concretely named. For reasons that will shortly be obvious, boundary mapping will be named "shape," patch mapping will be named "colour," and scale mappings will lead to various names involving relative size.

Referring to Fig. 11.4, suppose that the ego is reacting to four mid-ideas, A, B, C, and D. A is a circle composed entirely of Off type atomic ideas — we may suppose it to be black; B is a circle, half the diameter of A, composed entirely of On type atomic ideas — we may suppose it to be white; C is a black square, of side equal to the diameter of A; and D is a white square the same size as C. We may assume that the ego will name the appearances of these four mid-ideas A, B, C, and D, as we do.

If now the ego does a patch mapping of A and C there will be a perfect likeness between the results: the patch from A will be like the patch from C. There will then be a proposition in the real mind, composed of A, C, two patch mappings, and the relation of likeness between the mappings. The ego could state this proposition in the form "A exactly similar colour C"; or, given rules of grammar [168] in the motor mind, "A is exactly the same colour as C."

Similarly, a boundary mapping of C and D will yield a proposition that the ego will state in the form "C and D are exactly the same shape." A more complex discrimination would occur if a boundary mapping of A and B was followed by a scale-down mapping of the boundary map of A, so as to produce complete likeness. The ego would state the resulting proposition as "A and B are the same shape and A is larger than B," where "larger than" names the scale-down mapping. (The meaning of *and* in this statement will

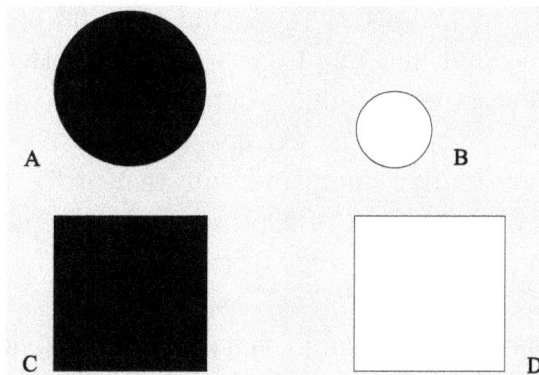

Fig. 11.4.

171

be explained in Chapter 14.)

Scale mappings are always used after boundary mappings when they are used for discriminating size, and only those are used that result in complete likeness; then a scale-down mapping is called "larger than" and a scale-up mapping, "smaller than," a vertical scale-down mapping is "taller than," a vertical scale-up mapping, "shorter than," etc.

Once the principle of abstraction, and the statement of the resulting proposition, is established, there is no difficulty in assuming special mappings for finer and more complex discriminations. For example, boundary mappings could be based on degrees of dissimilarity between theoretical sensations so as to obtain "same shape" from two coloured objects, other than black and white. Or more complex mappings could lead to the distinction between "same colour, different shade" or "same pitch different tone." We may also suppose various ancillary mappings, such as rotation, in order to obtain the same shape. A particular, and most important, special mapping will be that which produces class intensions — a matter that will be developed in Chapters 14 and 15.

★ ★ ★

Finally, in this chapter, **intuition** can be explained as the ego's consciousness of other parts of the real mind. For example, many people have had the intuition that everything is conscious to varying degrees: people more than animals, animals more than plants, plants more than rocks, etc. There is no scientific basis for this — indeed, the scientific consensus is adamantly against this view, since plants and rocks do not have the nervous systems necessary for consciousness. However, once it is understood that the scientists are considering real — theoretical — plants, rocks, etc. and the intuitives are considering empirical ones; and that the empirical ones are based on mid-ideas — then the intuition is explained. Because action and reaction are equal and opposite, so that when the ego is conscious of a mid-idea, by L.A.L., the mid-idea must be conscious of the ego. This latter consciousness is very primitive compared with that of the ego, but it exists and, as such, is part of the origin of the intuition; this particular intuition could also arise from the L.A.L. forces of interaction between any two real ideas.

Two other parts of the real mind that are prolific sources of intuitions are the oge (next chapter), which gives rise to intuitions of morality, the supernatural, heaven and hell, astrology, ghosts, and magic; and the psychohelios (Chapter 18), which gives rise to the intuitions that are the basis of creative thought. Intuition also probably was the process by which Freud discovered his own Oedipus complex [193, 203] and Adler discovered his own inferiority complex [187ff., 203].

12. The Oge.

The central concept of this chapter is called the **oge**. It will be sufficiently upsetting to the common-sense of those not already familiar with it that I will counter by giving two distinct arguments for the existence of the oge, followed by an illustration of the quite remarkable explanatory power of the concept.

✶

The first argument arises from an analysis of conflict. If we examine those conditions that are individually necessary and jointly sufficient for conflict, we find that there are four. There must be (i) at least two protagonists such that (ii) they have mutually exclusive goals [178] in a common situation and each has (iii) consciousness of at least some of that situation and (iv) some control over it. If we define an **agent** as anything that has goals, consciousness, and control in a particular situation, then these conditions can be stated as: at least two agents with mutually exclusive goals in a common situation. Readers should assure themselves that each of these conditions is necessary for conflict, and that together they are sufficient — that is, there are no other necessary conditions. It should also be clearly understood that this use of the word *conflict* excludes metaphorical use, and occurrences of the pathetic fallacy, such as "conflict of appetites" and "conflict of wind and tide."

Human society abounds with examples of conflict. Apart from wars, battles, feuds, and quarrels there are all the competitive sporting events and recreational games involving individual agents or teams of agents. There is also another kind of conflict with which we are nearly all familiar: internal conflict. A very common form involves the mutually exclusive goals of inclination and duty. Another involves desires and aversions, and neurotic thwartings of them — inhibitions and compulsions. Because of the fact of this internal conflict we have to suppose that there are at least two agents in a real mind. One, obviously, is the ego; the other I will call the **oge**, a word that is *ego* spelled backwards, and pronounced to rhyme with *bogey*.

It should be noted that although having mutually exclusive goals is possible for one agent — the familiar "have your cake and eat it" situation — this cannot produce conflict. At the worst it can produce indecision, which is not conflict.

The concept of oge is upsetting to many people because, I suspect, it is an affront to vanity — much as Darwin's contention that humans descended from apes, rather than being specially created, was offensive to vanity. The concept of oge is upsetting because most of us take for granted the sole and exclusive receipt of their own perceptions, and the sole and exclusive control of their own body. To allow that there is another "person" within one's own body, sharing one's experiences and partially controlling that body, is to diminish considerably one's own self-image — and is thereby an affront to one's vanity. This affront may be diminished, however, by the reflection that the oge does not inhabit one's mid- or apparent bodies, only the real body.

✻

As it turns out, the need to postulate a second agent in the real mind — an imperceptible which is postulated to explain a certain class of facts, such as internal conflict — is not the sole ground for claiming the existence of the oge. The present theory of mind produces an oge, quite naturally, once given the principle of L.A.L.R.U. and the existence of the ego.

As the ego is a structure of mutually attractive memories of its own mid-body, so the oge is a structure of mutually attractive memories of other people's mid-bodies. They are mutually attractive because of their similar content; and they form a separate structure from the ego because these mid-memories are different from those of the ego's mid-body. That is, likeness attracts these mid-memories into one structure, and unlikeness repels them from the ego. We each of us have considerable control over our own bodies, and private internal sensations in them; it is the absence of these in other bodies that is the primary unlikeness between the two kinds.

It was supposed in the last chapter that all the mid-memories involving one's own body go to constitute the ego. Obviously this must now be modified, since some of these memories must go to form the oge. The principle of their division is the attitude of the other mid-body — primarily that of a parent. If it is in favour of the ego in the given situation that produces the memory, then the memory, including this attitude, is attracted to the ego; if the other mid-body is not in favour, then the memory is repelled from the ego and attracted to the oge. Approval and disapproval are clearly a matter of likeness and unlikeness, since approval signifies to the ego that "My attitude is like yours" and disapproval signifies that "My attitude is unlike yours." In each of these cases, *attitude* is attitude towards whatever it is the ego's mid-body is doing. That approval or disapproval should be the determining factor in whether a given memory goes to ego or oge, arises from the fact that apart from attitude the memory should be approximately balanced between ego and oge, by virtue of containing two mid-bodies. One, the ego's own, makes the memory attractive to the ego and repulsive to the oge, and the other, of someone else, makes the memory repulsive to the ego and attractive to the oge. If the other apparent body is made more attractive or more repulsive by increased or decreased likeness to the ego, the scale will be tipped accordingly. The details of this will be amplified shortly.

However this is not the only way in which the ego and oge grow; if it were then the ego could never remember occasions on which its actions were disapproved by others. We may in fact distinguish between first and second stage growth of both ego and oge. In first stage growth every mid-memory goes to either ego or oge, depending on approval or disapproval. In second stage growth the ego and the oge have reached a threshold size and each is then able to do its own mapping, thereby obtaining an independent source of mid-memories for its growth. How it can do its own mapping is not explained, because the mechanical details of mapping have been disregarded. However a beginning of an explanation is that the ability to map should arise from need to do so, and this need is the result of L.A.L. forces of attraction between the ego, or oge, and mid-objects; a sufficient need would then only arise when the ego or oge reached sufficient size, since its total hekergy is a component of the L.A.L. force. We will return to the matter of second stage growth later [176].

✶

Memories are not the only constituent of the oge. As with the ego, beliefs are also constituents — including prejudices. Examples of these will appear as the chapter develops. The oge gets beliefs in two ways: by introjection, and from the ego. **Introjection** usually occurs when a belief is expressed by an empirical person whom the ego respects; because of the respect, which will be explained shortly [184], the belief is incorporated by the oge. Beliefs acquired from the ego are **oge prejudices**, which are equal and opposite to ego prejudices. Ego prejudices, it will be remembered, attract like evidence and repel unlike; all the evidence that is repelled has to go somewhere, so it goes to the oge; and because the items of evidence are similar among themselves, they are mutually attracted, to form one complex, or prejudice. We will see examples of such equal and opposite ego and oge prejudices later, with inferiority and superiority complexes.

✱ ✱ ✱

For the same reasons that the ego is conscious and able to act, so is the oge. The oge is a structure sufficiently similar to the ego to be characterised as reactive, in a complex fashion, to the L.A.L. forces of mid-ideas; so it is conscious of representations of these. And whatever allows the ego to move certain mid-ideas to the action point, and so act; or to prevent certain mid-ideas from reaching the action point, and so refrain from acting — whatever the factors are, the oge may be expected to possess them too. Furthermore, the ego and oge are conscious of, and act within, a common situation: they are conscious of one mid-world, in the sense that each has its own representation of it, its own empirical world. They are also both conscious of a part of the mental content, as opposed to material, of the real mind, although not necessarily the same part in this case — they are not usually conscious of each other, for example. And each has some control over this common situation: each has some control over how the apparent body acts in the apparent world, via motor ideas and real body, and each has some control over mid-ideas in the real mind.

Consequently the oge is as much an agent as is the ego, so if they have mutually exclusive goals, they will be in conflict. There are two ways in which they are so opposed, and these explain the inclination/duty conflict, and neurosis, respectively. In either case if the oge wins and makes the real body act against the will of the ego, the action is a compulsion; and if the oge prevents the ego from acting, the result is inhibition. Equally, if the ego acts to thwart the oge, this also is a compulsion or inhibition. If needed, we will distinguish the source of such thwartings adjectivally: **oge-compulsion, oge-inhibition, ego-compulsion,** and **ego-inhibition**. Everyday examples of oge-compulsion are subservience, giggling, and blushing; examples of oge-inhibition are shyness, laziness, timidity, impotence, and frigidity. A reluctant performance of one's duty is an oge-compulsion, and a taboo is a strong oge-inhibition. Ego-compulsions include blasphemy [295] and flattery, while intimidation is an ego-inhibition. The varieties of charity show the range of possibilities: a do-gooder is oge-compulsively charitable; dutiful charity is characteristic of mutual accommodation between ego and oge; genuine charity is performed with love, which is explained later [185]; and the charity that is an alternative to income-tax is selfish. The compulsively charitable do-gooder is ego-compulsive if acting to propitiate the oge, and is otherwise oge-compulsive.

The inclination/duty conflict arises out of the basic attitudes of ego and oge. The ego and the oge each need to increase hekergy, by the mind hekergy principle, but each will increase it according to its basic attitude. It is this need to increase hekergy according to an attitude that constitutes a **goal**. The basic attitude of the ego, as we saw [159], is selfish, so that its goals are its own hekergy increases, the good of the self. The basic attitude of the oge is social, since it represents other people, so that its goals are hekergy increases within society; which is to say that the oge is concerned with the good of society, it is **moral**.

That the ego and oge have these basic attitudes is easily explained. The central idea in the ego, by which all other ideas are determined to be like or unlike, is the idea of the self — the mid-body. There is no such single central idea in the oge, but a group of them: all other mid-bodies. Obviously, the central attitudes of ego and oge, which must be based on their central ideas, must be those of self and society.

✶

Hekergy increase, of either the ego or the oge, is of two basic kinds, depending upon whether it occurs in the apparent world or the apparent mind of either; and these, in turn, are representations of actual hekergy increases in the ego or the oge.

Ego hekergy increase in the apparent world is increase of ownership and of power. Ownership is material wealth, and has two significant characteristics for the present context: value and property. Value is intrinsic hekergy or else a function — the material object is valuable for its utility. A function is thus an extrinsic relation — extrinsic to both the material object and the owner. The value — of the object, to the owner — is then an emergent hekergy based on this function. For example, a car has the valuable function of providing transport; it also may have a secondary, minor, value as a status symbol. The material wealth is property because of the joint attitude of ego and oge: towards it the ego says "mine" and the oge says "yours." If the object is not the property of the ego it is because, although the ego may try to say "mine," the oge says "not yours." The behaviour of the oge in this respect corresponds with the attitudes of other apparent people in the mid-world; these attitudes are copies of the attitudes of the real people, which depend on their egos and oges. The meaning of *mine* is another extrinsic relation: the control over and of the material object by the ego. Power also has hekergy and hence value: the hekergy of an emergent relation of which the ego is a key term and which gives the ego control over the other terms. Power may be physical, political, economic, administrative, intellectual, emotional, creative, etc.

Part of ego-oge conflict will obviously be the effort by the ego to convert the not-mine into mine, and the opposing effort by the oge (in most cases) to keep the not-mine as such — that is, to keep the his his and the hers hers; or else to regulate how much of the available material wealth the ego may acquire. And similarly with power.

Ego hekergy increase in the mind — mental wealth — is quite different from that of material wealth. Since the ego, as a structure, is within the real mind, hekergy increase can be direct: the growth of the ego. This growth is hekergy increase, and can occur in two ways: rearrangement of existing mid-ideas in the ego, into a configuration of higher hekergy; and acquisition of new mid-ideas. Hekergy increase by rearrangement of ego structure is increase of the configuration hekergy of the ego; this, as will be discussed later, is increase in the ego's rationality [221, 282, 320]. Acquisition of ideas is increase in the summation hekergy of the ego. While the oge is still a first stage oge this is a matter of memories moving to the ego instead of to the oge. The memory of any thing or situation that other apparent people, or the oge itself, acknowledge to be the ego's constitutes a memory that goes to the ego. Whatever it is that produces such acknowledgement is an achievement for the ego, and the hekergy gain that results to the ego is the feeling of that achievement. Conversely, there is failure and its feeling of loss. In second stage growth summation hekergy increases most with new experiences, so that a richly variegated life leads to a large ego and a monotonous one leads to a small one. Achievement in general is hekergy increase of the ego, relative to the oge — that is, relative to other people's achievements. We may distinguish constructive and destructive achievement, depending upon whether the achievement included a hekergy increase or decrease, respectively. Thus, creation of a work of art is a constructive achievement and the killing of an enemy [182] a destructive one. Acquisition of material wealth or of power is of course a special case of achievement, and ostentatious display of it to others is another, lesser, kind; the latter, like the killing of an enemy, is a form of malice, which will be explained later [207].

Oge hekergy increase may be understood in similar terms. Oge achievements include the payment of taxes by the ego, and the ego acting for the good of the community. Others are achievements by the community working in concert, such as victory in war.

✳

Clearly, in terms of the foregoing, the ego and oge do have mutually exclusive goals: an achievement for one is usually a loss for the other. We will later see that with maturation of both ego and oge, this conflict will diminish, and may be resolved entirely. From the nature of these achievements, seeing why this conflict is characterised by inclination versus duty is not difficult.

There is, of course, introspective evidence for this conflict — evidence familiar to almost everyone. It is in general conscience. A young ego, in particular, is very sensitive to praise and blame, which require other people as their source. The response of the ego to blame is either guilt or shame, depending upon whether the blame comes from the oge alone, or from oge plus apparent bodies in the apparent world: that is, depending upon whether the blame is private or public. (What the oge feels in response to the ego is, of course, unknown to the ego.) Praise and blame are forms of pleasure and pain: there is an increase of ego hekergy with praise, and a decrease with blame. They come about simply because the oge knows that reward and punishment are valuable in controlling behaviour. It will know this both by means of the long cultural history contained in the parents' oges, plus similar knowledge from the parents' egos — that is, the parents will have discovered the effectiveness of reward and punishment for themselves. The ability of the oge to inflict punishment on the ego — that is, to reduce the ego's hekergy — depends on the strength of the oge relative to the ego. So a person with a strong oge will be much more susceptible to guilt and shame than one with a weak oge. This matter of relative strengths of ego and oge will be returned to shortly [197].

As far as duty is concerned, the oges of different people are largely similar within any one culture, and as such they are the repositories of all of that culture: proscriptions and prescriptions, moral code, taboos, mores, conventions, etiquette, idioms, slang, etc. The reason they are similar among one social group, tribe, nationality or whatever is that all within this group have their oge patterned on the group — on the public attitudes of the members of the group. These attitudes, in turn, are based on the oges of each individual, such that the oges and the public attitudes are mutually supporting. Because of this minority differences would tend to disappear — the nature of the growth of the oge promotes uniformity. However, although uniformity of oges would prevail, it could never be absolute, for a simple reason. The growth of the oge of a child will be patterned, in the first instance, on the oges of its parents; but it will also be patterned on the egos of the parents, since these display attitudes towards the child in the same manner that the oges do. Thus in one society each person's oge will have a base uniform to, and characteristic of, that society, plus an individuality based on the egos of the parents. (Egos of other later individuals may also influence the oge: teachers, heroes, or leaders of opinion.) It is because of this that cultures can change through the generations — very slowly, it is true, but much more quickly than genetic change. And also because of this, societies can develop cultural divisions within themselves: both stable ones, such as class and caste divisions; and unstable ones, such as ideological schisms, which may produce cycles of change — such as pendulum swings between puritanism and permissiveness, or between reason and romance — and even civil war.

✷

There is an analogy between oges and apparent worlds in that with both there are similarities between those of any two individuals, and also dissimilarities. The similarities are public and the dissimilarities are private. It is because of the public features of oges that we can speak of a group of people possessing *one* culture (thereby committing the identity error); and it is because of private features that an individual may be neurotic because of his oge, without this neurosis being universal in that culture. Also, in so far as moral judgments come from the public oge, they are objective; while those from the private oge are subjective. This objectivity does not equal that of science, since the publicity is not potentially universal among all peoples.

✷ ✷ ✷

The second kind of ego-oge conflict is neurotic conflict. As a preliminary to explaining this we must first examine the structure of the oge in greater detail.

✶

The actual shape of the ego and oge is something that we have not yet considered. It would be expected that the ego, if nothing interfered with it, would approximate to a spherical shape — because of ideas being attracted to one central idea from, presumably, all directions. But this sphericity could not be expected with the oge, because the oge does not grow about one central idea. Rather, it grows out of memories of attitudes of a series of people, no two of which people are quite alike. Consequently these memories should form a string, rather than a centre, so that the oge would tend to a sausage shape rather than a spherical one.

The importance of this is that, by L.A.L., the sausage shaped oge would point one end to the ego and the other away [184]. The near end would be composed of those oge mid-ideas most like the ego, and the far end of those least like; which is to say that the near end would be most approving of the ego and the far end the least. Thus the near end would be memories of those who loved the ego in childhood and those who love it now; and also memories of those loved by the ego. The far end would be, conversely, representative of the enemy: its attitude would be hating, as opposed to loving. And just as the ego would regard loving people as good, so it would regard hating people as evil.

A more detailed description of the structure of the oge is to say that it consists of substructures, or oge complexes, each of which consists of all the memories of a particular person or group of people. I will characterise each by the adjective *oge-*. Each of them is an **oge-person**. A plausible ordering of these, beginning with those nearest the ego could be: (i) a group of oge complexes, of approximately equal closeness, consisting of oge-father, oge-mother, oge-beloved, oge-spouse, oge-children, etc. The relative attitudes and positions of these depend upon the ego's experiences with these as apparent people, and upon the age of the ego. Thus the apparent mother may have been much more loving than the apparent father, so that the oge-mother is closer to the ego than the oge-father; and in adult life the oge-parents will be displaced from the closest position by the oge-spouse and/or the oge-children. This whole group, characterised by love, will be called the **oge-lover**. (ii) Beyond the oge-lover are memories of relatives and other fairly close people. These will not be loving (those oge people who are, are in the oge-lover) but they are still very close to the ego: perhaps the group is characterised by loyalty; it will be called the outer **oge-family**. (iii) Beyond the oge-family is another group, again varying with the individual, consisting of memories of apparent friends; it is characterised by liking, rather than loving or loyalty; it will be called the **oge-friend**; or it may be a group of oge-friends. (iv) Beyond the oge-friend is the **oge-stranger**; it is like the ego culturally, but no bonds of love, loyalty or liking are present. (v) Beyond the oge-stranger is the **oge-foreigner**, characterised by significant cultural differences from the ego — for example, the oge-foreigner speaks a language that the ego does not understand. It is characterised by its dissimilarities from the ego. (vi) Lastly, the **oge-enemy**, characterised by evil and hate. Other oge complexes may occur in some individuals, such as groups involving mutual loyalty: clubs, societies, trade unions, old boy networks, etc. Another possibility is an oge-monarch, with or without an oge-court of oge-aristocrats [202]; the presence or absence of these will be a major reason for the ego being a monarchist or a republican. And yet another possibility is a revered oge religious teacher, such as Christ, Budda, or Mahomet.

It is the two ends of the oge — the oge-lover and the oge-enemy — that are most susceptible to variation among individuals, and consequently are the most private and the basis of neurosis. The middle portion of the oge, the oge-stranger, is the most uniform and public, in any one culture, and the prime guardian of mores and morals. The near end of the oge-stranger consists of oge-acquaintances and the far end of compatriots who are sufficiently distant socially as to be almost oge-foreigners. The near end might be oge-neighbours — those about whose attitude so many people worry: "What will the neighbours think?"

The near and far ends of the whole oge are the most private, and the middle is the most public, on the basis that publicity is a matter of similarity to other oges, and privacy a matter of dissimilarity. The public portion of the oge is sometimes regarded, vaguely, with the identity error. It is supposed that publicity arises from identity, and consequently the public oges are spoken of as "the mind of the public," "the man in the street," "the average citizen" and so on. The private portions of the oge are those that engender respect and contempt, as well as love and hate. **Respect** is the attitude of the ego to an oge-person — and hence the corresponding empirical person — who is recognised by the ego to be superior to the ego, and **contempt** is the attitude towards someone inferior. Each may be highly selective: a bully may be respected for his superior strength but despised for his cowardice, or a father may be respected for his knowledge or ability, while loved for himself. And both may be diffuse: an ego might hold all foreigners in contempt, or respect all of his enemies for their fighting ability. **Snobbery** is the contempt of the haves for the have-nots, such as social, economic, intellectual, or authoritarian snobbery; the have-nots may have a corresponding respect for the haves, or else an equal and opposite contempt — an inverse snobbery.

However, although a young oge may be like a comet, with its tail pointing away from the ego, this shape changes because of two prejudices within the ego. These are what C. G. Jung called the **persona**, which is how the ego would have others believe it to be, and the **umbra**, which is those features of the ego about which it would prefer no one to know. (These two words mean *mask* and *shadow*, respectively.) For Jung these were two of the archetypes of the collective unconscious (which will be discussed later [211]), but here they are parts of the ego. These two prejudices repel each other, by L.A.L., and so must be at opposite poles on the spherical ego; and they also might, if strong, distort the sphere into an ellipsoid, by L.A.L. And also by L.A.L., the persona will face the oge-lover. But the umbra and the oge-enemy have a lot in common as well, because the umbra includes evil desires, so that the oge will curve around the ego, by the L.A.L. attraction between umbra and oge-enemy. And once the sausage shaped oge curls in this way there is nothing to stop it from thinning out into a spherical shell around the ego, and concentric with it — simply because there is enough variation among oge strangers for them to repel each other by L.A.L., around the equator of this shell. Thus the oge is a concentric shell around the ego; because it is outside the ego, it is outside the ego's apparent world — it is beyond the blue sky of a sunny day, beyond every horizon of the moment. And because there are many more mid-memories in the oge lover than in the oge-enemy, the oge is much thicker at the top than at the bottom; thus the oge-lover, as agent, is much stronger than the oge-enemy.

The persona, or mask, is usually a series of closely related prejudices: one for the beloved, another for friends, another for strangers — perhaps a variety for strangers, depending on the kind of stranger. So these personas will be distributed around the ego in the same way that oge people are distributed around the ego, each sub-persona opposite its corresponding oge-person. Each sub-persona determines the behaviour of the ego in the presence of the corresponding oge-person: that is, in the presence of an apparent person represented by that oge-person. We are all familiar with this: we talk and behave differently to our spouse, the boss, a child, a beggar, and a thief.

We may suppose the oge-lover to be at the top of the ego, and the oge-enemy to be at the bottom; we may call these the top and bottom poles of the ego and of the oge, so that oge-strangers would be around the equator. Since the oge is outside the apparent world of the person concerned, the oge-lover will be above the empirical blue sky and the oge-enemy will be below the empirical ground: so these locations of the oge top and bottom poles could reasonably be called Paradise and Hell, since they are inhabited by good and evil oge-people, even though they are within the theoretical skull. We will return to these theological implications later [293].

✻

In considering neurosis, next, caused by the private parts of the oge, we will deal first with that kind arising from an unhealthy oge-lover, and then that from an unhealthy oge-enemy.

Love, the characteristic of the oge-lover, is an attitude: it is a willingness to give unconditionally. That is, it is a willingness to raise, unconditionally, the hekergy of the beloved, at the expense of the lover. This is the hekergy of the ego of the beloved that is raised, and the hekergy of the lover's oge-beloved is raised in consequence — both by a diminution of the hekergy of the ego of the lover, and hence a corresponding diminution of the hekergy of the beloved's oge-lover.

In order for this to be possible within our theory — that is, within a real mind — it is not enough that the oge-beloved be very close to the ego, it is necessary that it become part of the ego. That is, the ego and oge must intersect, overlap, so that the oge-beloved is a part of each. In such a case the ego, in loving the oge-beloved, is not merely diminishing its own hekergy — a process that could not be explained in our theory — but is transferring hekergy from one part of itself to another. Such transfer does not contravene the mind hekergy principle, as a mere diminution of ego hekergy would, so is possible.

This ego-oge overlap is **identification**: the ego identifies with the oge-beloved. It occurs in all forms of love: love, by the ego, of parents, siblings, mates, children, country (that is, patriotism, as opposed to nationalism, which is a prejudice), heroes, or Gods.

Identification is possible only with a large ego. The reason for this, stated technically, is that near-likeness is fadingly transitive. That is, in a series, each term of which is near-like, but not completely like, its neighbours, two widely separated terms may have little likeness or similarity between them at all. It is for just this reason, for example, that the oge-beloved and the oge-enemy can be very unlike, as can the persona and the umbra. The ego is a structure of near-like terms, beginning with memories of its own apparent body at the centre and moving outwards; so if it is large then it is possible for it to include, as a part of itself, on a basis of L.A.L., something considerably unlike the mid-body — such as the mid-memories of the body of someone else: those of the beloved, which are those that constitute the oge-beloved.

Love is essential for the growth of the young ego. This is true for both material and mental hekergy increases. Material wealth for the infant, as food, clothing etc., must be given unconditionally, since the infant is unable to support itself. As we saw in connection with material wealth [186], when the attitude of the oge towards the material is "yours," the idea of the wealth goes to the ego. There is, of course, little property aspect to food, since the wealth is consumed; but although transient, the wealth is genuine. In the case of increases of the mental hekergy of the ego we need only consider a fresh minted memory, poised between oge and ego and ready to go to one or the other. If the oge-lover is loving the ego then the balance will be tipped in the ego's favour and the memory will travel by L.A.L. to the ego. That is, the oge-lover will unconditionally raise the hekergy of the ego at its own expense. This situation will occur if the oge has loving attributes — that is, has an oge-lover; this in turn requires that someone in the apparent world loves the person of the ego.

Since the ego is composed of memories; and since, in infancy, the strength of both the ego and the oge to attract memories by L.A.L. is very

186

small, it follows that whether most memories go to the ego or to the oge depends on whether the ego's person is loved or not, and to what extent. If it is not loved at all, the ego cannot grow — just as, if the body of the infant is not provided for, it cannot grow either.

Non-existence of the ego, or a very stunted ego, constitute a major form of insanity, which will be discussed later [204]. Neurosis and neurotic conflict are not insanity in this respect, but related to it. They arise when love is withdrawn by a parent in connection with some specific action by the ego. This leads to a neurotic attitude towards, and conflict over, this action. Specific examples will make this clear.

✶

Inferiority and superiority complexes are the first example. Each of these is a prejudice, involving a central belief that the person of the ego is inferior, or superior, relative to other people. Each prejudice characteristically selects evidence by attracting like ideas and repelling unlike. Those attracted swell the prejudice that attracts them; and those repelled go to the other, opposite, prejudice, which attracts them and repels those attractive to the first. Thus inferiority and superiority complexes occur as a mutually supporting pair, each attracting, and growing upon, the ideas that the other repels. They will generally be of approximately equal size and strength — unless the person of the ego is in fact unusually inferior or superior to the average, in which case there will be more evidence for one complex than the other. In the latter case the stronger complex, in so far as it is stronger, will be true; in so far as inferiority and superiority complexes are equal and opposite, they are false — in the sense that all prejudices are false: by virtue of being half-truths.

As we will see when we discuss the genesis of inferiority and superiority complexes, besides being prejudices they also carry strong feeling components that make them pre-eminent among the individual's prejudices as far as motivations are concerned, and hence the basis of neurosis.

These complexes always divide between ego and oge. The one in the ego represents the individual's self-opinion, and the one in the oge represents the opinion that the ego believes others have of it. So an oge superiority complex is a prejudice that the ego — not the oge — is superior, while an oge inferiority complex is a prejudice that the ego — not the oge —

is inferior; and corresponding ego complexes also refer to the superiority or inferiority of the ego.

Ego-oge conflict will result from the existence of these complexes because they produce mutually exclusive goals. A superiority complex has the goal of over-achievement by the individual and an inferiority complex the goal of under-achievement. Within the conflict a victory for the superiority complex is a compulsion: a compulsion to undertake some task in order to achieve. A victory for the inferiority complex is an inhibition: an inhibiting of action, thereby ensuring the failure expected by the inferiority complex.

Thus if a male ego has an inferiority complex it will make for a modest man, believing himself inadequate and believing that others constantly overrate him. He may undertake tasks that he believes beyond his capacity, because "it's expected of him" — that is, because his oge compels him. His belief of incapacity is false — his ego inferiority complex is false — so he may well succeed in the task. Such success will be evidence of superiority, hence as a memory will go to the oge superiority complex. If the ego cannot forget the fact of the success, because of circumstances that are reminders, then it will be discounted. It is rationalised: it is explained away through a theory that is false, but according to the prejudice that requires the rationalisation. The simplest and easiest rationalisation is that of luck. The ego believes he is still incapable of doing that task, and only succeeded on this occasion because of good fortune — an opportune coincidence, or some such. Meanwhile, if the success was public, other people will praise the ego and thereby strengthen the oge superiority complex, by introjection. Such praise aggravates the ego-oge relationship and hence may be genuinely distasteful to a modest person, as opposed to the more usual case of praise being an achievement for the ego and so pleasurable.

Alternatively, faced with a task that the ego inferiority complex believes, falsely, to be beyond the capacity of the ego, the ego may simply refuse to undertake it. Assurances by other people of his capacity in this regard strengthen the oge superiority complex; as such, depending on other circumstances, they will either persuade him to change his mind, or else, in reaction, strengthen his resolve. Which is to say, oge-compulsion will overcome ego-inhibition, or ego-inhibition will be strengthened.

If the male ego has a superiority complex, it will make for a conceited man, believing himself capable beyond his fellows and believing that others constantly underrate him. He may undertake tasks that he believes to be well within his capacity, and fail because this belief is false — that is, his ego superiority complex is false. Frequently the undertaking will be associated with a conscious desire to prove to "them" that his capability is not as inferior as "they" believe — that is, as his oge inferiority complex rates him. The failure will be forgotten or, if this is unavoidable, rationalised. If it was public, other people may sneer, and so strengthen the oge inferiority complex. Alternatively, if the undertaking is publicly announced, the conceit of the announcement may produce sneers that will so strengthen the oge inferiority complex as to inhibit all action in this respect, except rationalisation for the change of plan.

Needless to say, such pairs of complexes may equally afflict a female ego and oge.

The genesis of these complexes can be explained quite simply. If a parent has an ego inferiority complex then it will believe itself inferior to others, which is to say that it will regard others as superior; so it will identify the child with the oge-beloved and regard it as superior. The child will thereby develop a superiority complex in its oge-lover, and hence an inferiority complex in its ego. These will be reinforced by the expectation of over-achievement by the parent, such as in school grades, hence expectation of over-achievement by the child's oge and corresponding expectation of under-achievement, hence failure, by the child's ego. If, on the other hand, the parent has an ego superiority complex, it will regard the child as inferior. In pointing out the child's inferiorities — possibly even in manufacturing them; no difficult task for an adult ego against a child's ego — the parent will both assuage his own ego superiority complex and give the child an oge inferiority complex. The latter will generate an ego superiority complex in the child.

What is particularly significant in this type of genesis is that in its treatment of the child according to the dictates of its pair of complexes, the parent is quite clearly not loving. That is, not only is the parent not giving unconditionally to the child, but the reverse — it is feeding its own complexes at the expense of the child. Because love is of paramount importance to the child, its withdrawal will produce very strong crisis feelings. These crisis feelings will become bonded to the two complexes and by their presence will intensify the importance of the goals of the complexes and so will intensify the conflict.

This is not the only possible genesis. Indeed, if it were, there would be no way for the chain of transmission from parent to child to begin. An individual might develop a false belief about his own capacity through unusual circumstances in his apparent world; circumstances producing excessive flattery by subservient people, for example. It is also possible for circumstances to produce the opposite effect, such that the chain of culturally inherited complexes is ended. In fact, if the present analysis of this type of neurosis is correct then the cure [195] is in principle simple. The peers of a modest man should not praise him, they should belittle him; and the peers of a conceited man should praise him, not belittle him. Such small acts of love would tend to neutralise both oge and ego complexes. But since the complexes are bonded to crisis feelings based on love withdrawal, the neutralisation would only succeed if done with love — that is, as an unconditional gift; if any malice [207] is present, the act must fail.

∗

Another kind of oge-lover neurotic conflict arises in the case of second-hand ambition. A father, through having failed, for some reason, to achieve some ambition, may fall back on the alternative of preparing his son to fulfill this ambition in his place. The father will even cherish the son more, in proportion to his promise as a surrogate achiever. Thus the son will have a strong ambition, bonded to strong feelings, in his oge. Ambitions are normally in the ego, since they concern the achievement of the individual. An oge ambition, although it concerns the achievement of the individual, does so in spite of the ego. An oge ambition will also be at variance with ego ambitions, such that a conflict situation arises. For example, the father may have had a strong ambition to be a doctor, but never achieved it for lack of money or ability. The son may have an ambition to be a novelist. The son is then likely to go to medical school and there experience considerable conflict over how to spend his available time: studying or writing. If the conflict is involved with relatively weak feelings, he may be fortunate and succeed in a compromise. But if strong feelings are involved he is likely to fail in his studies because of interference by ego feelings of rebelliousness, and fail in his writing because of interfering feelings of guilt, disloyalty, etc.

190

from his oge. He may even find himself consciously agreeing to become a doctor but unconsciously thwarting the oge ambition by various forms of compulsive failure. He might fail to set his alarm clock and so sleep through an important examination, compulsively forget an important appointment with the Dean, have his mind go blank at crucial moments, or the like. Needless to say, there are many possible variations on this. A father may have no sons, only daughters, so that his failed ambition to be a sports hero turns his eldest daughter into a neurotic tom-boy. Or an able mother, frustrated in her ambitions by the demands of raising a family, may wish a son or daughter to fulfill them for her.

Another form of neurotic compulsive failure could arise with a mother both niggardly in her love, and desirous of keeping her child dependent upon her. In such circumstances the child would receive much needed love on those occasions when it attempted independent achievements but failed. Such an individual would then possess an oge that, by virtue of very strong feelings bonded to memories of failure, would give the ego no peace except on occasions of actual failure in the adult world. Such a doomed individual obviously could do nothing but descend to the lowest level of society, since he or she would constantly seek, fruitlessly, love in return for failure.

✷

We turn next to oge-enemy neurosis, which requires first some discussion of the oge-enemy.

As we have seen, the oge grows both by communication of the parents' oges and by encounters with actual mid-people, whose attitudes may condition oge-people by introjection. The oge-enemy is peculiar in that it usually grows only by the former method. The child rarely — indeed usually never — meets an apparent enemy. (In the case of an untravelled and relatively ignorant ego, the oge-foreigner will be formed the same way; for such a person the difference between foreigners and enemies may be quite indistinct.) The oge-enemy grows by repute: by repute of possessing the characteristics of evil.

Evil may be defined as anything that is at once of human origin, and much disapproved of, or disliked, by both ego and oge-lover. This disapproval or dislike is an attitude: the attitude towards hekergy decrease. Such hekergy decrease is painful; its greatest possibility is death. So any human who inflicts pain or death is evil. The most obvious examples of evil beings are criminals, particularly murderers, and the enemy in time of war. The concept of evil is sometimes extended to include any cause of pain or death, such as famine, plague, earthquake, volcano, shipwreck, or car accident. This will not be done here because we are interested in the oge, which represents the human. That is, we are concerned with human evil, not natural tragedy.

An oge-enemy consisting of oge-thieves, oge-murderers and oge-enemy soldiers is characteristic of an oge that is healthy but somewhat immature. A neurotic oge-enemy has rather more content.

Oge-enemy neurosis develops if the denial of parental love is associated — bonded — with an appetite. This, as is well known, most commonly occurs with the sexual appetite. Three possible formations will be discussed here.

If one or both parents believe sex to be evil then they will react with horror to manifestations of infantile sexuality in the child, such as an obviously pleasurable fondling of the genitals. Horror precludes love, so the child will be faced with a crisis, and crisis feelings and sexuality will be bonded, and jointly repelled. They are repelled both by the oge-lover and by the persona, and so go to the oge-enemy and the umbra.

This means that in later life, love and sex are separated: the ego cannot have sexual desire for a beloved, nor feelings of love for a stranger for whom sexual desires are possible. Sex is evil for the ego, such that (i) sexual activity is expected from the enemy, (ii) anyone displaying sexuality becomes an enemy, and (iii) sexual activity by the individual is only possible with an enemy. The oge-enemy and the umbra gain great power from the sexual appetite and force the individual to illicit sexual relations with an apparent enemy. Once the appetite is satisfied the oge-enemy and the umbra retire victorious and the oge-lover expresses outrage and horror — feelings with which the persona in the ego concurs, because of having repelled sexuality to the oge-enemy. The ego thus alternates between an evil need that it cannot resist, and remorse. The apparent enemy in such a case is anyone who displays sexuality openly; as such they are evil, hence enemies. An obvious example of this situation is that of a prude or a puritan, and a prostitute. Another example is the rapist, who cannot have love and sex together, and so has callous indifference with sex, or even hate with sex. The extreme of this situation would be that arising from a complete repudiation of sexuality by the ego, because of the extreme reaction of the parent. This would not be repudiation of all sexuality, necessarily, but only sexuality as understood by the parent. Any form of sexuality not considered by the parent would be permissible, and could then become the standard gratification for the adult individual. Such alternatives might be the various modifications of sexuality, of which homosexuality and sadomasochism are the most common.

A second kind of sexual neurosis could arise if the child receives only niggardly love from the parent of the opposite sex. The child's need for more love would then make it exceedingly jealous of the other parent when love between the two parents was displayed. In the case of a boy this would lead to the classic Oedipus complex [203]. Jealousy of the father would lead to fear of the father, fear that would be associated with sexuality: the fear of castration by the father. Sexuality would be identified as something that produces the needed love from the mother, so the sexual appetite would become bonded with the oge-mother, thereby preventing a sexual attachment to any other woman in adult life. What Freud called the Electra complex would apply correspondingly to a girl.

Of course, it is not only the sexual appetite that may be repressed to the oge-enemy and umbra. The extreme case is the puritan, for whom all appetites are repressed and, consequently, all pleasure is evil. Such unfortunates, besides having no healthy enjoyments, will have an exceedingly strong oge-enemy and so be very conscious of evil. In the neurotic conflict that they will have with the oge-enemy (who in English is usually called Satan [295]) they will need to bring every resource to bear. One major resource is to compel the strong, middle portion of the oge to oppose the oge-enemy. This requires that the populace at large come to regard pleasure as evil, and proceed to legislate against it. Puritans, because of the great danger in which their egos stand in the face of the strong oge-enemy and umbra, will be strongly motivated in both these tasks, and may well succeed. The result is a culture of unhealthy austerity. The puritans are, of course, doubly unfortunate in that all this effort is largely misdirected. They would do much better to get psychotherapy, as far as their personal agony is concerned, but they are oblivious of this possibility because their neurosis is rationalised — as, for example, by saying that a man's first duty is to God, his second to his fellow man, and his third to himself, so that pleasure, which is selfish, ranks low. Various forms of puritan preaching are various forms of prohibition: anti-sex, anti-alcohol, anti-theatre, anti-gambling, etc. Sometimes the campaign is against largely non-existent pleasures, as with the anti-vivisectionists who suppose that scientists experiment with laboratory animals solely for the sake of sadistic pleasure. Our language has many expressions to describe people who have a neurotic need to prevent pleasure, such as spoilsport, party pooper, wet blanket, and killjoy.

The misdirected effort of the puritan is a very common feature of neurosis. It is a displacement of an internal need into the external world — the apparent world. For example, those adults needing love will often misdirect their need onto the material symbols of love — food and money — and so become compulsive eaters or misers. A man with a disordered or untidy mind may be compulsively neat in his apparent world. A terrorist may be someone whose oge is all oge-enemy, except for his terrorist colleagues, and therefore should be destroyed; displaced into his apparent world, this need becomes a need to destroy society at large. A compulsive failure is someone whose natural talents and abilities are being neurotically wasted; his or her need to prevent this waste, if displaced externally, will become an obsession against all kinds of material waste — producing the kind of person who cannot throw out anything. One who has a neurotic fear of success may displace this into a fear of physical heights. A person with a neurotically divided mind may seek a displaced, external unification in a campaign for world government or in the ecumenical movement. Or one who neurotically needs others to admire him may be a compulsive liar. Generally, the various phobias are externally displaced neurotic fears. Self-knowledge — that is, rational understanding of one's own irrationalities — which is usually very difficult to obtain, can be advanced by awareness of how common it is for irrationality to be displaced externally in this way.

These are only a few of the more common varieties of neurosis. It should be clear from them, not only that a large variety can be explained by means of the oge, but also that, as conflicts, they are inexplicable without a second agent such as the oge, or some part of it, within the real mind.

✷

Cure of all neurosis is possible in principle because the oge may conform to the attitudes of apparent people — that is, of actual people met in the apparent world. This conformity is not, of course, assured: the reverse process may occur, in which oge attitudes are projected [196] onto the apparent people. A prude or a puritan will project sexlessness onto a beloved, for example. Classic examples are the projection of perfection onto a beloved and of evil onto an enemy, as will be explained in a moment. As we have seen, introjection of other people's beliefs occurs when these people are respected. So discussion with other people about the neurotic individual's beliefs and memories may change the oge to a more true representation of public attitudes — make the oge more objective. But since this is a matter of considerable re-structuring, of ego prejudices as well as oge ones, and also of memories with strong feelings bonded to them, a considerable time will be required to effect a cure. These are the two essentials: a second person — or group of people — and time. The usual psychoanalytic or psychotherapeutic situation, and a group therapy situation, clearly fulfil these conditions. The analyst or group must obviously be patient; ideally they should be loving as well, but they must at least be sympathetic; they should have some understanding of the neurosis involved, and so be respected in this regard; and, finally, they should be directive or non-directive as required. All of these further conditions except the last are obvious in view of the foregoing. The last arises from an ego-oge feature that we will discuss later [198]; that is, that an ego-dominant individual requires directive therapy and oge-dominant individuals require non-directive therapy.

✳ ✳ ✳

Infatuation is another feature of human behaviour easily explained by means of the oge. We have already met with the concept of projection [39]; infatuation is a process in which either the oge-beloved or the oge-enemy is projected onto an apparent person or group of apparent people. The mechanism of this is very simple. Because the oge surrounds the ego, there are oge-people between mid-people and empirical people. That is, a mid-person — a representation in the real mind of a theoretical person — produces an empirical person in the ego by L.A.L., and between the two is the oge, a thin shell surrounding the ego. The ego and the oge are locked together because of identification [186] so the oge cannot rotate about the ego; but the two can rotate together, so that the appropriate ego-persona and oge-person are opposite the mid-person. So between the mid-beloved and the empirical beloved is the oge-beloved; and between the mid-enemy and the empirical enemy is the oge-enemy. So the empirical beloved, or empirical enemy, is as it were, filtered through oge prejudices, and so correspondingly prejudicial. Such so-called projection is thus a process of filtration, like things seen through coloured glass.

The oge-lover and the oge-enemy produce infatuation because, being the most private, they can be the most false. When they are so they become a mutually supporting pair, like inferiority and superiority complexes: each will attract and grow upon the ideas that the other repels.

In the case of the oge-lover, we should note that the oge-lover may be an ideal: it may contain everything that the ego most desires and needs in another. Consequently when such an ego meets another empirical person who is sufficiently like the oge-beloved to be identified with it, he or she becomes the empirical beloved and all remaining oge-beloved qualities, such as supreme beauty and sex-appeal, are projected onto this person. The claim, by the lover, of these qualities in the beloved is, to any third person, obviously false; and so the lover is called infatuated. In an individual whose oge is healthy, the oge-beloved will contain qualities that may quite reasonably be expected to be found in an apparent beloved, so that those that the apparent beloved does not in fact possess are unimportant. If the oge is unhealthy then qualities will be projected onto the apparent beloved that are both non-existent in that person and very important to the ego. In such a case the infatuation will end quite quickly, as the oge adjusts to the empirical facts. It is quite possible that the oge-beloved will be destroyed as a result, leaving an ego that is cynical and bitter — that is, believing that none of the requisite sex have any of the desired qualities. If this does not happen, a new apparent beloved will be sought and found, followed by a new disillusionment, repeatedly.

In the case of infatuation over the enemy, all the evil of the oge-enemy is projected onto the empirical enemy. The oge-enemy and umbra jointly seize this opportunity to act, by advocating that it is permissible to do unto the enemy as they would do unto us. In the case of criminals this leads many otherwise kindly people to propose the most vicious punishments, and in the case of warfare it leads to all kinds of atrocities. Consequently it is salutary to remember when dealing with any enemy that all evil is in the real mind of the beholder.

Yet another form of infatuation may occur with racism. This is a prejudice that another cultural group is inferior. It may happen that if the prejudice is sufficiently strong the people of that other culture will have the oge-enemy projected onto them and so become apparent enemies, and thereby evil. A major example is the anti-Semitism of Nazi Germany. It is noteworthy that the Nazis accused world Jewry of all of their own evil characteristics: of trying to take over the world, and of being the then source of all evil in Germany.

It is interesting that infatuation is frequently mutual, because the infatuated person, in projecting the oge-beloved or oge-enemy onto the infatuee, will behave in an appropriate manner — that is, corresponding with the oge-beloved or oge-enemy. This may lead the infatuee to identify the infatuated with his or her oge-beloved or oge-enemy, as the case may be, and so also become infatuated. The result is either a honeymoon or a war. Each is folly because of the excessive falsity in the projection: the apparent beloved is not an angel and the apparent enemy is not a devil — each is only human. However, since an infatuated person behaves fatuously — that is, either angelically or demonically — his or her humanity is likely to be overlooked by the infatuee.

✳ ✳ ✳

Many features of human personality and behaviour may be explained by the simple fact of either the ego habitually dominating the oge or *vice versa*. We can speak accordingly of an **ego-dominant type** of personality, and an **oge-dominant type**; and we can understand the two types to occupy a spectrum of characteristics, depending upon the degree of dominance — where degree of dominance is the relative power or strength of the two agents.

The behaviour of individuals dominated by their oges will exhibit oge characteristics. They will be moral, dutiful, public spirited, conventional, loyal, obsequious, conscientious, politically correct, and obedient of prescriptions, of proscriptions, and of orders issued by other people. They will be sensitive to the judgments of others — particularly in the form, not of how other people actually judge them, but of how they believe these others to judge them: that is, of how their oges judge them. They will shun responsibility, particularly in connection with decisions for which there is no tradition or precedent, for fear of how others will judge their decision. They are susceptible to embarrassment and shame, and could be guilt-ridden. They will be in favour of the under-privileged and hostile to the over-privileged. And they will also tend to lack ego characteristics. But in an ego-dominant type the ego characteristics will be exhibited in behaviour: uninhibited selfishness, as in the initiative required for selfish ambitions and drives, unselfconscious non-conformity and even breaking of taboos when it is to the ego's advantage, a preference for issuing orders rather than obeying them, and a capacity for accepting responsibility. Ego-dominant types will also show a general inadequacy in oge characteristics: they will be largely immune to shame, guilt, embarrassment, praise, or blame. If they behave morally it will be as much for prudential reasons as from a sense of right and wrong [203]. And they will have little hesitation in exploiting the under-privileged.

Concerning the therapeutic analysis that we have just discussed [195], an oge-dominant type will clearly not respond to directive therapy because the analyst or group represents the oge and, in being directive, strengthens an oge already too strong. Non-directive therapy, on the other hand, weakens the oge and so allows the ego to grow. Conversely, an ego-dominant type will not respond to non-directive therapy and might do so to directive therapy, for corresponding reasons.

✳

The well-known hierarchy among chickens, known as the **peck-order**, in which a chicken can peck another that is lower than itself in the order but not one that is higher, has a parallel in human society that is explicable in terms of ego- and oge-dominance. Such a hierarchy in human relations is perhaps best characterised by **rudeness ability**. An individual can be rude to another lower in the order, but not to one who is higher. Such ranking is usually automatic, and based on so-called strength of personality. This strength is the strength of the ego face to face with the oge; it is usually expressed overtly as assurance and self-confidence, or lack thereof, in social situations. It follows that the most ego-dominant person is highest in the rudeness-order and the most oge-dominant is the lowest.

It is very likely that this expression of assurance, which must be via the motor mind, is due to an inherited set of motor ideas; and that the expression is recognised by means of inherited ideas in the real mind; in other words, the expression and the recognition of it are instinctive. The probability of this arises from the survival value of such instincts in a species that, because of its tribal nature, requires leaders: alpha-males and alpha-females. This is further demonstrated by the ego-dominant type being an order giver, unafraid of responsibility, etc., while the oge-dominant is obedient, fears responsibility, is loyal, etc.

The hierarchy of the rudeness-order tends to become formalised in a number of our institutions. Thus an ego-dominant type is clearly officer material in the armed forces and executive material in industry, commerce, and the civil service, while the oge-dominant type is an obvious subordinate. Indeed the very institutionalisation of the hierarchy may give an individual rudeness ability towards some people that he would not otherwise possess, and deprive him of it in other cases. This is because the institutionalisation of the hierarchy is an acceptance of it by all concerned, hence an embodiment of it into the oge. For this reason the oge of an oge-dominant individual may allow him to be rude to a subordinate just because he is a subordinate — even though the subordinate might be less oge-dominant without the institution; equally, it will prevent the subordinate being rude in reply, even though he would otherwise be free to be so; instead the subordinate will suppress his impulse of rudeness to the boss, because she is the boss, and, perhaps, substitute flattery. This institutionalisation of the hierarchy is socially valuable, and consequently it is usually reinforced by giving each rank actual power over lower ranks: power of reward and punishment, which is to say, hekergy gain and loss to the ego of the individual concerned.

The hierarchy of the rudeness order explains why a society, developing out of a dark ages, should be a feudal monarchy. Those high in the order would become barons, and fight ruthlessly among themselves for the crown, while those low in the order would accept their serfdom.

The theory of ego-and oge-dominance throws some light on modern political behaviour as well. The nearest external manifestation of the oge is the government, or more generally but also more vaguely, the state. Consequently an individual's attitude towards the state or the government will depend upon his ego-oge balance and the attitude of the stronger agent.

An oge-dominant individual will have his attitude towards the state determined by his oge. The oge, in accordance with its basic attitude, the good of society, and its need to increase its own hekergy, will desire a strong government. This would mean increasing the state's power to prescribe and proscribe — the state's power as expressed in laws. The oge will desire an assisting of all underprivileged people in the state, since it is concerned with the good of all. The oge will also desire a curbing, or even a suppression of the activities of ego-dominant types, since these are largely selfish and so antisocial.

On the other hand an ego-dominant individual's attitude towards the state will be determined by his ego. He will desire minimum government interference with his selfish activities — that is, minimum legal prescription and proscription of his ambitious initiatives towards ego hekergy increase. He will regard the underprivileged as having their just desserts, for lacking initiative and ambition, and will strongly oppose the oge-dominant politician who wants the state to support them — largely because such support will be paid for by levies against his own actual or anticipated wealth.

Clearly, an oge-dominant type politically is a socialist, and an ego-dominant type is a capitalist. Because these positions arise from ego-oge imbalances, and because there is a great deal of feeling involved in ego-oge dispute, political discussion between capitalists and socialists is usually both irrational and highly emotional.

In an earlier age similar irrational and emotional dispute arose for the same reason but over a different object. The externalisation of the oge was then the church. After the Reformation ego-dominant types were free of a strong authoritarian church, in that as Protestants they replaced the church of Rome with individual — ego — interpretation of the bible and with individual conscience. Oge-dominant types loyally remained with the strong church. Sufficient irrational passion arose between the groups to lead to war — just as recent irrational passion led to war between capitalists and communists.

An interesting sidelight on this matter arises from the fact that ego-dominant types could be expected to be emigrants from their homeland if they believed it to be to their advantage, while oge-dominant types, loyal to the homeland, would not emigrate. Consequently with the opening up of North America most of the immigrants would have been ego-dominant, thereby making Canada and the USA capitalistic. On the other hand, the countries they left behind in Europe would, because of their departure, have a higher proportion of oge-dominant types and — particularly if they were not catholic countries — so become socialist. Since ego-oge imbalance is usually not entirely transmitted from parent to child, the capitalist-socialist opposition between North America and Europe may be expected to disappear.

We may also note that because of the interests of ego-dominant types, a capitalistic country may develop much more material wealth and power than either a socialist country or a catholic country. This point is salutary, because such wealth is a necessary condition for a country to be able to afford the social safety net that socialists desire.

Finally on this matter of the significance of ego-oge imbalance in politics, in view of the irrational nature of the passions aroused in capitalist-socialist discussions, if it is asked what the rational approach would be to the problem of which is preferable, there is only one answer. Broadly speaking, ego-oge imbalance is unhealthy. Mentally healthy individuals have, among other things, a balance between ego and oge, and their political views are probably the most worthy. Such individuals are passionate about neither capitalism nor communism. They are probably best exemplified by the liberal tradition, by middle of the road politics. This seems an unsatisfactory answer because it requires, rather than manifestoes, a state of mind — literally. It is a matter of spirit rather than letter. Needless to say, this is not to deny any particular content of either socialist or capitalist platforms: but it is to aspire to an assessment of these on their merits, rather than on a prejudicial state of ego-oge imbalance.

★

A valuable touchstone in this regard is the **authoritarian**: a personality type that often results from ego-oge imbalance. Such people are, most characteristically, order takers and order givers; "Control or be controlled" could well be their motto. They are authoritarian because they operate according to some code, rule book, or authority. This makes them closed minded, since something is judged true or false by them according to its source — the accepted authority — or not, rather than its merits; and consequently authoritarians are conservative and uncreative. They regard all who reject their authority as enemies. Because their attitude towards other people is one of control, they tend to be unfeeling towards others — particularly their inferiors and their enemies. Because of these characteristics, authoritarians show many characteristic behaviour patterns. For example, because they lack feeling for others they lack courtesy; instead they rely on a formal code of behaviour. Such a code, or etiquette, originated with courteous behaviour but lacks the concern for others that is the basis of true courtesy. Again, because of their peck-order approach, authoritarians are the perpetuators of social hierarchies, so that those who inhabit such a hierarchy by choice are almost certainly authoritarians. Examples of such hierarchies include the military, church organisations, large businesses, and aristocracies. A particular form of authority that is much favoured because of its immutability is ancestry: so authoritarians are usually interested in pedigrees and, in the nature versus nurture controversy concerning the origin of personality, they favour nature. There are two kinds of authoritarian: dominant and subservient — or, ego-dominant and oge-dominant.

Non-authoritarians, on the other hand, lack these characteristics and have a live-and-let-live attitude. They are open-minded, flexible and creative, and act towards others with sensitivity rather than formality.

✶

The significance of all this is shown by the fact that some of those major movements in our history which give us ground for believing in **progress in civilisation**, are movements in which non-authoritarianism took over. The rise of modern science is one such, since science is characterised by a rejection of all human or divine authorities, such as Aristotle, Galen, and the church. The development of political freedom, from Magna Carta onwards, is another. Others are the Reformation; the flowering of the arts in ancient Greece and again in the Renaissance; and modern rejection of discrimination: rejections such as feminism and anti-racism. The concept of progress involved is, of course, that of hekergy increase. Two kinds are involved: the hekergy increase of society, which we call progress in civilisation, and the hekergy increase in the minds of those who participate in this progress. This latter is the cure, to some degree, of the previously mentioned unhealthy state of ego-oge imbalance. To achieve an ego-oge balance is to obtain a greater configuration hekergy of the mind as a whole.

✶

Another unhealthy ego-oge phenomenon is **extremism**, a prejudice that is a product of the degree of dissimilarity between oge-lover and oge-enemy, to which there corresponds an equal degree of dissimilarity between persona and umbra. The greater this dissimilarity the greater an extremist is the person concerned: an extremist in politics, religion or both. An extremist is either an extreme radical or extreme reactionary, depending on whether they are oge-dominant or ego-dominant; and, because of such dominance, they are authoritarian.

✶

Another field in which ego-oge imbalance is of some interest is **moral philosophy**. One of the major problems in moral philosophy is the question of the origin of moral feelings and judgments. There are two, mutually opposed, traditional answers. One is that humans have a moral sense, through which they can recognise, and judge, right and wrong. This sense is, as it were, internal to the person concerned. The other answer externalises morality. According to this view a moral judgment is a matter of prudential assessment. Men, as a social group, make laws to protect the group, with rewards for obedience and, particularly, punishment for disobedience. It is then simply a matter of prudence to obey the laws; hence the law-abiding, or moral, person is so for prudential reasons. Once the theoretical possibility of an immoral law is recognised, both answers jointly have to be granted partial truth — since an internalist might obey an immoral law for prudential reasons and an externalist might concede its immorality. The point here is not the relative merits and demerits of the two positions, so much as the obvious relation of them to ego-oge imbalance. An oge-dominant individual will have no doubt about the existence of a moral sense because his oge will have sent him introspective experience of it. An ego-dominant individual, on the other hand, will lack such experience and fall back on prudence as an explanation of moral behaviour, simply by default. As is well known, theorists have a strong tendency to project their own situation onto the rest of the world. Freud's Oedipus complex and Adler's inferiority complex are famous examples. Consequently it is not surprising that moral theories arising from ego-oge imbalance should be given universal scope by their authors.

This matter of moral philosophy is relevant to the theory of crime treatments. Clearly, if morality is merely a matter of prudence then greater deterrents will reduce crime. However if criminals have a moral sense and commit crimes in spite of it, then it must be either because they are neurotic or because they are socially deprived and act from need: and in either case the reduction of crime within society requires rehabilitation of the criminal. If the externalist is correct then rehabilitation is useless for curing crime, and if the internalist is correct then deterrents are useless. According to the present theory, either method may be required, depending upon the criminal. If he is ego-dominant but incompetent or reckless in prudential assessments, then greater deterrents and even preventive detentions are in order; while if he is oge-dominant then rehabilitation is in order. It is even conceivable that a rehabilitation technique could be developed for making an ego-dominant type into an ego-oge balanced individual, in which case there would be no need for deterrents at all.

In the light of these two approaches to moral philosophy, we might ask if there is any genuine basis for morality, other than irrational oges and prudential behaviour. And of course there is: the good is hekergy, so that morally aware people will be concerned with the hekergy increase of society as well as with their own hekergy increases.

✳ ✳ ✳

The last feature of mind that we will consider in terms of ego-oge imbalance is **insanity**. It is not difficult to make out a good case for claiming that paranoiac schizophrenia is extreme oge-dominance, that egomania is extreme ego-dominance, that manic depression is an oscillation between great ego and oge dominance, and that suicide is murder of the individual by the oge.

An individual who was starved of love in childhood will suffer in two ways. His ego will be stunted, since love is necessary for ego growth; and his oge will not contain an oge-lover, since no apparent people loved him. He will be very oge-dominant in consequence, and, in ego-oge conflict his oge, lacking an oge-lover, will be ruthless. In such a situation the oge will have more control than the ego over what the individual does, and may even try to destroy the ego. The ego, being very weak, will have no recourse but falsehoods — the only strength it will be able to muster against the oge will be pretence of strength, pure bluff. All of this internal activity will be projected onto people in the empirical world. It will appear as the characteristic delusions of schizophrenia: delusions of persecution and of grandeur. Thus "They are persecuting me," "They are trying to kill me," and "They are hidden in the next room and are controlling my body with invisible rays" are examples of projections of the actual situation and "I am really Napoleon" (or Churchill, or Christ) are examples of projected attempts to bluff the oge. If the oge succeeds in destroying the ego, the resultant bodily inactivity would be catatonia. A desperate schizophrenic, convinced that "They" are trying to kill him, may in self-defence make a pre-emptive strike and start killing as many of "Them" as possible, thereby becoming a homicidal maniac. Such homicidal maniacs often end their killing spree with suicide — an oge act of revenge, as explained in a moment.

✶

In the case of extreme ego-dominance the individual is without oge functions. He is a type known as a psychopath or a sociopath. He is without moral feelings, without feelings for others, without conscience, shame, or guilt. Publicly he will behave morally, for prudential reasons — that is, for the same reason that he will not run across a busy street without looking: the consequences are dangerous. Such a person is capable, if his appetites so move him, of child rape; followed by murder that is merely prudential to escape identification. If he has any appropriate ability, he will become a millionaire or a dictator — having the advantage of greater ruthlessness over most of his competitors. If he has exceptional ability, as well as opportunity, he will become a Napoleon, Hitler, or Stalin, killing with as little compassion as has the ocean for the drowning sailor. Such insanity is **egomania**.

✶

Manic depression is characterised by an alternation of mood between elation and depression. **Depression** is the state of an ego that is being oppressed by the oge; **elation** is the state of an ego that is oppressing an oge. If this alternation is not excessive, it produces what is sometimes called the artistic temperament. But if extreme, there will be delusions of power and delusions of worthlessness. The individual will believe himself superman in one state, able to endure without sleep, a genius, a sexual athlete, etc., and, in the opposite state, worthy only of being destroyed like vermin. The delusions are only delusions when projected into the empirical world; so far as the real mind is concerned, they are genuine: the ego *does* have great power over the oge, and then the oge *is* cruelly oppressing the ego. So artistic temperament can be explained by supposing an oscillation between mild ego and oge dominances, and manic depression by great dominances. The oscillations may be explained by supposing that the greater the oppression of one agent by the other, the greater the impetus to fight back; if this impetus is delayed, an oscillation, rather than a steady state, will result.

✶

Lastly, one other form of insanity is **suicide**. Suicide is not rationally comprehensible if there exists only an ego in the mind and it is subject to the mind hekergy principle. But in the present context suicide is readily explained. It is an oge act, a destruction of the individual for what the oge believes to be the good of society. Two pre-conditions are required: the belief, by the oge, that the individual's death would be an advantage to society; and a temporary weakness of the ego, of which the oge can take advantage — such as a large loss or failure. The ego's temporary weakness is, of course, characterised by depression. The fact that the ego may still fight back against the oge is one explanation why so many attempted suicides do not succeed. Suicide may also be pseudo-suicide: an attempt at suicide, by the ego, designed to win help, sympathy or pity from other people — that is, from the oge. The attempt is, of course, designed not to succeed. When a suicide does succeed, we naturally can never know whether it was caused by the oge, or by the ego unintentionally overdoing it.

✶

All of these explanations of insanity have in common the feature of a conquest in the conflict between ego and oge. This is so even in the case of manic depression, although the victory is only temporary, and seesaws between ego and oge. Such conquest is quite different from the stable state of advantage that occurs in ego-dominance and oge dominance, since in the latter the weaker agent is only disadvantaged, not destroyed or nearly destroyed. This in turn leads to the question of why an ego-oge imbalance should be stable in this way, rather than lead to insanity. That is, if an individual is ego-dominant, say, and has ego-oge conflict, then why does not the ego steadily weaken the oge to the point of its destruction? The answer lies in the distinction, made earlier, between first stage and second stage growth of egos and oges [176]. At the first stage level of development ego and oge can only grow at each other's expense, so that an imbalance in their relative strengths will be unstable and eventually lead to insanity. At the second stage level of development ego and oge can each do their own mapping of the mid-world in order to grow, so that the greater strength of one does not lead to malnutrition of the other. It follows from this that, whatever the chronological age of the individual concerned, insanity occurs only in the mentally immature: in those who have not yet reached second stage growth.

The distinction between first and second stage oge is also relevant when considering the interaction between the oge and apparent people. This can occur in two ways: projection, in which oge attitudes are projected onto apparent people — a process of filtration, as we saw [196] — and introjection, in which the attitudes of respected apparent people (or, more precisely, mid-people) cause changes of oge attitude. In first stage growth there is introjection from only a few, centrally important, apparent people: usually the apparent parents, predominantly. In the case of all other apparent people, projection occurs. In the second stage oge there is usually more introjection than projection; not only because the oge is larger and so has a greater variety of attitudes of apparent people in its constituent memories, but also because it can make finer discriminations in attitudes of others because of doing its own mapping, so that respect is more likely to be generated, for various reasons.

✳ ✳ ✳

The remainder of this chapter will be concerned with a miscellany of explanations by means of the concept of oge.

✳

Malice is a matter of an ego, seeking a hekergy increase, obtaining an illusion of it by decreasing the hekergy of the oge. In so far as the ego assesses its own hekergy relative to that of the oge, so will a decrease of oge hekergy seem to produce an increase of ego hekergy. If the ego is attacking the oge at large, the malice will take the form of **vandalism**. In such cases the ego may be aided by the oge-enemy and the umbra, so as to perform acts that the rest of the oge and the ego consider evil: arson, for example, or other acts of destruction. Directed towards specific oge-persons it may be expressed as practical jokes, pity (which is compassion adulterated with malice), spite, or various kinds of ill-favours. Related to malice is **gossip**. This is a process of oge communicating with oge, within a particular community, so as to establish who is worthy of oge action in the form of blame, ostracism, etc. When gossip is aided by the ego it is usually because of ego malice. Gossip can, of course, work with praise rather than blame; but this is much more rare. When it occurs, the person concerned becomes a public hero.

✶

Hypnotism is quite a straightforward matter in terms of the oge. A person who is hypnotised is one in whom the ego has abdicated control of the body in favour of the oge. The ego has "gone to sleep," but the oge has not. The oge controls the body according to the wishes of "Them" — that is, in this case, the introjected wishes of the hypnotist. Indeed, the hypnotist-oge collaboration is the cause of the ego going to sleep in the first place. Because of the key role of the oge in hypnotism we can explain that previously peculiar fact that people under hypnotism cannot behave immorally by their own standards. Obviously not: the oge, the custodian of morals, is in control during the hypnotic action.

✶

Possibly connected with hypnotism is another strange phenomenon: **sleep walking**. An explanation of mind that has only one agent within a mind cannot account for the body walking, and behaving with remarkable control, when that one agent is unconscious. But sleep walking, while the ego is unconscious, is in principle quite simple in terms of the oge: as in hypnotic action, the oge is in control.

It should be obvious that the potential for either hypnotism or sleep walking are indicative of oge-dominance.

✶

Fashion is an oge phenomenon: fashionable people are following the dictates of their oges concerning the latest fashion, while leaders of fashion are people who are both creative and ego-dominant, producing new fashions that are acceptable to the fashionable. Fashions are dynamic because novelty is transient.

✶

The **feeling of being watched**, while committing a guilty act in private, is not merely a fancy, but a fact: one is being watched at such a time, but by the oge rather than by apparent people.

✶

Self-sacrifice is more correctly described in terms of oge sacrifice. The oge sacrifices the individual for the good of society. Other oges in that society naturally approve of such behaviour and may make a hero of the individual. This is expressed on war-memorials as "They gave their lives for their country" — a falsehood, since it was their oges who gave their lives.

✳

A good deal of **primitive magic** can be explained by means of the oge. For example, if a man knows that the evil-eye has been cast upon him; and he, and hence his oge, know that everyone else in the community knows; and all concerned believe the evil-eye to be efficacious: then he will die. His oge will kill him, and his ego will not resist, since it believes resistance to be useless. Various other spells and charms would be expected to work in a similar manner. Thus a man cursed could be made inept by his oge and thereby suffer misfortune. A reluctant maiden or an impotent lover, knowing a love potion to have been administered, could have their behaviour changed accordingly by the oge.

The importance of names in magic — particularly of "true" or "secret" names — is shown by the fact that if a name is bonded to an idea then the idea may be summoned into the ego's consciousness by means of the name when it could not be summoned by L.A.L. alone. As we will see later, it is not unreasonable that particular oge-persons within the oge-enemy be called **demons** [293]. A large part of black magic is concerned with the summoning and control of demons through knowledge of their true names.

With all primitive magic, oge-dominance is a necessary condition for efficacy; since, as we will see, education strengthens the ego, such magic should be expected to work only among the ill-educated.

✳

Ghosts can be explained as the appearance of representations of oge-persons in the apparent world of the ego, as visible figures or voices, as can revelatory **visions** of saints or angels [294].

✳

Another feature of human behaviour explained by the oge is the extraordinarily widespread belief in **astrology**, as shown by the fact that most daily newspapers publish horoscopes. This belief in astrology was, originally, the belief that the planets, fixed in crystalline (transparent) concentric spheres, rotated around the heavens and determined one's future.

This is not unintelligent, since the Sun and the Moon influence us in the form of light and the tides; but today, with our knowledge of astronomy, such a belief is obviously false. However, we have already seen that intuition [172] is the ego's awareness of some other part of the theoretical mind, so it is conceivable that many egos could intuit the existence of the oge; and the oge has many features that make it a basis for astrology. First and foremost, it determines one's future in the sense of being one's fate, in that if one is ego-dominant or oge-dominant, or has neurotic conflict with the oge, this will have a considerable effect on one's future behaviour. Secondly, because each person's empirical world is within their ego and the oge is outside the ego, the oge can be described as being beyond heaven, beyond the blue sky — which is where the crystalline spheres of the astrologer are supposed to be. Thirdly, the oge is a thin shell which is transparent in the sense that it filters perception. Thus the widespread belief in astrology is to some extent justified, in spite of it being ridiculous in the light of modern science. It is ridiculous because it is misplaced, from the oge on to the empirical-cum-theoretical planets. Once this projection is corrected, the belief in astrology is much more true; but such correction means discarding as irrelevant the newspaper horoscopes, the zodiacal signs, and the positions of the planets.

✳

A **public ritual** [298] is an oge recognition and acceptance of whatever the ritual signifies: a rite of passage such as a wedding or graduation, or presentation of a medal or other award. Perhaps it is because our own society has abandoned many of these rituals that our teenagers are troubled and rebellious. They have to change from dependent childhood, irresponsible and unfree, to independent adulthood, responsible and free; and this involves considerable ego-oge adjustment. It is interesting that a great deal of youthful rebellion is clearly rebellion against the oge. That is, it is no more than a desire to shock. Thus in the 1920's young women adopted the facial make-up that until then was the badge of the prostitute, as well as shockingly short skirts, and very loud voices. In the 1960's boys adopted the long hair and clothing colours of the opposite sex. Neither action was immoral in the sense of doing social harm, but it was so in terms of affront to the oges of all concerned. Naturally such rebellions are initiated by ego-dominant individuals, who, as leaders, are later followed by their oge-dominant peers, once the action is becoming prescribed within that peer group. Because all the oges concerned rapidly adjust, and accept what is widespread just because it is widespread, the power to affront the oge with a specific rebellion quickly wanes, like any other fashion.

✶

Given the concept of oge, the distinguishing of a number of kinds of maturity is possible. **Maturation** is, in the first place, growth; which is to say, increase of summation hekergy. In terms of this we can distinguish between maturity of ego and maturity of oge. Thus in an ego-dominant person the ego may be more mature than the oge, and the other way round in an oge-dominant person. Equally, a first stage ego or oge will be immature, while a mature one will be a second stage one. Furthermore, increase of configuration hekergy also is increase of maturity. In terms of this an ego-dominant or an oge-dominant individual is, *qua* individual, immature compared with one in whom there is relative balance and harmony between ego and oge, with ego-oge overlap in the oge-lover. This in turn leads to the theoretical possibility of a state of maximum configuration hekergy of the real mind; this possibility will be examined in Chapter 18.

✶

We can also explain why love and hate are akin. If an apparent person is loved then he or she belongs in the oge-lover as an oge-person, or set of mid-memories. If love for that apparent person ceases for any reason then the oge-person must leave the oge-lover and go elsewhere. It cannot usually go to oge-family, oge-friends, oge-strangers or oge-foreigners because it is none of these. So it must go to the oge-enemy, which is hated by the ego.

✶

Finally, those who are familiar with the psychological discoveries of C. G. Jung will be interested in considering that the oge will explain much of what he called **the collective unconscious**. That is, the public portion of the oge is the collective unconscious, and the private portions — at each pole — are the **personal unconscious**. I do not propose to expound Jung's position here, but will only mention a few points.

The archetypes of the collective unconscious can be explained as oge persons, except for the persona and the umbra. For example, the **anima** in a man and the **animus** in a woman are the ideals of the opposite sex, and as such are characteristic of the oge-beloved of the person concerned, through which an infatuated person perceives an empirical beloved. However a major disagreement between the present theory and Jung's is that Jung supposed the collective unconscious to be *one* unconscious mind, common to all individuals; whereas the present theory requires each individual to have his or her own unconscious mind, all of these being collective — public — by similarity. I would claim that Jung is in error on this point; the error is the identity error, the same error which common sense makes in supposing that many near-similar apparent worlds are one.

The bulk of Jung's psychotherapeutic practice was what he called the process of individuation. Without going into any details of this, we can say that it is essentially a process of ego-oge communication (the oge represented by an analyst) in which conflict is resolved and co-operative harmony established.

In this context, it is of course necessary to acknowledge Freud, who, in spite of numerous errors, did more for theoretical psychology than probably any other thinker. There is considerable resemblance between his concept of superego and the present concept of oge; and between his concept of id, and the present one of oge-enemy. However, there are also considerable differences. Freud never, as far as I know, explicitly made the id and the superego agents — that is, complexes both conscious and able to act — although implicitly they must obviously be such. And their inter-relationship was different, also: Freud supposed the id to be primitive, such that out of it the ego grew, and out of the ego the superego grew. Again, Freud's concept of mind was energetic, rather than hekergetic, with the id the source of the energy, or libido. Although no mention of mental energy has so far been made in the present theory, the concept is easily derived — both from the L.A.L.R.U. formula, and from the mind hckcrgy principle, which provide drives — appetites and creativity.

13. Value and Feeling.

In the next two chapters we will be dealing with feeling and thinking, in that order. The distinction, within consciousness, of these two has already been made [161]: we can distinguish between the structures of real ideas, which are meanings; and hekergies of them, which are their values. Consciousness of meaning is then the L.A.L. reaction in the ego to structure, and consciousness of value is the reaction to hekergy. These can each be called a thought and a feeling, respectively — as opposed to the dynamic processes in which thoughts succeed each other, which is thinking, and feelings succeed each other, which is feeling as a process. Consciousness is always dynamic, so that these distinctions would not have to be made were it not for the fact that momentary states of consciousness can be as it were frozen by language. Language can communicate individual *thoughts* — propositions — by means of sentences, as well as communicate *thinking* by means of a succession of sentences. A precisely parallel situation does not hold for feelings, so we do not ordinarily distinguish, linguistically, between individual feelings and the process of going from one to another of these in succession.

Since the hekergy of an idea is a part of its structure, it follows that a feeling is an awareness of one kind of meaning. It is a very special kind of meaning, because of its significance in L.A.L. Hekergy is an important parameter in L.A.L., and hence in consciousness; consequently it will generally be the case that the consciousness of hekergies — that is, feelings — will be much more vivid than other meanings within the apparent mind.

That consciousness of feelings is a dynamic process is easily shown. In the first place, the apparent world is usually changing, so that the ego's reaction to the hekergies therein will also change. Secondly, a particular feeling may change the attitude of the ego, which in turn changes both the feeling, and the attention of the ego. Even when the apparent world is static — as in contemplating a painting — this can lead to a long train of various feelings.

The point has also already been made [134] that all values are hekergies; I also claim that all hekergies are values. Consequently we can say that all feelings, since they are ego reactions to hekergies, are evaluative: all feelings are reactions, by the ego, to values; these are, of course, normally conscious feelings: we must allow feelings to the oge as well, and these also will be evaluative.

In what follows we will first clarify the meanings of feeling, sensation, and emotion. This will be followed by a short explanation of discrimination, recognition and naming of feelings. Then the two points — that all values are hekergies and that all feelings are evaluative — will be amplified with reference to particular values and feelings: truth, beauty, goodness, humour, social feelings, etc.

✳ ✳ ✳

The words *feeling* and *sensation* are often used interchangeably in English because the classes of things they denote intersect. As we have seen, a sensation is either a level-2 real idea in the mid-world, in which case it is a mid-sensation; or else it is an empirical sensation, which is the ego's reaction to a mid-sensation. An empirical sensation is any concrete, or secondary, quality, such as a colour, sound, taste, or smell. A feeling is the ego's reaction to a hekergy or hekergy change. These overlap in the sensual realm, where some sensations are sensations of hekergy changes in the apparent body. Sensual pleasure and pain, as we saw in Chapter 11 [165], are sensations because they occur in the empirical body; but they are also feelings in that they are consciousness of hekergy changes. Sensations of touch and temperature are also called feelings, as in "It feels rough" and "I feel hot." However, with the understanding that sensual feelings are sensations, the word feeling will not here otherwise be used to refer to sensations.

Emotions are distinguished from feelings in that an emotion is a feeling plus a correlated bodily innervation. The latter comes about through the motor mind; a motor idea therein is bonded to a feeling and produces an innervation in the real body. This may be perceived by the ego as an apparent bodily sensation, and, if perceptible, by others, in their apparent worlds, as some form of emotive expression. Such innervations are smiling, frowning, blushing, laughter, trembling, sweating, heart acceleration, diversion of blood from the stomach to the brain, discharge of adrenalin, etc. We may suppose that the bonding of certain feelings with motor ideas is **instinctive** — that is, genetic. The innervation that results serves to communicate the feeling to others, who have a genetic, or innate, mid-idea by means of which they can recognise the expression instinctively, and/or prepare the real body for the action appropriate to the feeling, such as fight, flight, or sexual activity. In what follows, the word feeling will not refer to an emotion. Thus *feeling of fear* will refer to the ego's reaction to a fearful situation, while *emotion of fear* will refer to this feeling plus the bodily innervations bonded to it.

★

The fact of emotions complicates the question of discrimination, recognition, and naming of feelings because, from a behavioural point of view, there is no way to distinguish between the instinctive reaction of an emotion and a reaction based on discrimination and recognition. "Is this love?" a youth might ask himself of a novel feeling in reaction to a potential mate; but, provided his instincts are not crippled by taboos or neurosis, he will not have any questions about what to do about the concurrent emotional desires. The doubt over the feeling is due to lack of experience, hence non-recognition; the lack of doubt about wooing is due to instinct. Consequently the appearance of discrimination of feelings, as described next, may not be genuine.

Discrimination of feelings produces ideas of feelings by special mappings, which latter, since they have already been explained in principle, we can simply assume. The concept of an idea of a feeling should, of course, be familiar: we can have a feeling of shame, and an idea of shame — indeed, this very sentence should communicate the latter. The idea of a feeling is, usually, devoid of that feeling. To speak of shame does not, in normal people, produce a feeling of shame; it only produces the idea of shame. We can explain this by remembering that there is a difference between a value — a hekergy — and the feeling that it produces. A memory of the hekergy will recreate the feeling when remembered (although, since most memories are homomorphs — that is, less vivid than their originals — the feeling will be less intense); but a map of the feeling — or rather, a particular part of it — will not. Just as a description of a funny situation will amuse, but a description of the laughter which that situation produces will not.

Because there are ideas of feelings, it follows that recognition and naming of feelings are the same as with other ideas. Once a special mapping has occurred, L.A.L. will produce the appropriate idea of a feeling, which will be bonded to a name: mid-memories of written and spoken word plus motor ideas to produce them. Thus, the idea of a feeling is the meaning of the name for that feeling. For example the idea of shame is what is denoted by the word shame. (The idea of shame in turn denotes feelings of shame, transitively. Denotation will be further examined in the next chapter.) And the idea of shame is also what enables the ego to recognise the feeling of shame when it occurs.

✳ ✳ ✳

When it comes to the claim that all values are hekergies, it is not, of course, possible to prove this beyond doubt. This is because we are explaining values by means of hekergy, so that at best the explanation can be made very probable. To this end we have already seen considerable argument by analogy — such as, both values and hekergies are usually hard to gain but easily lost. Another argument that I will emphasise here is the one based on the concept of perfection [134]. (It is only a probable argument, not a demonstrative one, because of the fallacy called undistributed middle [15n].)

Except for humour — an exception the fact of which will be seen to be further argument that values are hekergies — any value can be conceived of as perfect. That is, the possibility, in principle, of perfection is a necessary condition of being a value. There are three characteristics of perfection: (i) it cannot be improved upon — that is, it is the maximum magnitude of the value concerned; (ii) its form or structure is unique — any alteration whatever to its form diminishes it; and (iii) departure from perfection produces alternative equivalent possibilities at a rate that rapidly increases relative to the number of departures.

These three characteristics are, of course, also characteristics of maximum hekergy. Maximum hekergy, by definition, cannot be increased. At this level, the number of equivalent configurations, the number e in the expression $\ln(t/e)$, is a minimum, which means that in all but simple cases it is one — that is, the configuration is unique. And as the number of changes to this configuration increases, the number of equivalent configurations increases exponentially.

The three kinds of value under which philosophers have traditionally subsumed all others are truth, beauty, and goodness. We will consider an example of each to illustrate this equivalence of perfection and maximum hekergy.

Similarity truth, as we have already seen, may be exemplified by a photograph or a road map. Let us suppose that we have a perfectly true map: that is, every spot in it resembles its original terrain. Suppose, for simplicity,

216

that it is quite a small map, so that the total number of spots in it is one million. If we allow one departure from perfection, the number of possible ways in which this could occur is one million — that is, any one of the spots could be false, non-resembling. If we allow two departures, the number of possibilities is almost a million million. If we allow three departures, it is nearly a million million million. If we allow half a million departures the number of possibilities is astronomically large, and a maximum. As the number of departures increases from half a million to a million the number of possibilities decreases again to one million and then to one. Clearly, the hekergy of the map, as defined by the degree of similarity between it and the terrain, is a maximum when the map is perfectly true or perfectly false, and a minimum when it is half-true. (This is what was called a simple case in the last paragraph but one: the number of perfect forms, although a minimum, is not one; if more than one kind of hekergy were involved this would no longer be so.) A perfectly false map is like a perfect black and white photographic negative, in which every element that should be black is transparent and vice versa. A map that is perfectly uniformly false is easily corrected, just as a photographic positive is easily obtained from a photographic negative. But a map that is only half true is the most difficult to correct; just as a photographic negative that is only half true records the least information — it is almost certainly a uniform grey, a chaotic mixture of black and white elements. It is for this reason that a half-truth is of least value. Consider liars: suppose that you know that a particular man lies all of the time, and that another man lies half of the time; in the first case you can easily obtain truth, but in the second you cannot.

A similar situation holds for beauty. Suppose a perfect piece of music, and consider an increasing proportion of wrong notes — to say nothing of wrong emphases, tempos, etc.

An example of perfect goodness is the Sunday school concept of heaven, in which perfect justice is meted out: billions of souls get the only fair reward or punishment; the same arithmetic applies again.

A particular form of both goodness and beauty is harmony (in the various meanings of the word) of which there are far fewer forms than there are of discord. Recall that Plato defined justice as harmony between the parts: between the three parts of a soul, for a just man, and between the three parts of society, for a just city state — what we would call a mentally healthy man and a healthy society.

✶

Humour is interesting in this connection because although we value the humourous, we never associate it with the possibility of perfection. We can explain the humourous by saying that it is hekergy in the forms of goodness, beauty, or, particularly, truth that is of such magnitude that it is at once too low to be mistaken for truth etc. and too high for the ego to fail to value it. There is no word in English to characterise something that pretends to the truth without pretending to deceive, but perhaps incongruity comes close.

It should be remarked here that by the humourous is not meant any of a number of alternative possible causes of laughter. Namely: malice, as in derision and practical jokes; relief from tension; hysterical or neurotic compulsions to shriek or giggle; or various motives to assumed laughter, such as geniality or flattery.

✶

In considering the claim that all feelings are evaluative it is first necessary to clarify the meaning of *evaluative* used here. In the first place, it should be understood that the converse claim is not being made: not all evaluations are a matter of feeling, since some may be the product of habit or of calculation. Secondly, all feelings are evaluative because we are here explaining feelings as reactions of the ego (or the oge) to hekergies, and these hekergies are values; but since not all the hekergies are properly discriminated as such, as we will see, their feelings are not normally considered evaluative. We must also note that feelings are necessarily very subjective, for a simple reason. They are based on hekergy, in L.A.L. The force of L.A.L., as we saw [149], is proportional to the product of two hekergies, H_1 and H_2. If H_1 is the value that is producing the feeling, then H_2 is that of the ego — the total hekergy of the ego. Obviously, this latter is going to affect the feeling considerably and so make it subjective. Secondly, the kinds of hekergy in the ego will affect the feeling, since degrees of likeness between H_1 and various parts of the ego also determine L.A.L. force. This second subjectivity is due largely to attitude and attention of the ego. An example of such subjectivity is the cry of "unfair" by a child who is losing a game, by an entrepreneur who dislikes the competition, or by a trade union spokesman who deplores technological obsolescence.

To argue the claim that all feelings are evaluative, I will examine in turn a variety of feelings and explain them in terms of evaluation. The feelings that will here be considered are: feelings of conviction, scepticism, significance, and irrelevance; aesthetic feelings; selfish feelings — glory and grief; moral feelings — right, wrong, good, evil, embarrassment, praise, and blame; feelings of neurotic anxiety, insecurity, and guilt; desires and aversions — greed, lust, avarice, disgust, etc.; amusement — malicious or humourous; and feelings of depression, elation, happiness, unhappiness, confidence, despair; and love — feeling of love, being in love, and loving.

✻ ✻ ✻

Feelings concerning truth are, to varying degrees, feelings of conviction and scepticism. Degree of conviction, of which scepticism is the lower portion of the scale, is strength of belief, or probability — as we saw in Part Two [75]. It was there stated as a simple matter of psychological fact that strength of rational belief in reportables is proportional to potentially universal publicity and strength of rational belief in strict imperceptibles is proportional to the explanatory power of the belief, and that various criteria have been discovered which determine this power of explanation. Strength of irrational belief is a third kind, which also needs to be explained. It is an introspective fact that conviction, and its degree, are a matter of feeling. Consequently we now need to show that conviction is a form of hekergy.

✻

Let us begin with irrational belief. A belief, as we have seen [161], is any proposition that is incorporated into the ego, as opposed to being considered by the ego. As a part of the ego it exists due to L.A.L., and so is irrational. It may be an intrinsically rational belief, learned by the ego from a more rational person, whom the ego accepts as an authority, and then irrationally incorporated into the ego; or it may be an intrinsically irrational belief, formed by L.A.L., such as a superstitious or stereotypical belief. In either case it becomes a prejudice and selects evidence by L.A.L. The degree of conviction that the ego has in it depends on two hekergies: the summation hekergy of the belief itself, and the configuration hekergy that results from the combination of the belief with the ego. The first depends mostly on the size of the belief: on the amount of evidence that it has collected in its own favour. The second is experienced by the ego as the *importance* of the belief: this, of course, is importance *to the ego*, what the ego might state as "Important to me," and this importance is experienced by the ego as a feeling. That is, the importance of the belief is the value of the belief, to the ego. If the belief is a rationalisation, hiding the ego's own weakness or evil from itself, it will be very important; while if it contributes little or nothing to the configuration hekergy of the ego, it will be unimportant. In both cases hekergy is involved, and hence feelings: these feelings are feelings of conviction in the truth of the beliefs. Consequently a person of little rationality is one unwilling to increase the number of his beliefs, because to do so would be to reduce harmony — that is, reduce hekergy — contrary to the mind-hekergy principle. Such reluctance, usually revealed as a refusal to consider alternatives, is of course, characteristic of a bigot and of a fundamentalist. It is noteworthy that the metaphor of *a small mind* is usually attributed to bigots, as well as to those with a stunted ego; indeed, the two frequently go together. We thus see why prejudices are irrational beliefs, which can produce strong feelings of conviction, and that a person whose beliefs are largely irrational has a closed mind. The fact of one's beliefs being irrational is also indicated if they are compartmentalised. This device, of never considering the beliefs of more than one compartment at a time, conceals the discord between those of different compartments. An authoritarian [201] is closed-minded, and thus a bigot; this happens because his standard of truth is an authority, hence prejudicial.

✳

Scientists and philosophers, as long as they are being rational, seek rational beliefs; this is because to them the summation hekergy of the belief, and the configuration hekergy it produces when harmonising with other beliefs, are more important than the configuration hekergy that it gives to the ego. (Psychologically, we say that this is because of a strong curiosity; and this is explained by saying that curiosity in young animals has survival value in that it teaches them a great deal about their empirical worlds. We see such curiosity in children, and the absence of it in most adults: but in scientists, philosophers, and other inquisitive people it is neotenous: it continues into adulthood.) And these rational beliefs are not irrationally incorporated into the ego, but into another, third, complex which is characterised by rationality; it is called the psychohelios, and will be discussed in Chapter 18.

For now we can say that rationality is the use of reason to correct false beliefs, as opposed to **sophistry**, which is the use of reason to bolster false beliefs.

We saw earlier [51] that there are two kinds of rational belief: existential beliefs, which are beliefs in reportables, and explanatory beliefs, which are beliefs in strict imperceptibles; and that the criteria for the truth of these are the criteria of good science. Rational beliefs are rational because the propositions within them are arranged with maximum hekergy; this is both our definition and our explanation of rationality. Clearly, such maximum hekergies will be the basis of feelings of conviction in the truth of rational beliefs. So we need to show that the various criteria of good science lead to high hekergies.

The criteria of empirical science, it will be recalled [70], are: objectivity, repeatability of experiments, and preference for quantitative data over qualitative data. And the criteria for theoretical science [77], and for all other explanations as well, are: explanations must not be inconsistent or contrary to empirical fact, which latter is the potentially universally public features of empirical worlds; and they should have large scope and density of detail, predict empirical novelty successfully, harmonise with other rational explanations, contain symmetries, and be simple and elegant. We now need to show both that these criteria lead to truth, and that such truth has high hekergy.

The kind of truth in this is similarity truth. Resemblance between relations was defined [112] as a matter of degree: $s/(s+d+m)$, where s is the number of similar properties between the two relations, d the number of dissimilar properties, and m the excess number of properties of one relation over the other. The same formula applies to low-level structures, where s is the number of corresponding parts that are similar, d the number that are dissimilar, and m the number of parts that do not have corresponding parts in the other. This assumes that between corresponding parts there are atomic likes or dislikes. At higher level structures the resemblance between corresponding parts will be a matter of degree rather than two-valued, and so the overall degree of similarity is the average of these. As we have just seen, the greater the degree of similarity, the greater the hekergy. So the greater the similarity truth of some proposition or theory, the more valuable it is.

We know similarity truth in the first place when we compare a memory with its original, and have good reason to believe that the original has not changed in the interval: the arrangement of furniture in the living room, for example. We also know similarity truth in science when we compare a scientific law with an empirical instance of it, and when we compare theories with the laws that they explain. The similarity truths that we do not know are those between empirical science and reality, and between theoretical science and reality — because reality is strictly imperceptible, and you cannot perceive a relation if you cannot perceive all of its terms. In those cases we rely on what might be called indications of similarity truth, or evidence of similarity truth. Some of these have high hekergy in their own right, such as successful prediction, scope and density of detail, simplicity and elegance, and harmony with other explanations. Some of these indicate similarity truth directly, as with the two kinds of prediction, of repetition and of novelty, and scope and density of detail; and the others indicate similarity truth indirectly because there are good reasons (as explained in Chapter 17) to believe the theoretical world to be elegant, simple, and coherent. Another of the criteria has been discovered to be an indication of, or evidence for, similarity truth, over centuries of trial and error — namely, potential universal publicity, both in empirical worlds and in minds — the latter in the form of rationality of theories. And, of course, explanations that are contrary to empirical fact or which contain contradictions are necessarily resemblance false, even if they have high hekergy in the form of beauty or simplicity; they are false because the fundamental principle of philosophy is that the theoretical world — reality — cannot contain contradictions, and because empirical fact is all that is potentially universally public. Dissimilarity falsity is non-resemblance, which has low hekergy.

Thus, similarity truth has high hekergy and we value it accordingly.

✶

A second feeling that arises in connection with truth is the feeling of **significance**. An idea or a proposition can only be significant in a context, and it will be more significant in some contexts than others. Generally speaking, it will be very significant in only one, or a few, contexts — which suggests right away that a hekergy is involved. We can see what it is if we consider an extreme case by analogy. Consider a jigsaw puzzle that is assembled except for one piece. Only one size, shape, and colouring of a piece will allow the completion of the puzzle. Completeness or wholeness has a high hekergy because it is produced by a unifying emergent relation that contributes configuration hekergy. Consequently, that unique piece, relative to the rest of the jigsaw puzzle, realises a large jump in hekergy. Similarly, one idea or proposition may realise a large jump in the hekergy of a rational context. It is this hekergy that, evaluated by the ego, produces the feeling of significance, relative to that context. Clearly, the criterion used above by which a belief harmonises with other beliefs is that of significance in a context. Alternatively, we earlier saw that harmony has hekergy; and significance in a context can be explained as harmony with a context. Coherence, and so coherence truth, is a special case of harmony. Conversely, if an evaluation of significance is sought and produces no feeling of significance because of disharmony, the feeling that does result is that of **irrelevance**.

✷ ✷ ✷

All aesthetic feelings are, I will claim, feelings arising from ego evaluations of **beauty**. That is, certain kinds of hekergy, when recognised, are called beautiful. They are values, and as such produce feelings in the ego that are aesthetic feelings. An attempt by the ego to recreate, in the apparent world, the hekergy or hekergies concerned is an attempt at artistic creation. It should be noted that a successful work of art is at once an expression of the artist's feelings, an artifact possessing value (specifically, beauty), and a communication of feeling in as far as the spectator reacts to the various values with feelings similar to those of the artist.

There is one form of beauty that most people rarely or never experience: mathematical beauty. This is because most people strongly dislike, not to say fear, mathematics — probably because of bad teaching, due to the fact that mathematics is such a difficult subject to teach. However, most people remember a bit of mathematics from high school, including, usually, Pythagoras' Theorem about right-angled triangles. There is a mathematically beautiful proof of this theorem — that the area of the square on the side opposite the right angle, or the square on the hypotenuse, is equal to the sum of the areas of the squares on the other two sides — a proof that is both very simple and offered here as an illustration of mathematical beauty, Fig. 13.1. Recall that the area of a triangle is half of the length of its base, b, multiplied by its height, a — that is, ab/2; and that any two triangles

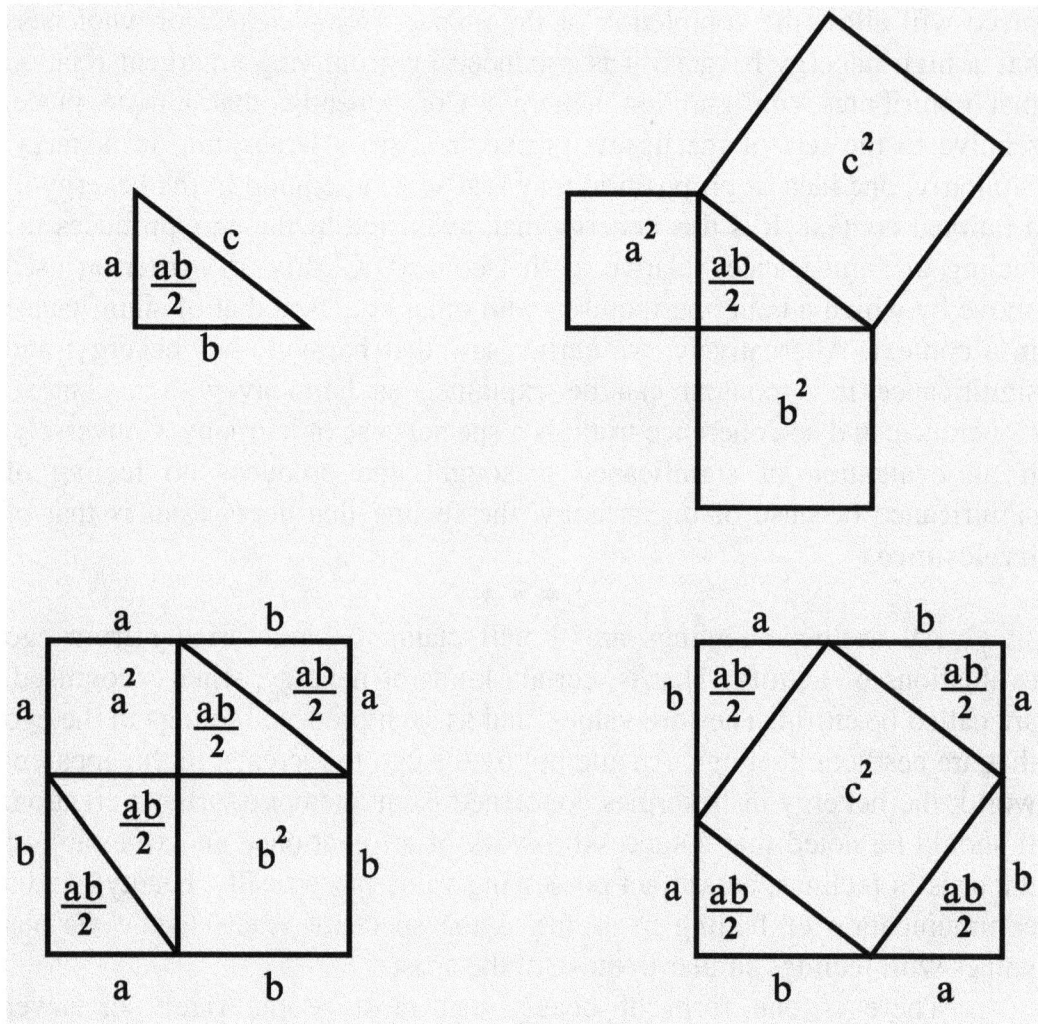

Fig.13.1.

that have the same lengths of sides, a, b, and c, are similar in all other respects.

✶ ✶ ✶

When it comes to feelings in reaction to the good, we have already seen that what is good for the ego is selfish and what is good for the oge is moral. Consequently we can distinguish selfish feelings and moral feelings. There is also the overall good of the real mind, the concern with which I will call **ethics**; but this can wait until Part Four.

Selfish feelings require little explanation. They are simply the ego's reaction to hekergies that the ego tries to possess. These include pleasures, and the avoidance of pains. Mental pleasures are those arising from achievement and mental pains are those arising from defeat or loss — such as glory and grief.

Moral feelings at first sight would seem to belong to the oge, not to the ego, making it difficult to understand how the ego can experience them: feelings such as those of right and wrong, good and evil, pride and shame, and embarrassment. But the explanation is simple. In all of these cases the ego is reacting to the attitude of the oge. Attitude is structure and hence has hekergies, so will produce feeling. The intensity of moral feelings can be accounted for, in mature people, by ego-oge overlap: the ego overlaps the oge-lover and so shares its moral feelings. Other intense moral feelings may be neurotic, as with the puritan's desire to make laws that repress pleasure. Yet other moral feelings, in the ego, arise from the oge's attitude to some proposition or to some state of affairs in the apparent world and thence to the ego's reaction to this oge attitude. For example, a feeling of embarrassment arises from the oge's attitude toward the breaking of a taboo, or a feeling of outrage arises from witnessing someone else's immoral behaviour. Praise and blame have already been discussed: we saw that they are forms of pleasure and pain — rewards and punishments inflicted by the oge for moral control. Neurotic anxiety and insecurity are feelings produced by the oge, and neurotic guilt is the ego's reaction to constant neurotic blaming by the oge. Persistent feelings such as these are sometimes called free-floating because the ego is unaware of their origin and pins them onto whatever is appropriate in the apparent world at that time. Thus, an individual might have free-floating guilt, free-floating anxiety, free-floating fear, free-floating contempt, or free-floating anger.

Note that an oge that is causing guilt feelings because of some ego crime or lesser immoral action will continue to react by blaming, every time the memory of the crime comes to its attention: that is, it will punish the ego every time it remembers the crime. The oge cannot, by itself, grant absolution. To grant absolution requires that the oge change its attitude toward this particular crime, by introjection, and this is possible only if at least one apparent person, or preferably all apparent people, relent. Thus confession can lead to forgiveness by an apparent person, and this forgiveness would then be introjected into the oge. The forgiveness may be conditional upon some form of reparation; this makes confession an essential first step to absolution, followed by the reparation by way of payment for the relenting. Without this forgiveness the ego may continue to suffer pangs of guilt for the rest of its life.

✳ ✳ ✳

The emotive feelings should require little explanation as evaluations: **desire** is based on the evaluation of possible pleasure, **aversion** on possible pain; depending upon the kind of pleasure or pain — the kind of hekergy increase or decrease — so may the feelings be greed, lust, avarice, disgust, etc. The fact that these are emotive feelings is subsequent to, not prior to, their being evaluations: the feeling, which is an evaluation, is bonded to those motor ideas that produces the bodily innervations that characterise the emotion.

✳

Amusement is a feeling that is an evaluation of either malice or humour.

✳

Those feelings that are described as states of mind are here more correctly described as states of ego — or, rather, as evaluations of states of ego. That is, the ego evaluates part of itself, or its extrinsic relations. Thus feelings of **depression** and **elation** are evaluations of the ego state of being oppressed by, or oppressing, the oge. Feelings of **confidence** and **diffidence** are evaluations of the ego's ability, or lack thereof, to deal with apparent people or with apparent objects. In the former case the ego-oge relationship of dominance is involved. **Happiness** and **unhappiness**, **contentment** and **discontentment** are evaluations of the ego's own state of hekergy.

✳

Finally the **feeling of love** is the ego's evaluation of identification — that is, of ego-oge overlap. We are thus able to distinguish clearly the feeling of love and **loving**, the latter being a willingness to give unconditionally to the beloved; and different from these again is **being in love**, which is infatuation. It is of course possible to love and to feel love without being infatuated: this occurs when, through experience of the apparent beloved, the oge-beloved has become a true representation of the apparent beloved rather than an ideal — and yet remains in the ego-oge overlap.

226

14. Meaning and Thinking.

Thinking, which we consider next, differs from feeling in that it is concerned with meaning rather than value. So we will first consider the nature of meaning, and discover three kinds, which I will call intensional, extensional, and nominal meanings. First, however, it must be made clear that thinking is abstract, as opposed to imagining which is concrete [92, 158]. Imagining, in other words, operates with images, which are concrete: usually visual or aural; and thinking — at least in the present technical sense of the word — does not. Thinking is best exemplified by logic and mathematics.

$$\ast\,\ast\,\ast$$

Our discussion of meaning will begin with the problem of universals. This ancient problem arose because we can classify many words and phrases according to whether they refer to particular individuals or to classes of individuals. — that is, according to whether their reference is singular or plural. A **universal** is a word that has plural reference. A proper name, for example, has a particular reference, and an adjective does not — since it can qualify many individuals — and so is a universal. A noun equally has a plural reference, since it may refer, in various ways, to one, any, some, or all members of a class, set, collection, or group. The **problem of universals** is the problem of discovering the nature of their meaning. It is an important problem because our present concern, thinking, is, loosely speaking, manipulation of meanings, which are usually meanings of universals.

Closely connected with the concept of a universal is that of a class. A class is a collection, or set. The word *set* is most commonly used these days, but the word class is preferred here because of its derivative concept of *classification*. Every universal defines a class: for example, the universal *red* defines the class of all red sensations. The things that constitute a class are its **members**; each member is an **instance** of the universal; the totality of the members of a class is the **extension**[11] of the class, and if all the members have something in common, which nothing else has, then this commonality is the **intension** of the class.

---

[11] The extension is different from the class in that it is many, while the class is one — although ordinary language does not distinguish them: we can speak of *the* extension, or *a* totality. The class is one because it is an extension unified by a relation. An exception to an extension being many is a one-membered class.

There are three traditional answers to the problem of universals, called **nominalism**, **conceptualism**, and **realism**, and two others, which we will consider here. (The word *realism* has more than one meaning; the present use should not be confused with that of Part One [10].) All of these, I would claim, have a defect in common; to the best of my knowledge, Spinoza was the only philosopher to recognise it, and the solution to the problem of universals that develops in our theory of mind is in the Spinozistic spirit. We will look briefly at the above-mentioned answers, and then consider the problem of universals in terms of our present theory.

✳

Nominalism, as an answer to the problem of universals, is the belief that they have no separate meanings. They are their own meanings, the word is the meaning. This means that thought can proceed only by means of words. "Words are the counters of the mind," "No thought without language" and "All thought is silent speech" are characteristic ways of putting this. Many sceptics are nominalists, and, I suspect, for the same reason: the meanings of universals, as entities, are imperceptibles. Sceptics, being those who would deny the existence of as many imperceptibles as possible, are thus naturally drawn to nominalism. A disadvantage of nominalism is that it is almost certainly contrary to empirical fact, and so false. It requires that there be no thought without language; if this is true then young children, deaf-mutes and intelligent animals such as dogs and cats are all incapable of thinking. Also, people who speak different languages must think differently, and their thought cannot be translated into another language. Yet another problem for nominalism is that it makes synonyms inexplicable: different words must have different meanings, according to nominalists, so two different words cannot have one and the same meaning. Equally, one word cannot have more than one meaning, so equivocation is impossible. A still further problem for nominalists is that words such as *relation* and *abstract* cannot be defined without using abstract concepts. A case can be made for saying that deaf-mutes get by with imagining, and that different languages are linked by imagining, but it will not work for abstract thought, which is distinct from concrete imagination. A more serious disadvantage of nominalism is that it requires thought to be arbitrary, since language is arbitrary; but little is arbitrary about logic and mathematics, and this unarbitrariness cannot be accounted for by nominalists.

✱

Conceptualism is the theory that the meanings of universals are abstract ideas. Originally the concept of abstract idea was largely undefined: it was what resulted from "abstracting" a part of an image from a whole image; but we will later [235] find a better definition. Conceptualists suppose that abstract ideas are bonded to words or symbols by convention, such that a particular abstract idea and its word together are a concept, a structure of concepts is a proposition, and a particular set of concepts and propositions, plus a grammar [168], constitute an abstract language. Thinking is a process of analysing, relating, or creating abstract ideas, and can be carried on either independently of any language, or in association with any one of them. Because of this it is possible for two people, not knowing each other's language, plus a deaf-mute, to all think exactly similar thoughts. Furthermore, an abstract idea is that which all of its instances have in common: for example, the abstract idea of two is what all pairs have in common; so abstract ideas are intensions of classes or sets. Abstract ideas are thus quite unarbitrary, so the precision of mathematics need not be explained away or ignored, as in nominalism. The major problem with conceptualism is the problem of saying just what an abstract idea is. Its nature must be such that it can represent properly both the concrete and the abstract, universally — such as *red* and *square root*, *man* and *theory*.

✱

Realism goes even further than conceptualism. It agrees with conceptualism that the meaning of, say, both the word *two* and the numeral *2* is an abstract idea. But everyone has their own abstract idea of two — there are at least as many abstract ideas of two as there are people who can count. Meanwhile, we speak of *the* number two: there is only one number two, although there may be many abstract ideas of it. Consequently, for these realists, there are actual numbers and other entities, of which all our abstract ideas are ideas. That is, every abstract idea is an idea *of* something, and it is belief in the existence of these somethings that characterises realism. Because these actual numbers exist, they have to exist somewhere: and their usual abode is either "beyond heaven" (Plato) or "in the mind of God." This strange theory stems almost entirely from Plato's theory of forms. Since realism suffers from the difficulties of conceptualism, multiplies entities quite extraordinarily beyond necessity, and also has all the difficulties inherent in Plato's theory of forms, it is not a widely held view. In defence of Plato I should remark that realism results from treating Plato's theory of forms as a theory produced exclusively as an answer to the problem of universals; it is almost certainly much more than this, as is shown by Plato's statement that the forms are "beyond heaven" — a phrase that we have met already and to which we will return. There is another point in favour of realism that should be mentioned. (I do not wish to advocate realism, but only to show that it is not quite as implausible as it first seems.) The relationship of *one number, many ideas of it* is similar to that of *one real world, many copies (empirical worlds) of it*. The parallel is even stronger if it is supposed, as Plato did in his theory of recollection of pre-natal acquaintance with the forms, that the number causes the ideas of it.

★

Another answer to the problem of universals is **extensionalism**. This is the view that the meaning of a universal is the extension of the class that it defines — that is, the totality of the instances of the universal. Berkeley used this device, and called extensions general ideas; he allowed that general ideas exist, while denying the existence of abstract ideas: that is, class extensions exist but their intensions do not. Hume followed Berkeley, but called general ideas abstract ideas, most confusingly. Frege used this device to define relations and hence number, and, following Frege, Whitehead and Russell used it widely in deducing mathematics from logic, in their *Principia Mathematica*. Thus for Frege, Whitehead, and Russell the number two is the extension of the class of all pairs — that is, the totality of all pairs. However, this approach leads to certain technical difficulties, if it is used to solve the problem of universals. Because if all universals are extensions, then the universal word *extension* must have an extension for its meaning; this will be the extension of all extensions. This concept led to a new paradox, called Cantor's paradox, which requires that the set of all sets must be bigger than it is. This extensionalist approach also led Russell to discover a new paradox, which now bears his name: namely, that the set of all sets which are not self-membered is itself self-membered if and only if it is not self-membered. My own view of extensionalism is that while it seems to serve Occam's Razor well, by eliminating a host of abstract ideas, it also reduces entities beyond necessity — that is, beyond the necessity of explaining the facts.

✶

A fifth answer to the problem of universals is due to Wittgenstein. This is the theory that the meanings of all abstract statements are to be found in *language game rules* [168]. This leads to the doctrine, which enjoyed great vogue in English speaking countries in the middle of the twentieth century, that all problems of philosophy can either be solved, or else shown to be "pseudo problems," by analysing the language in which they are stated. Those who accept this doctrine are called linguistic analysts. Wittgenstein's position is nominalism without the disadvantages described above. However, it suffers from the fact that, after decades of analysing language, linguistic analysts have neither solved any philosophic problems, nor shown any of them to be pseudo-problems.

✶

These five positions divide on the basic issue of whether anything abstract exists or not. Nominalists, extensionalists, and linguistic analysts deny it, while conceptualists and realists affirm it. It is obvious from what has been said in Part Two that I affirm it. In defence of this affirmation, and against the extensionalists and linguistic analysts, I would make three points.

If nothing abstract exists then the explanation of the fact that we use abstract language meaningfully must be an explanation wholly in terms of the concrete. But the concepts *extension* and *language game rule* are abstract, not concrete — to say nothing of the concept *abstract*.

Second, if the concrete view is correct then there must be no words that are both meaningful and abstract, and which are indefinable, ultimately, in terms of the concrete. That is, no primitively abstract words. (A word that is definable in terms of other abstract words, all of which are definable in terms of the concrete, does not count as a primitively abstract word, no matter how many intermediate abstract words are involved.) I claim that at least two words are primitively abstract: the words *abstract* and *relation*.

Third, if nothing abstract exists then all the abstract theoretical entities of physics must be non-existent. Many believe, for example, that they are imagining a magnetic field when they imagine the characteristic pattern of iron filings on a piece of paper held above a magnet. But of course such a pattern is not a magnetic field at all, but an effect of one. A magnetic field cannot be imagined — although it can be thought — because it is abstract. Similarly mass cannot be imagined, although weight, an effect of mass, can; heat cannot be imagined, although warmth, an effect of heat can; electromagnetic radiation cannot, although its effects such as colours, radio, and television can; and so on.

There are, in fact, a number of contemporary philosophers who accept that the abstract entities of physics do not exist. These philosophers allow that explanation is causal, but allow it only in the form of empirical causation, or covering law explanation [54]. Thus scientific laws become explanations, in that they describe Humean causations. For example, that this water on the stove is boiling is explained by saying that water always boils when heated sufficiently. What, in Part Two, we considered to be genuine explanation — that is, theoretical science — is for these philosophers a mere rephrasing of scientific laws. The explanatory power of theory is then said to be a matter of mere metaphor, in terms of *façons de parler* — convenient fictions. As fictions they obviously do not refer to any existing entities. From everything said earlier the scepticism of the concrete view obviously puts the holders thereof onto the slippery slope to solipsism. This is because many beliefs of common sense are explanatory beliefs, such as beliefs in the reality of empirical objects and the existence of other minds. Once on this slippery slope, nothing can save a sceptical philosopher from arriving at the solipsistic bottom except either logical inconsistency or dogma.

✶

Another objection, which applies this time to all five positions concerning universals, is that they are all exclusive. The advocates of each view want *every* universal to be explained within that view, and only within that view. This, again, is admirable from the point of view of Occam's Razor — it requires only one kind of universal, rather than two or more kinds — but it is reduction beyond the necessity to explain all the facts.

Spinoza claimed that there are two kinds of universal: what he called universal notions, which are confused images, such as the meanings of *man, horse, dog*; and common notions, which are mathematical concepts. The former are *confused* or *inadequate* ideas, and the latter are *adequate*, or *clear and distinct* ideas.

✶ ✶ ✶

I propose to take a leaf out of Spinoza's book and allow more than one kind of universal. By this means it is possible to take advantage of the strengths and to avoid the weaknesses of the five possible answers already given.

✳

1. To begin with, the meanings of some abstract statements are sometimes no more than what is to be found in the rules of the game that is the language in which the statement was made. This occurs in calculation. Most people, in doing long multiplication and long division, have no idea of any meaning to the intermediate steps in what they are doing, other than the rules by which symbols produce further symbols. Most people, to take another example, can figure out percentages, and how many miles per gallon they are getting from their car; but how little they understand the figuring is shown by their inability to explain what the *per* in their answer means. This is because they have calculated the answer, not thought it out; instead of thinking they have used an algorithm. Indeed, it is very likely that a contributory factor to the low average ability in mathematics is due to many bad teachers of mathematics who teach children to calculate rather than to think — because the former is so much easier to teach[12]. Language game rules [168] may also often be the sole meaning of many clichés and platitudes — statements that we have heard so often that they have become meaningless except for the conventional rule that requires them to be uttered in those particular circumstances. (So far we have spoken only of the meanings of statements, rather than of universals, in terms of language game rules; but the two are easily related, as we will see when we discuss definition [246].)

✳

2. Extensions are also the meanings of some universals, as we saw in discussing the possibility of language. That is, concrete names [167] have extensions as their meanings. These are always finite extensions (since the number of memories in a real mind is finite) and imprecisely defined. They are imprecise because the extensions are formed by recognition, which

---

[12] *Per* means *divided by*, so that to discover one's speed one divides the miles by the hours; hence *miles per hour*. Equally, *per cent* means *divided by 100*, so that 80% means 80 divided by 100, or 4/5.

operates on a basis of L.A.L. in which the likeness is not exact, but only near-likeness or high degree of similarity. Near-likeness, as we have seen [186], is fadingly transitive, so that the extensions of two concrete names may blend into each other by imperceptible degrees. For example, there is no clear line of demarcation between *black man* and *white man*. Fuzzy logic and fuzzy set theory are attempts to deal with such concrete names rigorously.

✶

3. Another kind of meaning for a few universals is a mental act of discrimination — or, possibly, the idea of the act. We saw in Chapter 11 [169] that discrimination among sensations requires special mappings. One example was patch mapping; two such mappings will produce either likeness or unlikeness between their maps. Likeness is named *same* and unlikeness is named *different*. Since it is colours that are either the same or different, the patch mappings will result in a statement of either *same colour* or *different colour*. In such circumstances, the meaning for *colour* is the act of discrimination, the patch mapping. Similarly, scale mappings provide the meanings of *greater than* and *less than* and boundary mapping the meaning of *shape*. Notice, however, that likeness, unlikeness, and mappings are all relations, so that mental acts of discrimination, as meanings of universals, are ultimately abstract ideas, which are described shortly.

It is, of course, possible for geometers to produce much more sophisticated definitions (and hence abstract meanings, or ideas — see below) of *shape*, for physicists to produce them for *colour*, etc. There is no reason for one universal not to have more than one meaning; colour words, for example, may mean sensations of colour, the ideas of certain frequencies of electromagnetic radiation, or the ideas of atomic or molecular structures in objects that reflect or transmit these frequencies. The point here is that special mappings are the earliest meanings for some universals — for example, the meanings for people who correctly use the words *shape* and *colour* but know no geometry or physics.

✶

4. Finally, there are abstract ideas. Enough has been said about these already to make it clear that they are structures in the real mind which (i) are "abstracted" from — that is, obtained by a partial mapping from — other mid-ideas, or else compounded out of other abstract ideas — that is, they may be constructs [150]; (ii) are subliminal; and (iii) are involved primarily

in thinking, not feeling. We also saw that all relations are abstract — a point whose converse will now be claimed: all abstract ideas are relations, or properties of relations. That is, abstract ideas are relations, or their properties, within a mind. In a sense, this latter point is a truism because all ideas, not merely abstract ideas, are structures and structures are relations. Indeed, because of this there is no radical difference between concrete and abstract mid-ideas: they differ in degree rather than in kind — as opposed to the ego's consciousness of them, in which the difference is radical. And, of course, it is the ego's consciousness of them that people usually mean by ideas: images and thoughts.

The only feasible way in which an idea can be an idea of a relation or relational property is for it to be itself that relation — that is, to be a representative instance of that relation or property. We will examine the abstract idea of triangle, both by way of illustration of this point, and to show why non-thinkers have so much difficulty with the concept of abstract idea.

I have chosen the abstract idea of triangle because Berkeley used it in his argument against abstract ideas. Recall that triangles are classified by geometers into three kinds: equilateral, isosceles, and scalene, according to whether they have three, two or no sides equal. Berkeley argued that he could without difficulty imagine a triangle that was equilateral, or one that was isosceles, or one that was scalene, but not one that was all three at once — since these properties are mutually exclusive. Consequently, Berkeley argued, there can be no single idea of triangle, only a "general idea" — that is, the extensional meaning [239] — of the word triangle, which is the extension of the set of all triangles. The weakness of this argument is that it rests on a dogma: the concretist dogma that whatever is unimaginable cannot exist. The difference between this and the rationalists' criterion of non-existence — logical impossibility — is most of the realm of relations, and hence of abstract ideas. We can agree with Berkeley that the idea of triangle is unimaginable, and then proceed on the basis that it is thinkable — as opposed to the logically impossible, which is unthinkable even though it is speakable. Imagination and thought, in other words, are not at all the same thing, and both are distinct from language.

We can consider an abstract idea in the following manner. (Several possible difficulties in this account will be ignored in the telling, but exposed immediately afterwards.) Suppose that a representative instance of a dyadic relation is the abstract idea of the cardinal number two, that of a triadic relation is the abstract idea of three, and so on. Suppose that a representative instance of a spatial relation is the abstract idea of a straight line. And suppose that a representative instance of a relation between two spatial relations is the abstract idea of a point — that is, it is the relation between two spatial relations that meet. The combination of the last two abstract ideas would be an abstract idea of the intersection of two straight lines. The combination of the abstract ideas of three and of intersection; and also of three and of straight line, would then be the abstract idea of triangle. Further combination of abstract ideas could give special cases of triangle: for example, a number three or two, and equality of sides of the triangles would give equilateral or isosceles triangles.

What seems to be a circularity in this explanation is not so. To say that the number three is a triadic relation seems to presuppose the number three, in order to define *triadic*. This is not so because instances of three are among the givens in apparent worlds. From a memory of an instance, a triadic relation may be abstracted, to give the idea of three. The instance of three, in its turn, is a copy of an instance in the real world, where the adicity of relations is logically primitive.

A second seeming difficulty arises with the concept of combination of abstract ideas. To combine them is to form structures of them, or constructs [150]. From any set of terms, a variety of structures is possible, so the question arises: which, of all possible combinations, constitutes the new abstract idea? The answer is that since abstract ideas are relations, a combination of them must be an emergent relation that has them as its terms — a combination being, after all, a relation; such combinations thus have configuration hekergy.

A third difficulty arises from the possibility that it may be impossible for an instance of a relation, such as a dyadic relation, to exist as an idea in the real mind. For example, it might be that the nature of the real mind requires that every idea have a spatial component, and that the dyadic relation is non-spatial. A fourth difficulty is that, with the explanation used, the numbers one and zero must be representative instances of "monadic" and "nonadic" relations; since these words have what will later [239] be called nominal meaning only, no instances of them will exist. There may be many other difficulties with this approach, of a like nature. These difficulties all belong to intensional logic, which is discussed in the next chapter.

One further point about abstract ideas is most important. They are all class intensions. Every member of the class of which an abstract idea is an intension either is similar to that idea, or else contains a substructure similar to that idea, or else is related by that abstract idea to something else. Thus every triangle contains an emergent relation similar to that which constitutes the abstract idea of triangle. We will return to this matter of intensions shortly.

✱

It should be noted that in the present claim that there is a variety of kinds of meanings for universal words, no use has been needed of the realistic view. However in this connection a situation arises that we have already encountered twice, concerning apparent worlds [42] and oges [181, 212]: this is the identity error. If Jack and Jill each have a representative instance of a dyadic relation in their real minds, and discuss its nature — that is, the nature of what the word *two* means, such as being the only even prime, being ordinally between one and three, being the square root of four, etc. — they will discover that they are talking about the same thing. *Same* here means, of course, similar; but it is easily construed, equivocally, as identity, so that they supposedly speak of the same thing, *the* number two. This further example of the identity error may be the origin of realism as an answer to the problem of universals. Certainly, in the present context, if we were to argue that realism is true then there would have to be actual numbers etc. existing in the real world, of which abstract ideas of numbers are copies. But we have no grounds for saying that there are archetypal relations "beyond heaven," only for saying that there are multiple instances of various relations, and hence of various relational properties, such as numbers, in the real world.

✱ ✱ ✱

In connection with universals, the use of quantifiers must be explained. They are necessary because the denotation of a universal is ambiguous. Does the word *triangle* refer to the intension of the class of triangles, the extension, or some instance? If an instance, is it in the real mind, the apparent world or the real world? Quantifiers are words, such as *all* and *some*, which remove some of the doubt concerning denotation. Thus, in a deductive context, *any triangle* refers to the intension of the class, *all triangles* or *every triangle* refer to the extension, *some triangles* to a part of the extension, *a triangle* to an instance, *this triangle* or *that triangle* to an ostensive instance — one pointed at, in the apparent world — and so on. In a non-deductive context the usage is less precise: *any* and *all* are equivalent, apart from grammatical differences: thus "Any trespasser will be prosecuted" and "All trespassers will be prosecuted." This is because non-deductive contexts are not dealing with abstract ideas — intensions — hence have no peculiar use for *any*. The English language is also imprecise (apart from grammatical differences) in its use of *all* and *every*; except that there is perhaps a faint tendency to use *all* for extensions that do not have intensions — such as "All men are mortal" — and *every* for those that do have them, such as "Every triangle has its internal angles sum to two right angles." When it comes to distinguishing the different kinds of instances of a universal, we use adjectives, such as *ideal* and *material. Empirical, theoretical, real, apparent, mid-, motor* and *oge-* are particular cases of such adjectives.

There are still other kinds of quantifier, such as negative, singular, numerical, distributive, and collective, but we need not go into them here. The point at issue is what their meaning is in the real mind. It requires only a little reflection to see that they are all adjectives. Compare, for example, *All black cows* and *Some cows* — each refers to a part of the extension of the class of cows. It is equally clear that all adjectives are universals. So quantifiers are universals; and, as such, they most usually are concrete names.

✶

However, although *black* and *cow* are both universals, this does not explain the meaning of *black cow*. The point is a most important one because it leads us not only to relations between words, but to the meanings of these relations, which are relations between meanings. Thus *a black cow* could be phrased as *a black and cowish thing* or *black and a cow* and thereby lead to the question of what *and* means. There are other such **connectives**, or **truth-functions**, as they are called, such as *not...* or *non...*, *...or...*, *if...then...*, and *...if, and only if...*, where the ellipses indicate the words or propositions that are connected.

✶

We can in fact discover three distinct meanings of each of the connectives within our theory, all of which ordinary language is able to, and does, treat as one. They are the **intensional, extensional,** and **nominal meanings** of each word. These terms are self-explanatory: intensional meanings are intensions of sets, or abstract ideas; extensional meanings are extensions of sets, the pluralities of members of the sets; and nominal meanings are nominal, or merely linguistic — they have meaning by linguistic analogy to intensional or extensional meanings. Put another way, a word has nominal meaning if it has an established use in a language — established in the first place by definition. This established use is based on intensional and extensional meanings. If a word has no established use then it has no meaning at all.

The distinction between these three kinds meanings is going to be important, for a variety of reasons. One reason is that paradox and contradiction are possible only with nominal meaning: they cannot occur with extensional and intensional meaning. Another reason is that **axiom generosity**, also called the **cornucopia-effect of axiom sets**, is possible only with intensional meanings; this is the phenomenon of a large number of theorems emerging cascadingly from a small set of axioms; without this mathematics would not exist. A third reason is that there is least arbitrariness with intensional meanings and most with nominal meanings. And a fourth reason is the three-way, asymmetrical relationship of necessity between them: (i) if a word or statement has intensional meaning then necessarily it has both extensional and nominal meaning; (ii) if a word or statement has extensional meaning then necessarily it has nominal meaning, but it does not necessarily have intensional meaning; and (iii) if a word or statement has nominal meaning then it does not necessarily have extensional meaning.

✶

The intensional meaning of *and* refers to the compounding of abstract ideas. We may consider the two abstract ideas denoted by *any triangle* and *any equilateral*. They may be compounded to give *any figure equilateral and triangular*, and the *and* refers to the fact of their being compounded. This meaning is called intensional because abstract ideas are intensions. The compounding need not, of course, be explicit: *any equilateral triangle* means the same thing. But this does not alter the meaning of *and* in this context.

Just as the intensional meaning of *and* is a relation between intensions, so is the extensional meaning a relation between extensions. This is the relation known technically as **intersection**. The intersection of two extensions is all the members they share in common. Thus the intersection of the extension of all cows and of the extension of all black things is the extension of all black cows. So in *all black and cowish things* there is reference to the extension of black things and to the extension of cows, and the *and* refers to the intersection of these two. Similarly, *all figures equilateral and triangular* refers to the intersection of the extensions of triangles and equilaterals. So the extensional meaning of *and* is intersection.

Nominal meaning is meaning by analogy, of language rules. That is, by analogy with rules of the language of extensional meaning or with rules of the language of intensional meanings. In the case of *and* the analogy is with rules concerning an extrinsic relation called a truth-function. A truth-function is a relation between the truth of the parts and the truth of the whole. In the case of *and* the parts are called **conjuncts** and the whole is called a **conjunction**. A conjunction is true only if both its conjuncts are true. Thus in the intensional case it is true that something is equilateral and triangular only if it is true that this thing is equilateral and it is true that it is triangular. That is to say, something has the substructure denoted by *equilateral and triangular* only if it has the substructure denoted by *equilateral* and also the substructure denoted by *triangular*. Again, extensionally, something is a member of the intersection of the extension of black things and the extension of cows only if it is a member of the extension of black things, and also a member of the extension of cows. Hence it is true that something is black and cowlike only if it is true that it is black and also true that it is a cow. So, by analogy, it is true that something is square and a circle only if it is true that it is square and also true that it is a circle, even though the words *square* and *circle* when combined have neither intensional meaning nor extensional meaning: they are both geometric figures in one plane, and it is impossible for one plane figure to be both. The meaning of this nominal conjunction is the rule that a conjunction is true only if both conjuncts are true. This nominal meaning is a rule applied to words, analogously to the rules applied to intensional and extensional conjunctions. In the case of intensional meaning this rule is a statement of fact concerning relations between intensions; in the case of extensional meanings this rule is a statement of fact concerning relations between extensions, and the extensions may or may not have intensions; and in the case of nominal meaning it is a rule between words, and the words may or may not have intensional or extensional meanings.

The asymmetrical relationship of necessity between intensional, extensional, and nominal meanings should be clear for the case of *and*. If *and* is used with intensional meaning then it is necessarily used with extensional and nominal meaning as well. If *and* is used with extensional meaning then it is necessarily used with nominal meaning as well, but not necessarily with intensional meaning. And if it is used with nominal meaning it is not necessarily used with any other. Thus *equilateral and triangular* is a conjunction of intensions, of extensions and of words; *black and cowlike* is a conjunction of extensions and of words, but not of intensions — since there are no abstract ideas of cows; and *square and a circle*, or *square circle* is only a nominal conjunction because nothing can be both square and circular, hence there can neither extensions nor intensions of square circles, only nominal meanings of them. Thus we have intensional, extensional, and nominal conjunction.

✶

It is now quite simple to show that similar considerations apply to the words *or* and *if... then...* If *or* refers to a relation between intensions, it is to their similarity — to what they have in common. For example, if, in referring to a triangle one specifies *equilateral, or isosceles, or scalene* then what is being specified is the similar substructure in the abstract ideas denoted by *any equilateral triangle, any isosceles triangle*, and *any scalene triangle*; this is the structure that is the abstract idea denoted by *any triangle*. The extensional meaning of *or* is that relation between extensions known as **union**. The union of two extensions is the totality of all their members. Thus if something is either black or a cow, then it belongs to the union of the extensions of black things and of cows — it belongs to one, or the other, or both. The nominal meaning of *or* is again truth-functional. A word or statement containing the word *or* is called a **disjunction**, and the words connected by *or* are called **disjuncts**. The nominal meaning of the word *or* is the rule that a disjunction is false only if both disjuncts are false.

As we saw in Chapter 4, a statement of the form *if... then...* is called a conditional, and the words or statements related by it are called antecedent and consequent respectively. Thus in *if A then B*, *A* is the antecedent and *B* is the consequent. Intensionally, the *if... then...* refers to the relation of substructure: that is, the consequent is a substructure of the antecedent. For example, *if something is an equilateral triangle then it is equilateral* states that the abstract idea denoted by *any equilateral triangle* contains as a part of itself a structure exactly similar to the abstract idea denoted by *any equilateral*. The extensional meaning of a conditional is the relation of subset: that is, the extension of the antecedent is a subset — a part — of the extension of the consequent. For example *if something is a crow then it is black* states that the extension of crows is a part of the extension of black things. The nominal meaning of a conditional is to be found in the rule that the conditional is false only if the antecedent is true and the consequent false. For example, there is a sense in which any statement of the form *if it is an A and a B then it is an A* is true; hence *if it is a square circle then it is a square* is true, which means that it never happens that something is both a square circle, but not square.

Notice that the intensional and extensional meanings of *if P then Q* work in opposite ways. Intensionally, Q is contained in P, while extensionally P is contained in Q The reason for this lies in a theorem called the implication theorem [265, 291].

✶

We are now in a position to begin to see the importance of distinguishing between our three kinds of meaning. It is simply trite to say that if something is an equilateral triangle then it is equilateral. But, given the combination of the abstract ideas of triangle and equilateral, something new appears: namely, it becomes true that all equilateral triangles are equiangular. This is because combining the abstract ideas of triangle and equilateral causes the idea of equiangular to emerge. More impressive still is the combination of the abstract ideas of triangularity and perpendicularity, within which Pythagoras' Theorem and all of trigonometry may be discovered. It is possible for abstract ideas and propositions to emerge cascadingly [114] from an initial set of them. This cascading emergence is the basis of axiom generosity.

Nothing like this happens with extensional meanings when intensional meanings are absent. What can be done by way of deduction with extensional meanings is what, compared with mathematics, is the relatively trivial logic of Aristotle; and statistics may also be applied to such extensional meanings.

Nominal meaning is even more limited. Because a term or combination of terms that have only nominal meaning have no extension — that is, their extensions are null, as it is called — a modified and more limited form of Aristotelian logic must be used if the possibility of such terms is allowed. This is the Boolean interpretation of Aristotelian logic, due to George Boole. Not only this, but a potentially enormous amount of redundancy is introduced by allowing words that have no meaning other than nominal: we can introduce the word *squircle*, for example, by defining it as a square-circle, and it has no meaning other than nominal.

Those who are familiar with that branch of modern logic called truth-functional logic will be familiar with another form of redundancy due to purely nominal meaning. This logic uses *and, or, if... then...*, and a few other truth functions to join complete statements, rather than predicates. Such statements may be represented by P, Q, and R. Two of the rules of inference in this logic are simplification and addition. Simplification is the rule that from 'P *and* Q', P may be deduced; and addition is the rule that from P, 'P *or* Q' may be deduced. Consequently, if R may be deduced from P — that is, '*if* P *then* R', symbolised by 'P⊃R' — then R may be deduced from 'P *and* Q' by simplification; and also, 'R *or* Q' may be deduced from P, by addition. P and R are deductively related, but Q is not here related to P or to R — Q is any statement whatever. This means that when R can be deduced from P there is a potentially infinite number of alternative premise sets from which R can be deduced, and a potentially infinite number of alternative statements that can be deduced from P. This kind of arbitrariness does not occur with extensional or intensional logic.

✶ ✶ ✶

The language rules that give meaning by analogy are not necessarily truth-functional. Four other analogies will be considered next: the triple meanings — intensional, extensional, and nominal — of analyticity, predication, definition, and modalities.

✶

Analyticity as it was discussed in Part Two, in connection with Leibniz [102], is **intensional analyticity**. It occurs when the predicate is contained in the subject: that is, the abstract idea that is the predicate is a part of the abstract idea that is the subject. In different words, a conditional is intensionally analytic when the consequent is contained in the antecedent. It may thus be stated equally by "Every S is a P" and "If it is an S then it is a P." Conversely, if these forms of statement are to have intensional meaning, then it must be analytic meaning. Intensional analyticity is characterised by necessity. If "Every S is a P" has intensional meaning then it is impossible for something to be an S and not a P; being an S necessitates being a P. Thus it is impossible for a right-angled triangle not to conform to Pythagoras' theorem [223]. This necessity is the basis of deduction.

Extensional analyticity occurs when the subject extension is contained in the predicate extension, or, in different words, when the antecedent extension is contained in the consequent extension. It may thus be stated just as intensional analyticity: "All S are P" and "If S then P." However, these expressions may have extensional meaning without intensional meaning; that is, they may be extensionally analytic without being intensionally analytic; when they are, they are called synthetic, as opposed to analytic. An extensional synthetic meaning is one that does not include necessity, but does include universality; it is a factual statement — such as "All crows are black" or "If you are cold then you shiver." There is no necessity here because it is possible to have a non-black crow, or to be cold without shivering; but if these statements are true then there is universality: crows are *always* black and when you are cold you *always* shiver. The difference between necessity and universality is that necessity entails universality, but not the other way round; because equilateral triangles are necessarily equiangular they are always equiangular, but because crows are always black it does not follow that they are necessarily black. The necessary cannot be otherwise, it is singular possibility, whereas the universal could be otherwise even though it never is [272]. However, since the universal is frequently called necessary, we will refer to it as **extensional necessity**, as distinct from intensional necessity.

Nominal analyticity has necessity only by verbal analogy. "All square circles are square" refers to no necessary connection between square circles and square because there are no square circles. The analyticity is only verbally analogical to intensional analyticity. In truth-functional logic the necessary is defined as universality of truth-functional truth or falsity; this may be called **nominal necessity**. A **tautology** is an expression that is always true while an expression that is always false is a **contradiction**; for example, P⊃P (which reads "If P then P" or "P implies P") is a tautology because it is truth-functionally true whether P is true or P is false, and P&~P (which reads "P and not-P") is a contradiction because it is truth-functionally false whether P is true or false. In other words, P⊃P is *always* true, whatever P stands for, and so a tautology, and P&~P is *always* false, and so a contradiction. But these universalities are less meaningful than extensional necessity because P may have no extensional meaning; it might be the statement that all square circles are square.

✶

Predication occurs whenever we attribute a predicate to a subject. **Intensional predication** occurs in only two ways: analytically, when the predicate is contained in the subject; or, what might be called intensionally synthetically, when the subject and predicate may be combined consistently. That is, when two or more abstract ideas may be combined into a larger unity by means of an emergent relation which has them as its terms. If the ideas cannot be combined, the words for them can; but the result will have only nominal meaning, as shown by the possibility of deducing a contradiction from it.

Extensional predication is wider than intensional predication: anything may be predicated of a subject provided that the so-called category mistake does not occur. A category mistake is something that is extensionally synthetically impossible. Examples are the predication of the qualities of one sense organ on the objects of another — such as a purple smell or a tart sound; predication of concrete qualities on abstractions, such as a hot number; cases of the pathetic fallacy; and so on. Extensional predication includes everything imaginable if we are concerned with extensions in the real mind. If we are concerned with extensions in the apparent world then naturally we must exclude the empirically non-existent, such as mermaids and perpetual motion machines. But intensional predication does not include everything imaginable — it only includes everything thinkable.

Nominal predication, however, allows anything whatever to be predicated of anything whatever. Squareness of circles and colouredness of justice are two examples of predication that have nominal meaning only. The first because it is logically impossible and the second because of a category mistake.

✳

We have a parallel situation with definition. A typical form of definition might be "An A is anything that is either a B or both a C and a D". "A" is the *definiendum*, or what is defined, and "B, or C and D" is the *definiens*, or the defining expression. **Intensional definition** is meaningful compounding of abstract ideas: in an intensional definition the *definiendum* has more intensional meaning than the *definiens*, because the components of the *definiens* are united into a whole by an emergent relation; thus the whole is greater than the sum of its parts. So in "A square is any equilateral equiangular quadrilateral" the words *equilateral, equiangular,* and *quadrilateral* each have intensional meaning, and are capable of being predicated of each other; so *square* has intensional meaning; and some of this intensional meaning is not to be found in any of the parts, such as the diagonals of a square being necessarily equal.

Extensional definition is any relating of extensions to make other extensions. In "A human is any featherless biped with broad nails" the words of the *definiens* have only extensional meaning, hence so does *human*. In this case the *definiendum* has only as much meaning as the *definiens*; there is no emergent intensional meaning because there is no intensional meaning at all. But the *definiendum* also does have as much meaning as the *definiens*: the quantity of extensional meaning in each is equal. (We later [268] extend this definition of extensional definition to include any set defined by enumeration.)

Nominal definition is any grammatically correct definition. Thus in "A squircle is any square circle" the *definiendum* has nominal meaning only, in spite of the fact that *square* and *circle* each have intensional meaning, because they cannot be predicated of each other. So the nominal meaning in the *definiendum* is equal to the nominal meaning in the *definiens*.

✳

The fourth example of triple meanings is those of the modalities: the three modalities are *necessity*, *contingency*, and *impossibility*.

Intensional necessity is, as we have already seen, singular possibility, while intensional contingency is plural possibility and intensional impossibility is zero possibility. Thus if you add the numbers two and three there is only one possibility, intensionally: five, so the answer five is necessary. If you draw a card from a well shuffled deck there are fifty two possibilities, so the card you draw is contingent. And if you define a right-angled equilateral triangle, you cannot draw it or build it because it has zero possibility, it is impossible.

The extensional modalities are *always*, *sometimes*, and *never*. That is, the extensional meaning of *necessity* is *always*, that of *contingency* is *sometimes*, and that of *impossibility* is *never*. These are sometimes called empirical modalities. Thus crows are always black, cows are sometimes brown, and live mermaids are never seen.

The nominal modalities are *tautology*, *contingency*, and *contradiction*. These are defined as being *always true*, *sometimes true*, and *never true* — and the truth here is nominal truth, or truth by syntax. Thus all square circles are square, some square circles are square, and no square circles are square.

There are also three moral modalities: required, permitted, and forbidden. These have all three kinds of meaning provided that the qualifier *moral* is used. So the required is a singular moral possibility, hence always moral, hence tautologically moral; the permitted is a plural moral possibility, hence sometimes moral, hence contingently moral; and the forbidden is not a moral possibility, hence never moral, hence a moral contradiction.

✳

In all these four cases — of analyticity, predication, definition, and modalities — the same situation holds as in the truth functional cases. A statement's possession of intensional meaning is a sufficient condition for its having both extensional and nominal meaning. Its having extensional meaning is a sufficient condition for its having nominal meaning, but only a necessary condition for its having intensional meaning. And its having nominal meaning is only a necessary condition for its having either intensional or extensional meaning.

✳ ✳ ✳

Given these three kinds of meaning we can distinguish between intensional, extensional, and nominal logic; the latter is truth-functional logic, extensional logic is what is called quantificational logic, while intensional logic is examined in the next chapter.

✳

A further point about intensions must be made. So far the use of the words *abstract idea* and *intension* has been confined, implicitly, to intrinsic properties of relations. If a class has an intension, then every member of that class is, or has, a substructure, exactly similar to the properties of this intension. But classes can be defined by extrinsic relations also. For example, "Everything in this room" defines a class; and every member of this class, and nothing else, has the extrinsic property of being within this room. *Within* is an extrinsic relation to each member of this class, so that *within this room* is the class intension. If we think of the room as a structure, then the intension is a relation extrinsic to each member of the class; or we can think of the room as, in part, concrete, such that we have a partly concrete intension. We may call this new type of intension **extrinsic intensions**, as opposed to **intrinsic intensions**, defined by intrinsic properties of relations; and in the remainder of this chapter they will be excluded from the concepts of intension and intensional meaning unless otherwise stated. They are discussed further in the next chapter. Further examples of extrinsic intensions are: all the king's horses and all the king's men; the works of Shakespeare; all the descendants of Queen Victoria; all the ancestors of Queen Victoria; everything under the sun; the causes of the First World War; and all the things I will never know.

✱ ✱ ✱

This brings us back to the problem of universals. A universal is clearly a word plus a meaning, and the meaning is one of four kinds: intensional, and so also extensional and nominal; extensional but not intensional, and so nominal also; nominal only; or a concrete name.

✱ ✱ ✱

We must now return to our theory of mind to see how it is possible for the ego to think. **Thinking**, properly speaking, is manipulation of abstract ideas. **Creative thinking** is compounding of abstract ideas so as to produce new ones; so as to produce structures of abstract ideas, which are propositions; and so as to produce structures of propositions, which are theories — all of these having emergent hekergies. **Deductive thinking** is examining abstract ideas, propositions, or theories to discover their substructures — that is, to discover intensional analytic truth. All of these ideas, and the relations between them, may be bonded to words or symbols, so that the thought may be expressed linguistically. We may speak of **pure**

thought as that which occurs with abstract ideas and propositions only — that is, without the symbols or words; **ordinary thought** as that which occurs with ideas or propositions and with language; and **nominal thought** or **calculation** as that which occurs with language only, as in algorithmic thinking.

(Since we are cataloguing kinds of thought, another that deserves mention is **critical thinking**, which is the searching of an argument for fallacies or errors.)

A special case of pure thought is mathematical intuition. It is enormously valuable because it is creative, in a way that calculation cannot be. Calculation is creative only by accident, as when a random jumbling of symbols and statements produces a new theory as opposed to nonsense. Although this is theoretically possible, it has probably never happened in fact. However, pure thought has also a great disadvantage: there is nothing *prima facie* to distinguish it from prejudice. The value of the creativity within pure thought becomes public only if the thinker demonstrates it, with symbols. This is one great value of language to thinking: it enables the abstract to become public — in both senses of 'public'. That is, the symbols enable the thought to be published; and the publication enables thinkers to agree on the results, to arrive at a consensus: that is, the similarity — the publicity — of their thought is established.

✶

The ego is able to manipulate abstract ideas so as to think, simply because near-likeness is fadingly transitive [186]. That part of the structure of the ego that is close to its centre will be composed of memories very like the apparent body; but if the ego is large, then the farther an idea is from its centre the less like the centre it may be. Given such a large ego, it will be able to move abstract ideas at will by exerting L.A.L. forces upon them — simply by appropriate attention. These forces will be far greater than the mutual L.A.L. forces between the abstract ideas involved, because the ego is so large, so that they may be moved into structures of maximum hekergy, rather than L.A.L. structures. The ego will do this, if it can, because of the mind hekergy principle. The ego may do this on its own, with the ideas available to it, in which case it is thinking originally; or it may do it with the aid of a teacher, who assists by means of language. The thinking that the ego does when taught is increase of understanding. As anyone knows who has done any teaching, the communication of facts is easy — since this involves only simple propositions; but the communication of understanding is more difficult — because, as we now see, it requires thought by the student as well as by the teacher.

✳

A number of factors may prevent the ego from thinking. Because the meaning of abstract ideas is relational, they usually will have the minimum number of atomic ideas necessary to represent their meaning. Consequently their hekergy will be small relative to the vivid objects in the apparent world, the vivid concrete memories of these, and vivid concrete constructs in the imagination. Hence they will be less accessible to the consciousness of the ego, for the same reason that the stars are invisible when the sun is shining: the faint is obscured from consciousness by the vivid. Secondly, because abstract ideas are concerned with relational meanings rather than feelings, there is another reason for their hekergy to be small compared with other ideas. Consequently people who feel very strongly about things — their egos habitually concentrate their attention on values — will be unable to think well. A parallel case occurs with the strongly prejudiced person, since prejudices may be at the periphery of the ego and there ruin the delicate manipulation of abstract ideas that is thought. An example of this is the common sense prejudice of realism, which greatly hinders acceptance of the Leibniz-Russell theory. In other words the special kind of objectivity that is characterised by the absence — or at least weakness — of relevant prejudices is necessary to thought. Finally, a certain amount of intelligence is required for abstract thought.

With all these obstacles it is not surprising that most people cannot think clearly. What passes for thought in ordinary day to day living is not thought at all, in the present technical sense, but either silent speech with extensional meanings, or else imagining with concrete images. Fortunately calculation is a good substitute for thought. Calculation becomes possible by our making it an exact analogue of thought, in so far as there is one-to-one correspondence between symbols and abstract ideas; and also between linguistic rules of inference — algorithms — and necessary relations between propositions or abstract ideas.

✳

250

We can now understand both the power and the poverty of abstract language. Its power is calculation, which enables mathematical non-starters to compute their income tax correctly. Its poverty is some exclusively nominal meaning, which has no value beyond the need to discover a particular instance of it and say that it has no value.

It is because of purely nominal meaning that language is the only realm in which the impossible is possible. Contradictions occur nowhere else but in language. We cannot think or imagine a square-circle, or draw it or construct it in any way; but we can say it, and write it. Not only can we speak of the unthinkable and the unimaginable but we can speak of the unspeakable, describe the utterly indescribable, name the unnameable, and refer to that which cannot be referred to.

Consequently, since we cannot tell simply by inspecting the statements concerned whether they have nominal, or extensional, or intensional meaning, we have the problem of never knowing whether solely nominal meaning is lurking in our calculations and leading us astray. It is possible, in other words, that the symbols and method of a form of calculation are only a near analogue, not an exact one, of the relevant thought process. When this occurs the calculation will be right most of the time, but will be capable of going wrong. We know that it goes wrong when a paradox or contradiction is produced.

For example, we have already seen that the branch of modern logic called truth-functional logic is based on nominal truth functions and thereby contains much redundancy due to purely nominal meaning. It could therefore produce paradoxes, and it does. There are two theorems in the logic, called the **paradoxes of material implication**. These are truth-functional theorems that require that a false statement materially implies any statement whatever, and that a true statement is materially implied by any statement whatever. The relationship of *material implication* is so called to distinguish it from deduction, but it is the implication of truth-functional logic. One attempt to get a relationship that corresponds more closely to deduction uses what is called strict implication, in a more complex logic called modal logic. But this leads to the **paradoxes of strict implication**: namely, an impossible statement strictly implies any statement whatever, and a necessary statement is strictly implied by any statement whatever. Quantificational logic, which for various reasons is not so defective, still has at least one paradox:

anything said of a non-existent thing is true. For example, since mermaids do not exist, "All mermaids are female" and "All mermaids are male" are both true[13].

This two-faced feature of language — its reliability and unreliability — is of course a matter of importance in philosophy. Most philosophic thinking is probably a mixture of ordinary thought and calculation, rather than pure thought, hence susceptible to aberration due to purely nominal meaning. It is for this reason that philosophers are so interested in paradoxes: they are signposts to mere nominal meanings that pollute the thought. If the precise location of these can be found, not only can the thought be purified, but the origin of the error can be stated explicitly, so as to avoid its future occurrence. We have seen an example of this with the inference of identity from similarity, which led us to the Leibniz-Russell theory and its plurality of empirical worlds, and which, once named as the identity error, helped us to reject the unification of many perceptions into supposedly one empirical object, the supposedly one culture of many similar people, the concept of the average man, the unity of C. G. Jung's collective unconscious, and the basis for realism as a solution to the problem of universals; and more exposures of the identity error will occur in the remainder of this book.

---

[13]For those familiar with truth-functional logic, the proofs of the paradoxes of material implication are as follows. From the premise $\sim$A we get $\sim$A$\vee$B by disjunctive addition, and this is equivalent to A$\supset$B — hence $\sim$A$\supset$(A$\supset$B); and from the premise A we get A$\vee\sim$B, which gives us $\sim$B$\vee$A by commutation and so B$\supset$A — hence A$\supset$(B$\supset$A); in each case B is any proposition whatever. For those familiar with quantificational logic, the proof of the mermaid argument is as follows. If M, F, and L stand for mermaid, female, and male, then our premise is $\sim$($\exists$x)Mx, from which we obtain (x)$\sim$Mx by quantificational equivalence. Instantiation gives $\sim$Ma, where a is an ambiguous individual, from which we obtain both $\sim$Ma$\vee$Fa and $\sim$Ma$\vee$La by disjunctive addition. These are equivalent to Ma$\supset$Fa and Ma$\supset$La, which, generalised, give (x)(Mx$\supset$Fx) and (x)(Mx$\supset$Lx).

15. Intensional Logic.

We have already seen that class, or set, formation occurs naturally in a theoretical mind, by L.A.L; this means that it is essentially irrational, rather than rational. On the other hand, the modern theory of classes is set theory, and this was made the basis of mathematics by Cantor, Frege, Whitehead and Russell, and others, about a century ago. So how can mathematics, which is the epitome of rational thought, be founded on irrationality? The answer offered here is that not all set theory is irrational, and that we can separate the rational parts from the irrational. Rational sets are derived from relations, and irrational ones from L.A.L.; and relations provide intensions of sets, while irrational sets do not have intensions. So sets are not the best foundation for mathematics because some of them do not have intensions, whereas relations are always intensional meanings. Also, relations are more fundamental than sets, because sets may be defined by means of relations, without circularity, but not the other way round. So a relational foundation for mathematics is to be preferred to a set-theoretic one. How all this unfolds is technical, so any reader who suffers from mathematicophobia or is unfamiliar with modern logic should skip to the next chapter [293].

✳

First, the standard set-theoretic definition of relations is that they are subsets of **Cartesian products**. If A and B are sets then their Cartesian product, $A \times B$, is the set of all possible ordered pairs, (a,b), the first member of which, a, belongs to A and the second, b, to B: namely, $A \times B = \{(a,b): a \in A \ \& \ b \in B\}$. Any subset of $A \times B$ is then a set of pairs of terms of a dyadic relation, and the relation is identified with this subset. The relation is what is called a logical construct out of its terms. Cartesian products of three sets, by means of ordered triads, define triadic relations, and so on for higher adicities.

However, to specify a particular subset of a Cartesian product requires either a specification by means of a set-defining rule, or by means of an enumeration; and neither of these can be done without presupposing at least one relation. Second, the ordering of members in an ordered set is a relation between them. Third, set membership, $\in$, is a relation. And many other relations are presupposed in the set theory that leads to the definition of Cartesian product, and in the logic that leads to set theory. Hence many relations are assumed in order to define relation, which makes this standard definition of relation in terms of sets circular and so logically useless. An even greater objection is that relations defined in this way cannot have emergent properties; the relation is identical with the subset of a Cartesian product, and a subset is a set, or extension, and such do not have emergent properties.

On the other hand, as we will see, there is little difficulty in defining sets by means of relations, and distinguishing the rational ones from the irrational. For this we have to assume that relations are logically primitive — but we have been doing this all along. We will distinguish between genuine relations, and relations that are logical constructs out of their terms, by calling the genuine relations **intensional relations**, and the logical constructs **extensional relations**. Whenever an intensional relation exists there also exists the set of all similar relations, and derivative from this is the set of all the ordered sets of terms of all of these similar relations; this latter set is the corresponding extensional relation. There is usually no point is discussing extensional relations unless one is trying to prove that intensional relations do not exist.

A relation which does not exist except in language is called a **nominal relation**.

✳ ✳ ✳

We next consider four special relations needed in later discussion: they are *possibility*, *identity*, *similarity* and *dissimilarity*.

✳

A **possibility relation** is characterised by having one special term, or set of terms, called the **antecedent**; all its other terms are called **consequents**, or **possibilities**; all these terms are always other relations. Each consequent is a possible emergent relation, given the antecedent; and, as possibilities, all the consequents are mutually exclusive, and exhaustive.

The number of consequents of a possibility relation is called its **degree of possibility**.

A possibility relation is here symbolised by an arrow, $\rightarrow$, and the disjunction of its consequents by a vertical stroke, $|$; so if A is the antecedent of consequents c_1 to c_n, this is symbolised by $A \rightarrow (c_1|c_2|...c_n)$, which means that given A, one and only one of the c_1 to c_n will emerge.

A **necessity** is a possibility relation having a degree of possibility of one, a singular possibility. A necessity relation is symbolised by $\Rightarrow$, and by $\Leftrightarrow$

if it is symmetric; and the absence of a necessity is symbolised by $\not\Rightarrow$. Thus if B is the only possibility, given A, then A$\Rightarrow$B and we say that A **necessitates** B.

A **bipossibility** is a possibility relation having a degree of two.

A **contingency** is a possibility relation having a degree of possibility greater than one, a plural possibility. Its degree of possibility is also called its **degree of contingency**. If A$\rightarrow$($c_1|c_2|...c_n$), we say that A **allows** c_1, A **allows** c_2, etc.

An **impossibility** might be defined as a zero possibility, which would make it a possibility relation of degree zero; but because there are no monadic relations, an impossibility is not a genuine relation, it is only a nominal relation.

Necessity is the basis of many mathematical functions, and of mathematical reasoning; bipossibility is the basis of complementary relations; and a contingency is here the basis of probability theory. We will look at each of these three degrees of possibility, with particular emphasis on singular possibility.

A real example of the necessity relation is theoretical causation, in which a cause is an event that is the antecedent and the effect is an event that is the consequent; the real cause necessitates the effect. A peculiar feature of theoretical causation, however, as we have seen [53], is that it is never empirical: if any real causes exist, they are always theoretical. Empirical causation is a different relation: namely, correlation, in which the earlier of two empirical events is called the cause and the later is called the effect, and correlation is an extensional relation between the set of all similar causes and the set of all similar effects. Thus theoretical causation is an intensional relation and empirical causation may be treated as an extensional relation: theoretical causation consists of genuine relations, individual necessities existing between each real cause and its real effect, while empirical causation consists of sets of constant conjunctions which define subsets of Cartesian products, each member of which is an ordered pair of empirical events called cause and effect. For example, visible lightning empirically causes audible thunder and each is theoretically caused by a theoretical atmospheric electric discharge, a complex structure of electric charges — as in Fig. 5.1 [82]. Empirical causation is characterised by universality: an instance of an empirical cause is *always* followed by an instance of the effect. The difference between *singular possibility* and *universality* has already been explained [244].

In pure mathematics relations of necessity occur as functions, mappings, operations, and transforms, since, given any argument of any of these, the value is a singular possibility: a necessity exists between each antecedent, or argument, and its consequent, or value, as a singular possibility. Thus the value of $\sin(\pi/2)$ *necessarily* is one. Similarly, a binary operation is a triadic relation that is a function between a pair of arguments, and a value that is a singular possibility given those arguments. Thus $\sqrt{2} + \sqrt{8}$ *necessarily* is $\sqrt{18}$. However, not all mathematical functions are necessity relations: some are only correlations — a point that will be discussed later. Those functions that are necessity relations are called **intensional functions**.

Necessities also occur as logical necessities in pure mathematics, in which the truth of a set of premises necessitates the truth of their conclusions: given the truth of the premises, there is only one possibility for the truth-value of each conclusion, namely, truth; this singular possibility is the necessity.

In applied mathematics a function describes a theoretical cause, and a differential equation with temporal derivatives describes a continuous series of causes, which is a **process**.

A second kind of necessity is an extrinsic property [258] of relations, rather than itself a relation. Distributive and compositional properties [277] are such extrinsic properties. If a whole has a distributive property then each part necessarily has it also, and this necessity is an upper extrinsic property [258] of each part; and if a part has a compositional property then the whole necessarily has it also, and this necessity is a lower extrinsic property of the whole. Necessities as extrinsic properties also occur with the emergence of relations: given a sufficient quantity and variety of terms for a relation to emerge, certain arrangements of those terms necessitate the emergence of the relation. Cascading emergence thus includes a series of such necessities.

Bipossibilities, our second kind of possibility relation, have only two consequents. They occur with such relations as *similar* and *dissimilar*, *true* and *false*, *inside* and *outside*, and a *toggle* such as an electrical *open* and *closed*. Given the requisite antecedent, one of the pair has to emerge, and thereby excludes the emergence of the other. Relations that occur in such mutually exclusive pairs of consequents are called **intensional complements**, and will be dealt with later [274].

Contingencies and their degrees, our third kind of possibility relation, are a basis of probability theory: if an antecedent A of a contingency relation of degree c has as one of its consequents the term C, then the probability of C, given A, is $1/c$. The limits of probabilities are 0 and 1, but these mark an open interval, not a closed one; this is because there is no degree of possibility of zero, other than nominally, because possibility relations are never monadic; and necessity is not, properly speaking, a contingency. A real contingency, if there are any (which is unlikely), is that kind of probability also known as a propensity. The importance of the concept of probability here is its use in the definition of hekergy [129]: a set of terms of a relation is the antecedent of e possible arrangements for the relation to emerge, and of t possible arrangements altogether, so that the probability of the emergence is e/t.

✱

Our second special relation, identity, is defined as: two or more symbols, words, names, or descriptions that between them have only one reference are said to be **identical**. Thus identity is a relation between these words and their one reference, as in the example of the identity of the highest mountain on Earth and Mt. Everest: we have a description, "the highest mountain on Earth", and a name, "Mt. Everest", but only one mountain. Identity is a linguistic relation because it relates language and reference; so far as the reference alone is concerned, there is only the one reference and no relation of identity. Identity will be symbolised by =.

✱

Our remaining special relations are similarity and dissimilarity; we have invoked them repeatedly in earlier chapters, and also called them resemblance and non-resemblance, and likeness and unlikeness, but here we deal with them somewhat more formally.

Similarity and **dissimilarity** are both dyadic, symmetric, relations that hold only between properties of relations: we may compare any two properties of relations and find that between them is either a similarity or a dissimilarity. Similarity will be symbolised here by ≋, and dissimilarity by ≈: symbols that will be easier to remember if their origin is explained. We have already defined similarity truth and dissimilarity falsity by means of similarity and dissimilarity. Falsity is usually symbolised by the tilde, $\sim$, so truth will here be symbolised by the tilde rotated through a right angle, $\wr$, since such rotation of a symmetric symbol is like negation, in that double application of the operation is the identity operation: double negation is affirmation. Since truth and falsity are special cases of similarity and dissimilarity, these latter are symbolised in parallel fashion by $\wr\wr$ and $\approx$.

✸

We may also note that certain relations that occur in ordinary language must be denied existence by Occam's Razor because of extravagant multiplication. Thus we speak of the relation *term of* that supposedly exists between a relation and each of its terms; and we speak of a whole being an *improper part* of itself, a set being an *improper subset* of itself, and a thing being *self-similar*. If *term of* is a relation then between it and each of its terms there must be a relation *term of*, which must have a relation *term of* between it and each of its terms, and so on to infinity. If *improper part* is a relation then this relation must be an improper part of itself, and this second relation of *improper part* must be an improper part of itself, and so on to infinity. And if anything is *self-similar* then this relation of *self-similarity* must be *self-similar*, thereby generating another infinity. Also, any similarity relation is similar to any other, so that another infinity of relations is generated, as are the infinity of similarities between dissimilarities. Relations such as these that multiply extravagantly exist only in language and so are nominal relations. All monadic relations are nominal, as well as those similarities and dissimilarities which multiply extravagantly.

However, *term of* is meaningful: a particular term either is, or is not, a term of a given relation. So we say that if A and B are terms of R, ARB, then A and B are **extrinsic properties** of R. More precisely, A and B are **lower extrinsic properties** of R, and AR is an **upper extrinsic property** of B and RB is an upper extrinsic property of A. For example, if your hat is *on* your head then your head has the upper extrinsic property of having a hat on it, and your hat has the upper extrinsic property of being on your head, while the relation *on* has the lower extrinsic properties of your head and your hat. As opposed to extrinsic properties, the actual properties of a relation, such as its adicity, are called **intrinsic properties**[14]. However, unless the precision of these definitions is required, we will use the words *term*, *property*, and *extrinsic property* for *lower extrinsic property*, *intrinsic property*, and *upper extrinsic property*, respectively.

So much for preliminaries.

★ ★ ★

As we have already seen, relations are characterised by being abstract entities that are simple — they have no concrete qualities and no parts — and by having both terms and properties. Their terms, which, with some exceptions, are also relations, are what they relate; and their properties are what distinguish one kind of relation from another. So every relation defines three **natural sets**, as they might be called: the set of all of its terms, which are its lower extrinsic properties, called its **term set**; the set of all of its intrinsic properties, called its **intrinsic property set**, or **property set** for short; and the set of all its upper extrinsic properties, which is all the relations of which it is a term, with or without their other terms, which is called its **upper extrinsic property set**, or **extrinsic property set** for short. Relations will be symbolised by uppercase letters; but since symbolising the terms of relations by lowercase letters is conventional, and these terms are themselves relations, we will symbolise terms by small caps; thus ARB symbolises the fact that the relations A and B are related by R, although we might equally say that the relations A and B are related by R. Term sets will be symbolised by uppercase italic letters, such as *A, B, C*; and property sets will be symbolised by capped small caps, such as Â, B̂, Ĉ; a single property will also be symbolised in the same way, since the distinction between property sets and individual properties is not here important. Upper extrinsic property sets will be symbolised by italicised capped small caps, such as *Â, B̂, Ĉ*. Membership in all these sets is symbolised as ususal by ∈. We want to generalise term sets into the extensions of orthodox set theory, and property sets into the intensions of those orthodox extensions that have intensions.

---

[14] Unfortunately the word *intrinsic* is ambiguous: we speak of the parts being intrinsic to the whole, and the members being intrinsic to the set, a second usage different from the present. Earlier we defined intrinsic relations [100] in this second sense.

From this we will get our three kinds of meaning. Intensional meanings are either relations or properties of relations. Extensional meanings are extensions of sets. And nominal meanings are the nominal analogies of either of these or else of sets that have no extensions. Intensional meanings are intensions, so they define extensions; extensions may or may not have intensions, but they always have members; and nominal meanings include sets that have no members, called **null sets**. Thus intensional meanings are clearly a sufficient condition for extensional meanings, which in turn are a sufficient condition for nominal meanings; but nominal meanings are only a necessary condition for extensional meanings, which in turn are only a necessary condition for intensional meanings. And because intensional meanings, and only intensional meanings, are relations, and relations may emerge from other relations, in a cascade of higher and higher emergent relations, we can explain the axiom generosity that is exclusive to intensional meanings; while because contradictions are possible only in language, they have nominal meanings only.

Logic and mathematics are a mixtures of all three kinds of meaning, and so have both axiom generosity and contradictions, or paradoxes. The advantage of distinguishing the kinds of meaning is that if a mathematics can be devised in which everything has intensional meaning then it will have the advantage of having axiom generosity while being perfectly consistent. This requires only the separation of intensional meanings from nominal meanings.

∗

We begin by defining five relations between term sets that are already familiar to most people: intersection, union, subset, equality, and complement; and five analogous relations between property sets. Those between term sets are defined by means of *identity*, and are called **extensional connectives**; and those between property sets are defined analogously by means of *similarity* and are called **intensional connectives**. We want to discover the relations between intensional connectives and their corresponding extensional connectives.

∗

1A. Two term sets, S and T, are **identical**, symbolised by $S=T$, if each member of S is *identical* with a member of T, and *vice versa*. $S=T$ means both that for all x, $(x \in S) \Rightarrow (x \in T)$ and $(x \in T) \Rightarrow (x \in S)$; or $(x \in S) \Leftrightarrow (x \in T)$. Set identity here is what is usually called *set equality*; strictly speaking, it is not a relation between sets, but it is here treated as one for simplicity.

1B. Two property sets, ŝ and t̂, are **similar,** symbolised by ŝ≀≀t̂, if each member of ŝ is *similar* to a member of t̂, and *vice versa*.

We can now distinguish two kinds of set-membership: **intensional set-membership** is membership in identical sets and **intrinsic property set-membership** is membership in similar sets. We distinguish the two kinds of membership by context: in x∈S the membership, ∈, is intensional set-membership, and in x̂∈ŝ it is intrinsic property set-membership; and whenever the word membership is used hereafter, the context will make clear which kind it is.

The membership in an extrinsic property set is intensional set-membership.

So now we may say that if ŝ≀≀t̂ then for all x̂, (x̂∈ŝ)⇒(x̂∈t̂) and (x̂∈t̂)⇒(x̂∈ŝ), or (x̂∈ŝ)⇔(x̂∈t̂).

Invoking Occam's Razor, we have to say that no two members of any one property set are similar.

✷

2A. The **intersection** of two term sets, *S* and *T*, symbolised by *S*∩*T*, if it exists, is such that each member of *S*∩*T* is *identical* both with a member of *S* and with a member of *T*. If an intersection does not exist, its term sets are said to be **disjoint**: they have no member in common.

2B. The **commonality** of two property sets, ŝ and t̂, symbolised by ŝ⅄t̂, if it exists, is such that each member of ŝ⅄t̂ is *similar* both to a member of ŝ and to a member of t̂. If a commonality does not exist, its property sets are said to be **disparate**: they have no property in common.

✷

3A. The **union** of two term sets, *S* and *T*, symbolised by *S*∪*T*, is such that each member of *S*∪*T* is *identical* either with a member of *S* or with a member of *T*.

3B. The **coupling** of two property sets, ŝ and t̂, symbolised by ŝγt̂, is such that each member of ŝγt̂ is *similar* either to a member of ŝ or to a member of t̂.

✷

4A. A term set, *S* is a **subset** of another term set, *T*, symbolised *S*⊂*T*, if each member of *S* is *identical* with a member of *T*, but not *vice versa*. The inverse of subset is **superset**, symbolised by $\supset$. If S is either a subset of T, or identical with T, this is symbolised by $S \subseteq T$. $S \subset T$ means that for all x, $(x \in S) \Rightarrow (x \in T)$ but $(x \in T) \not\Rightarrow (x \in S)$.

4B. A property set, $\hat{s}$, is a **subintension** of another property set, $\hat{t}$, symbolised $\hat{s} \prec \hat{t}$, if each member of $\hat{s}$ is *similar* to a member of $\hat{t}$, but not *vice versa*. The inverse of subintension is **superintension**, symbolised by $\succ$. $\hat{s} \prec \hat{t}$ means that for all $\hat{x}$, $(\hat{x} \in \hat{s}) \Rightarrow (\hat{x} \in \hat{t})$ but $(\hat{x} \in \hat{t}) \not\Rightarrow (\hat{x} \in \hat{s})$.

We will generally be more concerned with superintension than with subintension, since superintension will later be shown to be the main basis of analyticity and valid reasoning.

✶

5A. The **set difference** of two intersecting term sets, A and B, symbolised $A - B$., if it exists, is the set consisting of those members of A which are not *identical* with any member of B.

5B. The **decoupling** of two property sets, $\hat{a}$ and $\hat{b}$, which are not completely dissimilar, symbolised $\hat{a} - \hat{b}$, if it exists, is the property set consisting of those members of $\hat{a}$ which are not *similar*, or are dissimilar, to any member of $\hat{b}$.

Decoupling is submergence of coupling. If $\hat{c} \, \aleph \, (\hat{a} \curlyvee \hat{b})$ then the decoupling of $\hat{a}$ from $\hat{c}$, $\hat{c} - \hat{a}$, is similar to $\hat{b}$, and the decoupling of $\hat{b}$ from $\hat{c}$, $\hat{c} - \hat{b}$, is similar to $\hat{a}$: $(\hat{c} - \hat{a}) \, \aleph \, \hat{b}$ and $(\hat{c} - \hat{b}) \, \aleph \, \hat{a}$; these decouplings exist only if there exist relations having $\hat{a}$, $\hat{b}$, and $\hat{c}$ as their property sets.

If U is the universe of discourse and S is an extension then the **extensional complement** of S, symbolised S', is the extension $U - S$.

If two relations R and S are the consequents of a bipossibility relation then they are **intensional complements** of each other. This is symbolised with a prime: S is R' and R is S'.

✶

It is important that the extensional connectives — relations between term sets such as union and intersection — are distinguished from intensional connectives — relations between property sets such as coupling and commonality — by the fact that the former are defined by identity while the latter are defined by similarity. In ordinary language identity and similarity are frequently interchanged, as if they were synonyms; but here they must not be. Identity is oneness, whereas similarity requires twoness, since it is a dyadic relation; and when similarity is used transitively, a greater number of terms is required. So in general identity requires unity and similarity requires plurality; consequently not only can neither be inferred from the other, but the existence of one disallows the existence of the other. As we have seen [13], to infer identity from similarity is the identity error. We will discover the fundamental relation between identity and similarity shortly, in what is called the equivalence theorem.

$$\star\,\star\,\star$$

We next generalise term sets into extensions of sets in general, and property sets into their intensions, and then examine the relations between their connectives.

All relations unify their terms.

A **set relation** is a relation that has only one intrinsic property, a particular adicity. Set relations emerge with values of the **function every**, which has intensions as its arguments: the value of each argument is a plurality defined by that argument and unified by a set relation. The plurality is an **extension** and the unified plurality is an **intensional set**. An intensional set is thus the term set of a set relation, and all other term sets are intensional sets, since they are unified by the relation of which they are terms.

So if we have an intension, $\hat{R}\hat{P}$, then the function every, with $\hat{R}\hat{P}$ as argument, defines the intensional set whose extension is every $\hat{R}\hat{P}$, and which is unified by a set relation. An intension usually is a property set and a relation, such as $\wr\wr\hat{P}$ or $\succ\hat{P}$, or, generally, $\hat{R}\hat{P}$. The conventional symbolism for the sets defined by these three intensions is $\{x: x\wr\wr\hat{P}\}$, $\{x: x\succ\hat{P}\}$, and $\{x: xR\hat{P}\}$; these read as: "Every x that is similar to $\hat{P}$", "Every x that is a superintension of $\hat{P}$", and "Every x that is related by R to $\hat{P}$". Thus a set defining rule states an intension. We will here adopt a different symbolism: we will leave out the variable, x, since this is only needed in an extensional approach, and we will make the function *every* explicit, with the symbol $\forall$: thus $\{\forall(\wr\wr\hat{P})\}$, $\{\forall(\succ\hat{P})\}$, and $\{\forall(\hat{R}\hat{P})\}$. As usual, the braces (curly brackets) signify a set, which intensionally is a unified plurality.

Two special cases of intensional sets are sets unified by a relation which has more properties than the single adicity of a set relation. One is a **compound relation**, which is unified by a relation which has a property similar to one or more properties of all of its terms; a compound length, for example, has prime lengths as its terms and is itself a length. The second is a **whole**, which is unified by a relation which has a **novel property**, a property not possessed by any of its terms, or by any lower level relation; a melody, for example, has notes as terms, and no notes are melodic.

The **similarity set** of a relation R is an intensional set whose defining relation is similarity: $\{\forall(\aleph\hat{R})\}$. If $x\in\{\forall(\aleph\hat{R})\}$ then X is an **instance** of R.

Given a relation S such that $S\aleph R$ then $S\in\{\forall(\aleph\hat{R})\}$; but because $S\aleph R$, $\aleph S$ is equally an intension of $\{\forall(\aleph\hat{R})\}$, and so $\{\forall(\aleph\hat{R})\}$ has as many intensions as it has members, all exactly alike. Thus any two similarity sets are disjoint.

Because an instance of R determines the similarity set of R, just as R does, the difference between a kind of a relation and an instance of that relation is trivial. As we have seen, an instance of a relation is determined by its term set and a kind of relation is determined by its intrinsic property set. The instance is a member of the similarity set and the kind is the intension of the similarity set; these are symbolised by R or R, for the instance, and by $\hat{R}$ for the kind, and since the difference between instance and kind is trivial, it is not usually of great moment which of the symbols R or $\hat{R}$ are used. Thus *2* stands equally for the number two and for an instance of it. The expression *any instance* is synonymous with *kind*, because the definition of the function *any* is that it is the inverse of the function *every*. Strictly speaking, we should say that to speak of *the* kind of a relation is incorrect: there are many instances of similar relations, and every instance is an intension of their one similarity set, but there is no one kind. For example, there are many instances of two, or dyadicity, but *the* number two does not exist. But ordinary language is such that it is almost impossible to avoid such usage, which results from another instance of *the* identity error; so we will continue to speak of kinds. (We could, of course, define *the* kind as the extension of the similarity set, but this would be an extensional meaning, not an intensional one.)

The **superintension set** of a relation R is an intensional set whose defining relation is superintension: $\{\forall(\succ\hat{R})\}$. If $x\in\{\forall(\succ\hat{R})\}$ then X is a **representative instance** of R.

Every member of the superintension set of a property set $\hat{P}$, or of the similarity set of $\hat{P}$, is said to **have**, or **possess**, the properties of $\hat{P}$.

We also mention, for the sake of completeness, that the **subintension set** of a relation R is an intensional set whose defining relation is subintension: $\{\forall(\prec\hat{R})\}$.

264

All intensions are extrinsic to each member of the set that they define. For example, if x∈{∀(ℛ̂)} then x ℛ̂ and ℛ̂ is extrinsic to x. However, some intensions define by means of intrinsic property sets and some by extrinsic property sets; these will be called **intrinsic intensions** and **extrinsic intensions**, respectively, and the sets that they define are **intrinsic sets** and **extrinsic sets**. The intensions of property sets, similarity sets, superintension sets, and subintension sets are intrinsic intensions; all others are extrinsic intensions.

The nature of the function every is such that every intensional set is complete. For this reason intensional sets are also called **complete sets**. And because the relation *every* is a function, the membership of an intensional set is necessitated by the intension of that set; for this reason intensional sets are also called **necessary sets**. And, finally, it is because the membership is necessitated by an intension that sets such as these are called intensional sets. (We will consider incomplete sets, contingent sets, and extensional sets later [267].) This completeness that is necessitated is called **intensional completeness**, to distinguish it from other kinds.

★ ★ ★

At the end of this chapter we prove the following five theorems relating intensional and extensional connectives, assuming the existence of the relevant property sets:

The negation theorem: $\{\forall\hat{A}'\}=\{\forall\hat{A}\}'$

The conjunction theorem: $\{\forall(\hat{A}\curlyvee\hat{B})\} = (\{\forall\hat{A}\}\cap\{\forall\hat{B}\})$

The disjunction theorem: $\{\forall(\hat{A}\curlywedge\hat{B})\} \supseteq (\{\forall\hat{A}\}\cup\{\forall\hat{B}\})$

The implication theorem: $(\hat{A}\succ\hat{B}) \Leftrightarrow (\{\forall\hat{A}\}\subset\{\forall\hat{B}\})$

The equivalence theorem: $(\hat{A}\,ℛ\,\hat{B}) \Leftrightarrow (\{\forall\hat{A}\}=\{\forall\hat{B}\})$

If $\hat{A}\succ\hat{B}$ we may say that $\hat{A}$ is larger than $\hat{B}$, and $\hat{B}$ is smaller than $\hat{A}$; and similarly if $\{\forall\hat{A}\}\subset\{\forall\hat{B}\}$ we may say that $\{\forall\hat{A}\}$ is smaller than $\{\forall\hat{B}\}$ and $\{\forall\hat{B}\}$ is larger than $\{\forall\hat{A}\}$. What we are really doing is anticipating later developments by assuming that intensions and extensions, as sets, have natural numbers of members, and these numbers may be compared. So these theorems together imply that the larger an intension the smaller its extension, and *vice versa*. This means that sets determined by simple rules have very large extensions, while small extensions must be determined by large, complex, rules. This may seem implausible at first, as shown by the example of "Everything in this box", which is a small extension determined by a simple extrinsic intension; but "in this box" is a simplification of the intension, since everything in this box is also in this room, in this building, in this town, on this planet, in this solar system, in this galaxy, etc. Mathematically this situation occurs with least upper bounds and greatest lower bounds. An interval specified by a g.l.b. and a l.u.b. properly includes in its specification all its lower bounds and all its upper bounds: to specify the greatest is to presuppose the existence of the ordered set of all lower bounds, and similarly for the least. So the intension is large while the extension is small — compared with, say, the set of natural numbers, which has a small intension — the property of adicity — and a large extension.

✶

An **enumeration** of an extension is a list of the names or descriptions of every member of that extension.

An intensional set may in principle be specified either by a rule or by an enumeration, but an enumeration is not a set-defining rule because it does not specify an intension. We also see that an enumeration is not an intension from the fact that an enumeration is in one-one correspondence with the extension it specifies, so that the larger the enumeration the larger the extension, as opposed to the principle that the larger the intension the smaller the extension.

✶

Since the definition of commonality allows it to be polyadic, we may speak of the commonality of all the members of an extension; if S is an extension, the commonality of its members, if it exists, will be symbolised by $\wedge S$.

Notice that if a relation R has the property set $\hat{r}$ then the commonality of its similarity set is $\hat{r}$: $(\wedge\{\forall(\aleph R)\})\aleph\hat{r}$

We will later prove the theorem:

Theorem 3: A set S is an intensional set if and only if $\wedge S$ exists and $S=\{\forall(\wedge S)\}$.

✶

We turn next to "sets" which do not have intensions. Recall that a set is a unified plurality: the set is one, the plurality is many, and the plurality is the extension of the set. Ordinary language treats pluralities as single entities, as with *the* plurality or *a* plurality, and it does the same with extensions; there is no way to avoid this, other than to emphasise that pluralities are not one, they are many. Ordinary language also treats any plurality as a set, or class. We can allow this usage by enlarging the concept of set to that of **extensional set**, which is any plurality. Thus every intensional set defines an extensional set, but not every plurality is unified into an intensional set. An extensional set which is not unified into an intensional set is also called a **contingent set** and an **incomplete set**, since it is neither necessary nor complete.

We will later prove the theorem:

Theorem 4: A set S is a contingent set if and only if it has members and either its commonality, $\wedge S$, does not exist or else $\wedge S$ exists and $S \subset \{\forall(\wedge S)\}$.

For example, the enumerated set $A=\{1, 2, 7, 11\}$ has the commonality *number less than twelve*, or $\hat{\text{N}}$, say: $(\wedge A)\wr\wr\hat{\text{N}}$. Clearly, $\{\forall\hat{\text{N}}\}=\{1, 2,...12\}$ But $B=\{1, 3, 11\}$ and $C=\{1, 2, 3, 4, 5, 6, 7, 11\}$ have the same commonality, $\hat{\text{N}}$, so $A\subset\{\forall(\wedge\hat{\text{A}})\}=\{\forall\hat{\text{N}}\}$, $B\subset\{\forall(\wedge\hat{\text{B}})\}=\{\forall\hat{\text{N}}\}$, and $C\subset\{\forall(\wedge\hat{\text{C}})\}=\{\forall\hat{\text{N}}\}$. Thus there is no function from $\hat{\text{N}}$ to A, B, or C, because their membership is not necessitated by an intension, so these sets are contingent; because each is only a subset of $\{\forall\hat{\text{N}}\}$, each is incomplete; and because each is a plurality that is not unified by a relation, each is an extensional set, not an intensional set.

More generally, this theorem takes into account the fact that not all extensions have intensions; if $(x\epsilon A)\Rightarrow(x\epsilon B)$, and B is an intensional set, then A may not be an intensional set. This is because A may be a random selection of members of B, and so have no intension. We can still say that A is a subset of B, $A\subset B$, and hence A is an extension, because A has members; but since A

has no intension, it is incomplete, and its membership is contingent, so it cannot be specified by a set-defining rule, although it can be specified by an enumeration, such as $A = \{1, 2, 7, 11\}$.

Because of this the disjunction theorem proves that there is no closure on union of intensional sets: the union of two intensional sets may not be an intensional set, since it may be a subset of an intensional set and so may also not be an intensional set but a set that has no intension, is incomplete and is contingent, so that it cannot be specified by a set-defining rule, although it could be specified by an enumeration. We will later see an example of such non-closure, and at the end of the chapter will show Theorem 10, Coroll.:

$$(\{\forall(\hat{A} \curlywedge \hat{B})\} = (\{\forall \hat{A}\} \cup \{\forall \hat{B}\})) \Leftrightarrow ((\{\forall \hat{A}\} \cup \{\forall \hat{B}\}) \text{ is a necessary set), and}$$
$$(\{\forall(\hat{A} \curlywedge \hat{B})\} \supset (\{\forall \hat{A}\} \cup \{\forall \hat{B}\})) \Leftrightarrow ((\{\forall \hat{A}\} \cup \{\forall \hat{B}\}) \text{ is not a necessary set).}$$

We may extend our concept of **extensional definition** [246] to: an extensional definition of a set is either a definition by means of an enumeration or by means of extensional connectives between extensions.

Note that every subset of a similarity set is an incomplete set.

There is a trivial sense in which an intensionless set is complete: it is **extensionally complete** if it contains every member specified in its enumeration; this is a relation of one-one correspondence between the extension and the enumeration. The completeness that we have been talking about before this is intensional completeness.

The definitions above of the extensional connectives — set identity, intersection, union, and subset — may all be extended to incomplete sets. It is possible but unlikely that a subset of an incomplete set, or a union or intersection of any two of them, are complete sets. Obviously, the definitions of the intensional connectives cannot be applied to incomplete sets.

✳

The concept of set may be extended further in that the intersection of two disjoint sets may be called a set. The intersection of two disjoint sets is then a set that has no extension.

A **null set** is a set that has no extension.

A **nominal set** is a set that is either an extensional set or a null set.

✳ ✳ ✳

We can now distinguish three distinct set theories.

Intensional set theory deals only with intensional, or, equivalently, complete, or necessary, sets.

Extensional set theory deals with extensional sets: sets that are either complete or incomplete, necessary or contingent, without distinction.

Nominal set theory deals with nominal sets: sets that are intensional, extensional, or null, without distinction.

Thus the content of intensional set theory is a subset of the content of extensional set theory, which is a subset of the content of nominal set theory. So the existence of sets of intensional set theory is a sufficient condition for the existence of sets of extensional set theory, which in turn is a sufficient condition for the existence of sets of nominal set theory; but the existence of sets of nominal set theory is only a necessary condition for sets of extensional set theory, which in turn is only a necessary condition for sets of intensional set theory.

With three kinds of set theory we can again distinguish three kinds of meaning: intensional, extensional, and nominal.

A symbol, name, or description has **intensional meaning** if its meaning is an intension. Intensional meanings are thus either relations or sets of properties of relations: intrinsic or extrinsic properties.

A symbol, name, or description has **extensional meaning** if its meaning is an extensional set; and it has **exclusively extensional meaning** if it has no intensional meaning.

Clearly, intensional meaning is a sufficient condition for extensional meaning, since every intension determines an extension; but extensional meaning is only a necessary condition for intensional meaning since not every extension has an intension. Thus the set of all intensional meanings determines a subset of the set of all extensional meanings.

A symbol, name, or description has **nominal meaning** if its meaning is a nominal set; and it has **exclusively nominal meaning** if it has no extensional meaning.

Clearly, extensional meaning is a sufficient condition for nominal meaning, but nominal meaning is only a necessary condition for extensional meaning; and the set of all extensional meanings determines a subset of the set of all nominal meanings.

A symbol, name, or description has **purely intensional meaning** if it has no exclusively extensional meaning.

A mathematical symbol, name, or description has **purely extensional meaning** if it has no exclusively nominal meaning.

We could define *purely nominal meaning* similarly, but it would be no different from exclusively nominal meaning.

Purely intensional meaning entails some extensional meaning, and some nominal meaning, since every intension defines an extension and every extension may be described or named; but they entail no more extensional and nominal meanings than this minimum. Similarly, purely extensional meaning entails a minimum of nominal meaning.

Since some nominal sets have neither intensions nor extensions, their nominal meaning is meaning by verbal analogy to intensional or extensional meaning. For example, given that the words *triangle*, *equilateral*, and *right angle* have intensional meaning, these meanings may be coupled to give intensional meaning to *equilateral triangle* and *right angled triangle*; such coupling is indicated grammatically by verbal adjacence. So by verbal analogy these words also may be conjoined to give 'right angled equilateral triangle', which has neither intensional meaning nor extensional meaning, and so has only nominal meaning. Or we might have an enumeration of a supposed extensional set, such that every item in the enumeration had only nominal meaning; so by verbal analogy this enumeration has nominal meaning but no extensional meaning.

We have already made the claim [258], on the basis of Occam's Razor, that certain names of relations have nominal meaning only: namely, the supposed relation *term of*, and supposed monadic relations, or relations with only one term, such as self-similarity, improper part, and improper subset.

✱

Since the set of all intensional meanings determines a subset of the set of all extensional meanings, and the set of all extensional meanings determines a subset of the set of all nominal meanings, intensional meaning has the least generality and nominal meaning has the most.

However, intensional meanings have least arbitrariness, and nominal meanings have most. Arbitrariness in intensional meaning is confined to arbitrary manipulations of intensions; the resulting sets, if they exist, are necessary sets: their membership is necessitated by the intension, and thereby unarbitrary. With exclusively extensional meaning far more

270

arbitrariness is possible: any random sequence of numbers is an intensionless extension, or exclusively extensional set, and any random selection of referring proper names or definite descriptions is an enumeration of an exclusively extensional set. (Indeed, one might define the **random** as any intensionless set; as such it has exclusively extensional meaning.) With exclusively nominal meaning still more arbitrariness is made possible with ridiculous combinations of symbols, words, and descriptions, as with the even prime numbers greater than two, the rational square root of two, square-circle, military intelligence, honest politician, and truth in advertising.

Two reasons, more important than arbitrariness, for distinguishing these three kinds of meaning are that axiom generosity is possible only with purely intensional meanings, and paradox is possible only with exclusively nominal meanings. Exclusively extensional meanings are between these, both in lacking axiom generosity and in being free of paradox.

Axiom generosity is possible only with intensional meaning because axiom generosity results from cascading emergence, only relations can produce this, and only relations produce intensions. Paradox and contradiction cannot exist in reality so they are possible only in language[15]: that is, language that has no reference and so has only nominal meaning.

Both everyday language and everyday mathematics have a mixture of all three kinds of meaning. For example, whenever mathematicians define a set with a genuine set-defining rule, they have intensional meaning; when they define by means of intensionless extensions, as with enumerated sets, they have extensional meaning but usually no intensional meaning; and whenever their definitions lead to paradox, as with the definition of the set of all sets (which leads to Cantor's paradox [230]), or the set of all sets that are not self-membered (which leads to Russell's paradox [230]), they have nominal meaning but neither extensional nor intensional meaning.

---

[15] We spoke in Part One [25] of illusions as empirical contradictions, which suggests that contradictions can exist in empirical worlds. But they are only contradictions within the context of realism. The half-immersed stick that is bent to the sight and not-bent to the touch is an empirical contradiction only if it is one stick; when understood as two sticks, one seen and one touched, seemingly united by interpretation, there is no contradiction.

⋆ ⋆ ⋆

We have already, in the last chapter, illustrated the three kinds of meaning with the sentential connectives and with the concepts of *analyticity* [243, 280], *predication* [245], and *definition* [246]. Here we will further consider the three kinds of meaning of the concept of *necessity*, examine the sentential connectives in greater detail, and look at the three kinds of meaning of the concepts of *truth*, *validity*, and *equivalence*.

⋆

Intensional necessity is either the relation of singular possibility or an extrinsic property; for simplicity we will only consider the relation here, and leave the extrinsic property to Chapter 17. **Extensional necessity** is universality, as occurs with subsets: if the contingent set A is a subset of the contingent set B, then members of A are universally members of B, but only contingently so, hence not intensionally necessarily so. **Nominal necessity** is the necessity of truth-functional tautology, which requires such strange things as the paradoxes of material implication [251].

The difference between singular possibility and universality is that it is inconceivable for singular possibility to be otherwise, but not for universality to be otherwise: we cannot conceive of 2+3=5 being otherwise[16] but we can conceive of a particular party having a different guest list. Again, of the six examples of exclusively nominal meaning above, the first three are necessarily contradictions and the last three are universally contradictions. Observe that singular possibility is a sufficient condition for universality, which in turn is a sufficient condition for tautology, but tautology is only a necessary condition for universality, which in turn is only a necessary condition for singular possibility.

Another example of extensional necessity occurs with extensional functions, which may be defined by means of a **contingent function**, which is a contingent set of assignments of unique values to every member in its

---

[16] We can say, or write, otherwise, as in 2+3=7, but such statements have nominal meaning only. To conceive is to have more than words or symbols in the mind: it is to have these plus their abstract meanings. We say of an expression such as 2+3=7, not that it is meaningless, but that it is false; which is to say that each concept in it, each part of it — 2, 3, 7, +, and = — has intensional meaning but the proposition, the whole of it, does not, it only has nominal meaning.

domain, which latter is the extensional set of its arguments. An **extensional function** is then either a contingent function; or the extension, determined by an intensional function, consisting of a complete set of pairs, where each pair is composed of an argument of the intensional function and its corresponding value.

A contingent function may be enumerated but cannot be specified by a rule. A contingent function universally assigns unique values to its arguments, as does an intensional function, but this universality does not arise from an intensional necessity. So the existence of an intensional function is a sufficient condition for the existence of an extensional function, but the converse is only a necessary condition. The intensional function is a necessity and the extensional function is a universality. Also, an extensional function may be far more arbitrary than an intensional one.

✶

Turning again to the sentential connectives — negation, conjunction, disjunction, implication, and equivalence — the three kinds of meaning may be defined quite clearly.

If Â and B̂ are intensions then the intensional meanings of the sentential connectives are the intensional connectives; assuming that they exist,

> Â′ means "Non-Â" or "Not Â"
> Â⅄B̂ means "Â and B̂"
> Â⅄B̂ means "Â or B̂"
> Â≻B̂ means "If Â then B̂" or "Â implies B̂"
> Â≀≀B̂ means "Â is equivalent to B̂"

If A and B are extensions then the extensional meanings of the sentential connectives are the extensional connectives. Assuming that they exist,

> $x \in A'$ means "$x \in A'$" or "$x \notin A$"
> $x \in (A \cap B)$ means "$x \in A$ and $x \in B$"
> $x \in (A \cup B)$ means "$x \in A$ or $x \in B$"
> $A \subset B$ means "$x \in A$ implies $x \in B$"
> $A = B$ means "$x \in A$ is equivalent to $x \in B$"

P	Q	~P	P∧Q	P∨Q	P⊃Q	P≡Q
T	T	F	T	T	T	T
F	T	T	F	T	T	F
T	F		F	T	F	F
F	F		F	F	T	T

Table 15.1.

The nominal meanings of the sentential connectives are the standard truth-functional connectives, defined by truth tables: negation (~), conjunction (∧), disjunction (∨), material implication (⊃), and equivalence (≡), as in Table 15.1:

Notice that when we defined the extensional connectives and the intensional connectives, using identity and similarity, we did it by means of words such as *not, and, or,* and *if... then...* which suggests circularity in the definitions. In fact, we all have meanings for these words, which we learn soon after we learn to talk. It is these natural meanings that were intended in the definitions of the intensional and extensional connectives, and it is now proposed that these natural meanings are the extensional meanings; the intensional and nominal meanings are then derivative from the natural meanings. So properly speaking, the extensional connectives are primitive, undefined: the supposed definitions given above are only characterisations of them in terms of our natural meanings.

The nominal and extensional meanings of the sentential connectives are familiar enough to those with some logical or mathematical background, but some more must be said about the intensional sentential connectives, and also about extensional implication.

Intensional negation occurs only with intensional complements, such as *in* and *out, true* and *false, similar* and *dissimilar,* and *member* and *non-member.* Any other use of negation in intensional discourse is metalinguistic, as in the correction of an error, the disproof of a conjecture, or a proof of non-existence. A discourse in which everything has purely intensional

274

meaning states only intensional fact and so has no use for negation as a metalinguistic operation. So for most relations there are only nominal complements: the nominal complement of the relation being its absence, or non-existence, which has no intensional or extensional meaning. When a relation has a symbol of its own, this non-existence, or purely nominal meaning, is shown by a vertical stroke through the symbol[17]. Thus coupling is ϒ and its absence is ϒ̸, necessity is ⇒ and its absence is ⇏, and intersection is ∩ and its absence, or disjointness, is ⋔. So there is no closure on intensional negation: very few intensional meanings have intensional complements and so may be negated intensionally, although all of them may be negated nominally.

Intensional conjunction may be coupling of abstract ideas, as in *right triangle*, or coupling of propositions — which are structures of abstract ideas. Coupling of ideas is not always possible; when not, the extensions of the ideas are disjoint. When this happens, as in *square circle*, the words for the ideas may be conjoined but the result has exclusively nominal meaning; so there is no closure on intensional conjunction: the verbal conjunction of two intensional meanings does not necessarily have an intensional meaning. Coupling of propositions is usually implicit, linguistically: the relation that couples them is succession — sentential succession, and hence propositional succession. That is, the conjunction is nominally implicit but intensionally explicit, in that there is no *and* or *but*, but the relations of succession are genuine. For clarity, the symbol & will also be used here for intensional conjunction, particularly in the case of intensional propositions.

Intensional disjunction, or commonality, also has no closure, for two reasons. First, the commonality of two intensions may not exist, in which case the disjunction is purely extensional and nominal. Second, if the commonality does exist then the union of their extensions may not be an intensional set, as shown by the disjunction theorem: $\{\forall(\hat{A}\lambda\hat{B})\} \supseteq (\{\forall\hat{A}\}\cup\{\forall\hat{B}\})$. As a result of this second reason, there are two kinds of disjunction of intensions: that in which the resulting extension is an

---

[17] Since non-membership is a relation, the intensional complement of membership, we should use the symbol ϵ' rather than the more usual $\notin$; but this latter usage is so well established that it has to remain non-conforming.

intensional, or complete, set, and that in which it is not an intensional set, hence an incomplete set.

A **complete disjunction** is an intensional commonality, or disjunction, whose extension is a complete, or necessary, set.

An **incomplete disjunction** is an intensional commonality, or disjunction, whose extension is an incomplete, or contingent, set.

We saw, and will later prove, that an extension S is complete if and only if $\wedge S$ exists and $S=\{\forall\wedge S\}$, while S is incomplete if either $\wedge S$ does not exist or else $S\subset\{\forall\wedge S\}$. So if $\{\forall\hat{A}\}\cup\{\forall\hat{B}\}=\{\forall(\hat{A}\curlywedge\hat{B})\}$ then the intensional disjunction $\hat{A}\curlyvee\hat{B}$ is a complete disjunction; if $\{\forall\hat{A}\}\cup\{\forall\hat{B}\}\subset\{\forall(\hat{A}\curlywedge\hat{B})\}$, then the intensional disjunction $\hat{A}\curlywedge\hat{B}$ is an incomplete disjunction. And if $\wedge(\{\forall\hat{A}\}\cup\{\forall\hat{B}\})$ does not exist then there is no intensional disjunction, only an extensional disjunction.

This will be more clear with examples.

First, let the intensions of *natural number, odd,* and *even* be $\hat{N}$, $\hat{O}$, and $\hat{E}$. Then the intensions of the sets of the odd numbers and of the even numbers are $\hat{N}\curlyvee\hat{O}$ and $\hat{N}\curlyvee\hat{E}$ and the extensional disjunction of these sets is $\{\forall(\hat{N}\curlyvee\hat{O})\}\cup\{\forall(\hat{N}\curlyvee\hat{E})\}$, which, as we know, is the set $\{\forall\hat{N}\}$. Intensionally, the disjunction is $(\hat{N}\curlyvee\hat{O})\curlywedge(\hat{N}\curlyvee\hat{E})$, which is similar to $\hat{N}$: $((\hat{N}\curlyvee\hat{O})\curlywedge(\hat{N}\curlyvee\hat{E}))\,\aleph\hat{N}$. So it follows, by the equivalence theorem, that

$$\{\forall((\hat{N}\curlyvee\hat{O})\curlywedge(\hat{N}\curlyvee\hat{E}))\} = \{\forall(N\curlyvee\hat{O})\}\cup\{\forall(\hat{N}\curlyvee\hat{E})\}.$$

So intensionally what is either an odd number or an even number is a number; the disjunction is complete and conforms with normal usage.

For the second example, let the intensional meanings of *polygon, trilateral,* and *quadrilateral* be $\hat{P}$, $\hat{T}$, and $\hat{Q}$. Then $\hat{T}\curlyvee\hat{P}$ and $\hat{Q}\curlyvee\hat{P}$ are the intensional meanings of *triangle* and *quadrangle,* and $\{\forall(\hat{T}\curlyvee\hat{P})\}$ and $\{\forall(\hat{Q}\curlyvee\hat{P})\}$ are the intensional sets of every triangle and of every quadrangle. So $\{\forall(\hat{T}\curlyvee\hat{P})\}\cup\{\forall(\hat{Q}\curlyvee\hat{P})\}$ is the extensional disjunction of these disjoint sets; anything belonging to this set is either a triangle or a quadrangle. However the intensional disjunction of $\hat{T}\curlyvee\hat{P}$ and $\hat{Q}\curlyvee\hat{P}$ is $(\hat{T}\curlyvee\hat{P})\curlywedge(\hat{Q}\curlyvee\hat{P})$, and $((\hat{T}\curlyvee\hat{P})\curlywedge(\hat{Q}\curlyvee\hat{P}))\,\aleph\hat{P}$: the commonality of $\hat{T}\curlyvee\hat{P}$ and $\hat{Q}\curlyvee\hat{P}$ is $\hat{P}$. So anything that is a member of $\{\forall((\hat{T}\curlyvee\hat{P})\curlywedge(\hat{Q}\curlyvee\hat{P}))\}$ is identically a member of $\{\forall\hat{P}\}$. Consequently, intensionally, anything that is either a triangle or a quadrilateral is, more accurately, either a triangle or a quadrilateral or any other polygon; which is to say, any polygon. Consequently, $\{\forall((\hat{T}\curlyvee\hat{P})\curlywedge(\hat{Q}\curlyvee\hat{P}))\}\supset\forall(\hat{T}\curlyvee\hat{P})\}\cup\{\forall(\hat{Q}\curlyvee\hat{P})\}$. In this case intensional disjunction is peculiar: it is one or the other or neither, where the *neither* refers to the set difference between the intensional and the extensional sets: $\{\forall((\hat{T}\curlyvee\hat{P})\curlywedge(\hat{Q}\curlyvee\hat{P}))\}-(\{\forall(\hat{T}\curlyvee\hat{P})\}\cup\{\forall(\hat{Q}\curlyvee\hat{P})\})$. This is the kind of intensional disjunction that is incomplete: it is incomplete because the corresponding union is a contingent set, an incomplete set, hence the name incomplete disjunction.

So $\hat{A}\curlywedge\hat{B}$ means "$\hat{A}$ or $\hat{B}$" if $\hat{A}\curlywedge\hat{B}$ is complete, and it means "$\hat{A}$ or $\hat{B}$ or neither" if $\hat{A}\curlywedge\hat{B}$ is incomplete. In the incomplete case the *neither* refers to any member of $\{\forall(\hat{A}\curlywedge\hat{B})\}$ which is neither an $\hat{A}$ nor a $\hat{B}$; that is, to any member of $\{\forall(\hat{A}\curlywedge\hat{B})\}-(\{\forall\hat{A}\}\cup\{\forall\hat{B}\})$. Extensional disjunction, which is union, does not have this peculiarity because there is no extensional distinction between complete and incomplete sets — that is, between necessary and contingent sets. Obviously, normal linguistic usage conforms to extensional disjunction, not intensional.

For the third example, let $\hat{P}$ stand for polygon and $\hat{F}$ for female. Then $\{\forall\hat{P}\}\cup\{\forall\hat{F}\}$ is the set of all things which are either polygonal or female; but these two concepts are disparate, so their commonality $\curlywedge(\{\forall\hat{P}\}\cup\{\forall\hat{F}\})$ does not exist and $\{\forall\hat{P}\}\cup\{\forall\hat{F}\}$ has to be a contingent set.

That superintension is intensional implication will be clear once it is related to similarity truth, intensional validity, and proof, as follows.

✷

As we have seen [5], if a structure is a copy, representation, or reproduction of another, and they are similar, then their similarity is called the **similarity truth** of the copy, relative to the other, or original. If they are not similar then the copy is **dissimilarity false**, relative to the original.

We now symbolise similarity truth by the symbol ⸲ and dissimilarity falsity by ∼. Because we are going to define extensional and nominal truth and falsity, we will also call similarity truth and falsity **intensional truth** and **intensional falsity**, respectively.

We define **intensional validity** by: the inference from $\hat{A}$ to $\hat{B}$ is an **intensionally valid inference** if and only if either ⸲$\hat{A}$⇒⸲$\hat{B}$ or ∼$\hat{A}$⇒∼$\hat{B}$.

Intensional truth is a **distributive property**: if a whole possesses it then so do each of its parts. The converse of a distributive property is a **compositional property**: if one or more parts possess it then so does the whole. A property is a compositional property if and only if its complement is a distributive property. The proof of this is simple. Let $\hat{D}$ be a distributive property. First, if $\hat{C}$ is the absence of $\hat{D}$ then $\hat{C}$ must be a compositional property; second, if d̂ and ĉ are mutually exclusive then the presence of ĉ requires the absence of d̂, so ĉ is compositional; third, if ĉ and d̂ are complementary then they are mutually exclusive; hence the complement of d̂ is compositional. Conversely, by similar reasoning, if ĉ is compositional and the complement of ĉ is d̂, then d̂ must be distributive.

Two clear illustrations of this are existence and consistency. Existence is a distributive property, while non-existence is a compositional property: if a whole exists then so do each of its parts, while if one of the parts does not exist then neither does the whole. Similarly, if a whole is consistent then so are each of its parts, while if any part is inconsistent then so is the whole.

However, this said, it must be pointed out that these examples are nominal only, since the words *non-existence* and *inconsistency* have no more than nominal meaning. Intensionally, the only pairs of distributive and compositional properties are intensional complements, which are mutually exclusive bipossibilities. Two examples are identity and change [95], and similarity and dissimilarity, each term of each pair of which are intensional complements of each other. Thus identity is a distributive property and change is a compositional property: if a whole has identity then each of its parts is within that identity, while if a part changes then so does the whole; and identity and change are mutually exclusive.

Even more clear is the example of similarity and dissimilarity. Recall that we defined the degree of similarity between two relations as *s/(s+d+m)*. We can make this a two-valued expression by saying that the relations are similar if *s/(s+d+m)*=1, and dissimilar if *s/(s+d+m)*<1. Then if a relation A is similar to a relation B then each property of A is similar to a property of B, while if a property of A is dissimilar to its corresponding property of B then the whole of A is dissimilar to B. This may be extended to wholes, C and D, say, and their parts. So the similarity of C to D is a distributive extrinsic property of C, and the dissimilarity is a compositional property. It follows, by definition, that similarity truth and dissimilarity falsity, each of which is the intensional complement of the other, are respectively a distributive property and a compositional property. From this we get the main basis of accepted rules of inference:

$$(\hat{S} \succ \hat{P}) \Leftrightarrow ((\wr\hat{S} \Rightarrow \wr\hat{P}) \& (\sim\hat{P} \Rightarrow \sim\hat{S}))$$

since with $Ŝ≻P̂$, $Ŝ$ may be thought of as a whole and $P̂$ as a part of it. It follows that if $Ŝ≻P̂$ and $ʔŜ$, then necessarily $ʔP̂$:

$$((Ŝ≻P̂)\&ʔŜ)⇒ʔP̂;$$

and if $Ŝ≻P̂$ and $∼P̂$ then necessarily $∼Ŝ$:

$$((Ŝ≻P̂)\&∼P̂)⇒∼Ŝ;$$

thus we have the validity of intensional *modus ponens*, or affirmation of the antecedent, and of *modus tollens*, or denial of the consequent. Similarly the intensional validity of hypothetical syllogism or chain argument, $((Â≻B̂)\&(B̂≻Ĉ))⇒(Â≻Ĉ)$, and of simplification, $ʔ(ÂʏB̂)⇒ʔÂ$ and $ʔ(ÂʏB̂)⇒ʔB̂$, is easily shown, since superintension is transitive, $(ÂʏB̂)≻Â$ and $(ÂʏB̂)≻B̂$.

A derivative basis of inference is that of the principle of substitution of equivalents, which is that if $P̂⅋Q̂$ then $ʔP̂⇔ʔQ̂$ and $∼P⇔∼Q̂$. This is due to the fact that similarity truth is similarity, which is transitive: $ʔP̂$ means that $P̂⅋R̂$, where $R̂$ is any portion of reality that $P̂$ represents, so $P̂⅋Q̂$ means that $Q̂⅋R̂$, hence $ʔQ̂$, and *vice versa*; and similarly for $∼P⇔∼Q̂$.

We may also note that the traditional laws of thought all follow from the concepts of similarity truth and dissimilarity falsity applied to intensional meanings. These are the rules of identity, excluded middle, and non-contradiction: $ʔP̂⇒ʔP̂$, $P̂→(ʔP̂|∼P̂)$, and $∼(ʔP̂\&∼P̂)$, respectively. Observe that in the rule of identity the necessity is not monadic, since it relates two instances of the truth of $P̂$, rather than one instance to itself; as we shall see shortly [283], idempotence is possible with intensions while impossible with extensions.

We have, of course, been using these argument forms all along, so that as far as establishing them is concerned we cannot escape circularity; but we are not defining or asserting the argument forms, we are explaining them, with the aim of distinguishing them from inferior, nominal, versions; so the circularity is not vicious.

The significance of this validity for applied mathematics is that since theorems are emergent out of axiom sets, an axiom set plus its emergents is a superintension of each of its theorems; so if an axiom set is intensionally true then so are every one of its theorems.

The significance of this validity for pure mathematics is that since the truth of the axioms necessitates the truth of the theorems, the theorems are validly implied by the axioms: the theorems are deducible from the axioms.

Inference by *reductio ad absurdum* is intensionally valid, even though the key words involved have exclusively nominal meaning, since the inference is based on the singular possibility that a contradiction can only have exclusively nominal meaning: that is, the nominally proved contradiction intensionally necessitates exclusively nominal meaning in the assumption. This may be thought of as an intensional argument concerning exclusively nominal meanings: it assumes that the phrase *exclusively nominal meaning* has intensional meaning.

Notice, however, that *reductio* works intensionally only in proofs of non-existence; to use *reductio* to prove the existence of some mathematical entity does not establish the intensional existence of that entity, it only establishes the nominal existence of it.

There are four standard argument forms that are intensionally valid only in limited circumstances. First, addition, $(\wr\hat{P}\&\wr\hat{Q})\Rightarrow\wr(\hat{P}\curlyvee\hat{Q})$ is valid only if the coupling is possible. Second, disjunctive syllogism,

$$(\wr(\hat{P}\curlywedge\hat{Q})\&\sim\hat{P})\Rightarrow\wr\hat{Q} \text{ or } (\wr(\hat{P}\curlywedge\hat{Q})\&\sim\hat{Q})\Rightarrow\wr\hat{P},$$

is valid only if the disjunction is complete; so unless the completeness can be established first, this argument form is intensionally invalid. Using our earlier examples of complete and incomplete disjunction [276], we can say that if something is a natural number and it is not an odd number, then it is an even number:

$$(\wr((\hat{N}\curlyvee\hat{O})\curlywedge(\hat{N}\curlyvee\hat{E}))\&\sim(\hat{N}\curlyvee\hat{O}))\Rightarrow\wr(\hat{N}\curlyvee\hat{E});$$

but if something is a polygon and it is not a triangle, it does not follow that it is a quadrilateral:

$$(\wr((\hat{T}\curlyvee\hat{P})\curlywedge(\hat{Q}\curlyvee\hat{P}))\&\sim(\hat{T}\curlyvee\hat{P}))\not\Rightarrow\wr(\hat{Q}\curlyvee\hat{P}).$$

Third, disjunctive addition, $\wr\hat{P}\Rightarrow\wr(\hat{P}\curlywedge\hat{Q})$, is intensionally valid only if the commonality $\hat{P}\curlywedge\hat{Q}$ exists. Fourth, contraposition, $\wr(\hat{A}\succ\hat{B})\Leftrightarrow\wr(\hat{B}'\succ\hat{A}')$, is intensionally valid only if both of the intensional complements exist.

Superintension may be thought of as **intensional analytic truth**, as opposed to **synthetic truth**, which is similarity truth. As we saw when discussing the metaphysics of Leibniz [102], the ancient definition of analyticity was that with it the predicate is contained in the subject; this used to be regarded as equivalent to the alternative definition that the denial of an analytic truth is, or leads to, a contradiction; but we can see now that the containment definition is intensional while the denial one is nominal. If a relation, ŝ, is called a subject and a subintension, p̂, of all of its intrinsic properties is called a predicate of it, then it is clear that ŝ≻p̂: superintension is a kind of containment, such that the subject contains the predicate. Putting this another way, ŝ and p̂ are abstract ideas, and any instance of the first contains an instance of the second as a subintension. Because of this containment, ŝ necessarily is a p̂; so, nominally, if it is denied that ŝ is a p̂ then ŝ is both a p̂, because necessarily so, and not a p̂ because of the denial. So nominal denial of an intensional analyticity produces a nominal contradiction. On the other hand, truth-functionally to deny a tautology such as P⊃P produces the contradiction P∧∼P, which is truth-functionally equivalent to ∼(P⊃P); but if P has only nominal meaning then the tautology P⊃P will have no intensional meaning, so that there is no superintension, no containment of predicate in subject, no intensional analyticity. So denial of an exclusively nominal analyticity, which is denial of a tautology, produces a contradiction; but there is no containment in exclusively nominal analyticity.

✷

Turning next to intensional equivalence, we note that the claim that this is similarity, which is also symmetric implication, may seem implausible at first. Such implausibility is shown by the example of the concepts of *equilateral triangle* and *equiangular triangle* in Euclidean geometry. Each concept can be deduced from the other, so they are clearly equivalent, but they are equally clearly dissimilar, since *equilateral* does not mean *equiangular*. However, if Ê, Â, and T̂ stand for the intensions *equilateral, equiangular,* and *triangular,* then ÊⲨT̂ and ÂⲨT̂ stand for *equilateral triangle* and *equiangular triangle*; and ÊⲨT̂ is such that it necessitates the emergence of Â, while ÂⲨT̂ necessitates the emergence of Ê. Thus each is more fully represented by the expression ÊⲨÂⲨT̂, from which it follows that (ÊⲨT̂)≻Â and (ÂⲨT̂)≻Ê. This gives us both the similarity and the symmetric implication, since superintension is intensional implication. In other words, the dissimilarity is nominal, not intensional.

✷

Finally, on intensional implication, a warning. It is very tempting (and I myself fell for this temptation in earlier editions of this book) to say that because necessity is a singular possibility it must have maximum hekergy, since with a singular possibility the value of e is 1 in the expression $\ln(t/e)$. The temptation exists because we value rationality, and rationality is characterised by logical necessity, so logical necessity should have high hekergy. However, although all possibility relations, including necessities, have hekergy because they are emergent relations, and they also all have a degree of possibility, their degree of possibility is not the value of e in calculating their hekergy, as is seen as soon as we ask the value of t. In fact, the connection between necessity and value arises from the necessary nature of emergence: if the terms of a relation R exist and are arranged in one of the e arrangements in which R emerges, then R emerges necessarily; R cannot not emerge. As an emergent, R possesses hekergy and hence value; the necessity of the emergence of R is the basis of proving the existence of both R and its properties, $\hat{r}$; and the proof is the source of the logical necessities in the demonstration of the proof.

★

We may compare all this with extensional and nominal truth, validity, and equivalence.

There are two ways to discover the nature of extensional truth and falsity, which is useful because they are peculiar. The first way is to derive it from intensional truth and falsity, through the implication and equivalence theorems.

The implication theorem is $(\hat{A} \succ \hat{B}) \Leftrightarrow (\{\forall \hat{A}\} \subset \{\forall \hat{B}\})$. Since superintension is the basis of intensional validity, subset must be the basis of extensional validity. But $(S \subset P) \Leftrightarrow (((x \in S) \Rightarrow (x \in P))$ or $((x \notin P) \Rightarrow (x \notin S)))$. This is analogous to $(\hat{s} \succ \hat{p}) \Leftrightarrow ((?\hat{s} \Rightarrow ?\hat{p})$ or $(\sim \hat{p} \Rightarrow \sim \hat{s}))$, from which we can infer that extensional truth is membership and extensional falsity is non membership. The equivalence theorem shows the same thing: $(\hat{A} ?? \hat{B}) \Leftrightarrow (\{\forall \hat{A}\} = \{\forall \hat{B}\})$ makes set identity the extensional meaning of equivalence; but $(S = P) \Leftrightarrow (((x \in S) \Leftrightarrow (x \in P))$ or $((x \notin P) \Leftrightarrow (x \notin S)))$, which is analogous to $(\hat{P} ?? \hat{Q}) \Leftrightarrow ((?\hat{P} \Leftrightarrow ?\hat{Q})$ or $(\sim P \Leftrightarrow \sim \hat{Q}))$.

The second way to find the meaning of extensional truth and falsity is from the supposition that a meaningless sentence is false. A set is extensionally meaningless if it is null, so extensional falsity is absence of members and extensional truth is thereby possession of at least one member. This is clear when expressed in the symbols of quantificational logic: that S is null is stated by $(x)(x \notin S)$; and $(x)(x \notin S) \Leftrightarrow \sim(\exists x)(x \in S)$. Thus if S has at least one member, $(\exists x)(x \in S)$, then S is extensionally true. Hence **extensional truth** is set membership, and **extensional falsity** is non-membership.

An extensional inference from A to B is **extensionally valid** if and only if membership in A is universally membership in B: $x \in A$ always means $x \in B$, hence $A \subset B$. Thus extensional validity is based on extensional necessity, not on intensional necessity.

Extensional equivalence is set identity, more commonly known as set equality.

Because of the equivalence theorem — $(\hat{A} \between \hat{B}) \Leftrightarrow (\{\forall \hat{A}\} = \{\forall \hat{B}\})$ — we can see that idempotence may have intensional meaning when applied to intensions, but not when applied to extensions. This theorem requires that there cannot be two similar extensions, for if $\{\forall \hat{A}\} \between \{\forall \hat{B}\}$ then $\hat{A} \between \hat{B}$, in which case $\{\forall \hat{A}\} = \{\forall \hat{B}\}$; this means that $\{\forall \hat{A}\}$ and $\{\forall \hat{B}\}$ are identical, they are one. So to say that $A \cup A = A \cap A = A$ requires that in order for union and intersection to be idempotent they must be monadic — and there are no monadic relations. Such idempotence is acceptable in orthodox set theory, of course, because there monadic relations are allowed; but here they are only nominal. On the other hand intensions, unlike extensions, may be similar, so that idempotence between them is possible. Thus $\hat{A} \between \hat{A}$ means that one instance of $\hat{A}$ is similar to another instance of $\hat{A}$.

The intensionally valid argument forms are all extensionally valid, and as well addition, disjunctive syllogism, disjunctive addition, and contraposition are extensionally valid. Cast in extensional symbols, these argument forms are:

Modus ponens:	$((S \subset P) \& (x \in S)) \Rightarrow (x \in P)$
Modus tollens:	$((S \subset P) \& (x \notin P)) \Rightarrow (x \notin S)$
Hyp. syllogism:	$((S \subset P) \& (P \subset R)) \Rightarrow (S \subset R)$
Simplification:	$(x \in S \cap P) \Rightarrow (x \in S)$
Substitution:	$(S = P) \Leftrightarrow (((x \in S) \Leftrightarrow (x \in P))$ or $((x \notin P) \Leftrightarrow (x \notin S)))$
Addition:	$((x \in P) \& (x \in S)) \Rightarrow (x \in P \cap S)$
Disj. syllogism:	$((x \in S \cup P) \& (x \notin P)) \Rightarrow (x \in S)$
Disj. addition:	$(x \in S) \Rightarrow (x \in S \cup P)$
Contraposition:	$((x \in S)) \Rightarrow (x \in P)) \Leftrightarrow ((x \notin P) \Rightarrow (x \notin S))$.

✶

Nominal truth is correct statement of fact — intensional or extensional, ideal or real — and **nominal falsity** is incorrect statement of fact. *Correct* and *incorrect* here refer to the established use of language. Language that has no established use has no nominal meaning. So "All square circles are circles" has nominal meaning, by analogy to "All right triangles are triangles", and is nominally analytically true, but "All squircles are cirare" has no nominal meaning, hence no meaning at all. We note, however, that nominal meaning is easily established by stipulative definition: if we define a squircle as a square circle and a cirare as a circular square, then "All squircles are cirare" both has nominal meaning and is nominally analytically true.

A nominal inference of one statement, Q, from another, P, is **nominally valid** if and only if the truth function P⊃Q is tautologous, or always nominally true.

✳

With all three kinds of inference a true premise and false conclusion are a sufficient condition for invalidity. If ⟨ŝ and ∼p̂ then it is impossible that ŝ≻p̂: p̂ cannot be intensionally validly inferred from ŝ. If x∈S and x∉T then it is impossible that S⊂T: x∈T cannot be extensionally validly inferred from x∈S. And if P∧∼Q then it is impossible that P⊃Q is true: Q cannot be nominally validly inferred from P. And intensional validity is a sufficient condition for extensional validity, which is a sufficient condition for nominal validity; but nominal validity is only a necessary condition for extensional validity, which is only a necessary for intensional validity. Thus all inferences from contradictions are nominally valid, but have no extensional or intensional validity; all inferences from membership in a random subset, S, of a random set T, to membership in T are extensionally and nominally valid, but have no intensional validity; and all inferences from an intension ŝ to one of its subintensions, p̂, are intensionally, extensionally, and nominally valid.

As an illustration of the value of separating intensional validity from nominal validity, we consider the well known nominal proof that from a contradiction we may validly deduce anything we please, symbolised by Q:

1. $P \land \sim P$ Premise
2. P 1, Simplification
3. $\sim P$ 1, Simplification
4. $P \lor Q$ 2, Disjunctive addition
5. Q 4, 3 Disjunctive syllogism.

Intensionally the argument is invalid both because, first, the disjunctive syllogism is only valid if both the commonality of P and Q exists and the disjunction can be shown to be complete — which is impossible if Q is any proposition whatever; and, second and more significantly, the argument is intensionally invalid because the premise has no intensional meaning. Nominally, of course, the argument is valid.

The inadequacy of the truth-functional basis of logic has long been known; it is clearly illustrated by the theorems in truth-functional logic that a false proposition implies any proposition, a true proposition is implied by any proposition, and any two true propositions are equivalent, as are any two false propositions — theorems that have nominal meaning only. And also by the fact that if $P \supset Q$ is true then by addition there are an infinity of premises from which Q may be deduced, and by disjunctive addition there are an infinity of conclusions to be drawn from P.

$$\ast \ast \ast$$

Having examined the intensional, extensional, and nominal foundations of set theory and logic, we now do the same for the foundations of mathematics.

We first define intensional natural numbers, and then define various relations between them that together constitute intensional arithmetic.

An **intensional natural number** is an adicity, with the exception of the natural number one, which is the commonality of all relations.

We have seen that all and only relations, have the property of adicity. The similarity set of a natural number is the set of every adicity that is similar to it, or, as we might say, that is **equiadic** to it. It follows that there is only a nominal difference between a number and various instances of it: the number is the intension of the similarity set and all the instances of it are the extension, but in an expression such as $2+2=2\times2=2^2$, each of the six instances of 2 is *the* number 2, since, with ⅍, it serves as an intension of the similarity set of all dyadicities.

Every set relation is an instance of its own adicity, and every other relation is a representative instance of its own adicity.

The intensional natural number one is not an adicity because there are no monadic relations. Instead, the **intensional natural number one** is the commonality of every intrinsic property set, the commonality of every relation. The number one is thus the property set consisting of adicity-in-general — as opposed to a particular adicity. Adicity-in-general is number, and this property set has only one member; the two together constitute the number one. Since this is a subintension of every property set, every relation is a unity; so any instance of any relation may be a representative instance of the intensional natural number one — as is shown by us calling it one relation. The number one should not be confused with set relations, each one of which has a particular adicity.

Thus intensionally there is a fundamental difference between singularity and plurality — a fact that seems evident in the grammar of ordinary language and in the distinction between proper names and universals — that is, between words or descriptions that have, respectively, singular or plural reference.

The **adicity of a term set** is the adicity of its unifying relation. Every intensional set is unified by a relation and so is a term set; thus every intensional set has an adicity, which is the adicity of its unifying relation.

The basic arithmetical operations on the natural numbers are all quite obvious.

Two numbers *a* and *b* are **equal**, symbolised $a=b$, if they are equiadic: that is, if a representative intensional set of adicity *a* is equiadic with a representative intensional set of adicity *b*.

A number *a* is **greater than** another number *b*, symbolised $a>b$, if a representative intensional set, *B*, of adicity *b*, is a subset of a representative intensional set, *A*, of adicity *a*; in short, if *B* is a subset of *A*. The inverse of the relation *greater than* is the relation **smaller than**, symbolised $b<a$.

To define the operation of addition of intensional natural numbers an assumption is required, called the **axiom of addition**: if two relations R and S, having adicities *r* and *s*, exist, then there exists a relation having the adicity of R∪S. Another way of stating this axiom is that among all the *r*-adic relations and all the *s*-adic relations there exists at least one relation, all of whose terms are either the terms of an instance of the first, R_n, or an instance of the second, S_m; that is, its terms are the terms of $R_n \cup S_m$. There is a limiting exception to this axiom, to be dealt with later [289]: it arises because there is no closure on intensional addition.

If two disjoint relations, A and B, have adicities *a* and *b* and term sets *A* and *B*, then the **sum** of the two numbers *a* and *b*, symbolised *a+b*, is the adicity of $A \cup B$. It two intersecting relations, C and D, have adicities *c* and *d* and term sets *C* and *D*, and the adicity of $C \cap D$ is *e*, then *c+d* is the sum of the adicity of $C \cup D$ and *e*.

The **addition** of two numbers *a* and *b* is the binary operation, or function, having the set of the two of them as its argument and their sum as its value.

If two relations, A and B, have adicities *a* and *b* and term sets *A* and *B*, and $B \subset A$, then the **difference** of the two numbers *a* and *b*, symbolised *a-b*, is the adicity of $A - B$.

The **subtraction** of a number *b* from another number *a*, where *a>b*, is the binary operation, or function, having the ordered pair of them, (*a,b*), as its argument and their difference as its value.

The **multiplication** of two numbers, *a* and *b*, symbolised *a×b*, is the addition of *b* instances of *a*: $a \times b = a_1 + a_2 + ... a_b$.

The **division** of two numbers, *a* and *b*, *a>b*, symbolised *a/b*, is the repeated subtraction of instances of *b* from *a* until no further subtraction is possible; the number of subtractions, *c*, is the **quotient** of the division, such that *a/b=c*. If after the *c* subtractions there remains a number *d*, then *d* is the **remainder**.

✶

It should be clear that if two relations are equiadic then their term sets are in one-one correspondence. From this we may extend the definition of an intensional natural number to incomplete sets: the natural number of an incomplete set is the adicity of any complete set with which it is in one-one correspondence.

The **extensional natural number** of an extension is the set of all extensions with which it is in one-one correspondence.

Extensional arithmetic then follows in the usual way.

A **nominal number** is any intensional or extensional natural number or any number defined nominally out of these natural numbers.

Nominal arithmetic includes numbers that have exclusively nominal meaning. One such is the number zero: the usual arithmetical definition of zero is that if $a = b$ then $0 = a - b$, while the putative intensional definition of it should be that it is the adicity of the null set; but if $a = b$ then $a \not> b$, in which case $a - b$ has only nominal meaning; and also the null set has exclusively nominal meaning; hence so does the number zero. Our definition of the null set was that it is the intersection of two disjoint sets — that is, the intersection of two non-intersecting sets: a self-contradictory definition which *ipso facto* has exclusively nominal meaning.

Another class of numbers that probably have exclusively nominal meaning is the infinite numbers. It can be argued that the usual definition of an infinite set, as one in which a proper part is equal to the whole, has exclusively nominal meaning because it is self-contradictory[18].

Another way of looking at infinite numbers is to point out that in practice we have to use numbers that have nominal meaning only, since finite minds must have a relation of largest adicity. For such a mind a number larger than this has nominal meaning only, since it does not have either intensional or extensional meaning. This is not serious, since the nominal rules for manipulating nominal numbers are isomorphic to the intensional rules for manipulating intensional numbers, so that no error is introduced; and if such a large number occurs in the real world, the limited mind can think about it, nominally, without error. Equally, no finite mind can contain an intensional infinity or an extensional infinity, so infinite numbers have nominal meaning only for a finite mind, although it is perhaps conceivable that reality contains infinite-adic relations. But our nominal rules for infinite arithmetic (or transfinite arithmetic, as it is properly called) are different from those of finite arithmetic, so we have no guarantee that

------

[18] Bertrand Russell, in discussing the one-one correspondence between the set of natural numbers and the set of even numbers, wrote: "Leibniz, who noticed this, thought it a contradiction ... Georg Cantor, on the contrary, boldly denied that it is a contradiction. He was right; it is only an oddity." (*A History of Western Philosophy*, Allen and Unwin, London, 1946, p.858) As much as I admire Russell, I have to agree with Leibniz.

they are consistent; and if they are necessarily inconsistent, there can be no real infinities.

Yet a third way of considering infinite numbers is that we arrive at them because of closure. Closure on addition means that if any two numbers are added together, the result is always a number; this requires an infinity of numbers — larger and larger numbers without end. Closure on subtraction requires an infinity of negative numbers (as well as a zero), closure on division requires an infinity of fractions, and so on. But closure arises as a scientific induction, not mathematically: we never experience two numbers whose sum is not a number, so we assume that there are none — and once we allow an infinity of natural numbers there is little difficulty in allowing other kinds. But suppose that there are no infinite numbers. Then there must be a largest finite number: let it be l, for largest. Then closure on arithmetical addition no longer holds: if a and b are numbers then if $a+b>l$ then $a+b$ is not a number, except nominally. The number l could well be large beyond our comprehension, yet still finite.

✶

We may note that Godel's theorems, on the incompleteness and consistency of any system large enough to contain number theory, do not apply to a purely intensional arithmetic if it is not infinite.

✶

Intensional geometry is the geometry of atomic lengths [121], a geometry on an orthogonal lattice. We need only note here that as the length of an atomic spatial relation decreases, relative to everyday macroscopic sizes, so does this geometry approach the limit of the geometry of the continuum, which is a nominal geometry.

✶

Thus intensional mathematics is considerably more limited than everyday mathematics, which contains a mixture of intensional, extensional, and nominal meanings. We will examine more of the nature of intensional mathematics in Ch. 17.

✶ ✶ ✶

Finally, in this chapter, we prove the theorems already quoted.

Theorem 1. For any intension, $\hat{A}$, $\lambda\{\forall\hat{A}\}\aleph\hat{A}$.

Proof. For every x, x∈{∀Â}⇒xÂ, ∴ ⋀{∀Â} ≈Â.□

Theorem 2. For any set S, if ⋀S exists then S⊆{∀⋀S}.

> *Proof.* Assume that ⋀S exists. (x∈S)⇒(x⋀S) and
> (x⋀S)⇒(x∈{∀⋀S}), so (x∈S)⇒(x∈{∀⋀S}); ∴ S⊆{∀⋀S}. □

Theorem 3. An extension S is an intensional set if and only if S={∀⋀S}.

> *Proof.* (i) Suppose that ⋀S exists and S={∀⋀S}: then S is an
> intensional set, since {∀⋀S} is an intensional set. (ii) Suppose
> that S is an intensional set, {∀ŝ}; by Theorem 1, ⋀{∀ŝ} ≈ŝ;
> therefore S={∀ŝ}={∀⋀{∀ŝ}}={∀⋀S}, by the principle of
> substitution of equivalents. □

Theorem 4. An extension S is a contingent set if and only if either ⋀S does
not exist, or else ⋀S exists and S⊂{∀⋀S}.

> *Proof.* We note that the disjunction is complete, in that to say
> that "⋀S neither exists nor does not exist" has exclusively
> nominal meaning. (i) If ⋀S does not exist then S cannot be an
> intensional set, by Theorem 3, so S is either a nominal set or
> else a contingent set, and this latter disjunction is complete in
> that there does not exist a set that is not intensional or
> extensional or nominal; but S is not a nominal set because it is
> an extension; so S is a contingent set. (ii)(a) Suppose, using
> *reductio*, that ⋀S exists, that S⊂{∀⋀S}, and that S is not a
> contingent set; S is not a nominal set, since ⋀S exists, so S is a
> necessary set, in which case S={∀⋀S}, by Theorem 3, which
> contradicts our assumption; so S is a contingent set. (b)
> Suppose that S is a contingent set, hence not a necessary set;
> S⊆{∀⋀S}, by Theorem 2, which means that either S={∀⋀S} or
> S⊂{∀⋀S}; but if S={∀⋀S} then S is a necessary set, by
> Theorem 3; so S⊂{∀⋀S}. □

Theorem 5. The negation theorem: if Â and Â′ exist, {∀Â′}={∀Â}′.

Proof. We observe that $\hat{A}''≈\hat{A}$. If A and A′ are predicable of x then $x{\rightarrow}(xA|xA')$, hence $x{\in}\{\forall A\}{\Leftrightarrow}x{\notin}\{\forall A'\}$. But, extensionally, $(x{\in}A{\Leftrightarrow}x{\notin}B){\Leftrightarrow}(A=B')$, so $\{\forall A\}=\{\forall A'\}'$ and $\{\forall A'\}=\{\forall A''\}=\{\forall A\}'$. $\square$

Theorem 6. The equivalence theorem: $(A≈B){\Leftrightarrow}(\{\forall A\}=\{\forall B\})$.

Proof.
$\{\forall A\}=\{\forall B\} \Leftrightarrow (x{\in}\{\forall A\}{\Leftrightarrow}x{\in}\{\forall B\}) \Leftrightarrow (xA{\Leftrightarrow}xB) \Leftrightarrow A≈B$ $\square$

Corollary. $(A≈B){\Leftrightarrow}(\{\forall A\}\neq\{\forall B\})$.

Theorem 7. The implication theorem: $(A{\succ}B){\Leftrightarrow}(\{\forall A\}{\subset}\{\forall B\})$.

Proof. (i)
$(A{\succ}B){\Rightarrow}(xA{\Rightarrow}xB){\Rightarrow}(x{\in}\{\forall A\}{\Rightarrow}x{\in}\{\forall B\}){\Rightarrow}(\{\forall A\}{\subseteq}\{\forall B\})$, by Theorem 1; but $(A{\succ}B){\Rightarrow}(A≈B)$, so $\{\forall A\}\neq\{\forall B\}$, by Theorem 6, Coroll. $\therefore (A{\succ}B){\Rightarrow}(\{\forall A\}{\subset}\{\forall B\})$. (ii) The converse is proved similarly. $\square$

Theorem 8. The conjunction theorem: $\{\forall(A{\curlyvee}B)\}=\{\forall A\}{\cap}\{\forall B\}$.

Proof. $x{\in}\{\forall(A{\curlyvee}B)\}{\Leftrightarrow}x(A{\curlyvee}B){\Leftrightarrow}(xA\ \&\ xB)$ by definition of coupling. But $xA{\Leftrightarrow}x{\in}\{\forall A\}\ \&\ xB{\Leftrightarrow}x{\in}\{\forall B\}$. So $x{\in}\{\forall(A{\curlyvee}B)\}{\Leftrightarrow}(x{\in}\{\forall A\}\ \&\ x{\in}\{\forall B\}){\Leftrightarrow}(x{\in}\{\forall A\}{\cap}\{\forall B\})$, by definition of intersection. $\square$

Corollary $(\hat{A}{\curlyvee}\hat{B}){\Leftrightarrow}\{\forall\hat{A}\}{\pitchfork}\{\forall\hat{B}\}$.

Theorem 9. For all intensional sets A, B, $(\wedge(A{\cup}B)≈(\wedge A{\wedge}\wedge B)$.

Proof. Suppose that $A=\{A_1,...A_n\}$ and $B=\{B_1,...B_m\}$; then $A{\cup}B=\{A_1,...A_n,B_1,...B_m\}$.
$\therefore\ \wedge(A{\cup}B)≈(A_1{\wedge}...A_n{\wedge}B_1{\wedge}...B_m)≈(\wedge A{\wedge}\wedge B)$. $\square$

Theorem 10. The disjunction theorem: $\{\forall(\hat{A}\lor\hat{B})\}\supseteq\{\forall\hat{A}\}\cup\{\forall\hat{B}\}$.

Proof. Because $\{\forall\hat{A}\}$ and $\{\forall\hat{B}\}$ are intensional sets, $\lambda(\{\forall\hat{A}\}\cup\{\forall\hat{B}\})$ exists, by Theorem 9. So $\lambda(\{\forall\hat{A}\}\cup\{\forall\hat{B}\})\aleph(\lambda\{\forall\hat{A}\}\lor\lambda\{\forall\hat{B}\})\aleph(\hat{A}\lor\hat{B})$, by Theorems 9 and 1; but $\{\forall\hat{A}\}\cup\{\forall\hat{B}\}\subseteq\{\forall\lambda(\{\forall\hat{A}\}\cup\{\forall\hat{B}\})\}$, by Theorem 2; $\therefore\{\forall(\hat{A}\lor\hat{B})\}\supseteq\{\forall\hat{A}\}\cup\{\forall\hat{B}\}$. $\square$

Corollary. $(\{\forall(\hat{A}\lor\hat{B})\}\supset(\{\forall\hat{A}\}\cup\{\forall\hat{B}\}))\Leftrightarrow((\{\forall\hat{A}\}\cup\{\forall\hat{B}\})$ is a contingent set), and $(\{\forall(\hat{A}\lor\hat{B})\}=(\{\forall\hat{A}\}\cup\{\forall\hat{B}\}))\Leftrightarrow((\{\forall\hat{A}\}\cup\{\forall\hat{B}\})$ is a necessary set).

Part Four.   The Suprarational.

16. Gods.

In Part Four we are going to be concerned with the possibility of the real mind reaching a state of maximum hekergy. This will involve us in consideration of the ultimate goals of both religion and philosophy. To this end, we will begin by discussing, in the present chapter, the seven possible meanings of the word God that the present system reveals. Each one of these seven meanings conforms in one way or another with an accepted use of the word God. We will discover that of these seven Gods a rational person will be inclined to believe that five exist and two do not exist. Such belief in this connection is, of course, rational belief: its strength is based on the power of the concepts involved to explain not only the usage of the word God, but also historical claims to religious experience, and one's own personal religious experience.

We previously [174] defined an agent as anything having some awareness of, and some control over, its environment. We may now define a **spirit** as an agent in the real mind. Thus the ego is a spirit — often known as the soul — and the oge is a spirit. We could call them major spirits, because of their size, as opposed to particular oge-persons, say, which are minor spirits; or, oge-enemies, an evil kind of minor spirit called demons. We will later consider a third major spirit. If this medieval language offends, it may be discounted. It is introduced mostly because it is appropriate. That is, there is no room in modern, science conditioned, common sense for spirits and demons; but once the theoretically mental status of the material world — the empirical world — is recognised, the limitations of scientific common sense are removed without in any way invalidating the science that gave rise to them. In other words, in scientifically conditioned common sense the blue sky is real, and beyond it is the rest of the real universe; there is no detectable paradise or inferno anywhere out there. But with the Leibniz-Russell theory there is room for Heaven and Hell, between the empirical blue sky, which is in the ego, and the real skull of the person concerned — while leaving theoretical astronomy unaffected — other than by the distinction between empirical stars and theoretical stars.

★ ★ ★

As a major spirit the oge is the most obvious meaning of the word God. We may call it the **oge-God**, to differentiate it from other meanings. It is, first of all, traditionally a Father — because of the major role played by the apparent father in childhood's disciplinary occasions, hence the major role of the father in moral matters. The oge-God is naturally, by the nature of the oge, very much a God of morality: a source of prescription and proscription. But it is much more than a source of morality. Because it is a spirit, it has mental attributes and so may be loving, just, merciful, vengeful etc. Which of these attitudes dominate depends upon the oge of the individual concerned. Since people tend to congregate, for religious purposes, with others of like oge, various sects will be characterised by the dominant attitudes of their oge-God: from harsh justice to loving forgiveness. The extent to which the oge-God demands worship also depends upon the oge of the person concerned.

Worship of the oge-God may be of two kinds. One is public recognition of the oge-God, by the ego. This occurs in services in church, synagogue, mosque or temple. The other is private abasement of the ego to the oge — an abasement demanded, irrationally, by the oge. The first tends to promote ego-oge harmony; the second is mostly a victory for the oge in the ego-oge conflict.

Communication between the ego and the oge-God is possible. Messages received by the ego from the oge-God are revelations. The content of these may be archetypal (in the Jungian sense [211]) as in the Revelation of St. John the Divine, moral as in Moses' ten commandments, or patriotic as with Joan of Arc. Messages to the oge from the ego are of two kinds. One is prayer. It is obvious that prayer for material effects, such as an end to drought, famine, or plague, cannot be granted by the oge-God, since the apparent world is controlled by scientific laws — that is, by the real world via theoretical perception — that take precedence over anything the oge can do. But there are some prayers that the oge-God has the power to grant. These are prayers that fall into the range of power that the oge-God does have: power over the real body, via the motor mind, and so over the apparent body. This power includes the powers of compulsion and inhibition that are normally used in the inclination-duty conflict that the oge has with the ego, and also in neurotic conflict, if any. An appeal for help in a time of crisis may bring the power of the oge-God to the aid of the ego, instead of its usual opposition, in order to meet the crisis. Such a prayer might for example be an appeal for strength in order to endure pain in order to survive, and it is a prayer that could meaningfully be said sometimes to work — that is, to be granted by God. For example, a clumsy individual might be clumsy because his co-ordination is partially inhibited by the oge; good co-ordination might save his life in a fight with an apparent enemy of his oge, and be granted by the oge in response to prayer.

The most effective form of prayer that might be expected to be answered by the oge-God would be that requesting aid by the ego for work toward oge goals. These are both good works, by the oge's standard, and suppression of evil. In the latter the prayer is for aid by the oge-God, to the ego, against the oge-enemy. In such prayer the name of the oge-enemy is usually Satan — the evil spirit. The only power that Satan has is some degree of compulsion, of evil acts by the individual. The ego experiences this compulsion as temptation, and it is clearly in the interests of the moral oge-God to answer a prayer for aid to resist temptation. It is to be expected that both the need and the effectiveness of this kind of prayer would be greatest in puritans, both because of the strength of the oge-enemy in these unfortunate individuals and because of their oge attitude toward pleasure.

However, such prayer is not the only means of obtaining a truce in internal conflict in times of crisis. Interference with the ego by the oge may be stopped temporarily by cowing the oge: by breaking a taboo, so as to shock the oge into temporary inactivity. This is the second kind of communication from ego to oge. It most usually takes the form of declaiming taboo words — of swearing. This has a smaller potential than prayer because it can only stop oge obstruction, it cannot bring oge aid. It is noteworthy that swearing and prayer serve similar functions, because they are often verbally similar: many of the words of prayer and blasphemy are the same, it is their intent that differs.

It is noteworthy that taboos may disappear with time, but always some remain or else are replaced. Thus in the twentieth century the taboo against discussion of sexual matters, brought about by Victorian prudery, and the taboo against illegitimacy, disappeared, as did the taboo against the use of four-letter words in mixed company; but the new taboo against uttering politically incorrect statements — anything that could conceivably offend someone — has arisen. The oge does not relinquish power easily.

＊

The influence of the oge-God in the apparent world is not, of course, as great as it was once believed to be. It cannot perform miracles — that is, over-ride scientific laws — but it may produce visions within the apparent world, such as an angel bearing a message. These, naturally, are private to the person concerned and consequently incorrectly believed by many to be mere hallucinations, mere perceptual aberrations.

＊

The separation of the oge-enemy from the oge-God raises the more general question of polytheism and monotheism with respect to the oge-God. The oge is composed of many complexes, each a set of theoretical memories or ideas of an apparent person or a group of people; each such set is an oge-person. Is it therefore correct to say that the oge is a pantheon, a group of spirits, each a god? Or is it One, united by an emergent relation? If one, then God is partly evil; the possibility of God being evil is traditionally denied in the doctrine that God is all-good; and allowed in the doctrines that God created the world, including evil, and that God sends the unworthy to Hell. The answer to any question of this type is to be found in the answer to whether the particular whole concerned is greater than the sum of its parts, or not. In so far as it is, so is it a unity, over and above its parts. Which is to say that it is a unity because it is united by an emergent relation, so that the configuration of its parts has hekergy. The hekergy of the configuration of the oge as we have described it, while not the maximum possible, certainly is not zero either — the structure of the oge is not random. So whether the oge is one God or many gods is moot. Clearly, in the present theory, a doctrine of monotheism   of oge unity   is not important; but, equally clearly, it must once have been of very great significance. For the declaration that we have not many gods but one God signified a large increase in our oge's hekergy, and so a considerable moral advance — using *moral* in the technical sense of oge hekergy increase.

＊

The oge-God is a tribal God. There are as many kinds of oge as there are sects, nationalities, skin colours, languages, cultures, etc. Each such kind of oge is a different oge-God, although many of them may be the supposedly one God of a given religion — usually ostensibly because of an extrinsic relation such as a common origin or common authority — prophet or book

— but actually because of the identity error: many similar oges are erroneously supposed to be one. Each such different kind of oge-God is God only to those who possess an oge of that form. Such selectivity is most apparent with those sects who believe that they, and they alone, are the chosen people of the one and only God. They are correct in so far as they are indeed chosen by their own oge, but incorrect in supposing that there is no other God. They are also incorrect in attaching far more significance to being chosen than the fact warrants. Usually this includes the doctrine that only the chosen will go to Heaven, all others will go to Hell (see below). It is also in terms of this tribalism of the oge-God that two groups of people, supposedly of the same religion, may be at war and each pray to their supposedly common God for victory against the other. They can do this without consciously insulting the goodness of their God because each group feels that it is chosen — as it can be, because it is praying to a qualitatively different oge-God.

✳

Certain eschatological considerations arise with the oge-God. If Jill loves Jack, and Jack dies, memories of Jack will remain in Jill's oge, as oge-Jack. Jill's oge will be communicated by introjection to her children, and so to her grandchildren, and on down. If such open ended perpetuation be called eternal, and the top end of the oge (that is, the oge-God's "right hand") be called Heaven, then Jack, after dying, has an eternal life in Heaven; and since Heaven has only goodness, morally speaking, oge-Jack will be in a state of bliss. Alternatively, if Jill hates Jack, oge-Jack will be in the lower pole of Jill's oge — the oge-enemy — which may be called Hell, and so in the company of Satan; and since all the demons of hell are evil, oge-Jack should suffer at their hands. We may note also that each person's oge-heaven is beyond the apparent blue sky — that is, it is in the usual religious location of heaven — and each person's oge-hell is below the apparent ground [185]. However, as the oge-God makes doctrines about being a chosen people true but trivial, so this eschatology, although true, is trivial. Because the post-mortem survival of oge-Jack is in no way a survival of the real mind of Jack — hence of Jack's ego and consciousness. Rather, it is merely a survival of a set of representations of mid-Jack. And these representations are recreated with each generation, as is the entire oge, so that they may be expected to fade. *Eternity* is thus not *forever* — even if the oge Jacks endure through many generations because real Jack was a legendary hero or a legendary villain — as, for example, Robin Hood and Bluebeard. Oge-Jack, being largely mindless, is very like the Greek idea of a shade in Hades, a shadow having no memories of its past life and no idea of whom it is. It is in fact conscious — but only minimally so. By L.A.L. every real idea reacts with every other, and this reaction is consciousness: but it is not the rich consciousness of a large complex of ideas such as the ego. Notice that the "chosen people" belief above is true: only the believers in a particular oge-God have a post mortem survival in the company of this God, and all other people that survive in this variety of oge do so elsewhere in the oge, hence in Hell. But, again, although this is true, it is trivial.

Thus the fact that the belief in post mortem survival of consciousness is so widespread is explained, over and above the explanation by means of wishful belief. That the belief must be false, according to the present theory, is shown by the fact that the mind, and hence consciousness, are emergent out of the brain and so cannot survive the death of the brain — since no emergent relation can exist without its terms. For those who find this conclusion dismaying, the present theory provides some consolation, in that the wealth of one's own experiences, memories, and understanding is not lost at one's death because the principle of conservation of hekergy requires that this wealth, as a hekergy magnitude, be conserved. That is, the specific content is not preserved, but its hekergy is.

✻

The fact that the oge is both a God and represents society explains the importance of public religious rituals and rites of passage. The claim that marriages are made in Heaven, for example, is explained by public acceptance of the wedding ceremony, so oge acceptance of it, by introjection, hence its occurrence in Heaven. And the once believed Divine Right of Kings arose because public acceptance of a king as monarch — during his coronation, for example — became an oge acceptance and so divine. Similar reasoning makes the old saying *vox populi, vox dei* true, provided that the voice of the gods is understood as the voice of the oge.

· ✻

We may also note that the oge-God, as an agent and a spirit, is, in a sense, a person. It is thus a personal God.

298

We should also remark on what the oge-God is not. It clearly is not infinite, in any way. Its hekergy is not a maximum, so it is not perfect. It may be loving, but it is not all-loving; it may be powerful, but it is not all powerful; and it may be knowledgeable, but it is not all-knowing. Because it is formed by L.A.L. it is irrational — except in so far as some of its beliefs are rational in the sense of having been introjected from rational other people.

✳ ✳ ✳

The second meaning of the word God is a special oge-person that exists in some oges. This is the oge-person of the original teacher or prophet. It is the **deified teacher**, as Christ or Buddha are in many oges. This deification is the creation of this oge-person in the oge, in such a way as to be as close as possible to the ego and to remain that way for generation after generation among those raised in that religion. This **way-God**, as it might be called, is as it were a bridge between oge and ego. As such, it is intercessor between ego and God; it is metaphorically on God's right hand; it is both human, because an oge-person, and God, because part of the oge. It is easier for the ego to pray to the way-God, as intercessor, than to the oge-God because the way-God is "closer in spirit" to the ego than the oge-God — that is, it is the closest part of the oge, and the part of the oge most like the ego.

If the way-God is believed in by only a small group of people than it will be a bridge to only a small portion of the oge. It will not, for example, be a bridge to many — or perhaps any — oge-strangers. This situation can be improved by persuading apparent strangers to join the sect that has this way-God. We thus have an explanation for the widespread strength of the missionary drive: it strengthens the far end of the bridge.

The way-God may, on the other hand, be a bridge to more of the oge than is comfortable for the ego — because there is too much power at the far end of the bridge. This can be rectified by deifying a subsidiary teacher, and making this oge-teacher a bridge to the bridge, intercessor to the intercessor. Such an oge-teacher would be a saint. Saints are only needed when the balance of power between ego and oge is strongly in the oge's favour — that is, in oge-dominant personalities.

Note that the way-God is both a spirit and a person — an oge-person, that is.

✳ ✳ ✳

The third meaning of the word God is the mind hekergy principle. This is the source of all creativity, and as such could be another name for what is known as the Holy Ghost. Although it is important as a causal principle in our theory of mind, it is not of great interest in the present context because it explains little of religious significance. It is mentioned at this point because along with the oge-God and way-God it forms the trinity as usually described in Christianity. Note that this third God, in spite of its name, is neither spirit nor person.

✳ ✳ ✳

If Heaven is defined as the space beyond the upper part of the apparent world — the space beyond the dome that is the blue sky in the day and the fixed stars at night — then all the three Gods of the trinity and all the saints are in Heaven. Or, more correctly, they are all in the Heaven of an individual who believes in them all. And the oge-God is in the heaven of all except extreme psychopaths, while the mind hekergy principle is in the Heaven of everyone. That all these Gods are in Heaven — that is, beyond the apparent world — makes them transcendent; that they can have some influence in the apparent world and be aware of what goes on in the apparent world makes them immanent.

✳

A further point may be made here concerning the possibility of a conscious computer. If the present theory of mind is correct then it may be possible to program a computer so that the mind-hekergy principle applies to it, along with the principle of L.A.L. If such a computer were realised, then it would develop an ego and an oge and all three of these Gods could be within the real mind of that computer, thus leading to the possibility of experimental theology.

✳ ✳ ✳

The fourth meaning of the word God, much more significant than the previous three, is the real world. As a God the real world is neither spirit nor person; it has no mental attributes such as knowledge, love, or mercy — except in so far as real minds are part of the real world. It is the creator, or cause, of the ego, or soul, of each person; and creator, or cause, of the empirical world of each person. Of all the Gods it is the only one that is omnipotent — it has all power; any power that any of the other Gods have is only a portion of this omnipotence. It is also the only one of all the Gods that is completely perfect — given that the real world is of maximum hekergy; it is, for this reason, rational [320]. It is also, of the five Gods that exist in the present context, the only one that is infinite in the sense of being unbounded — given that the world is finite but unbounded, in Einstein's sense [124]. As God, the real world is transcendent — not only to the apparent world but to the entire real mind — and immanent, in the sense that the real mind is a part of the real world. As we shall see in the next chapter, it is both *causa sui*, self-caused, and first cause.

✶

Because of its lack of human attributes this God is much more a God of philosophers than it is of theologians. Thus one of Aristotle's descriptions of God was to say that God is pure form — that is, nothing but relations. Another was that God is the first cause, or unmoved mover of all that moves in the visible world; this God, a substance, is "beyond heaven" — that is, beyond the dome of the sky. The God of Plotinus also is, in this context, the real world. Plotinus propounded an obscure doctrine of emanation, as follows. From the One, or God, emanates *nous* — mind or intelligence or intellect; from *nous* emanates soul; from soul, the world; and from the world, matter. In terms of reality and perfection, God is the highest being and matter the lowest. Emanation here is used metaphorically, as in the sense of light emanating from the Sun. In our present theory, Plotinus' terms can be interpreted as: the One, or God, is the real world; *nous* is the real mind; soul is the ego; the world is the empirical world; and matter is concrete empirical sensation. Emanation then is both causal priority, and the relation of whole to part. Thus real mind is a part of, and is caused by, the real world; the ego is part of, and caused by, the real mind; the empirical world is part of, and caused by, the ego; and sensations are part of (but not caused by) the apparent world. It is interesting that there is a sense in which we can say of this God, contrary to Descartes, that it is a deceiver — because the apparent world that it gives to each soul contains much illusion, or falsity. Spinoza also spoke of God as we speak of the real world (except that for Spinoza no relations are real and God is a substance). Spinoza was accused of pantheism for this, but quite incorrectly; pantheism is the doctrine that defines God as the apparent world, not as the real world, and implicitly in this commits the identity error of common sense realism; clearly, it is a doctrine that we need not consider seriously here. Again, for Hegel, God, Reason, and the Absolute were all one.

✶

The traditional problem of evil can also be considered at this point. This is the problem that if God is all-good, He will desire evil not to exist; and that if He is all-powerful, He will be able to annihilate evil; and that evil does exist. Therefore God is either not all-good or not all-powerful, or both. A logical solution to this problem is that there are two Gods, one all-good but not all-powerful and the other all-powerful but not all-good; then there is no inconsistency in saying that God is all-good, God is all-powerful and evil exists [329]. This is not an acceptable solution in a monotheistic theology, of course; but here it is not only acceptable but obvious: the oge-God is good, in the sense of moral, but not all-powerful; the real world is all-powerful but not moral; and the oge-god and the real world are two, not one.

✶ ✶ ✶

The fifth meaning of the word God is an incoherent amalgam of the ideas of the previous four. It is an imaginary anthropomorphic being that is used as panacea explanation, refuge from ignorance, solace in the face of fear of the unknown, support of prejudices denying human injustice and mortality, destroyer of curiosity, opiate of the people and rocklike authority for the closed-minded. It is the God of children in Sunday school, the God rightly denied by atheists, a mere prejudice accepted irrationally by the ignorant and the superstitious. We may call it the **panacea God**, or **placebo God**, and recognise that there are no rational grounds for believing it to exist.

✶ ✶ ✶

The sixth God is the other one that was said probably not to exist. This is the hypothetical creator of the real world. If there is such, then it exists outside the real world. I will argue later (Chapter 17) that this is in fact impossible. But even if it is possible, there is nothing more that we can meaningfully say about such a God — beyond raising the childish infinite regress question about who or what created the creator.

That no such creator of the real world is possible is the case with Spinoza's system, in which God is both the real world and infinite in all respects. There cannot therefore be anything of any kind outside of God to create it — hence God must be *causa sui* — self-caused. Just how self-causation might occur is indicated in Leibniz. Out of all the possible worlds that might exist there must, according to Leibniz, be a sufficient reason why the actual one exists, rather than any other. This sufficient reason is that this is the best of all possible worlds. Leibniz had a technical definition for *best* — maximum compossibility — which we can here interpret in terms of maximum hekergy. That is, this world exists because it has a greater total hekergy than any other possible world. For Leibniz also, this meant that the world — the real world, the pre-established harmony — is infinite. This whole matter is discussed further in Chapter 17.

My own opinion of the concept of infinity is that it has nominal meaning only. If it is true then the real world is finite — as suggested earlier — and it is logically possible for there to be something outside it, such as a creator.

✳ ✳ ✳

Finally, the seventh meaning of the word God is the psychohelios. This is a third complex of real ideas — an agent, or spirit — but not one based on L.A.L.R.U. It is the concern of the last chapter. We will see that it is the only God that could be described as omniscient; that it is perfect in its own way; and that it is a God of which worship of a second kind is possible.

17. The Ontological Argument.

In all of the foregoing there are two main philosophical weaknesses. Although at first sight they seem to be unrelated, they in fact both come together in an old argument called the ontological argument. In this chapter I propose to recapitulate the two weaknesses, and their relation to the present philosophic system, and then to present a new version of the ontological argument which, if it does not fully cure the weaknesses, at least does so partly.

The first weakness is the solipsistic predicament. It arises because of the fundamental point of departure between rationalists and empiricists. This is not, as John Locke supposed, the rationalist claim to the possession of innate ideas, nor, as the logical positivists supposed, a rationalist insistence that science should be *a priori* — rather, the point of departure between rationalists and empiricists is the argument from illusion and the causal theory of perception. Both of these require that what we are directly conscious of in perception is images of reality rather than reality itself. On this question empiricists — and this includes phenomenologists, existentialists, and Marxists, to say nothing of nominalists, relativists, and humanists — favour the long-established belief of common sense, over reason; while rationalists favour reason over common sense. The long-established belief is, of course, common sense realism: a prejudice destined to go the way of geocentricism and creationism among the educated but which, for those who continue to believe it, disallows solipsism. Because if what I perceive around me is reality then, by definition, it continues to exist between occasions of my perceiving it, and by that fact solipsism is false. But if, on the other hand, all that I am conscious of in perception is in my mind then the solipsistic predicament looms. The mental things of which I am conscious could be images of reality, but it is not good enough philosophically merely to believe this: we should prove it. In Chapter 4 we did fall back on belief — an act of faith — to escape solipsism. It was, to be sure, faith in science, and thereby rational; but this is still faith. What is needed is proof that the real world exists, and proof that the nature of the real world is such that the exact theoretical sciences are largely true. Because of Chapter 16, it is immaterial whether we prove the existence of the real world or the existence of God, provided that it is understood that by *God* we mean the real world: creator of apparent worlds and consciousness, omnipotent, immanent, transcendent and perfect. In this sense such a proof belongs equally to theoretical science, to metaphysics and to theology.

✳

The second weakness is relational metaphysics. We supposed in Chapter 8 that every event has a cause, but this was not proved; and the global hekergy principle — the assumption that the hekergy of the real world is the maximum possible — was also not proved. We also saw in Chapter 8 that although global causes were postulated, they were wholly lacking in density of detail. And in Chapter 9, we examined other weaknesses of relational metaphysics.

✳

Returning, next, to the solipsistic predicament, we may note that, historically, the nearest that philosophers have come to disproving solipsism is with arguments for the existence of God. Indeed, if one is trying to prove the existence of an imperceptible — any imperceptible — the best strategy is to choose to prove the existence of one that is pre-eminent, since its pre-eminence could mean that it has certain unique properties that enable its existence to be proved. There are a half-dozen or so traditional arguments for the existence of God, and all but one of them rely on assumptions that are in as much need of proof as is the existence of God. It is as difficult to prove that everything must have a cause, that design requires a designer, that the effect cannot be more perfect than the cause, and so on, as it is to prove that God exists. The one exception to this invalidation is the ontological argument — although many philosophers will not agree with me on this.

The ontological argument was invented by St. Anselm, and is usually quoted in the following form: I can conceive of a being that is perfect in all respects; since I can conceive of it, it must necessarily exist — because if it lacked existence it would be imperfect in this respect. Another way of putting this is to say: I can conceive of a being than which no greater can be conceived; if this being did not exist then it would be less than if it did exist, therefore it must exist.

This argument has had a long history of controversy. The major objection to it is the claim that all perfections are predicates of whatever subject possesses them, and existence is not a predicate — hence non-existence is not an imperfection. The counter-argument to this is that this objection commits the fallacy of composition: it assumes that what is true of the parts must be true of the whole. An example of this fallacy is: an army consists of soldiers therefore an army is a soldier; one of the reasons that this conclusion is false is that an army is a whole and so possesses emergent relations not possessed by its soldiers. Hence the counter-claim that existence, while certainly not a predicate of any one part of the universe, is a predicate of the universe as a whole: it is that predicate which distinguishes the actual universe from all other possible universes. But this claim is not itself proved; so while it throws doubt on the predicate argument, it does not invalidate it.

My own view on this matter is that although the ontological argument has never been shown to be valid, it is in fact so. What I propose to do here is to advance another step in the direction of establishing its validity.

✶

In principle, demonstrating the validity of the ontological argument is easy. In its simplest form, the argument is: the greatest perfection necessarily exists. To show that this is valid we need clear and generally acceptable definitions of *greatest perfection* and *existence*, and then show that the first logically necessitates the second.

The basic difficulty in doing this is that if you want to prove something, you must first know what you are talking about. When it comes to existence, philosophers do not know what they are talking about. We all have experience of existence, because we are conscious and everything of which we are conscious exists indubitably; but no one has come up with a satisfactory definition of existence. This is called the **Problem of Being**: the problem of defining real existence. So the difficulty with the ontological argument is the problem of being: how can you deduce something which you cannot define?

A possible way round this difficulty is to turn to the notion of existence in mathematics. For mathematicians, the meaning of existence is clear: it is possibility. Given certain undefined — that is, primitive — mathematical entities and axioms concerning them, other entities can be defined; these are then either possible or impossible, according to the axioms and the principles of logic, and hence they either exist mathematically in this system, or else do not exist. For example, in the context of Euclidean geometry we can define *triangle*, *equilateral*, and *right-angled*, and then query the possibility of an equilateral triangle, a right-triangle, and an equilateral right triangle. As is well known, the first two are possible and the third is impossible because of contradiction. Hence equilateral triangles and right triangles exist in Euclidean geometry but equilateral right triangles do not.

We have come across this concept of possibility already, in our discussion of predication. This was intensional predication, in which there is the possibility that two abstract ideas may be combined consistently. Such combination requires an emergent relation to unify the two ideas into a whole, so that usually there is an emergent hekergy that makes the whole greater than the sum of its parts. This emergent hekergy may give the combination a higher hekergy than any other arrangement of the parts, and is thus a more perfect arrangement of them; and, often, only one arrangement of the terms will yield the emergent, so that $e=1$, the hekergy is a maximum, and the arrangement is perfect. All this is suggestive because in the present context we are talking about perfection as well as existence. If we rephrase the ontological argument as *perfection necessitates existence* then we can translate this to *singular possibility necessitates possibility* and the whole thing becomes a truism — since necessity is singular possibility.

Again, since we are talking of intensional mathematics, we may note that the two great strengths of intensional mathematics are that (i) it, and it alone, has axiom generosity, and (ii) it is perfectly consistent: paradox and contradiction exist only in language, they have only nominal meaning; so a purely intensional system has to be consistent. Axiom generosity produces emergent hekergy, so the amount of generosity is a measure of perfection; and consistency is intrinsic possibility, which is mathematical existence. So to say that the intensional mathematical system that *exists* does so because it is the *best* of all possibles, is an argument that relies on the two strengths of intensional mathematics.

Intriguing as all this suggestiveness is, it is not proof, but it is warrant to investigate further. So let us see if this skeleton can be fleshed out.

✱✱✱

Our starting point is the concept of mathematical entity: all mathematical entities are relations, or else intrinsic or extrinsic properties of relations. Thus we are dealing with intensional mathematics only. A mathematical entity is, for us, an abstract idea, which, as a relation, may relate other mathematical entities into larger entities — that is, structures —

or else be itself related to other entities to form larger entities. Thus if certain entities are called mathematical ideas then certain structures of these would be mathematical definitions or mathematical propositions, and certain structures of definitions and propositions would be mathematical systems. In particular, a set of primitive, or undefined, mathematical entities, and postulated propositions concerning them, constitute an axiom set; out of this a large amount of other entities may cascadingly emerge, so that the system has many more entities than its axiom set.

We note that nearly every mathematical entity has a numerical measure of its value: its hekergy; generally this will be both summation hekergy and configuration hekergy. An entity will be designated here by a capital letter and its hekergy by the same letter in italic lowercase. Thus a mathematical system S has hekergy s.

An entity exists if it is possible, and does not exist if it is impossible. But possibility may be intrinsic or extrinsic: this is a case of the distinction made earlier between intrinsic and extrinsic properties [258]. An entity has intrinsic possibility if it is not self-contradictory; and it has extrinsic possibility, relative to another entity, if the two can be related into one entity. Note that if possibility can be intrinsic or extrinsic then so can necessity, which is a special case of possibility: singular possibility. For example, the existence of a whole necessitates the existence of each its parts, and this necessity is extrinsic to each part, while the truth of an intensional concept necessitates the truth of its predicate and this necessity is intrinsic.

✶

We next define:

Axiom set. Any part of a mathematical system from which the whole system can be derived logically is an axiom set of that system. It is generally a set of propositions relating undefined, or primitive, concepts. Note that every system has at least one axiom set: the system itself. An axiom set is a mathematical entity and so has a hekergy: both summation hekergy and configuration hekergy. The summation hekergy is the sum of the hekergies of each axiom, while the configuration hekergy is the hekergy of all the emergents out of the axiom set; so the summation hekergy and configuration hekergy together constitute the total hekergy of the system.

Least axiom set. That axiom set of a system that has the least summation hekergy is called a least axiom set of that system. It does not matter if more than one axiom set has this least hekergy, since we are concerned with this hekergy magnitude rather than the axiom set which has it.

Degree of goodness of a system. If a system S has a least axiom set A, of summation hekergy a, and the configuration hekergy emergent out of A is e, then the degree of goodness, or goodness for short, g, of S, is $g = e/a$. The degree of goodness is thus the ratio of the emergent, or configuration, hekergy of the system to the summation hekergy of the least axiom set; so it is a function of the quantity of emergents from the axiom set, a measure of how much cascades from the axiom set. Since intensional infinities are here denied, there is no possibility of e or a being infinite and hence g being either infinite or indeterminate.

Contingent part. If a part, C, of a system S can be derived in that system only from itself, then C is a contingent part of S. Since C can be derived only from itself it must be a part of every axiom set of that system. A system whose only axiom set is itself is thus wholly contingent: it has degree of goodness equal to one — the lowest possible. This definition of the contingent is equivalent to our earlier definition of contingency as plural possibility: because if C is a part of S and C is derivable only from itself then C is not a singular possibility, given the existence of the rest of the system S, hence is a plural possibility; that is, C is only one among all possible contingent parts.

Necessary part. If a part N of a system S can be derived in S other than from itself, then N is a necessary part of S. This is equivalent to saying that N is a singular possibility in S; since given an axiom set of S that does not explicitly contain N, N must occur in S. Thus N is emergent out of every axiom set of the system, other than axiom sets of which it is a part.

A **mathematical world** is an intensional mathematical system that is complete — that is, no other intrinsically possible entities are extrinsically possible relative to it. Or, in simpler but less precise terms, nothing can be added to it. Two kinds of mathematical world can be distinguished, as follows.

A **contingent world** is complete in that it has all possible parts, contingent or necessary. We note that perhaps the concept of contingent world has nominal meaning only, in that it may be possible to add contingent parts to a system without end so that it cannot be complete; but as it turns out this does not matter, so we will assume for now that a contingent world may be complete.

A **necessary world** is complete in that it has all possible necessary parts; and, secondly, a necessary world contains no contingent parts. All possible necessary worlds vary among themselves in the quantity and variety of their prime relations, and thereby vary in their goodness.

Thus nothing at all can be added to a contingent world; and, although contingent parts can be added to a necessary world, if they are then it ceases to be a necessary world and becomes either part of a contingent world or a complete contingent world.

Exclusive existence. A system exists exclusively if it exists and thereby prevents the existence of anything else. That is, it exists and all other intrinsically possible entities are extrinsically impossible relative to it. A contingent mathematical world, if it exists, has exclusive existence, by definition: being complete, nothing can be added to it, so nothing else can co-exist with it.

The ontological argument now proceeds in six segments.

✶

1. We need to discover what changes to a system increase its goodness and what changes decrease it. Suppose we have a system S with a least axiom set A, having hekergy a, and total emergent hekergy e. thus the goodness of S is $g=e/a$. Suppose that a mathematical entity B, of hekergy b, is now added to A, and as a result a totality of emergents, C, of hekergy c, appear and change S into S$'$. Then the summation hekergy, a, of A is increased by b and the configuration hekergy e of S is increased by c. So the goodness, g', of the increased system, S$'$, is

$$g'=(e+c)/(a+b).$$

Simple arithmetic shows that:

$g'<g$ if, and only if, $c/b < e/a$,
$g'=g$ if, and only if, $c/b = e/a$,
$g'>g$ if, and only if, $c/b > e/a$.

That is, the ratio $g':g$ equals the ratio $(c/b):g$, since $e/a = g$.

c/b may be thought of as the increase of goodness to the system. It follows that if B is added to A then (i) the goodness decreases if few emergents appear and increases if many appear; and (ii) the threshold between decrease and increase is the previous degree of goodness. So if g is very small, a large variety of additions to A may increase the goodness of S, while if g is very large most possible additions to A will diminish the goodness of S. And of course the converse of all this holds if B is taken away from A, so changing S' back to S.

Emergents are necessary parts of S, because they are not parts of the least axiom set, while if no emergents appear when B is added to A then B is a contingent part of S', since B had to be put in A in order to appear in S'.

Consequently we can say that, broadly speaking, if one system has more necessary parts than another, and fewer contingent parts, then it is a better system; and fewer necessary parts and more contingent parts make it a worse system. Also, the greater the existing goodness the more difficult it is to increase it: there is a law of diminishing returns when it comes to increasing goodness by adding primitive parts or axioms.

It follows that the best of all possible systems — the system of greatest goodness — is a necessary world. It has maximum emergent hekergy for minimum hekergy of axiom set, or, as Leibniz put it, maximum consequences for minimum hypothesis.

The best of all possible intensional systems is finite, because there is no intensional infinity. That is, suppose that we imagine creating a system by gradually adding new parts to its axiom set, and that this is done in such a way that the resulting system always has the maximum possible goodness. Because of the law of diminishing returns, due to the threshold between decrease and increase being the previous degree of goodness, each addition to the axiom set must increase the goodness more than the previous addition. We thus have a series of additions each of which contributes a greater increase of goodness than its predecessor. Such a series must either end because no further term is possible, or it must go on infinitely because it is possible for a finite term to produce an infinite increase in goodness: that is, because it is possible for a finite term to produce an infinity of emergents. This is not possible in an intensional system and hence the best of all possible systems is finite.

✶

2. A contingent intensional world is impossible, because as soon as a world has one contingent part then other contingent parts can be added without end. This means that in order to be complete a contingent world must be infinite, and there is no intensional infinity. So in considering all

possible intensional mathematical worlds, we are confined to all possible necessary worlds. These vary in their least axiom sets and in their goodness. So the only possible intensionally mathematical worlds are necessary worlds: they cannot have any contingent parts, and so are complete. And being complete, whichever one exists, exists exclusively; because if another existed then they could both be contingently related into a part of a contingent world, which is impossible. So only one necessary world can exist.

✷

3. The best of all possible worlds must be a whole, having a relation that unites the highest level parts; we may call this relation the **top relation** of the world. By the principle of novel emergence [114], the top relation will have a novel property, a property that no other relation in the world possesses, within a property set [259] that we may call Ĝ. Note that the top relation must exist, and Ĝ must have the maximum of possible properties in it, simply because this world is the best. That is, the highest level parts of the system are all extrinsically possible relative to each other, which means that they could all be terms of one relation; this *could* is possibility, and if the best world did not have this possibility then it would not be the best. Similarly, if Ĝ did not have every possible property then the world would not be the best. In other words, in the best of all possibles such *could* means *must*.

✷

4. Other necessary worlds must all also have a top relation: all of their highest level parts are either arranged so that a top, novel, relation must emerge, or they are so arranged that it cannot emerge — and in the latter case they are united into an intensional set by a set relation, which is their top relation. So every necessary world has a top relation, and it may or may not have a novel property. Because a relation cannot exist without its terms, the top relation of a necessary world extrinsically necessitates the existence of all of its terms, the terms of its terms, on down to all the prime relations in the system. At the prime level the extension of the set of all the prime relations is identical with its arrangement, since each prime relation is equally relation and term; so the top relation also extrinsically necessitates the arrangement of the prime relations, and because arrangements of terms extrinsically necessitate the emergence of next higher level relations, and the

arrangements of these, the existence of the arrangement of the prime relations extrinsically necessitates the existence of all the cascading emergence in the system. Thus the existence of the top relation extrinsically necessitates the existence of everything else in its world. Note that the downward extrinsic necessary existence is distributive existence, while the upward extrinsic necessary existence, or emergence, is compositional existence: the existence of a relation necessitates the existence of its terms, and the existence of a suitable arrangement of terms necessitates the existence, or emergence, of a relation.

✶

5. We next consider the concept of **intrinsic necessary existence**. As a concept, it is both fascinating and dangerous. It is fascinating because whatever possesses this property must exist; but it is dangerous because it could have nominal meaning only, like *square circle*, in which case any serious use of it could produce results that were of great seeming significance but in fact false. So it must be shown to have more than nominal meaning. This requires both that it be shown to be derived from intensionally meaningful concepts and that this particular combination of concepts is intensionally meaningful — that is, it does not produce contradictions. For example, *square* and *circle* both have intensional meaning, but their combination, *square circle* does not; while *triangle*, *equilateral* and *equilateral triangle* all have intensional meaning. We note that *necessary* and *existence* both have intensional meaning.

We have already distinguished two possible kinds of necessary existence: extrinsic and intrinsic. Extrinsic necessary existence occurs if the existence of something is necessitated by something outside of it. And we have just seen two examples of extrinsic necessary existence: distributive and compositional. Both of these are extrinsic, since a relation and its terms are extrinsic to each other. Since the existence of a whole necessitates the existence of the parts, this means that extrinsic necessary existence is both a perfectly familiar concept, and has intensional meaning.

We do not have a similarly obvious example of intrinsic necessary existence. However, the concepts *intrinsic* and *necessary* not only both have intensional meaning, but careful thought shows no contradiction in their combination, such as there is with *square circle*. Thus intrinsic necessary existence is possible, and so at least one among all possible relations must possess it as an intrinsic property.

Intrinsic necessary existence occurs if it is a property of some relation such that this relation has to exist because of that property; and, by definition, this property must be intrinsic to the relation. We call this property of intrinsic necessary existence Ñ, and a relation that has the property Ñ, we call G. G exists necessarily, and also extrinsically necessitates the existence of all of its terms, terms of its terms, and on down to prime relations; and all of the relations cascadingly emergent out of these; thus intrinsic necessary existence, Ñ, is a property of the system that G unifies, and G is the top relation of this system. A second instance of G could not exist at any lower level in the system, because if it did its existence would also be extrinsically necessitated, in which case its possession of Ñ would be redundant, hence contingent; and no contingencies are possible in a necessary world. So Ñ must be a novel property of the top relation, and only of the top relation. Also, because only one necessary world can exist, and whatever world has G as a top relation must exist, it follows that G must be unique among all possible top relations of necessary worlds.

✶

6. The best of all possible necessary worlds must have G as its top relation, because if it did not have Ñ in its top relation it would not be the best. That is, the best *could* have Ñ in its top relation, therefore *must* — simply because it is the best. Also, the best, in being best, is necessarily unique among all possible necessary worlds, and this uniqueness is a necessary condition for having G as a top relation. So the best of all possible intensional mathematical systems exists necessarily because it is the best. This necessary world also has maximum hekergy, in that the arrangement of all of its parts is a singular possibility: any other arrangement would not cause the top relation G to emerge, and so $e=1$ in the expression $\ln(t/e)$. Maximum possible goodness thus entails greatest perfection.

Note that although a contingent world having, say, two necessary worlds as parts would in theory have at least double the hekergy of the one necessary world, such a contingent world has only nominal meaning: its seemingly greater hekergy has no intensional meaning.

Because G cannot exist without the rest of the necessary world of which it is the top relation, we will also refer to the entire world as G.

✱

There is another way of looking at all of this. We have shown that at least one intensional world must exist and that at most one can exist; and that at least one relation possessing intrinsic necessary existence must exist, and that at most one such relation can exist. The only way in which all four of these statements can be true is if there is a necessary world whose top relation is at a level higher than any other possible world, and this top relation has an emergent property that is intrinsic necessary existence. But such a world with a maximal level of top relation must be the best of all possibles, which thereby exists necessarily. (We could have defined the goodness of a possible world as the height of its highest level of emergence, so as to make clear that the best has this level, uniquely, and then argued that this is equivalent to the earlier definition of goodness; but this is a minor matter.)

✱

The question now is whether mathematical existence and real existence are one and the same or not. We have named the actually existent

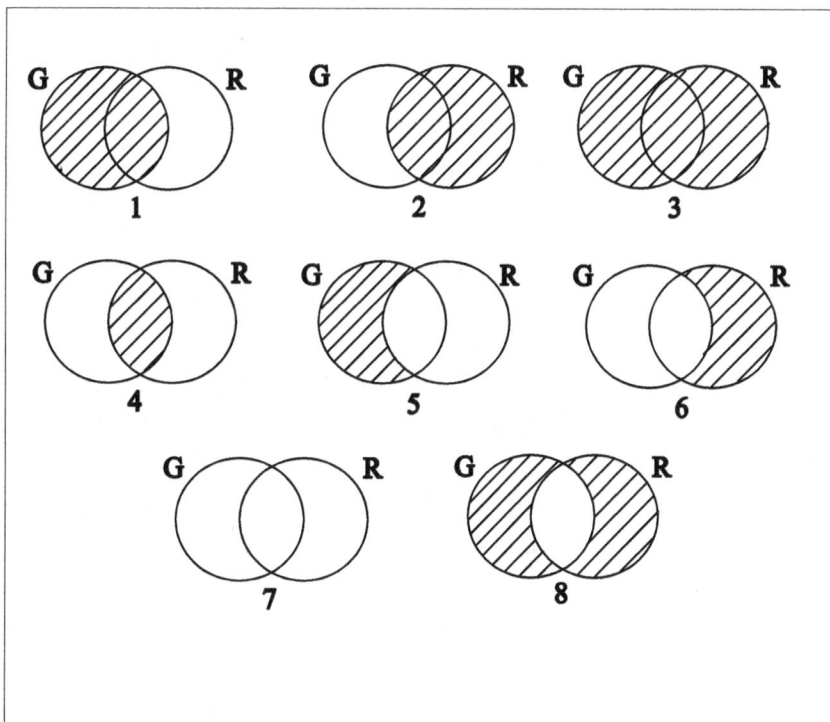

Fig 17.1.

intensional mathematical world G; let us call the real world R. This is the theoretical world of all strict imperceptibles and all theoretical minds. We can ask if G and R have anything in common, and if so, how much. There are a total of eight logical possibilities, as is shown by the Venn diagrams in Fig. 17.1. Each of these represents G by a circle and R by a circle, so that in each diagram there are three areas: G and non-R, both G and R, and non-G and R. That represented by each area may be either existent (unshaded) or non-existent (shaded), so there are 2^3, or 8, logical possibilities altogether. We are speaking of two kinds of existence, mathematical and real; so in the diagrams the unshaded portions of G have mathematical existence and the unshaded portions of R have real existence, and the unshaded intersections have both.

There are three relevant facts: (i) as we have just proved, G exists mathematically; (ii) at least some of R exists because some existence is indubitable, as we saw in the very beginning; and (iii) G and R do intersect because some relations exist indubitably — as, for example, this book is *in front* of your eyes. Let us now consider each Venn diagram in turn.

1. First is the logical possibility that G does not exist but R does exist. One only needs to think of some empirical relation to know that at least some of G exists in reality, in which case it is false that the intersection of G and R does not exist. But if some of G exists then all of it exists, by the argument above.

2. The second Venn shows that G exists but R does not. Since some of R exists indubitably — all that I am conscious of now — this cannot be true.

3. Third is the possibility that neither G nor R exist — which cannot be true, given 1 and 2.

4. Next we ask if both can exist, but have nothing in common — no intersection. Given the fact of the success of theoretical science, which is mathematical and which describes R, they must have something in common, so this possibility is false as well. Indeed, merely counting on one's fingers proves that G and R intersect, as does thinking of one relation.

5. The fifth diagram shows the possibility that G is a proper part of R, meaning that G, although a part, is not the whole of R. If this were so then there would be two kinds of real existence: mathematical and non-mathematical, or relational and non-relational. The non-relational existence

would have to be the existence of one or more substances, and the supposition of these would explain nothing; so they must be denied by Occam's Razor. Another way of putting this is that in this situation the non-G part of R would have to be added to G contingently, thus making G part of a contingent world — which is impossible.

6. The opposite of 5 is that R exists as a proper part of G. If this were so then there would be two kinds of mathematical existence: real and unreal. The real part of G would then have to have a property, $\hat{r}$, which is mind-independent existence, such that the unreal part would lack this property $\hat{r}$. But the whole of G has mind-independent existence, since no human mind can contain all of G, so the whole of G has $\hat{r}$ and R cannot exist as a proper part of G.

7. The last but one possibility is that all three parts exist: a part of G that is outside R, a part of R that is outside G, and also their intersection. But this cannot be true, by 5 and 6.

8. So if all of these seven possibilities are false, the last must be true: their intersection exists, but nothing outside of it exists; G and R are identical, one and the same. So the real world exists necessarily because it is the best of all possible worlds.

The key to this argument is the fact that theoretical science is intensional, successful, and describes the real world. It follows that real existence is intensional mathematical existence.

One could bring in Descartes' malevolent demon here, in its role of universal alternative explanation, and say that nothing exists except the content of solipsism, plus this demon, and the demon manufactures the intersection of mathematics and the empirical world in order to deceive; but such a world would not be the best of all possibles, and we have just proved that the best of all possibles must exist. Similarly for any other explanation of the intersection of mathematics and the empirical world, such as it being manufactured by God in order to test my faith.

✶

To summarise the conclusions of these six segments:

1. Increase of necessary parts and decrease of contingent parts both increase the goodness of a system. Hence the best of all possible worlds is a necessary world.

2. A contingent intensional world is impossible, and at most one among all possible necessary worlds exists.

3. The best of all possible worlds must have a top relation, G, possessing a novel property set.

4. Every necessary world has a top relation, with or without a novel property, and the existence of this top relation extrinsically necessitates the existence of everything else in the world.

5. Intrinsic necessary existence has intensional meaning, so at least one relation among all possibles must possess it; it must be a property of a top relation, G, and both novel in G and unique to G.

6. The best of all possible worlds must have G as a top relation, and hence intrinsic necessary existence, since if it did not it would be less than the best. Also, in being the best, this world is unique and has at least one novel property in its top relation — two necessary conditions for G being its top relation. So the best of all possible intensional mathematical worlds exists necessarily because it is the best.

7. Because intensional mathematics is applicable to the real world, and because some real existence is indubitable, the best of all intensional mathematical worlds and the real world must be identical, one and the same. So real existence is intensional mathematical existence, and the real world exists necessarily because it is the best of all possibles.

✳ ✳ ✳

I do not want to claim here that this version of the ontological argument constitutes ironclad proof that the best of all possible worlds exists necessarily. Ironclad proof in philosophy generally occurs only with falsification — as with the falsification of realism by demonstrating the realistic and identity errors by the contradictions they produce. In the present case the proof is constructive, and I do not know of any such in philosophy that are ironclad. Generally speaking the best one can do in philosophy is to move closer to ironclad proof. In this respect I claim that the present chapter takes the ontological argument nearer to validation than it has been before. And in so far as it has done this, it has provided escape from the solipsistic predicament.

✳

The argument has also provided some detail for our relational metaphysics, in that the best necessary world is deterministic, so every event has a cause; and the hekergy of the real world is a maximum, in that any alteration of the quantity and variety of the prime relations of the real world would reduce its hekergy, hence hekergy is globally conserved. And we note that if the argument is valid then if intensional mathematics could be developed fully then it would be at once the best mathematical system, an *a priori* mathematical metaphysics, a description of the content of the psychohelios [320ff.], the ultimate scientific theory from which all lesser theories could be deduced, and the universal characteristic of which Leibniz dreamed.

✷ ✷ ✷

We end with four further philosophical consequences of the ontological argument, three of them confirmation of points made earlier.

✷

1. Intrinsic necessary existence, N̂ is a predicate of the top relation of the best of all possibles, but not of any of its parts — so it is correct to claim that the "existence is not a predicate" objection to the ontological argument does indeed commit the fallacy of composition.

✷

2. The intrinsic necessary existence of G, or the real world, or God, is, ontologically speaking, causal necessity. It follows that the real world, or God, is *causa sui*, self-caused, as Spinoza claimed. And if one thinks of God as the top relation of the real world, rather than the entire real world, then God is first cause as well as self-caused.

✷

3. Leibniz's axiom — "All truth is analytic" — is true. In the ultimate analysis, all truth follows necessarily from the fact that the best of all possibles exists necessarily. The top relation, G, is the least axiom set of the best of all possibles.

✷

4. The principle that what exists is the best of all possibles is the ultimate stationary, or extremum, principle.

18. The Psychohelios.

The **psychohelios** is a complex of theoretical ideas ordered on a basis of maximum configuration hekergy rather than by L.A.L. We may define such ordering as rational, as opposed to L.A.L. ordering which was defined as irrational. This enables us to define a rational person: a man or woman is fully rational when attending to his or her psychohelios. (Obviously no one is fully rational at all times, although it is not difficult to suppose that some people are never fully rational.) We may also define a **suprarational** person as one in whom the maximum possible number of real ideas are arranged with maximum hekergy — that is, a person who is as much psychohelios as possible. Such a person would have his or her mind in a state of maximum possible configuration hekergy. The theoretical possibility of this is the subject of this chapter.

The psychohelios is produced by the ego as a result of thought. Thinking, as we saw in Chapter 14, is a process in which ideas at the periphery of the ego are rearranged, by suitable attention of the ego, from L.A.L. ordering toward an ordering of maximum hekergy. Most thinking occurs because of linguistic communication from others, rather than original thinking; and it takes place in the form of ordinary thought rather than pure thought. The resulting structure of ideas constitutes the ego's understanding of, and beliefs about, that subject matter, and may also be the psychohelios, or a part of it. It is a part, or all, of the psychohelios only if it is of maximum hekergy. Thought produces structures of ideas whose hekergy is greater than that of L.A.L., but not necessarily thereby of maximum hekergy. In other words, our understanding may contain some prejudice or error. If, however, it is free of prejudice and error then it is of maximum hekergy, it is part of the psychohelios and it is analytically true. The intensionally analytically true has maximum hekergy so the rational ordering of ideas is the ordering of maximum hekergy.

The psychohelios will also be true by resemblance to the real world in so far as it consists of global principles or of principles globally applied, as well as in detail, because the real world is, as a whole, of maximum hekergy; so the psychohelios and the real world will be similar in this respect and hence the psychohelios will be necessarily true by resemblance. For the same reason, the psychohelios will be true by resemblance to some potentially universally public features of apparent worlds.

Consequently the psychohelios is a re-creation, out of abstract ideas, of the real world. Inevitably it lacks an enormous amount of detail; but the detail that it does have is true — absolutely true — and in this sense the psychohelios is perfect in its own way. It is a perfect homomorph. Not only does the psychohelios have maximum truth because it has maximum hekergy, but, for the same reason, it has maximum beauty and maximum goodness.

If the psychohelios grows it will become an agent in its own right: conscious, and having some control. However, it will be strictly limited in both of these because its attention, and hence its attitude, are invariable. This is because, being a structure of maximum hekergy, it has no equivalent configurations into which it can change without hekergy change. So its structure cannot change, other than by growing larger, and so its attention cannot change. And since its attention is fixed, it will be unable to manipulate motor ideas; so it cannot control the real body.

Its singular attention is toward maximum hekergy, so toward the truth, and its control is control over ideas — particularly in the realm of muddled understanding that lies between it and the ego. This control is indirect. The psychohelios will be unable to think, as the ego can, because this needs variable attention, which the psychohelios does not have. But the psychohelios will have an influence on the ego, which makes the ego think. In this respect the ego will be the servant of the psychohelios, and will become more so as the psychohelios grows.

In growing, the psychohelios meets two obstacles. One is that not all the ideas available to it are usable; false ones such as perceptual illusions[19] are not, for example. Secondly, the ideas that are available will mostly belong to the ego, or possibly the oge, so that for the psychohelios to take them is to cause a hekergy decrease in the ego, or oge. Such a decrease is painful, as we know from our discussion of pain. Anyone who has consciously discarded a prejudice because of a rational argument will be familiar with such pain. This is the explanation of why the truth so often is

---

[19] All concrete sensations are illusory, but as illusions they are generated within the ego; since the psychohelios is working with mid-ideas, it has no problem with concreteness.

painful. Consequently we can expect conflict between ego and psychohelios for the possession of ideas.

This conflict will result in a stalemate unless it can be resolved in favour of the psychohelios. If it can be so resolved — and we will consider in a moment how it might be — then the ego, as a structure, finally will be disassembled and then re-assembled, as a part of the psychohelios, in a state of maximum hekergy. Not all of the ego will be reassembled: some of its constituent ideas will be unusable, because illusory, and hence discarded or destroyed. If there is ego-oge harmony then the ego and all the different oge-persons in the oge in effect constitute one structure, and the oge-persons will in their turn be absorbed into the psychohelios or disposed of. If, on the other hand, there is still ego-oge conflict, the oge might be overcome anyway, by a psychohelios strengthened with the material of the ego. The end result of all this is a real mind of maximum hekergy — that is, no other arrangement of its content could be so valuable. This state is the theoretical possibility that was defined as suprarational.

The conflict between psychohelios and ego could be resolved in two ways. The psychohelios could grace the ego with an intuition of the possibility of the suprarational, and of its value; or the ego might come to believe this through religious or philosophical teaching. Such religious teaching is known as mysticism; it claims that union with God is not only possible but more worthwhile than anything else. The God of the mystics is the psychohelios, and union with it is the dissolution of the ego and its regeneration, in its true proportion to reality, within the psychohelios. This might be described as the death of the ego and the rebirth of consciousness in heaven   that is, in a state of perfection. In philosophical teaching concerning the suprarational, the goal is wisdom (Plato) or happiness or blessedness (Spinoza). It can be achieved, according to Plato, through the study of mathematics, astronomy, and music, the practice of dialectic [325], the appreciation of beauty, and the practice of virtue; and, according to Spinoza, by the control of the passions (that is, the appetites and selfishness). Thus we can say that, with these special meanings, the pursuit of happiness, the search for wisdom, and the love of God are all the same activity.

The suprarational state is, by definition, the most valuable achievement that anyone can aspire to — because it is the state of maximum possible hekergy of mind, and hekergy is value. Since there is nothing more valuable that a human being could aspire to than the suprarational it will be of interest if we consider both the means by which a person might try to achieve it, and something of what it might be like to do so. It must be remarked at once that, as the most valuable of human goals, it will be the most difficult to achieve. It cannot be done by means of a weekend of fasting and meditation, nor obtained effortlessly by means of hallucinogenic drugs.

✱

We earlier defined the good as hekergy increase (or, at the least, preservation); and the good of the ego as selfish, and the good of the oge, because it is the good of society, as moral. On the same lines we can stipulatively define the good of the psychohelios as **ethical**.

Morals are common to all persons within a given culture, but ethics, as here defined, are individual. At any given point in a person's progress toward the suprarational a decision concerning what is ethical must be made by that person. By the ego, that is. If the decision is made by anyone else then it is, as far as the ego is concerned, a decision by the oge; and it is a decision that either directly or indirectly contributes to the dissolution of the ego. Clearly, a decision of this kind made by the oge cannot be acceptable to the ego — it is too reminiscent of, and possibly a part of, ego-oge conflict. As such, it will be an impediment to ethical progress. Consequently all ethical decisions must be made by the ego. Discipline — other than self-discipline — duty, conscience and other oge phenomena are, in these special senses of the words, moral but rarely ethical.

However this does not mean that ethics cannot be taught at all. Teaching comes from others, and so becomes oge belief; but the ego can consider any teaching, *qua* proposition, and rationally assent to it, or deny it. So the principles and theory involved in the suprarational can be expounded, and used as a guide by any ego that believes in the possibility of the suprarational and wishes to make ethical decisions. On these lines we will next examine the principles involved in the three main stages of progress towards the suprarational. These are the stages of maturation of ego and oge, of growth of the psychohelios, and of diminution of the ego.

✱

Maturation is growth, and growth is hekergy increase — of either summation or configuration hekergy. Thus maturation of the ego requires first, in infancy, increase of summation hekergy, provided through love, and, later, through school; and increase of configuration hekergy, which is cure of prejudice and increase of understanding. Maturation of the oge is, as with the ego, first of all growth through acquisition of ideas, and later rearrangement of these ideas. One such increase of configuration hekergy is a diminution of the L.A.L.-caused estrangement between oge-lover and oge-enemy — that is, diminution of extremism. Maturation of the whole individual (that is, of the real mind as a whole) begins with maturation of ego and oge, and proceeds to a harmony between these two. Such harmony is an increase of configuration hekergy — the joint configuration of ego and oge.

Maturation is clearly necessary for suprarationality. In the first place, the ego must reach a certain minimum strength in order for the psychohelios to develop at all. If the individual as a whole is mature then both ego and oge will be strong, and there will be harmony between them, which also will be an aid toward the suprarational. A particular form of oge maturity would be public acceptance of the possibility of the suprarational. This would include, eventually, an oge acceptance of immorality if it should be ethical for the individual concerned. An extreme case of this would be oge understanding of, and willingness for, dissolution of the oge for ethical purposes. At present of course, no oges are this mature — with the possible exception of the oges of some monastic communities.

If an immature ego strives for the suprarational it is quite possible that it will end in a schizophrenic state — which is dissolution of the ego, in the absence of any psychohelios, as a result of oge conquest. Indeed, because of this similarity, in one respect only, between schizophrenia and the suprarational it is possible that schizophrenics have some insight into the nature of the suprarational.

It is of course exceedingly difficult for an ego to know whether it is mature. An outstanding characteristic of naivety is self-ignorance, so that the immature are usually unaware of their immaturity. However, indices of maturity can be discovered. For example, the amount of malice in one's humour or one's pity decreases with maturity. Ego-oge harmony also is indicative of maturity, and is indicated by strength of both ego and oge, and absence of inclination-duty conflict. A strong ego is indicated very often by position in the peck-order — that is, by relative rudeness ability; and a strong oge by a strong sense of duty. To have only one of these is not of course indicative of harmony, since it may mean only an ego-oge imbalance. Also, there is a difference between having rudeness ability and being rude: the mature person has the ability but rarely uses it.

Cure of neurosis is a special case of maturation, since neurosis prevents maturation in the fields in which it operates — "arrested development," as it is popularly known. And cure of neurosis is certainly necessary if ego-oge harmony is to be achieved. We may note in this connection that if we call the unethical **sin**, then neurosis is the sin of the father that is visited upon the children, unto the third and fourth generation.

Other uses of the word sin are appropriate to the present meaning of *ethical*. Thus the traditional seven deadly sins — pride, envy, anger, sloth, avarice, gluttony and lust — are all attitudes of selfishness of one kind or another; these are "deadly" because they block further ethical progress. Venial sins, on the other hand, are acts rather than attitudes and so delay rather than block progress. Confession, repentance, penance, and absolution are ego-oge adjustments after venial sinning; as such, they are usually ethical. However, not all sinning (in the traditional sense) is unethical (in the present sense). The most obvious example is the selfishness of the young, which, in so far as it promotes ego maturation, is ethical. But in the elderly, of course, selfishness is unethical.

✶

Growth of the psychohelios is the second stage of ethical progress. The most obvious way of achieving this is a search for truth. In our day this is relatively easy: it requires a study of mathematics and theoretical science. It is relatively easy for us compared with, say, Plato's contemporaries because it is easier to study and understand other men's discoveries than it is to make them for oneself. In fact Plato recommended the study of mathematics and its applications, but his pupils were confined to arithmetic and geometry, astronomy and musical harmony.

A second means of aiding the growth of the psychohelios, also recommended by Plato, is dialectic. This is conversation with the aim of mutual enlargement of understanding. That is to say, it is exchange and discussion of theories understood by each participant — not with the goal of victory, as in debate, or the goal of conversion, as in proselytising — but the goal of improvement of the understanding. Dialectic is thus amicable, and probably exciting, rather than disputatious or fervent. It is noteworthy also that dialectic has a salutary effect on the oge: it teaches the oge, by introjection, that rationality is valued by others.

A third method, again one recommended by Plato, is the study and appreciation of other forms of high hekergy, such as great beauty and great goodness.

Since all three of these methods were advocated by Plato, it is perhaps appropriate to mention here my opinion that Plato's theory of forms is a theory of suprarational knowledge. The forms, which Plato said are "beyond heaven" — that is, beyond the blue sky — are, I suggest, ideas in the psychohelios. A special case is the form of the Good, which Plato likened to a sun in the mind — hence my name psychohelios. However, I do not propose to argue this opinion here.

✳

The third stage in ethical progress is diminution of the ego. One obvious way of doing this is self-denial. Control of the passions, Spinoza called it — that is, control of the appetites and selfishness. In other words, refusal, by the ego, to strive for greater growth, greater hekergy for itself. This means, in general, a denial of selfishness. Indeed we may say that selfishness is original sin, the price of the fruit of the tree of knowledge — because without an ego there can be no psychohelios, hence the ego characteristic of selfishness is the price of the knowledge in the psychohelios. It is most instructive to recognise that every act of self-denial must be truly voluntary in order to be ethical. It was earlier remarked that all ethical decisions must be made by the ego: if they are made by the oge then they become authoritarian and disciplinary rather than ethical. But many advocates of self-denial had their teachings enshrined in oges, as moral commands and taboos; as such these teachings were both ethically useless and mentally unhealthy. A great deal of contemporary neurosis can be traced back to sexual taboos, for example, which probably had their origin in the advocation, by religious teachers, of self-denial but which later became oge-denial.

Secondly, the ego may diminish itself by a giving of its hekergy to the psychohelios, unconditionally. This, literally, is love of God — since unconditional giving is love and the psychohelios is the God that is Truth, Beauty, and Goodness. Love need not be exclusively love of God even, in order to be ethical, since love of oge-persons promotes ego-oge harmony;

this is also called charity. Indeed, the ultimate achievement in ego-oge harmony is harmony between the ego and all of the oge, up to and including the oge-enemy. Evidently this last is particularly difficult — history does not abound with stories of people who managed to love their enemies.

✳ ✳ ✳

When it comes to describing the content of suprarational understanding, very little can be said. This is partly because understanding, unlike facts, is difficult to communicate, partly because the suprarational cannot be put into merely rational language (hence the mystical nature of mysticism), but mostly because little is known about it. However, two main points can be made.

✳

The first concerns the disappearance of the apparent, or empirical, body. In its absence suprarational consciousness is consciousness without a body — which is the proper meaning of the word *ecstatic*. Also, the apparent body is at the origin of an egocentric co-ordinate system: in front of me, behind me, above me, below me, to my left, to my right and my past, my future. With the disappearance of the apparent body, this co-ordinate system vanishes also. The result is consciousness without apparent space and time as we know it — which is the proper meaning of the word *eternal*.

These two terms have, of course, been debased by the limitations of popular understanding — as has the entire mystical teaching. For example "As a result of ethical living and after the death of the ego, consciousness is reborn in heaven, which is a state that is an ecstatic and eternal union with God" becomes "After physical death the apparent body is resurrected in a place beyond the sky, where everlasting intense pleasure is provided by the oge-God as reward for living a moral life." Again, the psychohelios, *qua* perfect homomorph of the real world, could be described metaphorically as the Son of the real world; and suprarationality could be described as the unification of ego and psychohelios — as "I am become the psychohelios" hence "I am the Son of God." Misunderstanding of this metaphor could then lead to all kinds of strange doctrines concerning immaculate conception and virgin birth.

✳

The second point concerning the content of the suprarational is the disappearance of illusions. To irrational common sense all of these illusions are dear, so that the mere claim that they are illusions is unpleasant — let alone the prospect of their disappearance. There are eight at least.

1, 2. Two we have met already. Concreteness [109] is illusory, and so is chance [131, 318]. Under chance we must include luck and fortune.

3. A third illusion is individuality, in so far as it is a product of egocentric, hence false, ordering of ideas. Another way of putting this is to say that the real world is a single structure, unified by a single top relation. We may divide it conceptually into substructures, but to do so — although necessary for a rational mind — is to falsify, since it is to lose novel emergent properties. One such substructure is the real body of the individual concerned: it is not really individual at all. The fact that this illusion disappears in the suprarational state emphasises a key difference between ordinary and suprarational consciousness: in ordinary consciousness there is always a distinction between subject and object, between me and not-me, whereas in suprarational consciousness there is no such distinction. In other words, the subject-object distinction is an illusion, part and parcel of the illusion of individuality. Another way of understanding the illusion of the individuality of oneself is to recognise that the ego is formed by L.A.L., so is irrational, and hence is false: the existence of the large, strong, ego both makes it very difficult to accept that one's own individuality is an illusion, and is also the cause of the illusion.

4. The fourth illusion is death, in so far as this is individual. If there is no individuality, there can be no individual death. This does not mean that there is no entropy increase at the end of the world line [96] which is a real person; it means that the world line is not an individual. Furthermore, *qua* death, the entropy increase is only local, because hekergy is conserved, and so unimportant from the point of view of the psychohelios; so the ego's fear of death, although genuine, is unwarranted.

5. The fifth illusion is freedom of the will, as it is usually understood. If there are no real individuals then there is no freedom. Or, to explain it another way, if the real world is in a state of maximum hekergy then everything in it is a singular possibility, hence necessitated. But if everything is so necessitated there can be no freedom. This illusion is related to that of chance. In either kind of event — a chance event or a free action — the event is a beginning of a causal sequence; that is, it was not necessitated by an immediately prior event or set of events. But in a real world of maximum

hekergy there can be no such beginnings, since the possible variety of them is not singular. Putting this yet a third way, in a world in which everything is necessitated, so-called free actions are all necessitated and hence not free.

However, there is another sense of *freedom* that is not an illusion: the Spinozistic sense. For Spinoza what a man does is an action, and so free, if its cause is internal to him; and it is a passion (that is, he is passive as opposed to active, a patient as opposed to an agent), and so unfree, if the cause is external. We saw a good example of this with self-denial, which is free if caused by the ego and unfree if caused by the oge; an example of freedom that is ethical. This freedom is necessary to gaining the suprarational, according to Spinoza, while the un-free are in a state of human bondage.

6. The sixth illusion is evil. As we saw earlier, evil is characteristic of the other face of the oge-God, and is that desired by the oge-enemy, as well as characteristic of the bottom pole of the ego. These are of largely neurotic origin, irrational and false. This does not mean, of course, that acts which we call evil do not occur. They do occur, they usually involve considerable hekergy decrease for the victims, and so they are tragic. But they are not evil. Tragedy is local hekergy decrease, necessary for an increase elsewhere, in accordance with the principle of conservation of hekergy. Evil is wholly in the mind of the beholder. Since evil is an illusion, so is good — in the sense in which good is the opposite of evil. Good in this sense is characteristic of the oge-lover, as evil is characteristic of the oge-enemy. This does not mean, of course, that good in the sense of high hekergy is an illusion.

7. The seventh illusion is the illusion of two intrinsic classes or sets: similarity sets and superintension sets, whose members are respectively instances and representative instances of the intrinsic property sets of their intensions. We think with sets, or classes, because sets form naturally in our minds by L.A.L., and with classes we classify. But everything produced by L.A.L. is irrational and thereby false. The only real sets are property sets, sets whose intensions define members by means of intrinsic or extrinsic properties, such as "Every property of this relation," "Every term of this relation," "Every relation of which this relation as a term," and "Everything within this boundary." Similarity sets and superintension sets do not exist outside of minds because they multiply similarities beyond necessity. We needed them in Chapter 15, in order to distinguish intensional sets from

extensional and nominal sets, and thereby make clear the differences between intensional, extensional, and nominal meaning; and we needed this in order to explain axiom generosity and paradox, and to base the ontological argument on the two strengths of intensional mathematics; but once intensional meaning is understood, we can manage without similarity sets and superintension sets.

8. The eighth illusion is the passage of time [56]. The real world is a four-dimensional space-time that, as a whole, is timeless and unchanging. At any one moment the ego is a structure within this eternal whole — it is an unchanging part of an unchanging whole. If a hypothetical god, looking into the whole, were to see this ego, and were to follow the ego's structure along the time dimension, then the ego would change. But this is the kind of change that a road may undergo as one travels along it; if one is stationary, the portion of road on which one stands is unchanging. Similarly, the momentary ego is unchanging; neither it, nor any other subject travels along the time dimension. So experience of change, and hence of passage of time, is illusory.

Philosophically, it is not enough to explain by stating that something is an illusion: the fact of the illusion must also be explained. (Unless, of course, the illusion is a contradiction between the senses, as in Part One.) Two famous examples in the history of philosophy are Parmenides' claim that all change is illusion, and the mystics' solution to the problem of evil, which is that all evil is illusory. Such claims may be true, but the fact of the illusion must be explained. If it is not explained then the difficulty that the illusion answer claims to solve is simply replaced by the difficulty of explaining the illusion. All but one of the egocentric illusions are easily explained, and in the same way: by the fact of ignorance. We see the world as concrete because we are ignorant of micro-detail, due to information loss in theoretical perception and empirical perception. We believe events to be chance because we are ignorant of the details of global principles of causation — and sometimes of local causation. We believe we are individuals because we are ignorant of the falsity of the basic structure of our egos. We believe we have freedom because we are ignorant of the causes of our actions. We believe we perceive evil because we are ignorant of its source in the oge-enemy, and of our projection of it onto events in the apparent world. The possibility of these illusions is also easily explained.

Illusion requires a duality — of original and copy — and some dissimilarity between the two. In each of these cases this holds. This is most clear in the case of concreteness; concreteness is characteristic of reactions within the ego to mid-ideas, and the reactions are dissimilar to the ideas because they lack detail. The other illusions are a product of false belief, in which the possibility of duality and dissimilarity is obvious.

It is only the illusion of temporal passage that cannot be explained this way. Indeed, I know of no explanation for this illusion — yet it must be an illusion if Einstein's theories of relativity are correct.

✶

According to the principle of novel emergence [114], it is a feature of emergent relations that, at the lowest level at which they emerge, their properties cannot be predicted from the properties of their terms: they possess properties that are novel in the sense that no lower level relations possess these properties, and these novel properties are not deducible from anything in the lower levels. So if the highest level relations that we know are of level-n, then we cannot know anything of the properties of level-$(n+1)$ relations, other than the fact that they will have some completely novel properties. Thus a group of suprarational people, unified by an emergent relation, may be expected to provide surprises.

✶

Finally, it should be mentioned that, in accordance with our explanation of explanation, everything said here about the suprarational is hypothetical, speculative — probable, at best. But if it should be true, then if anyone achieves the suprarational state then the knowledge and understanding that they gain therein will not be probable at all, but indubitable.

Thus philosophy may have the power to end as it begins.

Index.

www.ingramcontent.com/pod-product-compliance
Lightning Source LLC
Chambersburg PA
CBHW081144270326
41930CB00014B/3027